国学与文化传播通识系列教程

中国经典双语阅读
文化与思维(下卷)

顾　问　石　坚　彭青龙
主　编　冯文坤

科学出版社
北　京

内容简介

本书以华夏族群、区域文化和文化认知为主要内容，是一套以文化理解与思维认知为主旨、推动通用英语向通识英语过渡、实现语言工具性和人文性相融合的通识课读本。以中国经典（如《原道》《论衡》《传习录》《僧肇》《黄帝内经》《浮生六记》等）为阅读内容。全书起于《原道》而终于《浮生六记》，贯穿诗—思—情—意，落实于儒、道、释之和合与融合的华夏文化之精粹。易言之，本书旨在突出华夏民族的语言—文化—思维的话语构成体系，凸显文化中的思维，至民族认知的文化形态与表现，如修为、道德、文学、文艺、事工与医学。本书以英汉直观互参、双语对比的方式，使读者直接体会英文中的汉语文化，以及理解跨语言传播中的文化过滤和文化翻译。

本书适合高校本科生、研究生（硕士和博士）的中国文化通识课教学，英语专业的汉英翻译、中国语言文学专业、中国哲学专业和比较文学专业的跨文化教学，中国高校留学生和海外孔子学院的中国文化课教学，及作为语料供从事汉英对比研究的学者使用。同时，本书还可作为海外领事馆人员、驻外企业员工、海外留学生了解和传播中国文化的必备工具书。

图书在版编目(CIP)数据

中国经典双语阅读. 文化与思维. 下卷 / 冯文坤主编. — 北京：科学出版社, 2019.8

国学与文化传播通识系列教程

ISBN 978-7-03-056297-5

Ⅰ. ①中… Ⅱ. ①冯… Ⅲ. ①汉语-阅读教学-对外汉语教学-教学参考资料 Ⅳ. ①H195.4

中国版本图书馆 CIP 数据核字 (2018) 第 003537 号

责任编辑：张 展 于 楠 / 责任校对：彭 映
责任印制：罗 科 / 封面设计：陈 敬

科学出版社出版
北京东黄城根北街16号
邮政编码：100717
http://www.sciencep.com

成都锦瑞印刷有限责任公司印刷

科学出版社发行 各地新华书店经销

*

2019年8月第 一 版 开本：787×1092 1/16
2019年8月第一次印刷 印张：17 3/4
字数：410 000

定价：68.00 元

（如有印装质量问题，我社负责调换）

“国学与文化传播通识系列教程”编委会

“当代中国是历史中国的延续和发展，当代中国思想文化也是中国传统思想文化的传承和升华，要认识今天的中国、今天的中国人，就要深入了解中国的文化血脉，准确把握滋养中国人的文化土壤。”

——摘自习近平《人民日报》（2016年9月2日）

Contemporary China is the continuation and development of China in the midst of history. The ideology and culture possessed and shared by the Contemporary Chinese is also the inheritance and sublimation of traditional Chinese ideology and culture. To understand today's China and today's Chinese people, we need to have a thorough understanding of China's cultural heritage and an accurate understanding of the cultural soil that nourishes and nurtures the Chinese people.

—— Excerpt from Xi Jinping, *People's Daily* (09/02/2016)

“没有文明的继承和发展，没有文化的弘扬和繁荣，就没有中国梦的实现。中华民族的先人们早就向往人们的物质生活充实无忧、道德境界充分升华的大同世界。……实现中国梦，是物质文明和精神文明比翼双飞的发展过程。……让中华文明同世界各国人民创造的丰富多彩的文明一道，为人类提供正确的精神指引和强大的精神动力。”

——摘自习近平2014年3月27日在联合国教科文组织总部的演讲

“Without the inheritance and development of civilization and the promotion and prosperity of culture, there will be no realization of the Chinese dream. The ancestors of the Chinese nation have long yearned for a world of great harmony in which people's material life is substantial and their moral realm is fully sublimated. ...Realizing the Chinese Dream is a process in which material civilization and spiritual civilization fly together. ...Together with the rich and colorful civilizations created by people all over the world, Chinese civilization provides correct spiritual guidance and strong spiritual impetus for mankind.”

——Excerpt from Xi Jinping's Speech at UNESCO headquarters on March 27, 2014

前　言

首先向热爱、研习、诠释、传播、讲述中国优秀传统文化的国内外前辈和同行们表达真诚的敬意！他们是国际汉学研究者、中国族群典籍翻译者、传播者、教育者和那些满怀华夏情感的人们。

一个民族的文化在时间里进化，在语言里凝结，并与每个成员在貌、言、视、听、思、事工和认知等方面形成协调与约束。明天是昨天与今天的共舞，诚如僧肇言："吾犹昔人非昔人"。《易经·贲卦》讲："刚柔交错，天文也；文明以止，人文也。观乎天文，以察时变；观乎人文，以化成天下。"可见，文指一切现象或形相。天文就是指自然现象，也可以是由阴阳、刚柔、正负、动静等两种力量之交集而形成的多彩多姿的自然世界。人文连用，就是指自然现象经过人的劳动、认识、改造、重组的活动而形成的事、诗、思、情、意的统一，因此称为人文活动或称为属于人的社会活动。再就词的释意来说，"文"就是记录、储存、表达、讲述和诠释，也指已经被符号化或载体化的意义对象，如艺术、语言、文字、经典文本、技术产品等；"化"就是分析、理解、对话和融合，也就是人与自然对象相拂相荡，彼此涵摄。另外，"化"也指人与自然在劳动实践过程中的彼此扬弃和彼此成全，或人类心智、信念、认识的客观化和客观对象的主观化。马克思在《1844年经济学哲学手稿》中指出："社会是人同自然界的完成了的本质的统一，是自然界的真正复活，是人的实现了的自然主义和自然界的实现了的人道主义"。[1]马克思的文化认识观是一种历史唯物主义观，也是一种劳动实践观，是自然主义与人道主义的高度统一。根据马克思的观点，文化是人的类存在在实践活动中的对象化，它体现为形态化的精神世界，其中有历史、故事、记忆、意识等，并共同构成国家和民族的叙事，构成民族成员的身份。

学习中国传统优秀文化，除了知晓前人的行为事工，要进入文本并与文本对话，要与流觞着民族精神、饱含民族情感、存储和输出民族认知信息的语言共舞。听几场讲座能引起我们产生去了解它的意义和价值的动机，但意义总是与文本相联系，并以蕴含信息量(意义)的语言符号为其存在的形态。从价值层面看，意义内在于我们所习得的知识、信仰、道德、行为、习俗和作为一个社会成员在其中所获得的能量和习惯之中。因此，意义有两种主要表现形态，即观念形态的意义世界和现实形态的意义世界，语言的文本则是观念形态的符号载体。马克思把这两种形态称之为"社会通过行动的象征符号或意义特性而形成的关系"。[2]那么，我们了解和学习古人的思想，既要依据古代先贤们的著作，兼及他们的行为，更要联系其生成的社会背景并通过当下的社会实践为其赋新赋能赋意。

[1] 马克思著，《1844年经济学哲学手稿》，北京：人民出版社，2014年，第79-81页。

[2] 引自《多维视野中的文化理论》，庄锡昌、顾晓鸣、顾云等编，浙江人民出版社，1987年，第94页。

英国诗人亚历山大·蒲柏在《论人》一文中问道："如果不从我们所知出发，如何去推理？"（What can we reason，but from what we know?）若把这个问题引入对学习传统文化的讨论中，我们将进一步得出结论：我们只能通过"我们到底知道什么"或"我们已经知道什么"来知道"我们是谁"和我们将成为什么。在今天全球多元文化的融合与对话中，要接触他者文化和居住在某种文化之中的人民，我们首先要从已知的自我文化立场出发。不自知何以知他？因为我们总是在某个家庭中长大，在一定区域的文化中说一种影射出我们存在的语言，并在自己的文化中长大成人。"一方水土养一方人。"这一文化是祖先们和我们一起参与其中的知、行过程而呈现出的事、诗、思、情、意合一的品质，它们是我们身上的胎痕，始终伴随我们的物质世界和精神世界。我们能够享受来自异国文化中的各种乐趣和智慧，正是因为我们是有根底的、有前文本的世界公民。庄子讲："自彼则不见，自知则知之。故曰：彼出于是，是亦因彼。"庄子这句话，从认识论上解释，则是对此事物的认识不能出于此事物，对彼事物的认识也不能出于彼事物。彼与此互参，相互映照，才能实现"物我相与""人人相与"。这是一种建构的辩证认识观。因此，走进他者前，我们要有充分的自我文化装备，这套装备就是指记载自我文化的文本或话语。惟有具备这套文本和话语，才能带着信息能量走进与他者对话的视野，才能创造性地理解他者，才能产生自我文化的意义增值和文化赋新。宋代理学家朱熹《观书有感》讲："半亩方塘一鉴开，天光云影共徘徊。问渠那得清如许？为有源头活水来。"中国优秀传统文化就是这个"源头活水"，民族精神在其中汇集，民族成员在其中安身立命和生生不息。我们今天从中取水又向其输入时代的新知，因此而经久不息，生生不已。德国阐释哲学家伽达默尔提出视界融合的理解观，即理解的融合不是与"我们"同化，而是通过学习使"我们的"视界与"他们的"视界取得一致，因为不管是"他们"还是"我们"，都必须或多或少地重新修正现行的证明活动；因为学习是双方同时被卷入了的学习过程。[1]

我们的生活世界是由语言、文化、社会及个性结构四要素构成的，也构成了人们相互容纳和互相生成的意义语境。我们的身体栖居之所构成了自己的意义语域，它是生成思想与价值的具身源泉。人在充满情和意的物理环境中活动，同时又将各种文化意义融入自己的日常活动之中，如呼吸、脸红、行走、哭泣和笑等，还被历代的作者写进了由语言构成的文本之中，并且在变化的文化背景下对文本做出了不同的评价。马克思指出："思维本身的要素，思想的生命表现的要素，即语言，具有感性的性质"[2]，因此，对于心灵活动的可靠分析方法必然始于对意识现象和精神活动的语言表达。精神的反思活动始终处于用语言建构的各种特殊世界的语法范围内，因此，语言的边界即认知世界的边界。孔子讲："不学诗，无以言。"德国哲学家尤尔根·哈贝马斯也认为"主体一直都是出现在一个由语言建构和阐释的世界里，并且依赖着合乎语法的意义语境。"[3]由语言建构和阐释的生活世界成为人们的语言共同体和交往实践的立足点。对于具有言语和行为能力的主体来说，每种文化传统同时也都是一个教化的过程：主体在这个过程中树立自己，同时也确保了文化充满活力。文化传统的内涵永远都是个人的前知识和进入社会的前文本，而文化本

[1] 尤尔根·哈贝马斯著，《后形而上学思想》，曹卫东、付德根 译，译林出版社，2001年，第161页。

[2] 马克思著，《1844年经济学哲学手稿》，人民出版社，2014年，第87页。

[3] 尤尔根·哈贝马斯著，《后形而上学思想》，曹卫东、付德根 译，译林出版社，2001年，第42页。

身则是个人身份建构的资源。因此，个人与群体的关系总是一种彼此被建构的文化关系。

记忆总是及物的，没有不及物的记忆。记忆向着充满感知和携带意义的对象物聚集并保存在其中。被回忆的过去总是与特定的人、物、话语概念及事件融合一体。记忆总是扎根于传统的温暖、心照不宣的习俗之中并以集体无意识的方式提供给每个人。每个人通过它们去设计和建构着自己的身份。法国作家普鲁斯特把记忆称之为一本书："那本植入我们身体的书，带有不是我们自己写入其中的文字，它是我们唯一的书。"[1]文化记忆是我们的生命的最内层的底片，它们会随时显现在我们的生活里。没有文化记忆的自我，不会形成自我身份。僧肇讲，"吾犹昔人非昔人"。一个民族、一个国家总会有自己的语言、壮丽史诗、神话传说，令人心怀崇敬的英雄群体、庄严肃穆的纪念碑，还有那些写满情怀的山川河谷以及留情无限的故土和故园。它们构成一个民族的整体的象征意义体系。我们在这个共同拥有的象征意义体系之中寻觅到了集体的归属感和认同感及一个属于"我们"的"我"和因之属于我们的国家。个人身份认同归根到底是在这个"象征意义体系"中完成他的自我叙事。正是这个"象征意义体系"使得作为个体的"我"有资格说出"我们"。个体的"我"既是历史的又是共时的——历史的意义通过我们涌现，而空间是容纳历史(时间)和现在的共在，而今人与古人的关系是持续不断的无意识与有意识、无形与有形的对话。历史以及记载历史的文献和典籍，像一位媒人，穿梭于各种哲学观和各种世界观的间际之中，随时随地影响我们的生活世界和社会实践。

语言是复数，文化超越语言。文化可以通过语言获得理解与传播。德国现象学哲学家海德格尔认为，源于语言的道说，是对一个民族的历史赋形，因为"不仅诗在语言中发生，在其中，一个民族的世界历史性地展开出来。"[2]语言不仅仅是转译主观内容的工具，语言给一定区域的人们的世界观和思维方式打上了它们自身的烙印，因此使语言相互之间的转译变得比较困难。不可否认，历史的距离会掩藏它的意义，可距离也会使已发生的事件释放出新的理解，产生新的意义视域。美国诗人弗罗斯特认为翻译总是要担当对失去韵味与思想的切实风险，但同时肯定经过两种语言之间的触碰所产生的译文，却有一种格外的结合意义与优雅的分寸。因此，what is lost and what is gained co-exist in translation。前者是对文化输出主体而言，后者是对文化接受主体而言。文化超越语言的界限，因此语言是工具的，工具可以搬运文化，但惟有母语是存在之精神，是认知之缘起。惟有母语施与我们以无意识的教化和语词、语音、语法之用的价值尺度。须先有自我内涵的叙述，方有自我身份的语言表达。记住一语惊醒梦中人这句话。我们首先是母语中人。要讲述好中国故事，首先要走进和实践中国故事，成为故事中人。讲母语的人，从文化进入语言；学讲外语的人，从语言进入文化。创造总是在伴随中发生。两种语言彼此触碰，彼此照应，彼此交换视域，彼此自我包容也彼此向对方开放，彼此创造性地解读对方。文化从一种语言向另一种语言转渡，既给接受者带来新的认知，也让输出者的文化实现增值。

最后，没有一部奠定民族叙述之根基的整体的语义学，一个民族的灵魂、精神和经验是不可想象的。中国优秀传统文化这部不断聚集、融合和生成的语义学，不仅塑造了华夏

[1] 马塞尔·普鲁斯特：《追忆逝水年华》，引自《回忆空间——文化记忆的形式和变迁》，阿莱达·阿斯曼著，潘璐译，北京大学出版社，2016年，第9页。

[2] [德] 马丁·海德格尔著，孙周兴译，《林中路》，上海译文出版社，2008年，第52，53页。

族群形象和族群共同体，还赋予了每位华夏人的身份认同。这部语义学最凝聚的结晶就是写意无穷、留情不尽的文化经典，它描绘了中国人与日月同辉的精神品质。今天，我们是历史与当代中国经验的传承者，更是它的创造者和弘扬者。立足当代中国伟大实践，学习文化经典的意义，莫过于让我们明悟中华民族的思维和文化品格，明悟中国从哪里来，将要到哪里去。中华五千年文明，生生不息。一代代中国人前赴后继，战天斗地的精神品质——女娲补天、精卫填海、大禹治水、愚公移山……，"为天地立心，为生民立命，为往圣继绝学，为万世开太平""为有牺牲多壮志，敢教日月换新天"——已成为华夏族群的集体无意识，成为当代中国人精神的内里和底色。耕读传承，初心致远。中华族群的独特品格和延续需要自己的文化叙事，而国人的身份正是依靠话语叙事建立起来的。

以下是对本书内容组织与编辑的几点说明：

基本定位：一个集体、一个民族、一个国家的凝聚力总是因文化而聚集。《中国经典双语阅读》教材，从时间纵向上选择原文，使读者从具体原文的阅读中体验和感悟中华民族优秀传统文化与今天"中国精神""中国经验""中国实践""中国自信""中国表达"之间的传承关系，从而使读者树立起"不忘其所始，方求其所终"的中国情怀和人类情怀。

基本内容：本书是以文化理解与传承为主旨，推动高校通用英语教学向通识英语教学过度，实现语言工具性和人文性相融合的通识类读本。本书以中国经典(如《洪范 • 九筹》《易经 • 系辞》《道德经》《论语》《庄子》《孟子》《荀子》《传习录》《僧肇》《黄帝内经》等)为阅读内容。本书起于《诗经》而终于《浮生六记》，贯穿体现诗—思—情—意的民族整体认知与思维，落实于儒、道、释之和合与融合的华夏文化之精粹。易言之，本书旨在突出华夏民族文化的话语形成之体系，如"太极""阴阳""五行""元气""易""道""德""理""和""自然""中庸""仁""礼""兼爱""心""性""明心""大同"以及"言""象""意""韵""神"等，凸显文化之中的思维和思维中的文化形态与表现，如修为、道德、文学、文艺与医学等。

编辑策略：①本书最大的特点是汉英互参，直观呈现，双语烛照，使读者直接体会英文中的汉语文化与汉语思维及在跨语言传播中的文化意识和文化过滤中的文化信息欠缺与文化意义增益。编者认为语言既是认识工具又是认识价值，语言是价值和使用价值两者的高度统一。本书中针对部分汉语的字、词、句、概念、古代人物及用典等，采取文本内字句相邻加注或注音的方式，以方便读者能够直观阅读和有效理解。②针对本书中对应原文的英语译文，编者使用已经出版并有一定影响力的译者译文。选择的原则是：时间上先古译后今译，地域上先国外译者译文后国内译者译文。选择的原因是，编者认为，任何翻译的目的或所指向的读者对象应是该译语文化或目标语文化的接受者。③本书译文中出现部分对应中文的注释，其目的有二：一是突出读者在阅读时树立双语转换中的比较意识；二是在阅读时增强读者对汉英相互对应位置的意识，因为该书把文化传播确立为它的一个重要目标。④原文的选择、注释、解释和每篇旨在"点醒"的"思想指要"，其主要依据是武汉大学郭齐勇先生主编的《中国古典哲学名著选读》。至于所采用经典文献存在的"多解""选择性争议""汉语断句"等问题，读者可在多方调研的基础上提高自我甄别能力。郭齐勇先生的书于 2005 年由人民出版社出版。他在"编序"中指出："中国经典诠释的特点，不在于语言文字的锤炼、雕琢和知性系统的建构，而在于与圣贤对话，去感受、领悟经典，创造新的经典或新的理路。……我们只有进入先贤的语境，才能逐步把握、理解中国经典之精神”。这也是我们编辑这部中英对照本的原则和目的。⑤本书最初计划分成四卷出版，分别为“诗”“思”“情”“意”，即围绕华夏思维与认知的话语形成展开，发现难度较大，编者主观性较强，反而会割裂中国文化“诗”“思”“情”“意”的整体性与互涵性，故现在采取分三卷出版：上卷从《诗经》到《淮南子》；下卷从《原道》到《浮生六记》；中卷则集中于体现“道”之用的“器”上，如《抱朴子》《孙子兵法》和华夏族群特色文化等。这个分卷办法，除了考虑到中国文化重和合与融通的文化特征，还因为作为文化读本，更希望读者从整体上去把握中国族群文化的精粹，避免把文化经典轻龄化和通俗化。关于本书英语译文，编者只说一句话：与其“秘阁书房次第开”，孤芳自赏，何不江水共饮冷暖共知，推己及人！

该书编写初衷，源于我从 2016 年开始对本科生开设的中国哲学经典阅读课教学，继而获电子科技大学本科生通识课程和研究生思政课程的立项资助。编辑中，楚军、姚连兵、王凯凤、李冬青、刘淑珍、俞博、张铁俊等老师参与了本书的审阅、校核等任务。王蕾、蔡冰瑶、易建华等研究生同学参与了原文录入、英语译文收集、文献梳理等任务。全部工作用了近三年的时间。本书从纵向上以全面的、系统的、历史的方式反映了中国族群文化的话语表达与形成，尤其是以汉英互参、双语烛照的方式呈现给读者，无疑是同类书中最好的读本。本书编辑整理工作中的疏忽与偏差，在所难免，如在所选原译文中出现断译、漏译、改译、增译、减译、误译等以及保留了不同译者对同一人名地名的不同音译、同一核心术语的不同译法等，敬请读者诸君在阅读中予以识别和指正，并建议在一字一句阅读中体悟跨语际中的文化理解及话语传播策略，从而为当今中国文化走出去而收到“他山之石”之效果。

冯文坤
2019 年夏天于清水河

Contents

“文起八代之衰，而道济天下之溺。”

——苏轼《潮州韩文公庙碑》

中国经典双语阅读

韩愈《原道》（选）

Unit 1

韩愈《原道》（选）Han Yu：What Is the True Way[1]

[思想提要]韩愈（公元 768—公元 824 年），字退之，唐孟州河阳（今河南省孟州市）人，著名的文学家、哲学家。他从事古文运动，推崇儒家学说，创立了儒家“道统说”。哲学论著有《原道》《原性》《谏迎佛骨表》等。《原道》阐释儒家的“道”并进行了推原索宗，认为核心是仁，表现为“道德”，并通过礼乐刑政施于民，是治国平天下的根本手段。韩愈提出“道德论”，认为它的实质是沟通天人、贯串古今的根本大道。由此对佛道两家展开了激烈的批判。同时须指出，韩愈的批判是外在的，只是到了宋代理学家，才开始对佛道作内在的批判，消化吸收，融会贯通。

[Introduction] Han Yu (768 A.D.—824 A.D.), was a famous writer, outstanding literary thinker, philosopher and politician in the Tang Dynasty. He devoted himself to the initiation of the classical literary movement, advocating Confucianism and establishing the theory of Confucian Orthodoxy. He is well known for his philosophical works like “*What Is the True Way*”, “*What Is the True Nature*” and “*Memorial to Admonish the Remains of Buddha*”, etc. Among them, “*What Is the True Way*” explains the “Tao” of the Confucianism, trying to restore it to the true nature of ancient Confucianism. Han Yu holds that the hardcore of Confucianism is benevolence, it is manifested as morality, and it is applied to people through rites, music, penalties, and government, which serves the fundamental means of running the country and the world. Han Yu proposes his own “theory of morality”, which is considered to be the fundamental avenue of communication between man and nature, running through ancient and modern times. Therefore, he launches a fierce criticism of Buddhism and Taoism. At the same time, it should be pointed out that Han Yu’s criticism was external, and it was until the Song Dynasty that Neo-confucianists began to make an internal critique of Buddhism and Taoism by means of digestion, absorption and integration.

---

[1] 中文选自郭齐勇主编：《中国古典哲学名著选读》，北京：人民出版社，2005 年。
英文选自石峻主编：《汉英对照中国哲学名著选读》，北京：中国人民大学出版社，1988 年。

博爱之谓仁，行而宜之之谓义[博爱之谓仁：《孝经》曰：“先王见教之可以化民也，是故先之以博爱，而民莫遗其亲。”行而宜之：做起来与当时的制度相适合。]，由是而之焉之谓道，足乎己而无待于外之谓德。仁与义为定名，道与德为虚位[虚位：空虚的位置。]。故道有君子小人，而德有凶有吉[德有凶有吉：指德有凶、吉之分。]。老子之小仁义，非毁之也，其见者小也。坐井而观天，曰天小者，非天小也。彼以煦煦(xù xù)为仁，孑孑为义[孑孑(jié jié)：微小的样子。《庄子·天道篇》：“又何偈偈(jié jié)乎揭仁义若击鼓而求亡子焉？”庄子以此讥讽儒家仁义，韩愈又用以反讥之也。]，其小之也则宜。其所谓道，道其所道，非吾所谓道也；其所谓德，德其所德，非吾所谓德也。凡吾所谓道德云者，合仁与义言之也，天下之公言也。老子之所谓道德云者，去仁与义言之也，一人之私言也。

To love universally(“博爱”)is called humanity (*ren*)(“仁”); to apply this in a proper manner is called righteousness (*yi*)(“义”). The operation of these is the Way (*Tao*)(“道”), and its Inner Power (*te*)(“德”)is that it is self-sufficient, requiring nothing from outside itself. Humanity and righteousness are fixed principles(“仁与义为定名也”), but the Way and its Inner Power are speculative concepts(“道与德为虚位”). Thus we have the way of the gentleman and the way of the small man, and both good and evil power. Lao Tzu made light of humanity and righteousness, but he did not thereby abolish them. His view was narrow like that of a man who sits at the bottom of a well and looks up at the sky(“坐井观天”), say, “The sky is small.” This does not mean that the sky is really small. Lao Tzu understood humanity and righteousness in only a very limited sense, and therefore it is natural that he belittled them. What he called the Way was only the Way as he saw it, and not what I call the Way; what he called the Inner Power was only the power as he saw it, and not what I call the Inner Power. What I call the Way and power are a combination of humanity and righteousness and this is the definition accepted by the world at large(“凡吾所谓道德云者，合仁与义言之也，天下之公言也”). But what Lao Tzu called the Way and power are stripped of humanity and righteousness, and represent only the private view of one individual.

周道衰，孔子没，火于秦，黄老于汉，佛于晋、魏、梁、隋之间，其言道德仁义者，不入于杨，则归于墨；不入于老，则归于佛。入于彼，必出于此。入者主之，出者奴之；入者附之，出者汙之[汙(wū)：污辱、诋毁。]。噫！后之人其欲闻仁义道德之说，孰从而听之？老者曰：“孔子，吾师之弟子也。”佛者曰：“孔子，吾师之弟子也。”为孔子者，习闻其说，乐其诞而自小也，亦曰“吾师亦尝云尔。”不惟举之于口，而又笔之于其书[《礼记·曾子问》中有孔子“吾闻诸老聃曰”的话。]。噫！后之人虽欲闻仁义道德之说，其孰从而求之？

After the decline of the Chou(周)and the death of Confucius, in the time of Qin’s book burnings(“火于秦”), the Taoism(道教)of the Han(汉), and the Buddhism(佛教)of the Wei(魏), the Chin(晋), the Liang(梁), and the Sui(隋), when men spoke of the Way and power, of humanity and righteousness, they were approaching them either as followers of Yang Chu(杨朱)or of Mo Tzu(墨子), of Lao Tzu(老子) or of Buddha(佛陀). Being followers of these doctrines, they naturally rejected Confucianism. Acknowledging these men as their masters, they made of Confucius an outcast, adhering to new teachings and vilifying the old.

Alas! When people of the coming generations want to know the theory about humanity and righteousness, the Way and its Inner Power, upon whom should they follow to learn it? The Taoists said, "Confucius was merely a disciple of our master (Lao Tzu)." The Buddhists said alike, "Confucius was merely a disciple of our master (Buddha)"("孔子，吾师之弟子也"). Accustomed to these sayings, Confucians were fascinated by the absurdity and belittled their own master, saying, "Our master said the same as the Taoists and the Buddhists said." They not only acknowledged it with their mouths, but also wrote it in books. Alas! Though people of coming generations want to know the theory about humanity and righteousness, the Way and its Inner Power, upon whom should they follow to gain it?

甚矣，人之好怪也！不求其端，不讯其末，惟怪之欲闻。古之为民者四[古之为民者四：士、农、工、商。]，今之为民者六[今之为民者六：士、农、工、商、僧、道。]。古之教者处其一[古之教者处其一：指儒教，即儒家学派。]，今之教者处其三[今之教者处其三：儒、释、道三教。]。农之家一，而食粟之家六。工之家一，而用器之家六。贾之家一，而资焉之家六[资焉：取给于此。]。奈之何民不穷且盗也！

Too much do men crave for oddity! They neither want to investigate the beginning of things, nor want to carefully examine the end of them. The only thing they desire is to go in for what is of oddity. In ancient times, there were only four classes of people, but now there are six. There was only one teaching, where now there are three. For each family growing grain, there are now six consuming it; for each family producing utensils, there are now six using them; for one family engaged in trade six, others take their profits. Is it surprising then that the people are reduced to poverty and driven to theft?

古之时，人之害多矣。有圣人者立，然后教之以相生养之道。为之君，为之师。驱其虫蛇禽兽，而处之中土。寒，然后为之衣。饥，然后为之食。木处而颠[颠：从高处摔下来。]，土处而病也，然后为之宫室。为之工以赡其器用，为之贾以通其有无，为之医药以济其夭死，为之葬埋祭祀以长其恩爱，为之礼以次其先后，为之乐以宣其壹郁[壹：通"湮"。壹郁：心中积闷。]，为之政以率其怠勌[勌(juàn)：通"倦"。]，为之刑以锄其彊梗[彊：通"强"。梗：刚猛。]。相欺也，为之符玺斗斛(hú)权衡以信之；相夺也，为之城郭甲兵以守之。害至而为之备，患生而为之防。今其言曰："圣人不死，大盗不止；剖斗折衡，而民不争"[语引《庄子·胠箧》。]。呜呼！其亦不思而已矣。如古之无圣人，人之类灭久矣。何也？无羽毛鳞介以居寒热也，无爪牙以争食也。

In ancient times, men faced many perils, but sages arose who taught them how to protect and nourish their lives("相生养之道"), acting as their rulers and teachers. They drove away the harmful insects and reptiles, birds and beasts, and let men settle in the centre of the earth("中土"). The people were cold and they made them clothes. Hungry and they gave them food. Because men had dwelt in danger in the tops of trees or grew sick sleeping on the ground, they built them halls and dwellings. They taught them handicrafts that they might have utensils to use, trades so that they could supply their wants, medicine to save them from early death, proper burial and sacrifices to enhance their sense of love and gratitude, rites to order the rules of precedence, music to express their repressed feelings, government to lead the indolent, and punishments to suppress the overbearing. Because men cheated each other, they made tallies and seals, measures and scales to insure confidence; because men plundered, they made walls and fortifications, armor and weapons to protect them. Thus they taught men to prepare against danger and prevent injury to their lives. Now the Taoists tell us that "until the sages die off, robbers will never disappear, " or that "if we destroy our measures and break our scales, the people will cease their contention(“圣人不死，大盗不止；剖斗折衡，而民不争”)." Alas, how thoughtless are such sayings! If there had been no sages in ancient times, then mankind would have perished, for men have no feathers or fur, no scales or shells to protect them from cold and heat, no claws and teeth to contend for food.

是故君者，出令者也；臣者，行君之令而致之民者也；民者，出粟米麻丝，作器皿，通货财，以事其上者也。君不出令，则失其所以为君，臣不行君之令而致之民，则失其所以为臣；民不出粟米麻丝，作器皿，通货财，以事其上，则诛。今其法曰：必弃而君臣，去而父子，禁而相生养之道，以求其所谓清净寂灭者。呜呼！其亦幸而出于三代之后，不见黜于禹、汤、文、武、周公、孔子也；其亦不幸而不出于三代之前，不见正于禹、汤、文、武、周公、孔子也。

Therefore, those who are rulers give commands which are carried out by their officials and made known to the people, and the people produce grain, rice, hemp, and silk, make utensils and exchange commodities for the support of the superiors. If the ruler fails to issue commands, then he ceases to be a ruler, while if his subordinates do not carry them out and extend them to the people, and if the people do not produce goods for support of their superiors, they must be punished. Yet the Way of the Taoists and Buddhists teaches men to reject the ideas of ruler and subject and of father and son, to cease from activities which sustain life and seek for some so-called purity and Nirvana(“清净寂灭者”). Alas, it is fortunate for such doctrines that they appeared only after the time of the Three Reigns (“三代”)and thus escaped suppression at the hands of Yü(禹)and Tang(汤), Kings Wen(文)and Wu(武), the Duke of Chou(周公)and Confucius(孔子), but unfortunate for us that they did not appear before the Three Reigns so that they could have been rectified by those sages.

帝之与王，其号虽殊[帝：指尧舜。王：指禹、汤、文、武。]，其所以为圣一也。夏葛而冬裘(qiú)，渴饮而饥食，其事虽殊，其所以为智一也。今其言曰：“曷(hé)不为太古之无事？”是亦责冬之裘者曰：“曷不为葛之之易也？”责饥之食者曰：“曷不为饮之之易也？”

Emperors and kings are equal in their sageness though different in titles. Men are dressed in hemp in summer and fur in winter; they drink when they feel thirsty and eat when they feel hungry. Although they do not do the same in different cases, the reasoning of why they do these is the same. Now the Taoists say, "Why don't we behave in the same way as those who lived in the remote antiquity(“太古”) when people had nothing to do? " This is like the criticizing of those who are dressed in fur in winter: "Why aren't you dressed in hemp which could be made much easier than fur?" or those who are eating to satisfy their hunger: "Why don't you have a drink which could be prepared much more easily than a meal? "

《传》曰："古之欲明明德于天下者，先治其国；欲治其国者，先齐其家；欲齐其家者，先修其身；欲修其身者，先正其心；欲正其心者，先诚其意[引自《礼记·大学》。]。"然则古之所谓正心而诚意者，将以有为也。今也欲治其心而外天下国家，灭其天常[天常：指君臣父子夫妇等伦理关系。]，子焉而不父其父，臣焉而不君其君，民焉而不事其事。孔子之作《春秋》也，诸侯用夷礼则夷之，进于中国则中国之[诸侯用夷狄之礼，就把他当做夷狄看待；夷狄进而用中国之礼，就把他当做中国人看待。]。《经》曰："夷狄之有君，不如诸夏之亡也[引自《论语·八佾》。]。"《诗》曰："戎狄是膺，荆舒是惩[诗见《诗经·鲁颂·閟宫》。膺(yīng)：讨伐，打击。]。"今也举夷狄之法而加之先王之教之上，几何其不胥而为夷也[胥：相引。]？

The Book of *Rites* says, "The ancients who wished to illustrate illustrious virtue throughout the kingdom first ordered well their own states（"治国"）. Wishing to order well their states, they first regulated their families（"齐家"）. Wishing to regulate their families, they first cultivated their persons（"修身"）. Wishing to cultivate their persons, they first rectified their hearts（"正心"）. Wishing to rectify their hearts, they first sought to be sincere in their thoughts（"诚意"）". Thus when the ancients spoke of rectifying the heart and being sincere in their thoughts, they had this purpose in mind. But now the Taoists and Buddhists seek to govern their hearts by escaping from the world, the state and the family. They violate the natural law, so that the son does not regard his father as a father（"不父其父"）, the subject does not look upon his ruler as a ruler（"不君其君"）, and the people do not serve those whom they must serve（"不事其事"）. When Confucius wrote in *The Spring and Autumn Annals*（《春秋》）, he treated as barbarians those feudal lords who observed barbarian customs, and as Chinese those who had advanced to the use of Chinese ways（"诸侯用夷礼则夷之，进于中国则中国之"）. *The Analects*(《论语》) says, "The barbarians with rulers are not the equal of the Chinese without rulers." *The Book of Odes*（《诗》）says, "Fight against the barbarians of the west and north, punish those of *Ching* and *Shu*（"荆舒"）." Yet now the Buddhists come with their barbarian way and put them ahead of the teachings of our ancient kings. Are they not practically barbarians themselves ?

夫所谓先王之教者何也？博爱之谓仁，行而宜之之谓义，由是而之焉之谓道，足乎己无待于外之谓德。其文《诗》《书》《易》《春秋》，其法礼、乐、刑、政，其民士、农、工、贾，其位君臣、父子、师友、宾主、昆弟、夫妇，其服麻丝，其居宫室，其食粟米、果蔬、鱼肉，其为道易明，而其为教易行也。是故以之为己，则顺而祥；以之为人，则爱而公；以之为心，则和而平；以之为天下国家，无所处而不当。是故生则得其情，死则尽其常，郊焉而天神假[郊：祭天的礼仪。假：来到。]，庙焉而人鬼飨(xiǎng)。曰：斯道也，何道也？曰：斯吾所谓道也，非向所谓老与佛之道也。尧以是传之舜，舜以是传之禹，禹以是传之汤，汤以是传之文、武、周公，文、武、周公传之孔子，孔子传之孟轲。轲之死，不得其传焉。荀与扬也，择焉而不精，语焉而不详。由周公而上，上而为君，故其事行。由周公而下，下而为臣，故其说长。然则如之何而可也？曰：不塞不流，不止不行。人其人[人其人：当做“民其人”，因为避李世民之讳而然。]，火其书，庐其居。明先王之道以道之[“以道之”的“道”同“导”。]，鳏(guān)寡孤独废疾者有养也，其亦庶乎其可也。

What were these teachings of our ancient kings? To love universally, which is called humanity; to apply this in the proper manner, which is called righteousness; to proceed from these to the Way and to be self-sufficient without seeking anything outside, which is called Inner Power(“无待于外之谓德”). *The Odes*(《诗》)and *The History*(《书》), *The Changes*(《易》) and *The Spring and Autumn Annals*(《春秋》), are their writings; *rites* (礼) and *music*(乐), *punishments* (刑) and government(政), their methods. Their people were the four classes of officials(“士”), farmers(“农”), artisans(“工”), and merchants(“贾”); their relationships were those of sovereign and subject, father and son, teacher and friend, guest and host, elder and younger brother, and husband and wife. Their clothing was hemp and silk; their dwelling halls and houses; their food grain and rice, fruit and vegetables, fish and meat. Their ways were easy to understand; their teachings simple to follow. Applied to oneself, they brought harmony and blessing; applied to others, love and fairness. To the mind they gave peace; to the state and the family all that was just and fitting. Thus in life men were able to satisfy their emotions, and at death the obligations due to them were pleased; to the spirits of their ancestors and the ancestors received their offerings. What Way is this? It is what I call the Way, and not what the Taoists and Buddhists call the Way. Yao(尧)taught it to Shun(舜), Shun to Yü(禹), Yü to Tang(汤), and Tang to Kings Wen(文王) and Wu(武)and the Duke of Chou(周公). These men taught it to Confucius and Confucius to Mencius(孟子), but when Mencius died it was no longer handed down. Hsün Tzu(荀子)and Yang Hsiung(扬雄)understood elements of it, but their understanding lacked depth(“择焉而不精”); they spoke of it but incompletely(“语焉而不详”). In the days before the Duke of Chou, the sages were rulers and so they could put the Way into practice, but after the time of Duke of Chou they were only officials and so they wrote at length about the Way. What should be done now? I say that unless Taoism and Buddhism are suppressed, the Way will not prevail; unless these men are stopped, the Way will not be practiced. Let their priests be turned into ordinary men again, let their books be burned and their temples converted into homes. Let the Way of our former kings be made clear to lead them, and let the widower(“鳏”)and the widow(“寡”), the orphan(“孤”) and the lonely(“独”), the crippled(“废”)and the sick(“疾”)be nourished. Then all will be well.

“太史公执迁手而泣曰：‘余先周室之太史也。自上世尝显功名于虞夏，典天官事。后世中衰，绝于予乎？汝复为太史，则续吾祖矣。’”

——司马谈《命子迁》

Unit 2

司马谈《论六家要旨》

Sima Tan：The Discussion of the Essentials of the Six Schools [1]

[思想提要]司马谈(约公元前 165 —公元前 110 年)，夏阳(今陕西省韩城县)人，司马迁之父。西汉史学家，尊崇黄老之学，曾“学天官于唐都，受《易》于杨何，习道论于黄子”。《论六家要指》是司马谈写作的一篇重要学术史著作，对先秦至汉初诸子学说之长短得失作出评论，并概括为六大流派，与《庄子·天下》篇齐名。此篇从“为治异路”的角度入手，对阴阳、儒、墨、法、名、道六家思想作了评注，前五家各有得失，唯盛赞道家的思想。虚无因循、无为而无不为及先定神形等主张，都是道家思想的要点。此外，本篇首次以“六家”名义对先秦以来的诸子百家进行了高度概括，在学术史上具有重大意义。

[Introduction] Sima Tan (about 165 B.C.—110 B.C.) was born in Xia Yang (now Hancheng County, Shaanxi Province). Sima Tan is the father of Sima Qian. Sima Tan is a historian of the Western Han Dynasty. He highly values the Classical Taoism of Huang-Lao, as he himself said, “Tai Shi Gong studied astronomy in the capital of Tang Dynasty, immersed himself in the teachings on the arts of *Yin* and *Yang* from Yang He and concentrated himself on Taoism from Huangzi”. *The Discussion of the Essentials of the Six Schools* written by Sima Tan is an important work of academic history, in which he comments on the pros and cons of various theories from Pre-Qin to the early Han period, summarizing them and reducing them to Six Schools, which is as famous as Zhuangzi’s *The World*. Starting with the way of differentiating the thoughts of Six Schools, Sima Tan makes comments on the thoughts of Six Schools respectively—Yin-Yang, Confucianism, Mohism, Legalism, Logicism, and Taoism, of which he thinks that the first five have their own gains and losses, but he only praises the

---

[1] 中文选自郭齐勇主编：《中国古典哲学名著选读》，北京：人民出版社，2005 年。

Sima Tan：*The Discussion of the Essentials of the Six Schools*，selected from *Sima Qian：Grand Historican of China,* translated by Burton Watson. New York and London：Columbia University Press, 1958.

thought of Taoism. The propositions like "no action in life and yet action is present everywhere", "emptiness and accordance [with nature and the times] as its practice", and "the spirit of life is first and the vessel of life is next to it" constituted the key points of Taoism. In addition, in this treatise, for the first time, Sima Tan makes an outline of the various thoughts of the Six Schools since the Pre-Qin period, which is of great significance in the academic history of China.

《易大传》曰："天下一致而百虑，同归而殊途。"[《易大传》：可能别为一书，可能非指《系辞》。天下一致而百虑，同归而殊 途：今本《易·系辞》有此语。]夫阴阳、儒、墨、名、法、道德，此务为治者也，直所从言之异路，有省不省耳[有省不省耳：学或有传习省察，或有不省者耳。]。

The Great Commentary of The Book of Changes（《易大传》）says, "There is one moving force, but from it a hundred thoughts and schemes arise. All have the same objective, though their ways are different." The schools of the Yin-yang（"阴阳"）, the Confucianists（"儒"）, the Mohists（"墨"）, the Logicians（"名"）, the Legalists（"法"）, and the Taoists（"道德"）, all strive for good government. The difference among them is simply that they follow and teach different ways, and some are more penetrating than others.

尝窃观阴阳之术，大祥而众忌讳[大祥而众忌讳：大祥，重视吉凶之征兆；众，多。]，使人拘而多所畏。然其序四时之大顺，不可失也。

It has been my observation that the theories of the Yin-Yang School（"阴阳学派"）put strong emphasis upon omens and teach that a great many things are to be shunned and tabooed. Hence it causes men to feel restrained and bound by fear. But in its work of arranging correctly the all-important succession of the four seasons it fills the essential need.

儒者博而寡要，劳而少功，是以其事难尽从。然其序君臣父子之礼，列夫妇长幼之别，不可易也。

The Confucianists are very broad in their interests, but do not deal with much that is essential. They labor much and achieve but slight success. Therefore, their discipline is difficult to carry out to the fullest（"其事难尽从"）. But in the way in which they order the etiquette between lord and subject and father and son（"然其序君臣父子之礼"）, and the proper distinctions between husband and wife and elder and younger（"列夫妇长幼之别"）, they have something that cannot be altered.

墨者俭而难遵，是以其事不可遍循[俭：墨者节用、俭葬、非乐。遍循：普遍依从。]。然其强本节用，不可废也。

The Mohists are too stern in their parsimony to be followed and therefore, their teachings cannot be fully applied. But in their emphasis upon what is basic (i.e., agricultural production) and upon frugal usage（"强本节用"）they have a point which cannot be overlooked.

法家严而少恩[恩：仁恩，仁爱。]，然其正君臣、上下之分，不可改矣。

The Legalists are very strict and of small mercy. But they have correctly defined the distinctions between lord and subject and between superior and inferior, and these distinctions cannot be changed.

名家使人俭而善失真[俭而善失真：俭，同检，束缚。名家使人受名词概念的束缚，而丧失其真实。]。然其正名实，不可不察也。

The Logicians cause men to be overnice in reasoning and often to miss the truth. But the way in which they distinguish clearly between names and realities is something that people cannot afford not to look into.

道家使人精神专一，动合无形[无形：指道。]，赡足万物。其为术也，因阴阳之大顺，采儒、墨之善，撮名、法之要[撮(cuō)：选取，吸取。要：精要。]，与时迁移，应物变化；立俗施事，无所不宜，指约而易操[施：为。指：同旨。]，事少而功多。儒者则不然，以为人主天下之仪表也。君倡而臣和，主先而臣随，如此，则主劳而臣逸。至于大道之要，去健羡，绌聪明[健羡：健，强；羡，贪欲。聪明：指有为之智，道家崇尚清静无为。]，释此而任术[术：道术，道家治国的方法、思想策略。]。夫神大用则竭，形大劳则敝；形神骚动，欲与天地长久，非所闻也。

The Taoists teach men to live a life of spiritual concentration and to act in harmony with the Unseen(“动于无形”). Their teaching is all-sufficient and embraces all things. Its method consists in following the seasonal order of the Yin-Yang School, selecting what is good from the Confucian and Mohist teachings, and adopting the important points of the Logicist and Legalist schools. It modifies its position with the times and responds to the changes which come about in the world(“与时迁移，应物变化”). In establishing customs and practices and administering affairs, it does nothing that is not appropriate to the time and place. Its principles are simple and easy to practice; it undertakes few things but achieves many successes. It is not so with the Confucianists. They consider that the ruler of men must be the model of conduct for the world(“人主天下之仪表”). He shall set the example, they declare, with which his ministers need only to comply; he shall lead and his ministers follow. But if it were like this, then the ruler would have to labor while the ministers followed along at their ease. The essential of the *Great Tao*(大道) is to discard strength and envy and to do away with intelligence and understanding(“去健羡，绌聪明”); one must discard these and entrust himself to the practices of *Taoism*. If the spirit of a man is too much used, it will become exhausted; if his bodily substance is put to much labor, it will wear out. If a man has early in life exhausted his spirit and body, it is unheard of that he should hope to attain the long life of heaven and earth.

夫阴阳、四时、八位、十二度、二十四节，各有教令[八位：四正四维，即东、南、西、北、东北、东南、西南、西北八者。十二度：十二月。二十四节：二十四节气。教令：依时寄政，由政府按历法行事而规定的各种教令。]。顺之者昌，逆之者不死则亡，未必然也，故曰：“使人拘而多畏。”夫春生夏长，秋收冬藏，此天道之大经也，弗顺则无以为天下纲纪。故曰："四时之大顺，不可失也。"

The Yin-Yang School has its teachings and ordinances which apply to each of the four seasons(四时), the eight trigrams (八位/八卦), the twelve signs of the zodiac(十二度), and the twenty-four divisions of the year(二十四节), and it declares that anyone who follows these ordinances will meet with good fortune, while anyone who goes against them will die or at least lose his position in life("顺之者昌，逆之者不死则亡"). But this is not necessarily so. Therefore, I say that the Yin-Yang School causes men to feel restrained and bound by fear. Spring is the time for planting, summer for nurturing, fall for harvesting, and winter for storing away. This is the ever-constant principle of the way of Heaven and if one does not abide by this he cannot regulate and govern the world. Therefore, I say that in the all-important succession of the four seasons, the Yin-Yang teaching cannot be done without.

夫儒者以六艺为法[六艺：六经。法：准则。]。六艺经传以千万数，累世不能通其学，当年不能究其礼。故曰："博而寡要，劳而少功。"若夫列君臣父子之礼，序夫妇长幼之别，虽百家弗能易也。

The Confucianists consider *the Six Classics*("六艺")as their law and model. But the books and commentaries of *the Six Classics* run to thousands or tens of thousands. Generations of scholars could not master their study, nor could a man in his whole lifetime thoroughly comprehend all their rules. Therefore, I say that the Confucianists are broad in their interests but do not deal with much that is essential("博而寡要"), and that they labor much but achieve only slight success("劳而少功"). But as to the etiquette established by the Confucianists between ruler and subject and father and son and their distinctions between husband and wife and elder and younger, none of the other schools can change or improve upon this.

墨者亦尚尧、舜道，言其德行曰："堂高三尺，土阶三等；茅茨不剪，采椽不刮[茅茨不剪：指用茅草盖的房顶，而不加修剪。采椽(chuán)不刮：用杂木做的椽子，而不刮去树皮。]；食土簋啜土刑[簋(guǐ)：上古的食器、礼器。土簋，陶制的簋。土刑：刑，同型；土刑，土钵，盛羹器。]，粝粱之食，藜藿之羹；夏日葛衣，冬日鹿裘。"[粝(lì)粱：粝，粗米；粱，粟。藜藿(lí huò)：藜，与藿相似，外表赤色；藿，豆叶。]其送死，桐棺三寸，举音不尽其哀。教丧礼，必以此为万民之率[率：表率。]。使天下法若此，则尊卑无别也。夫世异时移，事业不必同。故曰："俭而难遵"。要曰强本节用，则人给家足之道也。此墨子之所长，虽百家弗能废也。

The Mohists also honor the ways of the emperors Yao(尧) and Shun(舜), and speak much of their virtuous actions, saying, "The foundations of the halls of Yao and Shun were three *ch'ih*(尺) high with three steps of earth leading up; their halls were roofed with untrimmed thatch and their timbers and rafters were untrimmed. These emperors ate from earthen plates and drank from earthen bowls. Their food was coarse grain with a soup of greens. In summer they wore clothes of coarse fiber and in winter the skins of deer." The Mohists bury their dead in coffins of *t'ung* wood three *ts'un* thick, and when they raise their voices in mourning they do not give full vent to their grief. They teach that funerals must be conducted in this way, setting this up as an example for all people(“万民之率”). But if everyone followed their rules, then there would be no distinction between the honorable and the lowly(“则尊卑无别”). Ages differ and the times change(“世异时移”), and the things people do need not always be the same. Therefore, I say that “The Mohists are too parsimonious to be followed.” But since they emphasize what is essential and are frugal in use(“强本节用”), theirs is the way to assure an ample supply for both individual and family. This is the point in which the Mohists excel and none of the other schools can afford to overlook it.

法家不别亲疏，不殊贵贱，一断于法，则亲亲尊尊之恩绝矣。可以行一时之计，而不可长用也。故曰：“严而少恩”。若尊主卑臣，明分职不得相逾越，虽百家弗能改也。

The Legalists do not distinguish between those who are close to oneself and those who are distant(“不别亲疏”); they do not differentiate between the honorable and the lowly(“不殊贵贱”), but judge all men alike by their laws(“一断于法”). If this is so, then the obligation to treat those near to oneself with special deference and to honor those who are worthy of honor is destroyed(“亲亲尊尊之恩绝”). Such laws can serve as an expedient for a particular time, but they cannot be used for long. Therefore, I say that “The Legalists are strict and show little mercy”(“严而少恩”). But in so far as they place the ruler in a lofty position and the subject in a lowly one and make clear the division of authority between the various officers of government so that there can be no usurping of unlawful power, they have a point which the other schools cannot improve upon.

名家苛察缴绕[缴绕(jiǎo rǎo)：缠绕，不切实际，不中大道。]，使人不得反其意，专决于名，而失人情。故曰：“使人检而善失真”。若夫控名责实，参伍不失[参伍：交互错综。]，此不可不察也。

The Logicians indulge in hair splitting and tortuous reasoning, making it impossible for people to follow their meaning. They decide everything on the basis of terms and overlook the realities(“专决于名，而失人情”). Therefore, I say that they cause men to be overnice and often to miss the truth. But if they can succeed in setting aside the names of things and get at their reality(“控名责实”) so that reason is not lost, then they have something that one cannot afford not to look into.

道家无为，又曰无不为，其实易行，其辞难知。其术以虚无为本，以因循为用。无成势，无常形，故能究万物之情。不为物先，不为物后，故能为万物主。有法无法，因时为业；有度无度，因物兴舍[兴舍：《史记•太史公自序》为“与合”，《汉书•司马迁传》为“兴舍”。此从《汉书》。颜师古曰：兴，起也。舍，废也，兴，提倡；舍，废弃。]。故曰：“圣人不朽，时变是守[圣人不朽：朽，当作巧，参见《汉书•司马迁传》和马王堆帛书《十大经•观》。]。”虚者，道之常也；因者，君之纲也。群臣并至，使各自明也。其实中其声者谓之端[中(zhòng)：符合。端：正。]，实不中其声者谓之窾[窾(kuǎn)：空。]。窾言不听，奸乃不生；贤不肖自分，白黑乃形。在所欲用耳，何事不成？乃合大道，混混冥冥。光耀天下，复反无名。凡人所生者神也，所托者形也。神大用则竭，形大劳则敝，形神离则死[神：精神。]。死者不可复生，离者不可复反，故圣人重之。由是观之，神者生之本也，形者生之具也。不先定其神(形)，而曰：“我有以治天下”，何由哉？

The Taoist School proposes the doctrine of “doing nothing”(“无为”), but it insists that thereby “there is nothing that is not done”(“无不为”). Its truths are easy to practice but its words difficult to understand(“其实易行，其辞难知”). Its teaching takes emptiness and inaction as its basis, and compliance and accordance (with nature and the times) as its practice. It recognizes as a fact that nothing is complete and finished, that nothing is constant in form. Therefore, it is able to penetrate the spirit of all things. It does not put material things first, nor does it put them last; therefore it is able to master all things. It has laws and yet it is as though it had no laws, for it follows the times in all its undertakings. It has rules and yet it is as though it did not have them, because it follows things and accords with them. Therefore, it is said that the Sage is without great skill but follows the changes of the times(“圣人不朽，时变是守”). Emptiness is the constant law of the *Tao*(“虚者，道之常也”). Accordance is the abiding principle of the ruler. Thus all the officers proceed to their business with a clear understanding of their respective duties. He who in reality comes up to what he claims to be is called upright, but he who does not actually measure up to his name is called vain. If a man pays no heed to vain words, then evil will not arise. The distinction between worthy and unworthy will become clear of itself, and white and black will become apparent. Thus one can choose the one and discard the other and thereby accomplish all things. He can be at one with *the Great Tao* which, formless and dark, yet lightens the whole world. Thus may one return again to the Nameless. It is spirit which gives life to all men and they assume their form in bodily substance(“凡人所生者神也，所托者形也”). If the spirit be put to great use, it will become exhausted. If the body be made to labor greatly, it will become worn out. When substance and spirit part, there is death. He who is dead cannot return to life, for that which has become separated cannot again be joined. Therefore, the Sage regards those things with gravity. From this we may see that the spirit is the basis of life and the substance is its vessel(“神者生之本也，形者生之具也”). If a man does not first put at rest his spirit and substance, but says instead, “I can govern the world!”, what reason can there be in his words?

“知屋漏者在宇下，知政失者在草野。”

——王充《论衡·书解》

中国经典双语阅读

王充《论衡》（选）

Unit 3

王充《论衡》（选）Selected from Wang Chong's Lun Heng [1]

［思想指要］《论衡》是东汉著名思想家王充的代表作品。王充（公元 27—约公元 97 年），字仲任，出身“细族孤门”，曾拜大学者班彪为师，通众流百家之言，自称其思想“违儒家之说，合黄老之义”，他的主要思想保留在《论衡》一书中。《论衡》共八十五篇，全书通过考察历史，特别是汲取当时自然科学的成果，发挥了以“元气”为核心的哲学思想，以及反对董仲舒以来的天人感应论，特别是谴告之说。

[Introduction] *Lun Heng* is a representative work of Wang Chong, who is a famous thinker in the Western Han Dynasty of China. Wang Chong (27 A.D.—about 97 A.D.), with the courtesy name of Zhong-Jen, was born in a less distinguished family. He once learned from Ban Biao, a great scholar. He came to know theories of hundreds of scholars, and called himself "contrary to the Confucian doctrine, but in compliance with the meaning of Huangti and Laotze". His thoughts are mainly manifested in *Lun Heng*. *Lun Heng* consists of a total of 85 articles. Through examining history, especially absorbing the natural sciences of his time, Wang Chong establishes his philosophical thought of "*Yuanqi*" and he definitely opposes the theory of "correspondence between man and Heaven", proposed by Dong Zhongshu, especially his Reprimand.

《自然》Spontaneity

本篇是王充阐述他的自然观的重要论文，在《论衡》一书中占有重要位置。在本篇中，王充扬弃了黄老之学的自然无为思想，使之与元气思想相结合。他指出，“天地合气，万物自生”，认为整个自然界都是自生而来的，是由元气形成

[1] 中文选自郭齐勇主编：《中国古典哲学名著选读》，北京：人民出版社，2005 年。
Lun Hêng（论衡）, selected from *Philosophical Essays of WANG CH'UNG*, translated by Alfred Forke, Paragon Book Gallery, New York, 1962, Book XVIII.

的。甚至天本身也是由元气构成的，没有感觉，没有意志。这样，王充就以“元气自然”的朴素唯物思想批判了天人感应的神学目的论。

[Introduction] *Spontaneity* which is a thesis of Wang Chong's view of nature occupies an important position in the book of *Lun Heng*. In this thesis, Wang Chong abandons the thought of non-action of nature insisted upon by Huang-Lao Taoism, but makes it combine with the theory of "*Yuanqi* (*primordial-Qi*) ". Instead, he proposes the idea that "By the fusion of the fluids of Heaven and Earth, all things of the world are produced spontaneously, " believing that the whole nature which is formed by "*Yuanqi*" can arise by its own. Even Heaven itself is made up of "*Yuanqi*", no feeling, no will. Accordingly, Wang Chong critically questions the theological teleology of interaction between Heaven and man from the perspective of "nature constructed by *Yuanqi*" — a simple view of materialism.

天地合气，万物自生，犹夫妇合气，子自生矣[气：指元气，一种极其精微的云烟状的物质实体。合气：指天地的阴阳二气相交合。]。万物之生，含血之类[含血之类：有血气的生物，这里特指人。]，知饥知寒。见五谷可食，取而食之；见丝麻可衣，取而衣之；或说，以为天生五谷以食人，生丝麻以衣人[或说：有的说法。这里特指董仲舒的天人目的论。食、衣：均用如动词，喂养、穿戴。]。此谓天为人作农夫、桑女之徒也[此句意为：这种说法意味着天在给人们充当农夫、桑女之类的角色。]，不合自然，故其义疑，未可从也。

By the fusion of the fluids of Heaven and Earth（“天地合气”）all things of the world are produced spontaneously（“万物自生”）, just as by the mixture of the fluids of husband and wife children are born spontaneously. Among the things thus produced, creatures with blood in their veins are sensitive of hunger and cold. Seeing that grain can be eaten, they use it as food, and discovering that silk and hemp can be worn, they take it as raiment. Some people are of opinion that Heaven produces grain for the purpose of feeding mankind, and silk and hemp to clothe them. That would be tantamount to making Heaven the farmer of man or his mulberry girl（“此谓天为人作农夫、桑女之徒也”）, it would not be in accordance with spontaneity（“自然”）, therefore, this opinion is very questionable and unacceptable.

试依道家论之。天者，普施气万物之中，谷愈饥而丝麻救寒[“万物”之前似脱一“于”字。愈：解除、治好。愈饥：充饥。救：抵御。]，故人食谷、衣丝麻也。夫天之不故生五谷丝麻以衣食人，由其有灾变不欲以谴告人也[故：故意，特意。由：同“犹”，就像。其：代指天。灾变：自然界的灾害和怪异现象。汉代士人喜谈灾异之说。谴告：谴责、告诫、预先警告。]。物自生而人衣食之，气自变而人畏惧之。以若说论之，厌于人心矣[若说：这种说法。厌：同“餍”，满足。厌于人心：指让人衷心满意。这是与上文“其义疑”相对的。]。如天瑞为故，自然焉在？无为何居[天瑞：上天所降下的祥瑞征兆。]？

Reasoning on Taoist principles we find that Heaven emits its fluid everywhere. Among the many things of this world grain dispels hunger, and silk and hemp protect from cold. For that reason man eats grain, and wears silk and hemp. That Heaven does not produce grain, silk, and hemp purposely, in order to feed and clothe mankind, follows from the fact that by calamitous changes it does not intend to reprove man. Things are produced spontaneously, and man wears and eats them; the fluid changes spontaneously, and man is frightened by it, for the usual theory is disheartening. Where would be spontaneity, if the heavenly signs were intentional, and where inaction?

何以知天之自然也？以天无口目也。案有为者，口目之类也[案：提语，提起下面的重要内容。有为者：有意识的、有作为的(生物)。]。口欲食而目欲视，有嗜欲于内，发之于外，口目求之，得以为利欲之为也。今无口目之欲，于物无所求索，夫何为乎！何以知天无口目也？以地知之。地以土为体，土本无口目。天地，夫妇也[“天地，夫妇也”：天地就像夫与妇一样匹配对应。]；地体无口目，亦知天无口目也。使天体乎？宜与地同[体：有形体。宜：应当。]。使天气乎？气若云烟；云烟之属，安得口目[“使天气乎”：假设天是像气一样虚渺无形的。属：类。]！

Why must we assume that Heaven acts spontaneously? Because it has neither mouth nor eyes. Activity is connected with the mouth and the eyes: the mouth wishes to eat, and the eyes to see. These desires within manifest themselves outward(“有嗜欲于内，发之于外”). That the mouth and the eyes are craving for something, which is considered an advantage, is due to those desires. Now, provided that the mouth and the eye do not affect things, there is nothing that they might long for, why should there be activity then? How do we know that Heaven possesses neither mouth nor eyes? From Earth. The body of the Earth is formed of earth, and earth has neither mouth nor eyes. Heaven and Earth are like husband and wife(“天地，夫妇也”). Since the body of the Earth is not provided with a mouth or eyes, we know that Heaven has no mouth or eyes neither. Supposing that Heaven has a body, then it must be like that of the Earth, and should it be air only, this air would be like clouds and fog. How can a cloudy or nebular substance have a mouth or an eye?

或曰：“凡动行之类，皆本有为[“皆本有为”的“有”字前原有一“无”字，据文意删。不过刘盼遂认为“有”才是衍文，应当作“皆本无为”。]。有欲故动，动则有为。今天动行与人相似，安得无为？”曰：天之动行也，施气也；体动，气乃出，物乃生矣。由人动气也，体动气乃出，子亦生也[由：通“犹”，就像。体：形体。]。夫人之施气也，非欲以生子，气施而子自生矣[欲：打算，有意，特意。]。天动不欲以生物，而物自生，此则自然也；施气不欲为物，而物自为，此则无为也。谓天自然无为者何？气也！恬淡无欲，无为无事者也，老聃得以寿矣[恬淡：淡漠。此指气没有情感欲望，是针对董仲舒的“阳气爱、阴气恶”的主张提出的反驳。]。老聃禀之于天，使天无此气[使：假设，假使。]，老聃安所禀受此性？师无其说而弟子独言者，未之有也[这句的意思是：老师没有讲过的，学生却能够独自讲出来，这样的事情从来没有过。它是在比喻“天无此气，则人无此性”。]。

Someone might argue that every movement is originally inaction. There is desire provoking the movement, and, as soon as there is motion, there is action. The movements of Heaven are similar to those of man, how could they be inactive? I reply that, when Heaven moves, it emits its fluid. Its body moves, the fluid comes forth, and things are produced. When man moves his fluid, his body moves, his fluid then comes forth, and a child is produced(“由人动气也，体动气乃出，子亦生也”). Man emitting his fluid does not intend to beget a child, yet the fluid being emitted, the child is born of itself. When Heaven is moving, it does not desire to produce things thereby, but things are produced of their own accord. That is spontaneity. Letting out its fluid it does not desire to create things, but things are created of themselves（“而物自为”）. That is inaction. But how is the fluid of Heaven, which we credit with spontaneity and inaction? It is placid, tranquil, desireless, inactive, and unbusied. Laotse（老聃）acquired long life by it. He obtained it from Heaven. If Heaven did not possess this fluid, how could Lao Tse have obtained this nature? For it does not happen that the disciples alone speak of something, which their master never mentioned.

或复于桓公，公曰：“以告仲父。”[或：有人。复：复命，报告执行使命的情况。“以告仲父”可以读作“以之告仲父”。仲父：指管仲，是对管仲的尊称。]左右曰：“一则仲父，二则仲父，为君乃易乎[为君乃易乎：做君主就那么容易吗？]？”桓公曰：“吾未得仲父，故难；已得仲父，何为不易？”夫桓公得仲父，任之以事，委之以政，不复与知[任：任命，使之担负。事：管理国家的大事。委：委托，托付。与知：参与，过问。此言自己就不再参与过问。]。皇天以至优之德与王政，而谴告之，则天德不若桓公，而霸君之操过上帝也[皇：大。与：给予，赋予。“而谴告之”的“之”当作“人”。霸君：在诸侯中称霸的君主，此指齐桓公。操：操行。这句话的意思是：天的道德还不如齐桓公，而霸君的操行反而超过上天了。王充以此来揭示“谴告说”的荒谬。]。

Perhaps this nature appeared again in Duke Huan（桓公）, who was wont to say, “Let Kuan Chung（管仲）know.” His attendants replied, “Is it so easy to rule, if Kuan Chung is always the first and second word?” The Duke rejoined, “Before I had secured the services of Kuan Chung, I was in the greatest difficulties, now, after I have got him, I find everything easy.”（“吾未得仲父，故难；已得仲父，何为不易？”）When Duke Huan had taken Kuan Chung into his service, he left the affairs to him, entrusted him with the administration, and did not trouble any more about it. Should high Heaven, which in its exalted virtue confers the government upon an emperor, reprove man, its virtue would be inferior to that of Duke Huan, and the conduct of a feudatory prince surpasses that of great Heaven.

或曰：“桓公知管仲贤，故委任之；如非管仲，亦将谴告之矣。使天遭尧、舜[遭：遇到。]，必无谴告之变。”曰：天能谴告人君，则亦能故命圣君，择才若尧、舜，受以王命，委以王事，勿复与知[受：通“授”。勿复与知：（上天）不再参与过问。]。今则不然，生庸庸之君，失道废德，随谴告之，何天不惮劳也[随：接着。不惮劳：不怕劳碌、不嫌麻烦。]！曹参为汉相，纵酒歌乐，不听政治，其子谏之，笞之二百[曹参及下文汲黯，均是西汉实行无为之道的官吏。笞（chī）：用鞭子抽打的刑罚。]。当时天下无扰乱之变。淮阳铸伪钱，吏不能禁，汲黯为太守，不坏一炉，不刑一人，高枕安卧，而淮阳政清。夫曹参为相，若不为相；汲黯为太守，若郡无人。然而汉朝无事，淮阳刑错者，参德优而黯威重也[错：通“措”，废弃。]。计天之威德，孰与曹参、汲黯[计：衡量、比较。]？而谓天与王政，随而谴告之，是谓天德不若曹参厚，而威不若汲黯重也。蘧（qú）伯玉治卫，子贡使人问之：“何以治卫？”对曰：“以不治治之。”夫不治之治，无为之道也。

Somebody might object that Duke Huan knew Kuan Chung to be a wise man, and therefore appointed him, and that but for Kuan Chung he would also have given vent to his displeasure. Meeting with men like Yao and Shun, Heaven would certainly not have reprimanded people either. I beg to reply, that, if Heaven can reprimand, it might as well purposely appoint a wise prince, select a genius like Yao and Shun, confer the imperial dignity upon him, and leave the affairs of the Empire to him without taking further notice of them. Now it is different. Heaven creates very inferior princes, who have no principles, and neglect virtue, and therefore has to reprove them every now and then. Would it not be afraid of the trouble? Ts'ao Ts'an, a minister of the Han, was given to wine, songs, and music, and did not care about government(“曹参为汉相，纵酒歌乐，不听政治”). When his son remonstrated with him, he gave him two hundred blows with the bamboo. At that period there was no insurrection in the Empire. In Huaiyang, people (淮阳人) coined counterfeit money, and the officials were powerless to check the abuse. Chi Yen(汲黯)was prefect then. He did not destroy a single furnace, or punish a single individual. Quite indifferent, he was comfortably reclining on his couch, and the conditions of Huaiyang became well ordered again. Ts'ao Ts'an(曹参)behaved himself, as though he were not a minister, and Chi Yen administered his prefecture, as if nobody were living in it. Albeit yet the empire of the Han had no troubles, and in Huaiyang the punishments could be discontinued. So perfect was the virtue of Ts'ao Ts'an, and so imposing Chi Yen's dignity. The majesty of Heaven and its virtue are quite something else than those of Ts'ao Ts'an and Chi Yen, but to affirm that Heaven entrusts an emperor with the government, and then reproves him, would amount to nothing less than that Heaven's virtue is not as exalted as that of Ts'ao Ts'an, and its majesty not as imposing as that of Chi Yen. When Chü Po Yü (蘧伯玉)was governing Wei(卫国), Tse Kung(子贡)asked him through somebody, how he governed Wei. The reply was, “I govern it by not governing.”— Government by not governing is inaction as a principle.

或曰：“太平之应，河出图，洛出书。不画不就，不为不成，天地出之，有为之验也[应：瑞应，吉祥的征兆。“河出图、洛出书”：原话见《易•系辞》，传说古代有龙马自黄河出，其背上有图，称为“河图”；又有灵龟自洛水出，其背上有书，称为“洛书'；就：完成，成就。此句意为：无论是河图还是洛书，都必须要画、刻才能形成。所以，这些可以看作是天有意识地谴告人间的明证。验：证据。]。张良游泗水之上，遇黄石公授太公书，盖天佐汉诛秦，故命令神石为鬼书授人[神石：指“黄石公”，传说他是由一块黄色的神石变成的。鬼书：指《太公兵法》，以其来源莫测，故称为“鬼书”。]，复为有为之效也。”曰：此皆自然也。夫天安得以笔墨而为图书乎？天道自然，故图书自成。晋唐叔虞、鲁成季友生，文在其手，故叔曰“虞”，季曰“友”[晋唐叔虞：是周武王的儿子；鲁成季友：鲁桓公的儿子。传说他们出生的时候，手上就已经分别有了“虞”、“友”的字样。]。宋仲子生，有文在其手，曰“为鲁夫人”。三者在母之时，文字成矣，而谓天为文字，在母之时，天使神持锥笔墨刻其身乎[宋仲子：宋武公的女儿，传说生下来手上就有“为鲁夫人”的字样，后来嫁给了鲁惠公。]？自然之化，固疑难知，外若有为，内实自然。是以太史公纪黄石事，疑而不能实也[实：证实。]。赵简子梦上天，见一男子在帝之侧。后出，见人当道[赵简子：即赵鞅，晋国大夫，赵国奠基人。帝：天帝。当：同“挡”，阻挡。]，则前所梦见在帝侧者也。论之以为赵国且昌之状也。黄石授书，亦汉且兴之象也[论：议论。且：将要。昌：兴盛。状：征兆。象：征兆。]。妖气为鬼，鬼象人形，自然之道，非或为之也[这句话的意思是：这些征兆(如黄石公授书、帝侧之男子挡道)其实都是元气中的妖气所变化形成的。妖气变化成像人的样子。但这也没有什么好奇怪的，它只不过是自然的一种变化之道，并非有人或神灵有意识造成的。这里，王充试图用元气说来解释鬼神现象，但仍有错陋之处。]。

Some opponent might say that as a sequel of universal peace a plan came forth from the Yellow River, and a scroll from the Luo River(“河出图，洛出书”). Without drawing no plan can be made, and without action nothing is completed. The fact that Heaven and Earth produced the plan and the scroll shows that they are active, they think. When Chang Liang(张良)was walking on the banks of the River *Sse*(泗水), he met the Yellow Stone Genius, who gave him the minister’ s book. Heaven was supporting the Han and destroying the Chin(秦), therefore he ordered a spiritual stone to change into a ghost. That a book was handed to somebody is again considered a proof of activity. I am of opinion that all this was spontaneous, for how could Heaven take a brush and ink, and draw the plan, or write the scroll? The principle of Heaven is spontaneity, consequently the plan and the book must have been produced of themselves. Tang Shuyü of Chin(“晋唐叔虞”)and Ch’êng Chi Yo of Lu(“鲁成季友生”)had a character in their hands, when they were born, therefore one was called Yü, the other Yo. When Ch’ung Tse of Sung(“宋仲子”)was born, the characters “Duchess of Lu(“为鲁夫人”)” were written on her palm. These letters must have been written, while the three persons were still in their mother’ s wombs. If we say that Heaven wrote them, while they were in their mother’ s wombs, did Heaven perhaps send a spirit with a style, a brush, and ink to engrave and write the characters on their bodies? The spontaneity of these processes seems dubious, and is difficult to understand. Externally there seemed to be activity, but as a matter of fact, there was spontaneity internally. Thus the Grand Annalist(太史公)recording the story of the yellow stone(“黄石事”), has his doubts, but cannot find the truth. Viscount Chien of Chao(赵简子)had a dream that he was ascending to heaven. There he saw a lad by the side of the Ruler of Heaven(“在帝之侧”). When he went out subsequently, he perceived a young man in the street, who was the one whom he had seen previously in his dream by the side of the Ruler of Heaven. This must be regarded as a lucky augury——the future flourishing of the Chao State(赵国), as the transmission of the book by the “yellow stone” was a sign of the rise of the Han Dynasty. That the supernatural fluid becomes a ghost, and that the ghost is shaped like a man, is spontaneous, and not the work of anybody.

草木之生，华叶青葱，皆有曲折，象类文章[华：同“花”。象类文章：好像文字、图案。]。谓天为文字，复为华叶乎[这句话的意思是：如果我们说天有意识地造出文字，那么是不是也要说天有意识地造出花和叶呢？王充以此反驳天人目的论。]？宋人或刻木为楮[楮(chǔ)：树名。]叶者，三年乃成。列子曰：“使天地三年乃成一叶，则万物之有叶者寡矣”。如列子之言，万物之叶自为生也。自为生也，故能并成[并成：同时产生出这么多花和叶。]。如天为之，其迟当若宋人刻楮叶矣。观鸟兽之毛羽，毛羽之采色，通可为乎[采：同“彩”。通：都。]？鸟兽未能尽实。春观万物之生，秋观其成，天地为之乎？物自然也。如谓天地为之，为之宜用手，天地安得万万千千手，并为万万千千物乎？诸物在天地之间也，犹子在母腹中也。母怀子气，十月而生，鼻口耳目，发肤毛理，血脉脂腴，骨节爪齿，自然成腹中乎[理：皮肤的纹理。腴：肥厚多肉。]？母为之也？偶人千万，不名为人者[偶人：泥塑木雕的假人。]，何也？鼻口耳目，非性自然也。武帝幸王夫人[幸：宠爱。]，王夫人死，思见其形[思见其形：思念她而希望能再看到她的形像。]。道士以方术作夫人形，形成，出入宫门，武帝大惊，立而迎之，忽不复见。盖非自然之真，方士巧妄之伪，故一见恍忽，消散灭亡。有为之化，其不可久行，犹王夫人形不可久见也[有为之化：有意识造作的东西。]。道家论自然，不知引物事以验其言行，故自然之说未见信也[引：援引。物事：具体的事件和物体。验：验证。见：被。信：信任，相信。]。

When plants and trees grow, their flowers and leaves are onion green and have crooked and broken veins like ornaments. If Heaven is credited with having written the above-mentioned characters, does it make these flowers and leaves also? In the State of *Sung* a man carved a mulberry leaf out of wood, (“宋人或刻木为楮叶者”) and it took him three years to complete it. *Confucius* said “If the Earth required three years to complete one leaf, few plants would have leaves.” According to this dictum of *Confucius* the leaves of plants grow spontaneously, and for that reason they can grow simultaneously. If Heaven made them, their growth would be as much delayed as the carving of the mulberry leaf by the man of the *Sung* State (宋国). Let us look at the hair and feathers of animals and birds, and their various colours. Can they all have been made? If so, animals and birds would never be quite finished. In spring we see the plants growing, and in autumn we see them full-grown. Can Heaven and Earth have done this, or do things grow spontaneously? If we may say that Heaven and Earth have done it, they must have used hands for the purpose. Do Heaven and Earth possess many thousand or many ten thousand hands to produce thousands and ten thousands of things at the same time? (“如谓天地为之，为之宜用手，天地安得万万千千手，并为万万千千物乎？”) The things between Heaven and Earth are like a child in his mother’s womb. After ten months, pregnancy the mother gives birth to the child. Are his nose, his mouth, his ears, his hair, his eyes, his skin with down, the arteries, the fat, the bones, the joints, the claws, and the teeth grown of themselves in the womb, or has the mother made them? Why is a dummy never called a man? Because it has a nose, a mouth, ears, and eyes, but not a spontaneous nature. Wu Ti (武帝) was very fond of his consort Wang (“王夫人”). When she had died, he pondered, whether he could not see her figure again. The Taoists made an artificial figure of the lady. When it was ready, it passed through the palace gate. Wu Ti was greatly alarmed and rose to meet her, but, all of a sudden, she was not seen any more. Since it was not a real, spontaneous being, but a semblance, artificially made by jugglers, it became diffuse at first sight, dispersed, and vanished. Everything that has been made does not last long, like the image of the empress, which appeared only for a short while. The Taoist school argues on spontaneity, but it does not know how to substantiate its cause by evidence. Therefore their theory of spontaneity has not yet found credence (“故自然之说未见信也”).

物虽自然，亦须有为辅助。耒耜耕耘，因春播种者，人为之也[耒耜：古代的农具。耕：翻土。耘：锄草。因：应顺，依随。]。及谷入地，日夜长大[“大”原作“夫”，据刘盼遂说改。]，人不能为也。或为之者，败之道也。宋人有闵其苗之不长者，就而揠之，明日枯死[闵：同“悯”，忧虑。就：走近。揠：拔。]。夫欲为自然者，宋人之徒也[欲为自然：欲有为于自然。徒：一类的人。]。

However, in spite of spontaneity there may be activity for a while in support of it. Ploughing, tilling, weeding, and sowing in Spring are human actions. But as soon as the grain has entered the soil, it begins growing day and night. Man can do nothing for it, or if he does, he spoils the thing. A man of *Sung* was sorry that his sprouts were not high enough, therefore he pulled them out, but, on the following day, they were dry, and died. He who wishes to do what is spontaneous, is on a par with this man of *Sung*.

问曰："人生于天地，天地无为，人禀天性者，亦当无为，而有为，何也[而有为：然而有为造作。]？"曰：至德纯渥之人，禀天气多，故能则天，自然无为[纯渥：纯朴笃厚。渥：厚。则：效法，以……为则。]。禀气薄少，不遵道德，不似天地，故曰不肖。不肖者，不似也[不肖：不肖似，不像。]。不似天地，不类圣贤，故有为也。天地为炉，造化为工，禀气不一，安能皆贤！贤之纯者，黄、老是也。黄者，黄帝也；老者，老子也。黄、老之操，身中恬淡，其治无为，正身共己而阴阳自和[操：道德操守。共：同"恭"，庄严，端庄。]，无心于为而物自化，无意于生而物自成。

The following question may be raised: "Man is born from Heaven and Earth. Since Heaven and Earth are inactive, man who has received the fluid of Heaven, ought to be inactive likewise, wherefore does he act nevertheless?" For the following reason. A man with the highest, purest, and fullest virtue has been endowed with a large quantity of the heavenly fluid, therefore he can follow the example of Heaven, and be spontaneous and inactive like it. He who has received but a small quota of the fluid, does not live in accordance with righteousness and virtue, and does not resemble Heaven and Earth. Hence he is called unlike, which means that he does not resemble Heaven and Earth. Not resembling Heaven and Earth he cannot be accounted a wise man or a sage. Therefore he is active. Heaven and Earth are the furnace, and the Creater is the melting process("天地为炉，造化为工"). How can all be wise, since the fluid of which they are formed is not the same? Huang (黄) and Lao (老) were truly wise. Huang is Huang Ti(黄帝), and Lao is Lao Tse(老子). Huang and Lao' s conduct was such, that their bodies were in a state of quietude and indifference. Their government consisted in inaction. They took care of their persons, and behaved with reverence, hence *Yin* and *Yang* were in harmony. They did not long for action, and things were produced of themselves; they did not think of creating anything, and things were completed spontaneously.

《易》曰："黄帝、尧、舜垂衣裳而天下治。"垂衣裳者，垂拱无为也[垂：手垂下。拱：双臂交于胸前。垂拱：形容清闲无事的样子。]。孔子曰："大哉，尧之为君也！惟天为大，惟尧则之[则：效法。]。"又曰："巍巍乎！舜、禹之有天下也，而不与焉[巍巍乎：崇高的样子。不与：不参与，不干预。]。"周公曰上帝引佚[引：长。佚：同"逸"，安乐。]。上帝，谓舜、禹也[此句意为：这里所说的"上帝"，就是指舜禹之类。舜禹：一本作"虞舜"。]。舜、禹承安继治，任贤使能，恭己无为而天下治。舜、禹承亮之安，尧则天而行，不作功邀名，无为之化自成，故曰"荡荡乎民无能名焉[荡荡乎：形容广大的样子。无能名：说不出，无法称颂它。]"。年五十者击壤[击壤：古代的一种游戏，置一片木板于地，在远处以另一木块投掷它，投中者得胜。涂：同"途"，道路。]于涂，不能知尧之德，盖自然之化也[此句意为：一群五十多岁的老人在路边玩击壤的游戏，很舒适平逸的样子。但他们并没有意识到这是尧的德政功劳，而把这当成是自然的变化而已。］。《易》曰：“大人与天地合其德。”黄帝、尧、舜，大人也，其德与天地合，故知无为也。天道无为，故春不为［不为：不是为了。］生，而夏不为长，秋不为成，冬不为藏。阳气自出，物自生长；阴气自起，物自成藏。汲井决陂，灌概园田，物亦生长［汲井：从井中引水。陂(bēi)：池塘。决陂：从池塘中放水。］。霈［霈(pèi)：雨多的样子］然而雨，物之茎叶根荄，莫不洽濡［荄(gāi)：草根。荄原作“垓”，据文意改。洽(qià)濡(rú)：湿润］。程量澍(shù)泽，孰与汲井决陂哉［程量：衡量、比较。澍泽：雨水滋润的程度。句意为：比较一下天然下雨与人工汲水决池的功效。］？故无为之为大矣。本不求功，故其功立；本不求名，故其名成。沛然之雨，功名大矣，而天地不为也，气和而雨自集［沛然：同“霈然”气和：阴阳二气合和。集：降落，栖止。］。

The Yi-king（《易》）says that Huang Ti, Yao, and Shun let their robes fall, and the empire was governed. That they let their robes fall means that their robes fell down, and that they folded their arms, doing nothing. *Confucius* said, “Grand indeed was Yao as a sovereign（“大哉，尧之为君也！”）! Heaven alone is great, and *yao* alone emulated it! ”（“惟天为大，惟尧则之！”）and, “How imposing was the way in which Shun（舜）and Yü（禹）swayed the empire, but did not much care for it.” The Duke of *Chou*（周公）makes the remark that the supreme ruler enjoyed his ease. By the supreme ruler Shun and Yü are meant. Shun and Yü took over the peaceful government, which they continued, appointing wise men and men of talent. They respected themselves, and did no work themselves, and the empire was governed. Shun and Yü received the peaceful government from Yao. Yao imitated Heaven; he did not do meritorious deeds or strive for a name, and reforms, for which nothing was done, were completed of themselves. Hence it was said, “Excellent indeed”, but the people did not find the right name for it.（“荡荡乎民无能名焉”）Those aged 50 years were beating clods of earth together on their land, but they did not understand Yao's virtue, because the reforms were spontaneous. The *Yi-king* says, “The great man equals Heaven and Earth in virtue.” Huang Ti, Yao, and Shun were such great men. Their virtue was on a level with that of Heaven and Earth, therefore they knew inaction. The principle of Heaven is inaction. Accordingly in spring it does not do the germinating, in summer the growing, in autumn the ripening, or in winter the hiding of the seeds. When the *Yang* fluid comes forth spontaneously, plants will germinate and grow of themselves, and, when the *Yin* fluid rises, they ripen and disappear of their own accord（“阳气自出，物自生长；阴气自起，物自成藏”）. When we irrigate garden land with water drawn from wells or drained from ponds, plants germinate and grow also, but, when showers of rain come down, the stalks, leaves, and roots are all abundantly soaked. Natural moisture is much more copious than artificial irrigation from wells and ponds. Thus inactive action brings the greatest results. By not seeking it, merit is acquired, and by not pursuing fame, fame is obtained. Rain-showers, merit, and fame are something great, yet Heaven and Earth do not work for them. When the fluid harmonizes, rain gathers spontaneously.

儒家说夫妇之道取法于天地。知夫妇法天地，不知推夫妇之道以论天地之性，可谓惑矣。夫天覆于上，地偃于下，下气蒸上，上气降下，万物自生其中间矣［偃(yǎn)：仰卧。烝(zhēng)：气上升，犹“蒸”。］。当其生也，天不须复与也，由子在母怀中，父不能知也［与：干预，过问。由：同“犹”。知：

主管，过问。]。物自生，子自成，天地父母何与知哉！及其生也，人道有教训之义。天道无为，听恣其性[人道：与天道自然相对，指人间的有意识的努力。听：听任。恣：放纵，不拘束。]，故放鱼于川，纵兽于山，从其性命之欲也。不驱鱼令上陵，不逐兽令入渊者，何哉？拂诡其性，失其所宜也[拂诡：违背，违反。所宜：所适宜的环境。]。夫百姓，鱼兽之类也，上德治之，若烹小鲜，与天地同操也[“上德治之，若烹小鲜”：取义自《老子》“治大国若烹小鲜”。烹：烧菜。小鲜：小菜，或曰为鱼。操：德操。]。商鞅变秦法，欲为殊异之功，不听赵良之议，以取车裂之患，德薄多欲，君臣相憎怨也。道家德厚，下当其上，上安其下，纯蒙无为，何复谴告[赵良：秦国儒生，曾以“恃德者昌、恃力者亡”来反对商鞅的变法。]？故曰：政之适也，君臣相忘于治，鱼相忘于水，兽相忘于林，人相忘于世，故曰天也[当：适合；一说解作“向往”。纯蒙：纯朴浑厚。]。孔子谓颜渊曰：“吾服汝，忘也；汝之服于我，亦忘也[服：佩服，信服。]。”以孔子为君，颜渊为臣，尚不能谴告，况以老子为君，文子为臣乎？老子、文子，似天地者也[文子：传说中老子的弟子，著有《文子》一书。似天地者：就像天与地的关系一样。]。淳酒味甘，饮之者醉不相知；薄酒酸苦，宾主嚬蹙[淳酒：味道纯厚的酒。淳：同“醇”。薄酒：与醇酒相对，味道浅涩的酒。嚬(pín)蹙(cù)：皱眉不快的样子。]。夫相谴告，道薄之验也。谓天谴告，曾谓天德不若淳酒乎[验：明证。曾：岂，难道。]！

The Confucianists insist that the relation of husband and wife establish similarities with Heaven and Earth. For husband and wife they find similarities with Heaven and Earth, but in so far as they are unable to make use of the relation of husband and wife, when discussing the nature of Heaven and Earth, they show a regrettable lack of acumen. Heaven expands above, and Earth below(“夫天覆于上，地偃于下”). When the fluid from below rises, and the fluid on high descends, all things are created in the middle(“下气蒸上，上气降下，万物自生其中间矣”). While they are growing, it is not necessary that Heaven should still care for them, just as the father does not know the embryo, after it is in the mother’s womb. Things grow spontaneously, and the child is formed of itself. Heaven and Earth, and father and mother can take no further cognisance of it. But after birth, the way of man is instruction and teaching, the way of Heaven, inaction and yielding to nature. Therefore Heaven allows the fish to swim in the rivers, and the wild beasts to roam in the mountains, following their natural propensities. It does not drive the fish up the hills, or the wild beasts into the water. Why? Because that would be an outrage upon their nature, and a complete disregard of what suits them. The people resemble fish and beasts. High virtue governs them as easily, as one fries small fish, and as Heaven and Earth would act. Shang Yang(商鞅) changed the laws of *Ch’in* (秦)wishing to acquire extraordinary merit. He did not hear the advice of Chang Liang(张良), consequently he incurred the horrible penalty of being torn asunder by carts. If the virtue be poor, and the desires many, prince and minister hate one another. The Taoists possess real virtue: the inferiors agree with the superiors, and the superiors are at peace with their inferiors. Being genuinely ignorant, they do nothing, and there is no reason, why they should be reproved. This is what they call a well-balanced government. Prince and minister forget one another in governing, the fish forget each other in the water, and so do the beasts in the forests, and men in life. That is Heaven. *Confucius* said to Yen Yuan(颜渊), “When I deferred to you, I did not think of it, and when you deferred to me, you likewise did not think of it(‘吾服汝，忘也；汝之服于我，亦忘也’).”Although *Confucius* was like a prince, and Yen Yuan like a minister, he could not make up his mind to reprimand Yen Yüen, how much less would Lao Tse have been able to do so, if we consider him as a prince and Wên Tse (文子) as his minister? Lao Tse and Wên Tse were like Heaven and Earth. Generous wine tastes sweet. When those who drink it, become drunk, they do not know each other. Bad wine is sour and bitter. Hosts and guests knit the brows. Now, reprimands are a proof of the badness of one' s principles. To say that Heaven reprimands would be like pretending that Heaven' s excellence is inferior to that of generous wine.

“礼者，忠信之薄，乱之首也[引自《老子》三十八章。薄：衰微。首：开端。]。”相讥以礼，故相谴告[讥：指责、埋怨。]。三皇之时，坐者于于，行者居居，乍自以为马，乍自以为牛[三皇：一说指天皇、地皇、人皇；一说指上古燧人氏、伏羲氏、神农氏。于于、居居：均指悠然无知的样子。乍：一会儿、时而。]。纯德行而民瞳矇，晓惠之心未形生也[纯德：纯朴的道德。瞳矇：浑昧无知的样子。晓惠：聪明，此指机巧伪诈。惠：同“慧”。形：形成。]。当时亦无灾异。如有灾异，不名曰谴告。何则？时人愚蠢，不知相绳责也[愚蠢：指单纯、无知。在这里，指道家的质朴状态，不具有贬义。绳：绳墨、标准。绳责：以某一标准相互指责。]。末世衰微，上下相非，灾异时至，则造谴告之言矣。夫今之天，古之天也。非古之天厚，而今之天薄也。谴告之言生于今者，人以心准况之也[准况：比照。]。诰、誓不及五帝，要盟不及三王，交质子不及五伯，德弥薄者信弥衰[诰、誓：《尚书》中的两种文体，君王对臣下作文告誓约的演说词。五帝：传说中上古的帝王，指黄帝、颛顼、帝喾、尧、舜。要盟：以武力胁迫而订下的盟约。要：要挟。三王：三代之王，指禹、汤、文、武。交：相互交换。质子：换至别国作抵押的太子。五伯：同“五霸”，春秋时称霸的五个诸侯国君，指齐桓公、秦穆公、晋文公、宋襄公、楚庄王。信：诚信，信誉。弥：愈。]。心险而行诐，则犯约而负教[诐(bì)：偏颇，邪僻。犯、负：均指违背。约：盟约。教：教令。指上文诰誓、要盟的内容。]。教约不行，则相谴告。谴告不改，举兵相灭[此句意为：已经谴告了还不改正过错，则兴兵而灭之。]。由此言之，谴告之言，衰乱之语也，而谓之上天为之，斯盖所以疑也。

Ceremonies originate from a want of loyalty and good faith, and are the beginning of confusion. On that score people find fault with one another, which leads to reproof. At the time of the Three Rulers (“三黄”) people were sitting down self-satisfied, and walking about at perfect ease. Sometimes they took themselves for horses, and sometimes for oxen. Virtuous actions were out of the question, and the people were dull and beclouded. Knowledge and wisdom did not yet make their appearance. Originally, there happened no calamities or catastrophes either, or, if they did, they were not denoted as reprimands. Why? Because at that time people were feeble-minded, and did not restrain or reproach one another. Later generations have gradually declined: superiors and inferiors recriminate, and calamitous events continually happen. Hence the hypothesis of reprimands has been developed (“末世衰微，上下相非，灾异时至，则造谴告之言矣”). The Heaven of today is the Heaven of old, and it is not the case that the Heaven of old was benign, whereas now Heaven is harsh. The hypothesis of reprimands (“谴告之言”) has been put forward at present, as surmise made by men from their own feelings. Declarations and oaths do not reach up to the Five Emperors (五帝), agreements and covenants to the Three Rulers, and the giving of hostages to the Five Princes (五伯). The more people' s virtue declined, the more faith began to fail them. In their guile and treachery they broke treaties, and were deaf to admonitions. Treaties and admonitions being of no avail, they reproached one another, and if no change was brought about by these reproaches, they took up arms, and fought, till one was exterminated. Consequently reprimands point to a state of decay and disorder. Therefore it appears very dubious that Heaven should make reprimands.

且凡言谴告者，以人道验之也[且：况且。句意为：况且凡是宣扬谴告之说的人，都只是用人间的道理来验证它的。]。人道，君谴告臣，上天谴告君也，谓灾异为谴告。夫人道，臣亦有谏君，以灾异为谴告，而王者亦当时有谏上天之义，其效何在[其效何在：它的表现在哪里呢？效：表现。]？苟谓天德优，人不能谏，优德亦宜玄默，不当谴告[玄默：沉默。]。万石君子有过，不言，对案不食，至优之验也[万石(dàn)君：即西汉人石奋，一家父子五人奉禄都达二千石，故汉景帝称他为“万石君”。案：食案，饭桌。]。夫人之优者犹能不言，皇天德大，而乃谓之谴告乎！夫天无为，故不言。灾变时至，气自为之。夫天地不能为，亦不能知也。腹中有寒，腹中疾痛，人不使也，气自为之。夫天地之间，犹人背腹之中也，谓天为灾变，凡诸怪异之类，无小大薄厚，皆天所为乎？牛生马，桃生李，如论者之言，天神入牛腹中为马，把李实提桃间乎[把：握，拿着。提：提放到。]？牢曰：“子云：‘吾不试，故艺[牢：姓琴，字子开，孔子的学生。试：任用，做官。艺：技能。]。’”又曰：“‘吾少也贱，故多能鄙事。’”人之贱不用于大者，类多伎能[类：一般，大都。伎，同“技”。]。天尊贵高大，安能撰为灾变以谴告人[撰为：制造，造作。]！且吉凶蜚色见于面，人不能为，色自发也[蜚(fěi)色：反常的神色。]。天地犹人身，气变犹蜚色，人不能为蜚色，天地安能为气变！然则气变之见，殆自然也。变自见，色自发，占侯之家因以言也[见：同“现”。殆：大概。占侯之家：以占卜、观相为生的人。]。

Those, who believe in reprimands, refer to human ways as a proof. Among men a sovereign reprimands his minister, and high Heaven reprimands the sovereign. It does so by means of calamitous events, they say. However, among men it also happens that the minister remonstrates with his sovereign. When Heaven reprimands an emperor by visiting him with calamities, and the latter wishes at that time to remonstrate with high Heaven, how can he do it? If they say that Heaven' s virtue is so perfect that man cannot remonstrate with it, then Heaven possessed of such virtue, ought likewise to keep quiet, and ought not to reprimand. When the sovereign of *Wan Dan* (万石) did wrong, the latter did not say a word, but at table he did not eat, which showed his perfection. An excellent man can remain silent, and august Heaven with his sublime virtue should reprimand? Heaven does not act, therefore it does not speak. The disasters, which so frequently occur, are the work of the spontaneous fluid. Heaven and Earth cannot act, nor do they possess any knowledge (“夫天地不能为，亦不能知也”). When there is a cold in the stomach, it aches. This is not caused by man, but the spontaneous working of the fluid (“腹中有寒，腹中疾痛，人不使也，气自为之”). The space between Heaven and Earth is like that between the back and the stomach. If Heaven is regarded as the author of every calamity, are all abnormities, great or small, complicated or simple, caused by Heaven also? A cow may give birth to a horse, and on a cherry-tree a plum may grow. Does, according to the theory under discussion, the spirit of Heaven enter the belly of the cow to create the horse, or stick a plum upon a cherry-tree? *Lao* said, “The Master said, ‘Having no official employment, I acquired many arts, ’ ” and he said, “When I was young, my condition was low, and therefore I acquired my ability in many things, but they were mean matters." What is low in people, such as ability and skillfulness, is not practised by the great ones. How could Heaven, which is so majestic and sublime, choose to bring about catastrophes with a view to reprimanding people? Moreover, auspicious and inauspicious events are like the flushed colour appearing on the face. Man cannot produce it, the colour comes out of itself. Heaven and Earth are like the human body ("天地犹人身"), the transformation of their fluid, like the flushed colour. How can Heaven and Earth cause the sudden change of their fluid, since man cannot produce the flushed colour? The change of the fluid is spontaneous, it appears of itself, as the colour comes out of itself. The soothsayers (占候之家) rely on this, when they foretell the future.

夫寒温、谴告、变动、招致，四疑皆已论矣[王充先后写过《寒温》《谴告》《变动》《招致》四篇文章来驳斥当时的几种谬论。]。谴告于天道尤诡，故重论之，论之所以难别也[诡：违背。重：重新，再一次。难：责难；别：辨别。意即明辨其是非。]。说合于人事，不入于道意[说：谴告之说。合：符合。人事：人世间的事情。道意：天道自然的道理。]。从道不随事，虽违儒家之说，合黄老之义也[从：服从，依。随：迁就，随顺。]。

Heat and cold, reprimands, phenomenal changes, and attraction, all these four queries have already been treated. Reprimands are more contrary to the ways of Heaven than anything else, therefore I have discussed them twice, explaining where the difficulties in the way of the two antagonistic views lie. The one is in accordance with human affairs, but does not fall in with Taoism, the other agrees with Taoism, but is not in harmony with human affairs. But though opposed to the belief of the Confucianists, it corresponds to the ideas of Huang Ti (黄帝) and Lao Tse (老子).

“法谓法则也。人不违地，乃得安全，法地也。地不违天，乃得全载，法天也。天不违道，乃得全覆，法道也。道不违自然，乃得其性，法自然也。法自然者，在方法方，在圆法圆，于自然无违也。”

——王弼《老子注》第 25 章

Unit 4

王弼《老子指略》

Wang Pi: The Structure of the Laozi's Pointers [1]

[思想指要]王弼(公元 226—公元 249 年)，字辅嗣，三国时期魏山阳(今河南焦作)人。自幼“好老庄，通辩能言”，曾任尚书郎。他著有《周易注》《周易略例》《老子注》《老子指略》和《论语释疑》等，是魏晋玄学的主要代表人物及创始人之一。通过对有无、动静、言意之论证，建立了一套以贵无、主静、圣人体无、言不尽意等为主要内容的哲学体系。《老子指略》是王弼哲学思想的重要作品。他认为《老子》之书一以贯之，“崇本息末”而已矣。本者，无形无名者，万物之宗；“道”“玄”“深”“大”“远”及“素朴”等等，皆言崇其本者也。王弼的哲学思想重在对《老子》和《周易》等进行形上的揭明和阐释。

[Introduction] Wang Bi (226 A.D.— 249 A.D.), who styled himself Fusi, was born in Wei Shanyang (now Jiaozuo, Henan Province) during the Three Kingdoms Period of China. Since childhood he was “good at Lao and Zhuang and known for his sharp mind and witty words”, and later served as a minister in the court of the Tang dynasty. He wrote books, such as *Notes to The Book of Changes*, *Illustrated Examples of The Book of Changes*, *Notes to Lao Tzu*, *The Pointers of Lao Tzu* and *Questions and Problems of The Analects of Confucius*. He was one of the representatives and the founders of the School of Metaphysics which was popular in Wei and Jin dynasties. Through the argumentation of “existence and non-existence”, “action and inaction”, “word and meaning”, he established a set of philosophical system whose content was composed by “valuing non-assertion”, “advocating tranquilization”, “sage being con-substantial with nothing”, “language does not exhaust the concept in the mind”, and etc. Among his

---

[1] 中文选自郭齐勇主编：《中国古典哲学名著选读》，北京：人民出版社，2005 年。
Wang Bi, The Structure of the Laozi's Pointers (Laozi weizhi lilüe)— *A Philological Study and Translation*, by Rudolf G. Wagner. from ***T'oung Pao***, Second Series, Vol. 72, Livr. 1/3 (1986), 72 (1): 92-129.

writings, *The Pointers of Lao Tzu* is the most important work of philosophy. He said of what was consistent in *Laozi,* "Ah, exalting the root to soothe the branches, that is all!" Being ontic and invisible and nameless is the Mother of all things. In his opinion, "Tao", "Xuan"(玄), "Depth", "Greatness", "Remoteness" and "Simplicity" all exalt the root. Wang Bi's philosophical thought is essentially focused on providing a metaphysical exposition and interpretation of *Lao Tzu* and *Zhou Yi*.

夫物之所以生，功之所以成，必生乎无形，由乎无名。无形无名者，万物之宗也[无形无名：指常道常名。宗：宗极。]。不温不凉，不宫不商。听之不可得而闻，视之不可得而彰，体之不可得而知，味之不可得而尝。

That by which beings are created, that by which achievements are brought about, (beings) are necessarily created out of the featureless, and (achievements) are (necessarily) based on the nameless. The featureless and the nameless is the "ancestor of the 10,000 entities." (Being featureless) it neither warms nor cools. (Being nameless) it neither (lets sound forth the notes) *gong*（宫）nor *shang*（商）. (Even when) straining one's ear for it, one is (still) unable to hear it. (Even when) looking for it, one is (still) unable to perceive it. (Even when) fumbling for it, one is (still) unable to identify it. (Even when) going after its taste, one is (still) unable to get its flavour.

故其为物也则混成，为象也则无形，为音也则希声，为味也则无呈[呈：呈现。]。故能为品物之宗主，苞通天地，靡使不经也[靡使不经：靡，不；经，经纶，贯通。]。若温也则不能凉矣，宫也则不能商矣；形必有所分，声必有所属。

Therefore (Laozi says), "as a being" it "completes out of the muddy" , as a "figure" it is "without features, " as a "sound" it is "toneless, " as a "taste" it is without flavour. For this reason it is able to be the "principle" and the "master" of all (different) categories of beings, to embrace and permeate Heaven and Earth so that there is nothing which it does not thread through. Would it be warming, then it would not be cool. Would it (let sound forth) *gong*(宫), then it would not be able to (let sound forth) *shang*（商）. A feature necessarily has something which specifies it. A note necessarily has (a place in the scale) to which it belongs.

故象而形者非大象也，音而声者非大音也。然则四象不形则大象无以畅[四象：春、夏、秋、冬。]，五音不声则大音无以至[五音：宫、商、角(jué)、徵(zhǐ)、羽。]。四象形则物无所主焉，则大象畅矣。五音声而心无所适焉，则大音至矣。故执大象则天下往，用大音则风俗移也。

Therefore, A figure which takes on features(“故象而形者”) is not the "Great Figure." A sound which takes on a note(“音而声者”) is not the "Great Sound." However, if the Four Figures(“四象”) did not take on features, then the "Great Figure" would have nothing in which to shine forth. If the Five Sounds(“五音”) did not take on notes, the "Great Sound" would have nothing in which to come about. (Thus) when the Four Figures take on features and beings have nothing (else) by which they are dominated, then the Great Figure shines forth. When the Five Sounds take on notes and the minds have nothing (else) that engages them, then the reat Sound comes about. Therefore, "if (the lord) keeps to the Great Figure, the all-under-Heaven will flock to him" (Laozi says). If (the lord) makes use of the Great Sound, then the customs and habits will change for the better.

无形畅，天下虽往，往而不能释也[释：说明。]。希声至，风俗虽移，移而不能辩也。是故天生五物[五物：五行。]，无物为用。圣行五教[五教：五品之教，父义、母慈、兄友、弟恭、子孝，一说为父子有亲、君臣有义、夫妇有别、长幼有序、朋友有信。]，不言教化。

As the featureless is shining forth, although all-under-Heaven are flocking (to him), this flocking "to" they are not able to explain. As the toneless is coming about, although the customs and habits do change for the better, this change (the people) are not able to analyze. Thus, Heaven creates the Five Things, but it is a nothing that brings about their usefulness. the Sage (Confucius) spreads the Five Teachings, but it is "no-words" which brings about the improvement.

是以"道可道非常道，名可名非常名"也[《老子》第1章。]。"五物之母，不炎不寒，不柔不刚。五教之母，不皦不昧[皦(jiǎo)：明亮。]，不恩不伤。虽古今不同，时移俗易，此不变也，所谓"自古及今，其名不去"者也[《老子》第21章。]。天不以此则物不生，治不以此则功不成。故古今通，终始同。执古可以御今，证今可以知古始。

Therefore (Laozi says), "The *Tao* that can be spoken about is not the eternal *Tao*." The mother of the Five Things is neither hot nor cold, neither soft nor hard. The mother of the Five Teachings is neither "bright" nor "dark", neither kind nor harsh. Although old and new are not the same, the times have changed and the habits differ, she has not changed. This is what (Laozi) calls "from antlquity to the present her name has not disappeared." If Heaven would not rely on her, then beings would not be created. If government would not rely on her, then achievements would not be brought about. Therefore, as antiquity and present are connected, and as end and beginning have the same (structure). keeping to the old, (the lord) can regulate the present, and taking the present as evidence the "oldest beginning can be cognized."

此所谓"常"者也。无皦昧之状，温凉之象，故"知常曰明"也[《老子》第16章。]。物生功成，莫不由乎此，故"以阅众甫"也[《老子》第21章]。

This is what (*the Laozi*) styles "the eternal." It has neither a "bright" nor a "dark" appearance, a warming or a cooling feature. Therefore (Laozi says), "To cognize the eternal is called enlightenment." In the creation of beings, in the completion of achievements, there is nothing which is not based on this (eternal). Therefore (Laozi says), "It is said to be the beginning of the multitude."

夫奔电之疾犹不足以一时周[一时周：一时，与下文一息同，指在极短的时间内。周：周遍。]，御风之行犹不足以一息期[期(jī)：周还。]。善速在不疾，善至在不行。故可道之盛未足以官天地，有形之极未足以府万物[官：裁任，任用。府：包藏。]。

The speed of racing lightening is still insufficient to go full round in one single moment. Advancing by riding on the wind is still insufficient to arrive in one single breath. "To be good at being fast lies in not speeding" (say *the Xici*). "To be good at arriving lies in not rushing"(say *the Xici*). Therefore, the bloom of that "which can be spoken about" is still insufficient to "administer Heaven and Earth." The maximum of that which has features is still insufficient to "store the ten thousand entities."

是故叹之者不能尽乎斯美，咏之者不能畅乎斯弘。名之不能当，称之不能既[既：已。]。名必有所分，称必有所由。有分则有不兼，有由则有不尽。不兼则大殊其真，不尽则不可以名。

Therefore, he who praises it is unable to fully account for such a beauty. He who sings of it is unable indeed to expound such a width. Giving it a name cannot match it. Giving it a designation can not fully grasp it. A name necessarily has something which makes it specific. Having a specification, there will, as a consequence, be something which is not included. There being something not included, (the name), as a consequence, greatly deviates from the truth. A designation necessarily has something on which it is based. Having a base, there will, as a consequence, be something which is not exhausted. There being something not exhausted, (the designation), as a consequence, cannot be taken as a name.

此可演而明也。夫"道"也者，取乎万物之所由也[取：取名，称名。]。"玄"也者，取乎幽冥之所出也。"深"也者，取乎探赜而不可究也。"大"也者，取乎弥纶而不可极也[极：穷尽。]。"远"也者，取乎绵邈而不可及也[绵邈：长远。]。"微"也者，取乎幽微而不可睹也。然则道、玄、深、大、微、远之言，各有其义，未尽其极者也。

This can be further clarified. "*Tao*" is taken for (its aspect) of being that on which the 10,000 entities are based. "Dark" is taken for (its aspect) of being that which lets the recondite emanate. "Deep" is taken for (its aspect) that in searching out (its) mystery one cannot examine it. "Great" is taken for (its aspect) that one "adds and adds" but cannot top it. "Distant" is taken for (its aspect) that it is wide and remote and that one cannot reach it. "Subtle" is taken for (its aspect) that it is so recondite and subtle that one cannot perceive it. Thus the words "*Tao*, " "Dark, " "Deep, " "Great, " "Subtle, " and "Distant" each have their meaning, but do not exhaust its totality.

然弥纶无极不可名细，微妙无形不可名大。是以篇云[篇：指《老子》书。]："字之曰道"，"谓之曰玄"，[别见《老子》第 25 章、第 1 章。]而不名也。然则言之者失其常，名之者离其真，为之者则败其性，执之者则失其原矣。是以圣人不以言为主，则不违其常。不以名为常，则不离其真。不以为为事，则不败其性。不以执为制，则不失其原矣。

That to which one “adds and adds” without topping it cannot be given the name “minute”. That which is subtle and fine and without features cannot be given the name “great”. Therefore, Laozi says, “It is given the character ‘*Tao’*,” and “ it is styled ‘*Dark’*,” but no name is given. Thus he who talks about it, misses its (all-under-Heaven’s) eternal; he who gives a name to it, becomes separated from its (all-under-Heaven’s) truth; he “who acts upon it, destroys” its (all-under-Heaven’s) nature; he “who holds on to it, loses” its (all-under-Heaven’s source. Therefore, the Sage (Confucius) does not take words as the master so that he does not deviate from its eternal; does not take a name for the eternal so that he does not become separated from its truth; does not take actions for his business so that he does not destroy its nature; does not take holding on for control, and thus does not lose its source.

然则《老子》之文，欲辩而诘者则失其旨也[诘：诘问。]，欲名而责者则违其义也[责：追问。]。故其大归也[大归：根本宗旨，中心思想。]，论太始之原以明自然之性，演幽冥之极以定惑罔之迷。因而不为，损而不施。崇本以息末，守母以存子[母：道根。子：万物。]。贱夫巧术，为在未有。无责于人，必求诸己。此其大要也。

Hence, he who imposes discursive analysis upon the textual patterns of the *Laozi* will miss what he points at, and he who wishes to burden (the *Laozi*) with names deviates from his meaning. Thus it is the (*Laozi* text’s) great purport to expound the source of the Great Beginning in order to elucidate the nature of that—which is by itself what—these are its (i.e. the *Laozi* text’ s) key points.

而法者尚乎齐同，而刑以检之。名者尚乎定真，而言以正之。儒者尚乎全爱，而誉以进之[誉以进之：用称誉来推崇全爱之人。]。墨者尚乎俭啬，而矫以立之[矫：矫拂，指墨者违背人性之自然而强求节用等行为主张。]。杂者尚乎众美，而总以行之。夫刑以检物[检：苛察。]，巧伪必生。名以定物，理恕必失[理恕：恕字恐有误。]。

But the Legalists（“法家”）promote equality and egality, and apply punishment to supervise them (the people); the Name-school promotes the fixation of the true, and uses words to make them (the people) orthodox; the *Ru*-school（“儒家”）promotes complete love, and uses praise to further them (the people); the Mohists（“墨家”）promote parsimony and simplicity, and use enforced reform to settle them (the people) on this; the Eclectics（“杂家”）promote all sorts of goodies and use a variety (of means) to let (the people) act accordingly. When (however,) punishments are applied to supervise beings, craft and deceit will inevitably arise; When names are used to make beings orthodox, order and con considerateness will inevitably be lost;

誉以进物，争尚必起。矫以立物，乖违必作。杂以行物，秽乱必兴。斯皆用其子而弃其母。物失所载，未足守也。然致同途异，至合趣乖，而学者惑其所致，迷其所趣。

When praises are used to further beings, competition will inevitably arise; When enforced reform is used to settle beings, heresy and rebellion will inevitably come about; When mixed (goodies) are used to make beings act, defilement and chaos will inevitably come about. All these schools make use of the sons but discard their mother so that beings lose what supports them and that they cannot be guarded. However, (in *Laozi*) the destination (of the various arguments) is the same, though the ways thither differ, what (the various arguments) amount to coincides, but the approaches vary, but the scholars are bewildered as to their (the arguments') destination, are befuddled as to their amount.

观其齐同则谓之法，睹其定真则谓之名，察其纯爱则谓之儒，鉴其俭啬则谓之墨，见其不系则谓之杂[系：关系，联系。]。随其所鉴而正名焉，顺其所好而执意焉，故使有纷纭愦错之论[愦(kuì)：昏乱。]，殊趣辩析之争，盖由斯矣。又其为文也，举终以证始，本始以尽终，开而弗达，导而弗牵[导：引导。牵：牵引。]。寻而后既其义，推而后尽其理。善发事始以首其论[首其论：作为言论的开端。]，明夫会归以终其文。

When they observe them (i.e. some of the arguments) to be equalizing, they style him (*Laozi*) Legalist; when they perceive them (i.e. some of the arguments) fixing the true, they style him (*Laozi*) a member of the Name-school; when they find out about their (i.e. some of the arguments') pure love, they style him (*Laozi*) a *Ru*-ist; when they reflect on their (i.e. some of the arguments') parsimony and simplicity, they style him a Mohist; when they see their (i.e. some of the arguments') unsystematical (thoughts), they style him an Eclecticist. According to what their eyes happen to perceive, they fix the name; depending on what they like, they cling to that meaning. That there are confused and faulty exegeses and struggles between different tendencies and interpretations is caused by this (faulty attitude of scholars). Furthermore (Wang Bi's treatise says): As for literary form (*wen*), (the individual arguments of the *Laozi*) take up the end in order to give evidence of the beginning, and they do not relate the beginning in order to fully exhaust the end. They open up but do not go all the way, they show the way but do not lead forward (in accordance with the practice of the *junzi* in the *Liji*). (Thus) only after careful searching does one fully realize his meaning, and only after making inferences does one fully understand the principle (which) he (is pointing at). Fine indeed his exposition of a theme's beginning with which he starts his exegesis! Brilliant truly his conclusion with which he ends his texts!

故使同趣而感发者，莫不美其兴言之始，因而演焉。异旨而独构者[异旨而独构者：旨趣不同而独立思考的人。构：架构，建构。]，莫不说其会归之徵(zhēng)，以为证焉。夫途虽殊必同其归，虑虽百必均其致。而举夫归致以明至理，故使触类而思者，莫不欣其思之所应，以为得其义焉。

Of those who are motivated by the same tendency (as the *Laozi*), there is none who does not relish his beginnings in which he makes the exposition, and they will proceed from there to elaborate; of those with a different orientation who compose writings on their own, there is none who does not enjoy the proofs with which he concludes, and will take them as evidence. The ways may differ, but by necessity they must lead to the same purport. The thoughts may be hundredfold, but by necessity they are equal in their destination, and he (the *Laozi*) takes up indeed their purport and destination in order to elucidate the highest principle. Therefore, of those thinking about kindred things, there is none who does not delight in the correspondence (of the *Laozi*) with his thoughts, surmising that he grasps the meaning thereof.

凡物之所以存，乃反其形[乃：而。物之所以存，无形；物，有形；所以说“乃反其形”。]。功之所以尅，乃反其名[尅(kēi)：同克，成就。]。夫存者不以存为存，以其不忘亡也。安者不以安为安，以其不忘危也。故保其存者亡，不忘亡者存。安其位者危，不忘危者安。善力举秋毫，善听闻雷霆，圣功实存，而曰绝圣之所立。仁德实著，而曰弃仁之所存。

Generally, that by which beings persist is the negative opposite indeed to their features. That by which achievements are performed is the negative opposite indeed to their name. That is to say, he who persists does not take persistence for (the cause) of his persisting, but (this is due) to his not forgetting about (the danger of) perishing. He who is secure does not take security for (the cause) of his being secure, but (this is due) to his not forgetting about perils. Therefore (according to the Sage)， he who guards his persistence perishes, while he who does not forget about (the danger of) perishing persists. He who secures his position is in peril, while he who does not forget about peril is secure. He who is good at strength lifts an autumn down. He who is good at hearing listens to the thunderclap. The achievements of the Sage persist indeed, but (Laozi) says they are established by (his) “cutting off sageliness”. The influence of benevolence is manifest indeed, but (Laozi) says it persists through the “rejection of benevolence”.

故使见形而不及道者，莫不忿其言焉[不忿其言焉：忿，愤慨，反对；其，老子。]。夫欲定物之本者，则虽近而必自远以证其始。欲明物之所由者，则虽显而必自幽以叙其本。故取天地之外，以明形骸之内。明侯王孤寡之义，而从道、一以宣其始[宣：阐明。]。故使察近而不及流统之原者，莫不诞其言以为虚焉。是以云云者各申其说，人美其乱[乱：概括出来的结论。]。或迂其言，或讥其论，若晓而昧，若分而乱[乱：混乱，紊乱。]。斯之由矣。

Therefore, among those who see the features but do not reach as far as the *Tao*, there is no one who does not loathe his (the *Laozi's*) words. However, he who wants to define the root of entities must, though they (the entities) are near, from afar give evidence of their beginning. He who wants to elucidate the basis of the entities must, though these (entities) be evident, start from the recondite in order to point out their root. Therefore, (the *Laozi*) takes things external like Heaven and Earth in order to elucidate that which is inside the shape and bones (i.e. the body). Elucidating the meaning of (the fact that) dukes and kings (style themselves) orphaned and alone, he starts the deduction from the Tao and the One in order to display the origin of this. Therefore, among those researching that which is close at hand but not reaching to the source controlling the currents, there is none who does not dismiss his words, taking them for empty talk. Thus the bubblers each proclaim their own theory, and the others relish their confusion. They either water down (Laozi) words or ridicule (Laozi) arguments. When the clear becomes obscure and the separate confused——here is the reason!

名也者定彼者也，称也者从谓者也[名也者定彼者也，称也者从谓也：彼，所名之对象物；从谓，顺从人之所称谓。名称，与主客双方皆相关。]。名生乎彼，称出乎我。故涉之乎无物而不由，则称之曰道。求之乎无妙而不出，则谓之曰玄。妙出乎玄，众由乎道。故“生之畜之”，不壅不塞，通物之性，道之谓也。“生而不有，为而不恃，长而不宰”[《老子》第51章。]。有德而无主，玄之德也。“玄”，谓之深者也。“道”，称之大者也。名号生乎形状，称谓出乎涉求。名号不虚生，称谓不虚出。故名号则大失其旨[名号则大失其旨：以名号称呼道就大大违反道的本旨。]，称谓则未尽其极。是以谓玄则“玄之又玄”，称道则“域中有四大”也[《老子》第25章。]。

A “name” is that which defines an object. A “designation” is an inferred style. The name is born from the object(“名生乎彼”). The designation comes from the subject(“称出乎我”). Therefore, when concerned with it as that for which there is no entity which is not based on it, he (Laozi) designates it as “*Tao*.” When searching for it as that for which there is no subtlety which is not emanating from it, he (Laozi) styles it “the Dark.” As the subtleties emanate from the Dark, the many are based on the *Tao*, therefore, (Laozi’s statement) “it generates them and nourishes them”(“生之畜之”) (i.e.) that it does not block them and permeates the nature of entities, is styling the *Tao*. (Laozi subsequent statement) “generating (them) it does not take hold of them, acting (on them) it does not make them dependent, letting (them) grow it does not direct, ” (i.e.) that there is an influence (from it) but no dominance, (refers to) the influence of the Dark(“玄”). The Dark is the most profound of styles(“谓之深者也”). The *Tao* is the greatest of designations. Names and marks are born from the features and appearances. Designations and styles come out of the “being concerned with” and the “searching”. Names and marks are no hollow products. Designations and styles are no hollow emanations. Therefore, with names and marks one greatly misses its significance. With designations and styles one does not exhaust its absoluteness(“称谓则未尽其极”). For this reason when styling it “Dark” (Laozi says) “Dark and Dark again”. When designating it as “*Tao*” (Laozi says) “in the Beyond there are Four Great Ones(“域中有四大”)”.

《老子》之书其几乎可一言而蔽之：噫，崇本息末而已矣！观其所由，寻其所归，言不远宗，事不失主。文虽五千，贯之者一。义虽广瞻[广瞻：大观。]，众则同类。解其一言而蔽之，则无幽而不识。每事各为意，则虽辩而愈惑。尝试论之曰：夫邪之兴也，岂邪者之所为乎？淫之所起也，岂淫者之所造乎？

The book of *Laozi* can almost be summed up in one phrase: Ah, exalting the root to soothe the branches, that is all! In observing on what (the ten thousand entities) are based, and in investigating whereto (they) return, (the *Laozi*’s) words do not depart from the ancestor, and (his) themes do not lose (sight) of the master. Although the text has five thousand characters, what threads through them is one. Although (its) ideas are broad and far flung, in their multitude they are of the same kind. Once it is understood that it can be "summed up in one phrase" there is nothing recondite which is not cognized; but when each theme is (interpreted) as having a (separate) meaning, then, analytical skill notwithstanding, the delusions will only increase. (I will) venture to analyze this: The rise of depravity—how could it be the work of the depraved? The upsurge of debauchery—how could it be operated by the debauched?

故闲邪在乎存诚[闲邪在乎存诚：见《易传•系辞》。闲，防。]。不在善察。息淫在乎去华，不在滋章。绝盗在乎去欲，不在严刑。止讼存乎不尚，不在善听[讼：狱讼。不尚：不推崇争夺。善听：善于断狱。]。故不攻其为也，使其无心于为也。不害其欲也，使其无心于欲也。

(It cannot.) Therefore (Confucius says), "To ward off depravity lies in holding on to sincerity", but not in the improvement of surveillance. To bring debauchery to rest lies in keeping (oneself) aloof of embellishments and not in making more (laws and orders) public. To cut off robbery lies in keeping aloof of desires (oneself), but not in aggravating punishments. To stop litigation lies in not honouring (worthies oneself), but not in listening better (to charges). Therefore, (the sage-emperor) does not attack their (the people's) actions, but brings it about that they do not have any inclination to act, and does not thwart their (the people's) desires, but brings it about that they have no inclination towards desires.

谋之于未兆，为之于未始，如斯而已矣。故竭圣智以治巧伪，未若见质素以静民欲。兴仁义以敦薄俗，未若抱朴以全笃实。多巧利以兴事用，未若寡私欲以息华竞。故绝司察，潜聪明，去劝进，剪华誉，弃巧用，贱宝货，唯在使民爱欲不生，不在攻其为邪也。故见素抱朴以绝圣智，寡私欲以弃巧利，皆崇本以息末之谓也。

(According to the *Laozi*) to make precautions before something has sprung up and "to act on something before it has started"—that is all! Therefore, to exert wisdom and knowledge in order to control tricks and pretensions(“竭圣智以治巧伪”) does not compare to manifesting simplicity and plainness in order to calm down people's desires(“未若抱朴以全笃实”); to promote benevolence and justice in order to finish off the shallow and vulgar does not compare to embracing the uncouth in order to complete the sound and unadorned; to multiply skill and profit interests in order to raise the utility of affairs does not compare to the diminishing of egotism and desires (in oneself) in order to bring the competition for adornments to rest. Therefore, (the *Laozi*'s advocating the) cutting off of the surveillance and the submerging of one's intelligence, elimination of encouragement and promotion, and cutting off of adornments and eulogies, and the dismissal of skills and utility as well as the despising of precious goods all have only the purpose of preventing the people's cravings and desires from being born, but they do not emphasize attacks on their being depraved. Therefore, manifesting simplicity and uncouthness for the benefit of cutting off wisdom and knowledge, reducing egotism and desires for the benefit of discarding skill and profit interests —these are all but styles for exalting the root to soothe the branches!（“皆崇本以息末之谓也”）

夫素朴之道不著，而好欲之美不隐[好欲之美：疑作好美之欲。]，虽极圣明以察之，竭智虑以攻之，巧愈思精，伪愈多变，攻之弥甚，避之弥勤。则乃智愚相欺，六亲相疑，朴散真离，事有其奸。盖舍本而攻末，虽极圣智，愈致斯灾。况术之下此者乎！夫镇之以素朴，则无为而自正。攻之以圣智，则民穷而巧殷[殷：盛。]。故素朴可抱，而圣智可弃。夫察司之简[司：伺，察。]，则避之亦简。竭其聪明，则逃之亦察[察：详]。简则害朴寡，密则巧伪深矣。夫能为至深探幽之术者，匪唯圣智哉？其为害也，岂可记乎！故百倍之利未渠多也[未渠多：不算多。]。

If（, however,）the Tao of the plain and uncouthdoes not shine forth（“素朴之道不著”）while the amenities of predilections and desires are not hidden, (the ruler) might go to extremes with (his) wisdom and enlightenment in the attempt to keep them (the people), under surveillance might exhaust (his) knowledge and wit in the attempt to attack them (the people), but the more spirited the skills are, the more variegated their (the people's) pretensions become, the more intensely his attacks on them proceed, the more efforts they will make to evade him, and then, indeed, the dull-witted and the intelligent will get the better of each other, the (relatives in) the six relation ships will distrust each other（“六亲相疑”）, the un couth dissolves and the true disintegrates（“朴散真离”）, and there is debauchery in (all) affairs. Once the root is abandoned and the off spring is being attacked, wisdom and knowledge might be applied to the maximum, there will only be more of sure disasters—and how much greater (will they be) when one's art is inferior to this(maximum wisdom and knowledge)! If (on the other hand) one subdues them (the people) with the plain and uncouth then they will “without being acted upon” “rectify themselves.” If（, however,）one attacks them with wisdom and knowledge, the people will become exhausted and tricks will proliferate. Therefore, once one is able to embrace the plain and uncouth, wisdom and knowledge can be discarded（“故素朴可抱，而圣智可弃”）. When surveillance (by the ruler) is simple, then (the people's) evasion of it will be simple as well. When (the ruler) exerts his intelligence, then (the people's eluding him will be come more perspicacious. Being simple, damage to (people's) uncouth (nature) will be small（“简则害朴寡”）. Being perspicacious, tricks and pretensions will become deeper（“密则巧伪深矣”）. But who masters the art of supreme surveillance and of ferreting out the hidden if not (he who has) wisdom and knowledge? How can the damage be calculated which he inflicts! Therefore, (Laozi's statement about) “hundredfold gain” (if wisdom and knowledge are discarded) is certainly not exaggerated.

夫不能辩名，即不可与言理。不能定名，则不可论实也。凡名生于形，未有形生于名者也。故有此名必有此形。有此形必有其分。仁不得谓之圣，智不得谓之仁，则各有其实矣。夫察见至微者，明之极也。探射隐伏者[射(shè)：猜测。]，虑之极也。能尽极明，匪唯圣乎？能尽极虑，匪唯智乎？校实定名，以观绝圣，可无惑矣。

If names cannot be differentiated, there is no possibility to talk with someone about principles. If names cannot be defined, then there is no possibility to discourse with someone about reality（“不能定名，则不可论实也”）. In general, names are born from the features, and it does not occur that features are born from names. Therefore, if there is this (specific) name, there must be these (specific) features; if there are these features, they must have their specification. As benevolence can by no means be styled wisdom, as knowledge can by no means be styled benevolence, each one of them has its own reality（“各有其实”）. Now, he who searches out the most subtle is at the epitome of enlightenment. He who investigates and goes after the hidden and crouching at the epitome of heedfulness. What if not wisdom is able to reach the epitome of enlightenment? What if not knowledge is able to top the epitome of heedfulness. (Thus) by checking reality and defining the names in the intention to find out about (Laozi's statement concerning) the "cutting off of wisdom" one can be without error.

夫敦朴之德不著，而名行之美显尚。则修其所尚而望其誉，修其所道而冀其利。望誉冀利以勤其行，名弥美而诚愈外，利弥重而心愈竞。父子兄弟，怀情失直。孝不任诚，慈不任实，盖显名行之所招也。患俗薄而名兴行[名兴行：当作兴名行。]，崇仁义，愈致斯伪，况术之贱此者乎？故绝仁弃义 以复孝慈，未渠弘也[未渠弘：不算过甚。]。

If the influence of the honest and uncouth does not shine forth while the amenities of the fame and deeds are praised and exalted, then (people will) strive for that which is being exalted and they hope for fame. (People will) strive for that which is being talked about and they will long for profit. If hoping for fame and longing for profit motivates their activity, then the more beautiful the name becomes, the more alienated will one be from sincerity, the heavier the profits becomes, the more competitive the mind will be. Between father and son, elder and younger brother the affection which they harbour will lose its straightforwardness（“父子兄弟，怀情失直”）: filial piety will not be displayed with sincerity and compassion will not be displayed truthfully. This is provoked by the praising of names and deeds. When out of disgust for the vulgar and shallow, for the purpose of promoting names and deeds, benevolence and righteousness are venerated, they will only bring more of those pretensions, and how much more will this be the case when the art (applied) is even inferior to these (to benevolence and righteousness). Therefore, (Laozi's statement concerning) the "cutting off of benevolence and the throwing away of righteousness for the purpose of restoring filial piety and com passion" is not exaggerated.

夫城高则冲生[冲：攻城的战车。]，利兴则求深。苟存无欲，则足赏而不窃。私欲苟行，则巧利愈昏。故绝巧弃利，代以寡欲，盗贼无有，未足美也。夫圣智，才之杰也，仁义，行之大者也，巧利，用之善也。本苟不存，而用此三美，害犹如之，况术之有利斯以忽素朴乎{忽：轻视，忽视。[说明：王弼三篇注释参考了楼宇烈《王弼集校释》和中华书局《中国哲学史教学资料汇编》（魏晋南北朝）二书。]}！故古人有叹曰：甚矣，何物之难悟也！既知不圣为不圣，未知圣之不圣也；既知不仁为不仁，未知仁之为不仁也。故绝圣而后圣功全，弃仁而后仁德厚。

When the city walls rise, war chariots make their appearance. When profits up, greed (among those not benefitting) becomes deepened. If one would (being the ruler) keep to desirelessness, then one would not be robbed even if a premium were set on it. If one (being the ruler) acts out one's egotism and desires, then tricks and lust for profit (among the people) will become even more sombre. Therefore, there is nothing better than to "cut off tricks and discard the lust for profit"（"绝巧弃利"）(as the *Laozi* says), (i.e.) to replace them with a reduction of desires, whereupon (according to Laozi) "there will be no robbers and thieves." Wisdom and knowledge are the heroes among the talents. Benevolence and righteousness are the heroes among the forms of conduct. Trickery and lust for profit are the best in employment. If to the root, however, one does not keep, but lets these amenities flourish, the damage is already such (as described), but how much worse (will the damage be) if the arts (applied) go even further than these (which have been mentioned) in forgetting about the plain and uncouth! Therefore, the people of old had this sigh: "Indeed! Why are things so difficult to understand!" Having already understood that non-wisdom is non-wisdom, one still fails to understand that wisdom (itself) is non-wisdom. Having already understood that non-benevolence is non-benevolence, one still fails to understand that benevolence (itself) is non-benevolence. Therefore once wisdom is cut off, then (only) will the achievements of wisdom be completed. Once benevolence is discarded, then (only) will the influence of benevolence be rich.

夫恶强非欲不强也，为强则失强也。绝仁非欲不仁也，为仁则伪成也。有其治而乃乱，保其安而乃危。后其身而身先，身先非先身之所能也。外其身而身存，身存非存身之所为也。功不可取，美不可用。故必取其为功之母而已矣。篇云："既知其子"，而必"复守其母"。寻斯理也，何往而不畅哉！

To despise strength does not mean that one does desire not to be strong, but he who acts strong loses his strength. To cut off benevolence does not mean that one desires to be non-benevolent, but in acting out benevolence pretensions (among its objects) are brought about. By clinging to order, chaos indeed is brought about. By protecting one's security, peril indeed is brought about. (In Laozi's statement) "putting one's own person behind, (one's) person will stand in the fore, "（"后其身而身先"）the standing of one's person in the fore is not brought about by one's putting one's person in the fore. (In Laozi's statement) "treating one's person as extraneous, (one's) person will persist," the persistence of one person is not achieved by having one's person persist. As achievements cannot be taken hold of, and as amenities cannot be made use of, therefore, one must take hold of the mother which brings about the achievements, and that is all. The chapter (of the *Laozi*) says "when the sons are already known" one must "again keep to their mother."（"既知其子"，而必"复守其母"。）Having come to an understanding of this principle, where could one come to with out being in the clear.

“合同异，离坚白，然不然，可不可，困百家之知，穷众口之辩。”

——《庄子·秋水》

中国经典双语阅读

公孙龙子《白马论》（选）

Unit 5

公孙龙子《白马论》

"A Discussion on the White Horse" Selected from Gongsun Longzi[1]

[思想指要]《公孙龙子》是先秦的杰出代表公孙龙的思想论著。公孙龙，战国赵人，大约与荀子同时。他精通明辨，提出"白马非马""离坚白"等一系列名家论题，成为先秦名家最重要的代表之一。他的思想主要保留在《公孙龙子》一书中。据《汉书·艺文志》记载，《公孙龙子》共十四篇，今存六篇。其中《白马论》《指物论》《通辨论》《坚白论》《名实论》五篇大体可确定为公孙龙子的著作。此书是先秦明辨思潮的代表性著作，也是中国逻辑思想史上的典范。在《白马论》篇中，公孙龙深入地分析了"概念"当中的"共名"与"别名"的关系，从外延与内涵两个方面论证了一般与特殊、属名与种名所指对象(范围)和属性(内容)是不相等的。这一学说肯定了不同概念的确定性和不矛盾性。作者表达了对个别与一般的辩证洞识。

[Introduction] *Gongsun Longzi* was written by Gongsun Long, who was an outstanding thinker of the Pre-Qin period. Gongsun Long was born in the state of Zhao in the Warring States Period, nearly the same time as Xunzi. He was proficient in discernment and raised a series of famous propositions such as "white horse is not horse" and "separation of the hard and the white (*Li Jianbai*)", which made him become one of the most important representatives of logicians in the Pre-Qin period. His thoughts are mainly preserved in the book of *Gongsun Longzi*. According to the records of *Art and Literature of Han Shu*, *Gongsun Longzi* has 14 articles, of which six remain. Among them, five articles, such as *On White Horse, On Reference to Things*, *General Debate*, *On Separation of the Hard and the White*, *On Names and Reality,* can be generally identified as the works of Gongsun Longzi. This book is the representative of the thought of discernment in the Pre-Qin dynasty, and also a model in the history of Chinese

[1] 中文选自郭齐勇主编：《中国古典哲学名著选读》，北京：人民出版社，2005 年。
英文选自石峻主编：《汉英对照中国哲学名著选读》，北京：中国人民大学出版社，1988 年。

logic thought. In *On White Horse*, Gongsun Long deeply analyzes the relation between common name and alias in the concept, proving that the object (scope) and the attribute (content) referred to by generic name and specific generic name are not equal in terms of its denotation and its connotation. His theory affirms the certainty and non-contradiction of different concepts, and also reflects his dialectical insight of specific and general.

曰：“白马非马，可乎[本篇是主、客问答体的论文，采取一问一答的方式。白马：白色的马。非：有异于，不等于。“白马非(异于)马”并不否认“白马是(属于)马”中的逻辑包含关系。这一“非”字，只是表示“有异”，不表示“全异”。]？”

曰：“可。”

曰：“何哉?”

曰：“马者所以命形也，白者所以命色也，命色者非命形也；故曰白马非马[命：或作“名”，称谓。形：形体。]。”

A: “Is it correct to say that a white horse is not a horse?”

B: “It is.”

A: “Why?”

B: “Because ‘horse’ denotes the form and ‘white’ denotes the color. What denotes the color does not denote the form. Therefore, we say that a white horse is not a horse. ”

曰：“有白马，不可谓无马也；不可谓无马者，非马也[马：没有马的性质。非马也：“也”读“邪”，那(白马)不是“马”吗？]？有白马为有马，白之非马，何也[白之：用白去称呼马。]？”

A: “There being a white horse, one cannot say there is no horse. If one cannot say that there is no horse, then isn’t (it) a horse? Since there being a white horse means that there is a horse, why does being white make it not a horse?”

曰：“求马，黄黑马皆可致；求白马，黄黑马不可致[致：给与，奉送。]。使白马乃马也，是所求一也[使：假设，假如。乃：就是。一：一致，相同。]；所求一者，白者不异马也。所求不异，如黄黑马有可有不可，何也可与不可[白者：白色的马。如：而，然而。可：谓求马而黄黑马可致。不可：谓求白马而黄黑马不可致。]，其相非，明[相非：情形不同。明：明显。]。故黄黑马一也，而可以应有马，而不可以应有白马，是白马之非马，审矣[一：作为一样事物。第二个“而”，指然而，却。应：应答，称之为。是：由是。审：清楚无疑。]！”

B: “Ask for a horse, and either a yellow or a black one may answer. Ask for a white horse, and neither the yellow horse nor the black one may answer. If a white horse were a horse, then what is asked in both cases would be the same. If what is asked is the same, then a white horse would be no different from a horse. If what is asked is no different, then why is it that yellow and black horses may yet answer in the one case but not in the other? Clearly the two cases are incompatible. Now the yellow horse and the black horse remain the same. And yet they answer to a horse but not to a white horse. Obviously a white horse is not a horse.”

曰：“以马之有色为非马，天下非有无色之马也，天下无马，可乎[以：因。非有：没有。此句意为：

因为马有颜色我们就说它不等同于马，而天下并没有无色的马，那么我们能够说天下没有马吗？]？”

A: “You consider a horse with color as not a horse. Since there is no horse in the world without color, is it all right (to say) that there is no horse in the world?”

曰：“马固有色，故有白马。使马无色，有马如已耳，安取白马[固：本来。使：假设。如：而。如已：而已，罢了。安：如何。取：取得，出现。]？故白者非马也。白马者，马与白也；马与白，马也[与：加上。马与白：“马”的形体加上“白”的颜色。“马与白，马也？”：意为：(白马)是“马形”与“白色”加在一起所构成的，又怎么能单独地称它为“马”呢？]？马也故曰白马非马也。”

B: “Horses of course have color. Therefore, there are white horses. If horses had no color, there would be simply horses. Where do white horses come in? Therefore, whiteness is different from horse. A white horse means a horse combined with whiteness. (Thus in one case it is) horse and (in the other it is) a white horse. Therefore, we say that a white horse is not a horse.”

曰：“马未与白为马；白未与马为白[此句意为“马”在它尚未与“白”合在一起时才叫“马”；“白”在它尚未与“马”合在一起时才叫“白”。当我们把“马”与“白”合在一起时，它才有了一个重名叫“白马”。复名：重复叠加的名字。]；合马与白，复名白马是相与以不相与为名，未可[相与：“马”与“白”相结合。不相与：“马”与“白”不相结合。此言把“马”与“白”相合的(白马)称作是“马”与“白”不相结合的(马)。]。故曰白马非马未可。”

A: “ (Since you say that) before the horse is combined with whiteness, it is simply a horse; before whiteness is combined with a horse it is simply whiteness, and when the horse and whiteness are combined they are collectively called a white horse, you are calling a combination by what is not a combination. This is incorrect. Therefore, it is incorrect to say that a white horse is not a horse.”

曰：“以有白马为有马，谓有白马为有黄马，可乎[“谓有白马为有黄马”：一说“白”字为衍文。]？”

B: “If you regard a white horse as a horse, is it correct to say that a white horse is a yellow horse?”

曰：“未可。”

A: “No.”

曰：“以有马为异有黄马，是异黄马于马也。异黄马于马，是以黄马为非马。以黄马为非马，而以白马为有马，此飞者入池而棺椁异处，此天下之悖言乱辞也[飞者入池：飞鸟入于水池。棺椁异处：棺和椁分散于不同的地方。棺是埋葬死者的内棺，椁是外棺；棺本应在椁之中。悖言乱辞：胡言乱语。]。”

B: “If you regard a white horse as different from a yellow horse, you are differentiating a yellow horse from a horse. To differentiate a yellow horse from a horse is to regard the yellow horse as not a horse. Now to regard a yellow horse as not a horse and yet to regard a white horse as a horse is like a bird flying into a pool or like the inner and outer coffins being in different places. This would be the most contradictory argument and the wildest talks.”

曰："有白马不可谓无马者，离白之谓也[此段不是客问，而是主人进一步阐释。庞朴认为句首"曰"字当作"以"，下段同此。离白：分离出"白色"，仅指"马形"而言。]。不离者，有白马不可谓有马也。故所以为有马者，独以马为有马耳，非以白马为有马。故其为有马也，不可以谓马马也[独：仅，只。以马为有马耳：因为"马"有"马"的形体。"马马"：若以"白马"为"马"，则"白马"中的"马"是"马"，"白"亦是"马"，那么"白马"就成了"马马"。]。"

A: "(When we say that) a white horse cannot be said to be not a horse, we are separating the whiteness from the horse. If (the whiteness) is not separated from (the horse), then there would be a white horse and we should not say that there is (just) a horse. Therefore, when we say that there is a horse, we do so simply because it is a horse and not because it is a white horse. When we say that there is a horse, we do not mean that there are a horse (as such) and another horse (as white horse)."

曰："白者不定所白，忘之而可也[白者不定所白：指尚未固定到任何具体事物上的"白"。忘之而可也：指可以置之不理，暂时不讨论它。]。白马者言白定所白也。定所白者，非白也["定所白者，非白也"：指已经固定到某一具体事物(如马)上的"白"，就不同于作为共相的"白"了。]。马者，无去取于色，故黄黑皆所以应[去取：取舍，选择，限定。或曰"黄黑"之后当补一"马"字。]。白马者，有去取于色，黄黑马皆以所色去[所色：所具有的颜色(不合于白色)。去：排除，舍弃。此句道藏本作"黄黑马皆所以色去"，从胡适说改。]。故唯白马独可以应耳。无去者，非有去也[去者：指不限定、不选择(马的颜色)。有去：指限定、选择(马的颜色)。]。故曰：白马非马。"

B: "It is all right to ignore the whiteness that is not fixed on any object. But in speaking of the white horse, we are talking about the whiteness that is fixed on the object. The object on which whiteness is fixed is not whiteness (itself). The term 'horse' does not involve any choice of color and therefore either a yellow horse or a black one may answer. But the term 'white horse' does involves the choice of color. Both the yellow horse and the black one are excluded because of their color. Only a white horse may answer. What does not exclude color is not the same as what excludes (color). Therefore, we say that a white horse is not a horse."

“等闲识得东风面，万紫千红总是春。”

——朱熹《春日》

Unit 6

朱熹(选) Selected from ZhuXi's Works

[思想指要]朱熹(公元 1130—公元 1200年)，宋朝著名的理学家、思想家、哲学家、教育家、诗人，儒学集大成者，世人尊称为朱子。程颐的四传弟子，继承并发展了二程(程颢和程颐)理学而成为理学的集大成者。朱熹在哲学上建立了理先气后、理本气末的道本论思想体系，认为“理生万物”，主张“理一分殊”。在认识论上发展了程颐格物穷理的思想，倾向于日积月累的学问研究。主要哲学著作有《太极图说解》《四书章句集注》《周易本义》等。后世编的《朱子语类》亦涉及到文、史、哲等方面的内容。哲学、论文和书信则在其子朱在所编的《朱文公文集》中。朱熹把天地万物的总根据三纲五常称为理，“太极只是一个理字”。太极即万物之理之一般，万物也可以分别体现太极。诚如朱熹所说：“物物有一太极，人人有一太极，事事有一太极，时时有一太极。”他又说：“月印万川，洒在江湖，则随处可见。”实则只有一月，此即“理一”之谓也。

[Introduction] Chu Hsi (1130 A.D. —1200 A.D.) is a famous thinker, philosopher, educator, poet, and master of Neo-Confucianism in the Song Dynasty. He is addressed respectfully as Zhuzi. He inherited and developed Neo-Confucianism initiated by Chenghao and Chengyi and was Chengyi's disciple of the fourth generation. In philosophy, Zhuxi establishes the tao-based ideological system which holds that " *Qi* originates from *Li* " and "*Li* is the source of *Qi*", believing that "all things emanates from *Li* (reason)" and advocating "everything is unified by only one principle." In epistemology, he develops Chengyi's thoughts on " the investigation of things so as to probe the principle", tending to accumulate knowledge day by day. His main philosophical works include *An Illustrated Explanation By Taiji Diagram*, *An Annotation on Chapters and Sentences of the Four Books*, *A Searching For Original Meaning of Zhouyi*, etc.. Besides, the book of *What Zhuzi Said,* edited by his disciples of later generations, is related to literature, history and philosophy, etc. Philosophy, essays and letters are also collected in *The Collected Works of Zhu Wengong* which was edited by Chu Tsai, his own son. Chu Hsi reduced the entirety of the whole universe to *li*, thinking "*Taichi* means just a word of *li*". *Taichi* includes the reason of all things, and all things are just an emanation of reason. *Taichi* provides the reason for all things, and all things share the whole *Taichi* separately. As Chu Hsi said, "All things possess a *taichi*—everyone has a *taichi*, all events have a *taichi*—*taichi* is always present all the time." He said again, "Moonlight imprints thousands of mountains and sprinkles in rivers and lakes and is present everywhere and in everything." This is "one principle running throughout all things".

《仁说》A Treatise on *Ren* [1]

本文是一篇哲学论文，选自《朱文公文集》卷六七。全篇主要论述在儒家思想体系中很有分量的重要概念——仁的基本内涵。作者自认为是"以爱之理而名仁者也"。仁虽包含着智，却非因其而得名。

[Introduction] *A Treatise on Ren* is a philosophical essay, which is selected from Volume 67 of *The Collected Works of Zhu Wengong*. It mainly deals with the intrinsic value of benevolence, which is a weighty concept in the Confucian ideological system. Its author thinks that "(we should) elucidate the term of '*Ren*' in terms of the principle of love". Benevolence, though it contains wisdom, does not get its name for wisdom.

天地以生物为心者也，而人物之生，又各得夫天地之心以为心者也。故语心之德，虽其总摄贯通，无所不备，然一言以蔽之，则曰仁而已矣。请试详之：

"The mind of Heaven and Earth is to produce things." In the production of man and things, they receive the mind of Heaven and Earth as their mind. Therefore, with reference to the character of the mind, although it embraces and penetrates all and leaves nothing to be desired, nevertheless, one word will cover all of it（"一言以蔽之"）, namely, *Ren* (humanity). Let me try to explain fully.

盖天地之心，其德有四，曰元亨利贞[元、亨、利、贞，《周易·乾卦》卦辞。]，而元无不统，其运行焉，则为春夏秋冬之序，而春生之气无所不通。故人之为心，其德亦有四，曰仁义礼智，而仁无不包；其发用焉，则为爱恭宜别之情，而恻隐之心无所不贯。故论天地之心者，则曰乾元坤元[《乾卦》彖辞："大哉乾元，万物资始，乃统天。"《坤卦》彖辞："至哉坤元，万物资生，乃顺承天。"乾代表天，坤代表地，所以说天地之心。]，则四德之体用不待悉数而足；论人心之妙者，则曰"仁，人心也"，则四德之体用亦不待遍举而该。盖仁之为道，乃天地生物之心即物而在；情之未发而此体已具，情之既发而其用不穷，诚能体而存之，则众善之源，百行之本，莫不在是。此孔门之教所以必使学者汲

[1] 中文选自郭齐勇主编：《中国古典哲学名著选读》，北京：人民出版社，2005 年。

Chan, Wing-tsit（trans. and ed.）, *A Source Book In Chinese Philosophy*, Princeton：Princeton University Press, 1963. pp. 593-596.

汲於求仁也。其言有曰“克己复礼为仁”，言能克去己私，复乎天理，则此心之体无不在，而此心之用无不行也。又曰：“居处恭，执事敬，与人忠”[语见《论语·子路》。]，则亦所以存此心也。又曰：“事亲孝”，“事兄弟”[语见《孝经·广扬名章》。]，及物恕，则亦所以行此心也。又曰：“求仁得仁”，则以让国而逃，谏伐而饿[《论语·述而》：“子贡问孔子曰：‘伯夷叔齐何人也？’曰：‘古之贤人也。’曰：‘怨乎？’曰：‘求仁而得仁，又何怨！’”让国而逃，谏伐而饿，事见《史记·伯夷列传》。]，为能不失乎此心也。又曰：“杀身成仁”，则以欲甚於生，恶甚於死，为能不害乎此心也[《论语·卫灵公》：“志士仁人，无求生以害仁，有杀身以成仁。”《孟子·告子上》：“生亦我所欲，所欲有甚於生者，故不为苟得也；死亦我所恶，所恶有甚於死者，故患有所不辟也”。]。此心何心也？在天地则块然生物之心，在人则温然爱人利物之心，包四德而贯四端者也。

The moral qualities of the mind of Heaven and Earth are four: origination(元), flourish(亨), advantage(利), and firmness(贞). And the principle of origination unites and controls them all. In their operation they constitute the course of the four seasons, and the vital force of spring permeates all. Therefore, in the mind of man, there are also four moral qualities(“其德有四”)—namely, *ren*(仁), righteousness(义), propriety(礼), and wisdom(智)—and *ren* embraces them all. In their emanation and function, they constitute the feeling of love, respect, being right, and discrimination between right and wrong and the feeling of sympathy pervades them all. Therefore, in discussing the mind of Heaven and Earth, it is said, “Great is *chien* (Heaven), the originator!” and “Great is *kun* (Earth), the originator.” Both substance and function of the four moral qualities are thus fully implied without enumerating them. In discussing the excellence of man’s mind, it is said, “*ren* is man’s mind.” Both substance and function of the four moral qualities are thus fully presented without mentioning them. For *ren* as constituting the Way (Tao) consists of the fact that the mind of Heaven and Earth to produce things is present in everything. Before feelings are aroused, this substance is already existent in its completeness. After feelings are aroused, its function is infinite. If we can truly practice love and preserve it, then we have in it the spring of all virtues and the root of all good deeds. This is why in the teachings of the Confucian School, students are always urged to exert anxious and unceasing effort in the pursuit of *ren*. In the teachings (of Confucius, it is said), “Master oneself and return to propriety.” This means that if we can overcome and eliminate selfishness and return to the Principle of Nature (*Tien-li*, Principle of Heaven), then the substance of this mind (that is, *ren*) will be present everywhere and its function will always be operative. It is also said, “Be respectful in private life, be serious in handling affairs, and be loyal in dealing with others.” These are also ways to preserve this mind. Again, it is said, “Be filial in serving parents” “Be respectful in serving elder brothers.” and “Be loving in dealing with all things.” These are the ways to put this mind into practice. It is again said, “They sought *ren* and found it, ” for (Po-i) declined a kingdom and left the country (in favor of his younger brother, Shu-chi) and they both remonstrated their superior against a punitive expedition and chose retirement and hunger, and in doing so, they prevented losing this mind. Again it is said, “Sacrifice life in order to realize *ren*.” This means that we desire something more than life and hate something more than death, so as not to injure this mind. What mind is this? In Heaven and

Earth it is the mind to produce things infinitely. In man it is the mind to love people gently and to benefit things. It includes the four virtues（“四德”）(of humanity, righteousness, propriety, and wisdom) and penetrates the Four Beginnings（“四端”）(of the sense of sympathy, the sense of shame, the sense of deference and compliance, and the sense of right and wrong).

或曰：若子之言，则程子所谓爱情仁性，不可以爱为仁者，非欤？曰：不然。程子之所论，以爱之发而名仁者也；吾之所论，以爱之理而名仁者也。盖所谓性情者，虽其分域之不同，然其脉络之通各有攸属者，则曷尝判然离绝而不相管哉！吾方病夫学者诵程子之言而不求其意，遂至於判然离爱而言仁，故特论此以发明其遗意，而子顾以为异乎程子之说，不亦误哉！

Someone said: According to our explanation, is it not wrong for Master Cheng to say that love is feeling while *ren* is nature and that love should not be regarded as *ren*?

Answer: Not so. What Master Cheng criticized was the application of the term to the expression of love. What I maintain is that the term should be applied to the principle of love. For although the spheres of man's nature and feelings are different, their mutual penetration is like the blood system in which each part has its own relationship. When have they become sharply separated and been made to have nothing to do with each other? I was just now worrying about students' reciting Master Cheng's words without inquiring into their meaning, and thereby coming to talk about *ren* as clearly apart from love. I have therefore purposely talked about this to reveal the hidden meaning of Master Cheng's words, and you regard my ideas as being different from his. Are you not mistaken?

或曰：程氏之徒言仁多矣，盖有谓爱非仁而以“万物与我为一”为仁之体者矣，亦有谓爱非仁而以“心有知觉”释仁之名者矣。今子之言若是，然则彼皆非欤？曰：彼谓物我为一者，可以见仁之无不爱矣，而非仁之所以为体之真也；彼谓心有知觉者，可以见仁之包乎智矣，而非仁之所以得名之实也。观孔子答子贡博施济众之问［《论语•雍也》：“子贡曰：‘如有博施於民而能济众何如？可谓仁乎？’子曰：‘何事於仁？必也圣乎！尧舜其犹病诸！’”］与程子所谓觉不可以训仁者，则可见矣，子尚安得复以此而论仁哉！抑泛言同体者，使人含糊昏缓而无警切之功，其弊或至于认物为己者有之矣；专言知觉者，使人张皇迫躁而无沉潜之味，其弊或至于认欲为理者有之矣。一忘一助［助：即揠苗助长］，二者盖胥失之。而知觉之云者，于圣门所示乐山能守之气象尤不相似，子尚安得复以此而论仁哉！

Someone said: The followers of Master Cheng have given many explanations of *ren*. Some say that love is not *ren*, and regard the unity of all things and the self（“万物与我为一”）as the substance of *ren*. Others maintain that love is not *ren* but explain *ren* in terms of the possession of consciousness by the mind. If what you say is correct, are they all wrong?

Answer: From what they call the unity of all things and the self, it can be seen that *ren* involves love for all, but unity is not the reality which makes *ren* a substance. From what they call the mind's possession of consciousness, it can be seen that *ren* includes wisdom, but that is not the real reason why *ren* is so called. If you look up Confucius'answer to (his pupil) Tzu-kung's question whether conferring extensive benefit on the people and bringing salvation to all (will constitute *ren*) and also Master Cheng's statement that *ren* is not to be explained in terms of consciousness, you will see the point. How can you still explain *ren* in these terms?

Furthermore, to talk about *ren* in general terms of the unity of things and the self will lead people to be vague, confused, neglectful, and make no effort to be alert. The bad effect—and there has been—may be to consider other things as oneself. To talk about love in specific terms of consciousness will lead people to be nervous, irascible, and devoid of any quality of depth. The bad effect—and there has been—may be to consider desire as principle. In one case, (the mind) forgets (its objective). In the other (there is artificial effort to) help (it grow). Both are wrong. Furthermore, the explanation in terms of consciousness does not in any way approach the manner of (a man of *ren* who) "delights in mountains" (while a man of wisdom delights in water) or the idea that (*ren* alone) "can preserve" (what knowledge has attained), as taught his pupil are taught by Confucius. How then can you still explain love in those terms?

因并记其语，作《仁说》。

I hereby record what they said and write this treatise on *ren*.

《观心说》A Treatise on the Examination of the Mind [1]

本文选自《朱文公文集》卷六七。本文以问答的形式叙述作者关于心的观念，从心是身之主宰的角度，阐释儒家的道德修养论，发扬孟子“尽心”“知性”“知天”“存心”“养性”“事天”的观点。

[Introduction] *A Treatise on the Examination of the Mind* is selected from Volume 67 of *The Collected Works of Zhu Wengong*. This paper, in the form of question and answer, describes the author's ideas about the mind; from the point of view that the mind is the master of the body, it explains the cultivation theory of Confucian moral; and thereby carries forward Mencius' view of "fully developing one's mind", "thoroughly knowing one's nature", "thoroughly knowing Heaven", "preserving one's mind", "nourishing one's nature" and "serving Heaven".

或问：佛者有观心说[佛家有“四观”：“观身”、“观受”、“观心”、“观法”。]，然乎？曰：夫心者，人之所以主乎身者也，一而不二者也，为主而不为客者也，命物而不命於物者也。故以心观物，则物之理得，今复有物以反观乎心，则是此心之外复有一心而能管乎此心也。然则所谓心者，为

[1] 中文选自郭齐勇编著：《中国古典哲学名著选读》，北京：人民出版社，2005 年。
Chan, Wing-tsit (trans. and ed.), *A Source Book in Chinese Philosophy*, Princeton: Princeton University Press, 1963. pp.602-604.

一耶，为二耶？为主耶，为客耶？为命物者耶，为命於物者耶？此亦不待教而审其言之谬矣。

Someone asked whether it is true that the Buddhists have a doctrine of the examination of the mind.

Answer: The mind is that with which man rules his body. It is one and not a duality, is subject and not object, and controls the external world instead of being controlled by it. Therefore, if we examine external objects with the mind, their principles will be apprehended. Now (in the Buddhist view), there is another thing to examine the mind. If this is true, then outside this mind there is another one which is capable of controlling it. But is what we call the mind a unity or a duality? Is it subject or object? Does it control the external world or is it controlled by the external world? We do not need to be taught to see the fallacy of the Buddhist doctrine.

或者曰：若子之言，则圣贤所谓精一，所谓操存，所谓尽心知性，存心养性，所谓见其参於前而倚於衡者[《论语•卫灵公》：“立则见其参於前也；在舆则见其倚於衡也，夫然后行”。]，皆何谓哉？应之曰：此言之相似而不同，正苗莠朱紫之间，而学者之所当辨者也。夫谓人心之危者，人欲之萌也；道心之微者，天理之奥也；心则一也，以正不正而异其名耳。惟精惟一，则居其正而审其差者也，绌其异而反其同者也。能如是，则信执其中而无过不及之偏矣；非以道为一心，人为一心，而又有一心以精一之也。夫谓操而存者，非以彼操此而存之也；舍而亡者，非以彼舍此而亡之也；心而自操，则亡者存；舍而不操，则存者亡耳。然其操之也，亦曰不使旦昼之所为得以梏亡其仁义之良心云尔[梏：桎梏]，非块然兀坐以守其炯然不用之知觉，而谓之操存也。若尽心云者，则格物穷理，廓然贯通，而有以极夫心之所具之理也；存心云者，则“敬以直内，义以方外”，若前所谓精一操存之道也。故尽其心而可以知性知天，以其体之不蔽而有以究夫理之自然也；存心而可以养性事天，以其体之不失而有以顺夫理之自然也。是岂以心尽心，以心存心，如两物之相持而不相舍哉！若参前倚衡之云者，则为忠信笃敬而发也；盖曰忠信笃敬不忘乎心，则无所适而不见其在是云尔，亦非有以见夫心之谓也。且身在此而心参於前，身在舆而心倚於衡，是果何理也耶？

Someone may say: In the light of what you have said, how are we to understand such expressions by sages and worthies as “absolute refinement and singleness (of mind) , ” “Hold it fast and you preserve it. Let it go and you lose it, ” “Exert the mind to the utmost and know one’s nature (“尽心知性”). Preserve one’s mind and nourish one’s nature, ” and “(Standing) let a man see (truthful words and serious action) in front of him, and (riding in a carriage), let him see them attached to the yoke.”

Answer: These expressions and (the Buddhist doctrine) sound similar but are different, just like the difference between seedlings and weed, or between vermilion and purple, and the student should clearly distinguish them. What is meant by the precariousness of the human mind is the budding of human selfish desires (“人心之危者，人欲之萌也”), and what is meant by the subtlety of the moral mind is the all-embracing depth of the Principle of Heaven (Nature). The mind is one; it is called differently depending on whether or not it is rectified. The meaning of the saying “Have absolute refinement and singleness (of mind)” is to abide by what is right and discern what is wrong, as well as to discard the wrong and restore the right. If we can do this, we shall indeed "hold fast to the Mean, " and avoid the partiality of too much or too little. The saying does not mean that the moral mind is one mind, the human mind another, and then still a third one to make them absolutely refined and single. By "holding it fast and preserving it" is not meant that one mind holds fast to another and so preserves it. Neither does "letting it go and losing it" mean that one mind lets go another and so loses it. It merely means that if the mind holds fast to itself, what might be lost will be saved, and if the mind does not hold fast but lets itself go, then what is preserved will be lost. "Holding it fast" is another way of saying that we should not allow our conduct during the day to fetter and destroy our innate mind characterized by humanity and righteousness. It does not mean that we should sit in a rigid position to preserve the obviously idle consciousness and declare that "This is holding it fast and preserving it!" As to the exerting of the mind to the utmost, it is to investigate things and study their principles to the utmost, to arrive at broad penetration(“格物穷理，廓然贯通”), and thus to be able to fully realize the principle (*li*) embodied in the mind. By preserving the mind is meant seriousness (*ching*) to straighten the internal life and righteousness to square the external life, a way of cultivation similar to what has just been called absolute refinement, singleness, holding fast, and preserving. Therefore, one who has fully developed his mind can know his nature and know Heaven, because the substance of the mind is unbeclouded and he is equipped to search into principle in its natural state, and one who has preserved the mind can nourish his nature and serve Heaven, because the substance of the mind is not lost and he is equipped to follow principle in its natural state. Is this the same as using one mind to fully develop another, or one mind to preserve another, like two things holding on to each other and refusing to let go? The expressions "in front of him" and "attached to the yoke" are intended to teach loyalty, faithfulness, earnestness, and seriousness(“忠信笃敬”), as if saying that if these moral qualities are always borne in mind, we will see them no matter where we may go. But it does not mean that we observe the mind. Furthermore, suppose the body is here while the mind is in the front beholding it, and the body is in the carriage while the mind is attached to its yoke. Is that not absurd?

大抵圣人之学，本心以穷理，而顺理以应物，如身使臂，如臂使指；其道夷而通，其居广而安，其理实而行自然。释氏之学，以心求心，以心使心，如口龁口，如目视目；其机危而迫，其途险而塞，其理虚而其势逆。盖其言虽有若相似者，而其实之不同盖如此也，然非夫审思明辨之君子，其亦孰能无惑於斯耶！

Generally speaking, the doctrine of the sage is to base one's mind on investigating principle to the utmost and to respond to things by following it. It is like the body using the arm and the arm using the finger. The road will be level and open, the abiding place will be broad and easy, and the principle concrete and its operation natural. According to the doctrine of the Buddhists, one seeks the mind with the mind, and one employs the mind with the mind(“以心

求心”), like the mouth gnawing the mouth or the eye seeing the eye. Such an operation is precarious and oppressive, the road dangerous and obstructed, and the principle empty and running against its own course. If their doctrine seems to have something similar (to the Confucian), in reality, it is different like this. But unless one is a superior man who thinks accurately and sifts clearly, how can he avoid being deluded in this matter?

"身之主宰便是心，心之所发便是意，意之本体便是知，意之所在便是物。"

——王阳明《传习录》

中国经典双语阅读

王阳明（选）

Unit 7

王阳明(选) Selected from Wang Yangming

[思想指要]王守仁(公元 *1472*—公元 *1529* 年)，字伯安，浙江余姚(今绍兴地区余姚县)人。因曾筑室于会稽山阳明洞，自号阳明子，后世学者称之为阳明先生，亦称王阳明。明代中叶著名的思想家、文学家、哲学家、军事家和政治家，“心学”的代表人物。其思想学说发展到晚明时影响甚大，形成了阳明学派。王阳明所提出的“致良知”“知行合一”学说在历史上独树一帜。在知与行的关系上，强调要知，更要行，知中有行，行中有知，所谓“知行合一”，二者互为表里，不可分离。知必然要表现为行，不行则不能算真知。其影响不仅在当时很大，而且几乎动摇了程朱理学在传统社会后期思想的正统地位。阳明学是明朝中晚期的主流学说之一，后传于日本，对日本及东亚都有较大影响。著作被后人编辑为三十八卷的《王文成公全集》，现有上海古籍出版社出版之《王阳明全集》。他的主要哲学代表著作为《传习录》和《大学问》。

[Introduction] Wang Shouren (1472 A.D.—1529 A.D.), with the courtesy name of Bo An, was born in Yuyao County, Zhejiang (now Yuyao County, Shaoxing, Zhejiang Province). Because he once built his house in the Yangming Cave of Kuaiji Mountain, he claimed himself to be Yangmingzi, and late comers called him Mr. Yangming, accordingly he was also known as Wang Yangming. He was the famous thinker, writer, philosopher, strategist and statesman and also representative of the “concept of mind” in the middle of the Ming Dynasty. He proposed his unique theory of “the extension of innate knowledge” and “unity of knowledge and action”, which was widely known in the late Ming Dynasty. In terms of the relation between knowledge and action, he thought that it was more important to practise things than to know them, emphasizing that in knowledge there is action and in action there is knowledge, of which each is inextricably interconnected and still each varies mutually outside and inside. This is what he called the “unity of knowledge and action”. In Yangming’s view, knowledge must manifest itself as action, while knowledge without action cannot be regarded as true knowledge. His thought of “unity of knowledge and action” exerted a great influence not only at his time, but also almost shook the orthodox position of Cheng / Zhu's Neo-Confucianism in the later period of Chinese traditional society. Meanwhile, Yangmingism is one of the mainstream theories in the middle and late Ming Dynasty, and later, it spread to Japan and had a great impact on Japan and East Asia. His works have been edited by later generations into *The Complete Works of Wang Wen-Cheng* in 38 volumes. Now *The Complete Works of Wang Yangming* was published by Shanghai Chinese Classics Publishing House, of which *Instructions for Practical Living* and *On Great Learning* are two master treatises concerning his principal philosophy.

《传习录》（上篇）Instructions for Practical Living（Part I）[1]

本文所选出自《传习录》上篇。王阳明于此从“心外无理”出发，认为《大学》之“格物”只是“诚意”。这样，作为道德意识的知识和作为道德行为的行或实践便是一体之两面，知与行是合一的。无行之知不是真知，无知之行只是冥行。王阳明的“知行合一”学说在中国古代哲学中独树一帜，影响颇大，乃至今天依然具有重要的思想价值和实践意义。

[Introduction] This text is selected from *Instructions for Practical Living* (Part I) . Wang Yang-ming began with the premise that “There is no principle outside the mind; there is no event outside the mind, ” believing that “the investigation of things” in *Great Learning* means “nothing more than the effort to make the will sincere. ” Thus, knowledge as a moral consciousness and action as a moral act are two sides of one; knowledge and action are two in one. Knowledge without action is not real knowledge; action without knowledge is only blind action in shadow. Wang Yang-ming's theory of “unity of knowledge and action” is unique in ancient Chinese philosophy and until today it still has important ideological value and practical significance.

爱问[爱：徐爱，字曰仁，号横山，余姚人，王守仁的大弟子。]：“‘知止而后有定’，朱子以为‘事事物物皆有定理’，似与先生之说相戾[戾(lì)：违背。]。”

I said, “With reference to the sentence, ‘only after knowing what to abide in can one be calm’ in *Great Learning*(《大学》), Chu Hsi(朱熹)considered that ‘All events and things possess in them a definite principle’ . This seems to contradict your theory.”

先生曰：“于事事物物上求至善，却是义外也。至善是心之本体，只是‘明明德’到

[1] 中文选自郭齐勇主编：《中国古典哲学名著选读》，北京：人民出版社，2005 年。
Instructions for Practical Living and Other Neo-Confucian Writings by Wang Yang-ming, translated, with notes, by Wing-tsit Chan, New York and London：Columbia University Press, 1963.

‘至精至一’处便是。然亦未尝离却事物，本注所谓‘尽夫天理之极，而无一毫人欲之私’者得之[本注：指朱熹《大学章句》第一章注：“明明德新民，皆当止于善之地而不迁。盖必其有以尽夫天理之极，而无一毫人欲之私也。”]”

The Teacher said, “To seek the highest good (the abiding point)(‘至善’)in individual events and things（‘事事物物’）is to regard righteousness as external. The highest good is the original substance of the mind(‘至善是心之本体’). It is no other than manifesting one’s clear character to the point of refinement and singleness of mind. And yet it is not separated from events and things. When Chu Hsi said ‘in his commentary that (manifesting the clear character is) the realization of the Principle of Nature(‘尽天理’)to the fullest extent without an iota of selfish human desire, ’ he got the point.”

爱问：“至善只求诸心，恐于天下事理有不能尽。”

I said, “If the highest good is to be sought only in the mind, I am afraid not all principles of things in the world will be covered.”

先生曰：“心即理也。天下又有心外之事、心外之理乎？”

The Teacher said, “The mind is principle. Is there any affair in the world outside of the mind? Is there any principle outside of the mind?”

爱曰：“如事父之孝，事君之忠，交友之信，治民之仁，其间有许多理在，恐亦不可不察。”

I said, “In filial piety in serving one’s parents, in loyalty in serving one’s ruler, in faithfulness in intercourse with friends, or in humanity in governing the people, there are many principles which I believe should not be left unexamined.”

先生叹曰：“此说之蔽久矣，岂一语所能悟！今姑就所问者言之：且如事父不成，去父上求个孝的理[不成：不见得。]；事君不成，去君上求个忠的理；交友治民不成，去友上、民上求个信与仁的理：都只在此心，心即理也。此心无私欲之蔽，即是天理，不须外面添一分。以此纯乎天理之心，发之事父便是孝，发之事君便是忠，发之交友治民便是信与仁。只在此心去人欲、存天理上用功便是。”

The Teacher said with a sigh, “This idea has been obscuring the understanding of people for a long time. Can they be awakened by one word? However, I shall comment along the line of your question. For instance, in thc matter of serving one’s parents, one cannot seek for the principle of filial piety in the parent. In serving one’s ruler, one cannot seek for the principle of loyalty in the ruler. In the intercourse with friends and in governing the people, one cannot seek for the principles of faithfulness and humanity in friends and the people. They are all in the mind, that is all, for the mind and principle are identical(‘心即理也’). When the mind is free from the obscuration of selfish desires, it is the embodiment of the Principle of Nature, which requires not an iota added from the outside(‘此心无私欲之蔽，即是天理，不须外面

添一分’). When this mind, which has become completely identical with the Principle of Nature(‘天理’), is applied and arises to serve parents, there is filial piety; when it arises to serve the ruler, there is loyalty; when it arises to deal with friends or to govern the people, there are faithfulness and humanity. The main thing is for the mind to make an effort to get rid of selfish human desires and preserve the Principle of Nature."

爱曰："如今人尽有知得父当孝、兄当弟者，却不能孝、不能弟，便是知与行分明是两件。"

I said, "For example, there are people who know that parents should be served with filial piety and elder brothers with respect but cannot put these things into practice. This shows that knowledge and action(‘知与行’)are clearly two different things."

先生曰："此已被私欲隔断，不是知行的本体了。未有知而不行者；知而不行，只是未知。圣贤教人知行，正是要复那本体，不是着你只恁的便罢[恁(rèn)的：如此，这样。]。故《大学》指个真知行与人看，说‘如好(hào)好(hǎo)色，如恶(wù)恶(è)臭’。见好色属知，好好色属行。只见那好色时已自好了，不是见了后又立个心去好。闻恶臭属知，恶恶臭属行。只闻那恶臭时已自恶了，不是闻了后别立个心去恶。如鼻塞人虽见恶臭在前，臭中不曾闻得，便亦不甚恶，亦只是不曾知臭。就如称某人知孝、某人知弟，必是其人已曾行孝弟，方可称他知孝知弟，不成只是晓得说些孝弟的话，便可称为知孝弟。又如知痛，必已自痛了方知痛；知寒，必已自寒了；知饥，必已自饥了；知行如何分得开？此便是知行的本体，不曾有私意隔断的。圣人教人，必要是如此，方可谓之知。不然，只是不曾知。此却是何等紧切着实的工夫！如今苦苦定要说知行做两个，是甚么意？某要说做一个是甚么意？若不知立言宗旨，只管说一个两个，亦有甚用？"

The Teacher said, "The knowledge and action you refer to are already separated by selfish desires and are no longer knowledge and action in their original substance. There have never been people who know but do not act. Those who are supposed to know but do not act simply do not yet know(‘知而不行，只是未知’). When sages and worthies taught people about knowledge and action, it was precisely because they wanted them to restore the original substance(‘复那本体’), and not simply to do this or that and be satisfied. Therefore *The Great Learning*(《大学》) points to true knowledge and action for people to see, saying, they are ‘like loving beautiful colors and hating bad odors(‘如好好色，如恶恶臭’).’ Seeing beautiful colors appertains to knowledge, while loving beautiful colors appertains to action(‘见好色属知，好好色属行’). However, as soon as one sees that beautiful color, he has already loved it. It is not that he sees it first and then makes up his mind to love it. Smelling a bad odor appertains to knowledge, while hating a bad odor appertains to action(‘见好色属知，好好色属行’). However, as soon as one smells a bad odor, he has already hated it. It is not that he smells it first and then makes up his mind to hate it. A person with his nose stuffed up does not smell the bad odor even if he sees a malodorous object before him, and so he does not hate it.

This amounts to not knowing bad odor. Suppose we say that so-and-so knows filial piety and so-and-so knows brotherly respect. They must have actually practiced filial piety and brotherly respect before they can be said to know them. It will not do to say that they know filial piety and brotherly respect simply because they show them in words. Or take one's knowledge of pain. Only after one has experienced pain can one know pain. The same is true of cold or hunger. How can knowledge and action be separated(‘知行如何分得开？’)? This is the original substance of knowledge and action, which have not been separated by selfish desires. In teaching people, the Sage insisted that only this can be called knowledge. Otherwise, this is not yet knowledge. This is serious and practical business. What is the objective of desperately insisting on knowledge and action being two different things? And what is the objective of my insisting that they are one? What is the use of insisting on their being one or two unless one knows the basic purpose of the doctrine?"

爱曰："古人说知行做两个，亦是要人见个分晓，一行做知的功夫，一行做行的功夫，即功夫始有下落。"

I said, "In saying that knowledge and action are two different things, the ancients intended to have people distinguish and understand them, so that on the one hand they make an effort to know and, on the other, make an effort to act, and only then can the effort find any solution."

先生曰："此却失了古人宗旨也。某尝说知是行的主意，行是知的功夫；知是行之始，行是知之成。若会得时，只说一个知已自有行在，只说一个行已自有知在。古人所以既说一个知又说一个行者，只为世间有一种人，懵懵懂懂的任意去做，全不解思惟省察，也只是个冥行妄作，所以必说个知，方才行得是；又有一种人，茫茫荡荡悬空去思索，全不肯着实躬行，也只是个揣摸影响，所以必说一个行，方才知得真。此是古人不得已补偏救弊的说话，若见得这个意时，即一言而足，今人却就将知行分作两件去做，以为必先知了然后能行，我如今且去讲习讨论做知的工夫，待知得真了方去做行的工夫，故遂终身不行，亦遂终身不知。此不是小病痛，其来已非一日矣。某今说个知行合一，正是对病的药。又不是某凿空杜撰，知行本体原是如此。今若知得宗旨时，即说两个亦不妨，亦只是一个；若不会宗旨，便说一个，亦济得甚事？只是闲说话。"

The Teacher said, "This is to lose sight of the basic purpose of the ancients. I have said that knowledge is the direction for action and action the effort of knowledge, and that knowledge is the beginning of action and action the completion of knowledge(‘知是行之始，行是知之成’). If this is understood, then when only knowledge is mentioned, action is included, and when only action is mentioned, knowledge is included. The reason why the ancients talked about knowledge and action separately is that there are people in the world who are confused and act on impulse without any sense of deliberation or self-examination, and who thus only behave blindly and erroneously. Therefore, it is necessary to talk about knowledge to them before their action becomes correct. There are also those who are intellectually vague and undisciplined and think in a vacuum. They are not at all willing to make the effort of concrete practice. They only pursue shadows and echoes, as it were. It is therefore necessary to talk about action to them before their knowledge becomes true. The ancient teachers could not help talking this way in order to restore balance and avoid any defect. If we understand this motive, then a single word (either knowledge or action) will do. "But people today distinguish between knowledge and action and pursue them separately, believing that one must know before he can act. They will discuss and learn the business of knowledge first, they say, and wait till they truly know before they put their knowledge into practice. Consequently, to the last day of life, they will never act and also will never know（'故遂终身不行，亦遂终身不知'）. This doctrine of knowledge first and action later is not a minor disease and it did not come about only yesterday. My present advocacy of the unity of knowledge and action is precisely the medicine for that disease. The doctrine is not my baseless imagination, for it is the original substance of knowledge and action that they are one（'又不是某凿空杜撰，知行本体原是如此'）. Now that we know this basic purpose, it will do no harm to talk about them separately, for they are only one. If the basic purpose is not understood, however, even if we say they are one, what is the use? It is just idle talk."

爱曰："昨闻先生之教，亦影影见得功夫须是如此。今闻此说，盖无可疑。爱昨晓思格物的物字即是事字，皆从心上说。"

I said, "Yesterday when I heard your teaching, I vaguely realized that one's effort must follow this procedure. Now that I have heard what you said, I have no further doubt. Last night I came to the conclusion that the word 'thing' (*wu,* 物) in the phrase 'the investigation of things' (*ko-wu,* 格物) has the same meaning as the word 'event' (*shih*, 事), both referring to the mind."

先生曰："然。身之主宰便是心；心之所发便是意；意之本体便是知；意之所在便是物。如意在于事亲，即事亲便是一物；意在于事君，即事君便是一物；意在于仁民爱物，即仁民爱物便是一物；意在于视听言动，即视听言动便是一物。所以某说无心外之理，无心外之物。《中庸》言'不诚无物'，《大学》'明明德'之功，只是个诚意。诚意之功只是个格物。"

The Teacher said, "Correct. The master of the body is the mind. What emanates from the mind（'心之所发'）is the will. The original substance of the will（'意之本体'）is knowledge, and wherever the will is directed is a thing. For example, when the will is directed toward serving one's parents, then serving one's parents is a 'thing'. When the will is directed toward serving one's ruler, then serving one's ruler is a 'thing'. When the will is directed toward being humane to all people（'仁民'）and feeling love toward things（'爱物'）, then being humane to all people and feeling love toward things are 'things,' and when the will is directed toward seeing, hearing, speaking, and acting, then each of these is a 'thing'. Therefore, I say that there are neither principles nor things outside the mind（‘无心外之物，无心外之理’）. The teaching in *The Doctrine of the Mean*（《中庸》）said that ‘Without sincerity there would be nothing（‘不诚无物’）,’ and the effort to manifest one’s clear character（‘明明德之功’）described in *The Great Learning* means nothing more than the effort to make the will sincere. And the work of making the will sincere is none other than the investigation of things.”

先生又曰：“格物，如孟子‘大人格君心’之格[格：纠正。]，是去其心之不正，以全其本体之正。但意念所在，即要去其不正以全其正，即无时无处不是存天理，即是穷理。天理即是‘明德’，穷理即是‘明明德’。”

The Teacher further said, “The word *ko* in *ko-wu* is the same as the *ko* in Mencius’saying that ‘A great man rectified (*ko*) the ruler’s mind.’ It means to eliminate what is incorrect in the mind so as to preserve the correctness of its original substance. Wherever the will is, the incorrectness must be eliminated so correctness may be preserved. In other words, in all places and at all times the Principle of Nature（‘天理’）must be preserved. This is the investigation of principles to the utmost（‘穷理’）. The Principle of Nature is clear character（‘明德’）, and to investigate the principle of things to the utmost is to manifest the clear character.”

“虚灵不昧[虚灵：指心。]，众理具而万事出。心外无理，心外无事。”

The Teacher said, “The original mind（‘虚灵’）is vacuous (devoid of selfish desires, and not beclouded). All principles are contained therein and all events proceed from it. There is no principle outside the mind; there is no event outside the mind.”

《答顾东桥书》(中篇)[1] Reply to the Letter from Gu Dongqiao (Part II)[2]

此文乃阳明就有关问题而回复顾东桥的信函。选自《王阳明全集》卷二。此段文字中，阳明申论其“知行合一”思想与“心即理”的观念，为王氏的重要思想。阳明先生于此文中提出了“生而知之”“学而知之”“困而知之”的不同学习方法以及以仁爱为道，得道多助；以小慧为道，失道寡助，道胜于术的主张。但王氏之学就是在同时代亦有被讥为“立说过高”之嫌。

[Introduction] It is Wang Yang-ming’s *Reply to the Letter from Gu Dongqiao* concerning some questions and problems, selected from Volume 2 of *The Complete Works of Wang*

[1] 东桥：顾璘(公元1476—公元1545年)，别号东桥，字华玉，明苏州人，寄寓上元(今南京)。弘治进士，官至南京刑部尚书。著有《浮湘集》《山中集》《凭几集》等。

[2] 中文选自郭齐勇主编，《中国古典哲学名著选读》，北京：人民出版社，2005年。
The Philosophy of Wang Yang-ming, trans. by Frederick Goodrich Henke, London and Chicago: The Open Court Publishing Co., 1916.

Yangming. In his reply, Yang-ming firmly proposes his important idea that "knowledge and action are united " and "mind is the principle". And Mr. Yangming also raises different methods of learning in his reply, such as "being born with the possession of knowledge", "acquiring it as the result of education", and "acquiring it as the result of hard experience", and complying oneself with the Way of benevolence and righteousness, so as to enjoy abundant support for a just cause. On the contrary, he is definitely opposed to some claims such as "approaching Tao with small tricks", "being unjust, it lacks popular support", and "Tao is superior to art". However, Wang Yangming's theory of high morality was ridiculed by his contemporaries as being too high to attain to.

来书云："近时学者务外遗内，博而寡要，故先生特倡'诚意'一义，针砭膏肓，诚大惠也。"

Your letter says: "Recent scholars have devoted themselves to external things and have lost interest in the internal (subjective)（'务外遗内'）. They study extensively and get few fundamental principles. For this reason you (the Teacher) especially introduce the idea of making the will sincere（'诚意'）. Thus to probe into fundamentals (to use the acupuncture needle in the vitals) is truly a great kindness."

吾子洞见时弊如此矣，亦将何以救之乎？然则鄙人之心，吾子固已一句道尽，复何言哉！复何言哉！若'诚意'之说，自是圣门教人用功第一义。但近世学者乃作第二义看，故稍与提掇(duō)系要出来，非鄙人所能特倡也。

My disciple, you thoroughly apprehend the defects of the present age（"洞见时弊"）. How shall they be removed? Moreover, my mind has been fully expressed by you in a sentence. Why should I elaborate it further? Making the purpose sincere is naturally the first principle which the sages teach others to use, but present-day students view it as being of secondary importance. For this reason I simply select some of the more important things. This does not imply that I am especially able to introduce them.

来书云："但恐立说太高，用功太捷，后生师传，影响谬误，未免坠于佛氏明心见性、定慧顿悟之机，无怪闻者见疑。"

Your letter says, "But perhaps you have discussed learning too profoundly and have executed the task too cleverly. Later scholars and students, exaggerating the message (tidings), will not be able to avoid coming under the influence of the Buddhist doctrines of seeing one's nature by the light of one's intelligence（'佛氏明心见性'）and of fixing intelligence by sudden inspiration（'定慧顿悟'）. It is not strange that those who hear your views are in doubt."

区区"格致诚正"之说，是就学者本心日用事为间，体究践履，实地用功，是多少次第、多少积累在，正与空虚顿悟之说相反。闻者本无求为圣人之志，又未尝讲究其详，遂以见疑，亦无足怪。若吾子之高明，自当一语之下便瞭然矣！乃亦谓立说太高，用功太捷，何邪？

My sayings regarding the investigation of things(“格”), the development of the intuitive faculty(“致”), the making sincere of the purpose(“诚”), and the rectifying of the mind(“正”), refer to the students’ use of his original nature in his various daily tasks in order to investigate and firmly maintain the truth. This implies a great deal of orderly advance and development. Surely it is just the opposite of the empty, meaningless, sudden enlightenment(“空虚顿悟”) of the Buddhists. My hearers do not intend to be sages, nor have they ever investigated this matter minutely. That they should be in doubt is not enough to disturb me. A man of your high intelligence naturally should understand it in a moment. Why should you, too, say that I discuss learning too profoundly and execute my task too cleverly?

来书云：“所喻知行并进，不宜分别前后，即《中庸》尊德性而道问学之功交养互发、内外本末一以贯之之道。然工夫次第不能无先后之差，如知食乃食，知汤乃饮，知衣乃服，知路乃行，未有不见是物，先有是事。此亦毫厘倏(shū)忽之间，非谓有等今日知之而明日乃行也。”

Your letter says, “You give instruction that knowledge and practice advance *pari passu*(“知行并进”), that no distinction should be made as to the precedence of the one or the other, and that this is what is meant in *The Doctrine of the Mean*(《中庸》) by saying, ‘The superior man honors his virtuous nature, and maintains constant inquiry and study.’ It implies mutually cultivating and conjointly manifesting the internal and the external, the source and the result(“交养互发、内外本末”). We have here the doctrine of an all-pervading unity(“一以贯之之道”). But in the progress of the task there must be a distinction between that which is first and that which follows. If one knows what food is, one may eat; if one knows what soup is, one may drink; if one knows what clothes are, one may wear them; if one knows the road, one may traverse it. There is no ease in which one performs the act before one has a realization of the thing in question. This all happens in a moment. It does not mean that I wait until I know it today and act tomorrow.”

既云“交养互发、内外本末一以贯之”，则知行并进之说无复可疑矣。又云“工夫次第不能不无先后之差”，无乃自相矛盾已乎？“知食乃食”等说，此尤明白易见，但吾子为近闻障蔽，自不察耳。夫人必有欲食之心然后知食：欲食之心即是意，即是行之始矣。食味之美恶必待入口而后知，岂有不待入口而已先知食味之美恶者邪？必有欲行之心然后知路：欲行之心即是意，即是行之始矣。路歧之险夷必待身亲履历而后知，岂有不待身亲履历而已先知路歧之险夷者邪？“知汤乃饮”，“知衣乃服”，以此例之，皆无可疑。若如吾子之喻，是乃所谓不见是物而先有是事者矣。吾子又谓“此亦毫厘倏忽之间，非谓截然有等今日知之而明日乃行也”，是亦察之尚有未精。然就如吾子之说，则知行之为合一并进，亦自断无可疑矣。

Since you have said that the cultivation and mutual manifestation of the internal (referring to knowledge) and the external (referring to practice), of the source and the result once having been considered as a unity are to be identified with the mutual advance of knowledge and practice, there should be no further doubt arising in your mind. You further say that in the progress of the task there must be a distinction between that which is first and that which follows. Is not this a case in which the spear and shield oppose each other (self-contradiction) (“无乃自相矛盾已乎？”)? Your sayings that knowledge of food, for example, precedes eating it are easily comprehended. But you, my disciple, are obscured in mind as a result of what you have recently heard, so that you do not examine yourself. The individual must first have a desire for food, and after that he knows what it means to eat. Having this desire for food, he immediately gets the purpose to acquire it; and this is the beginning of the act. The good or evil taste of the food must first enter his mouth, and after that he knows it. Is there anyone who does not need to wait until he has experienced the taste, before he knows whether the food is good or bad? One must first have the desire to traverse the road, and after that he may learn to know it(“必有欲行之心然后知路”). Having the desire to traverse it, he forthwith determines to do so; and this is the beginning of the act. He knows the dangers and the advantages of the forks of the road after he himself has traversed them. Is there anyone who does not need to wait until he himself has traversed the forks in the road, before he knows their disadvantages and advantages? That one drinks after one knows the soup, and wears the clothes after one knows them, all these usages cannot be doubted. As for your comparisons, they mean that before one sees the thing, the act is already present. You say that this all occurs in an instant and does not mean that today's knowledge is followed by tomorrow's act. This also shows that your investigation has not reached fundamentals. However, in accordance with your discussion, knowledge and practice are united and advance together(“知行之为合一并进”). That, of course, cannot be questioned.

来书云：“真知即所以为行，不行不足谓之知。此为学者吃紧立教，俾务躬行则可。若真谓行即是知，恐其专求本心，遂遗物理，必有暗而不达之处。抑岂圣门知行并进之成法哉?”

Your letter says: “If one truly has knowledge, he practices it; if he does not practice it, he cannot be said to know it. This is the most important instruction for the student in causing him to devote himself to practicing his learning. If he says that genuine practice is to be identified with knowledge, he may merely seek to attain his original nature(“专求本心”) and thus lose the principle of things(“遂遗物理”). There will thus be points at which he is confused and not intelligent. Or is this, also, a method by means of which the sages advance knowledge and practice together? ”

知之真切笃实处，即是行；行之明觉精察处，即是知，知行工夫本不可离。只为后世学者分作两截用功，失却知行本体，故有合一并进之说。“真知即所以为行，不行不足谓之知”，即如来书所云“知食乃食”等说可见，前已略言之矣。此虽吃紧救弊而发，然知行之体本来如是，非以己意抑扬其间，姑为是说以苟一时之效者也。“专求本心，遂遗物理”，此盖失其本心者也。夫物理不外于吾心，外吾心而求物理，无物理矣；遗物理而求吾心，吾心又何物邪？心之体，性也；性即理也。故有孝亲之心，即有孝之理，无孝亲之心，即无孝之理矣。有忠君之心，即有忠之理，无忠君之心，即无忠之理矣。理岂外于吾心邪？晦庵谓“人之所以为学者，心与理而已。”[晦庵：朱熹别号。引语见《大学或问》。]心虽主乎一身，而实管乎天下之理，理虽散在万事，而实不外乎一人之心。是其一分一合之间，而未免已启学者心理为二之弊。此后世所以有专求本心，遂遗物理之患，正由不知心即理耳。夫外心以求物理，是以有暗而不达之处；此告子“义外”之说，孟子所以谓之不知义也。心，一而已。以其全体恻怛而言谓之仁[恻怛(dá)：怜悯。]，以其得宜而言谓之义，以其条理而言谓之理；不可外心以求仁，不可外心以求义，独可外心以求理乎？外心以求理，此知行之所以二也。求理于吾心，此圣门知行合一之教，吾子又何疑乎？……

When knowledge is genuine and sincere, practice is included; when practice is clear and minutely adjusted, knowledge is present. The two cannot be separated. Unfortunately, later scholars have separated them and thereby have lost the original character of knowledge and practice. It is for this reason that I say that they are united and advance together. Genuine knowledge is practice(“真知即所以为行”). Where practice is absent there is no real knowledge(“不行不足谓之知”). This is in accordance with the illustrations your letter gives regarding knowing food and then eating, etc. You will observe that I have already discussed that in a general way. Though this was really said in order to remove a defect, knowledge and practice are by nature like this. It is not a case of using one’s own purpose to assist or repress. Merely to carry out this saying implies following the impulse of the moment; merely to seek the original nature of the mind and thus to lose sight of the principles of things is an instance of losing sight of the original nature of the mind(“专求本心，遂遗物理”). The principles of things are not to be found external to the mind. To seek the principles of things outside the mind results in there being no principles of things. If I neglect the principles of things, but seek to attain the original nature of my mind, what things are there then in my mind? The mind in its original character is nature (disposition), and nature is principles(“心之体，性也；性即理也”). Since the mind has the experience of being filial, there is a principle of filial piety. If the mind lacks filial piety, there is no principle of filial piety. Since the mind has the experience of being loyal to the prince, there is a principle of loyalty. Without a mind that is loyal to the prince there can be no principle of loyalty. Are these principles external to the mind? Hui-an(晦庵)said: “He who devotes himself to study should devote himself to a study of the mind and of principles(“人之所以为学者,心与理而已”).” Though the mind in one aspect controls merely the body, it really exercises control over all the principles under the heavens. Though these principles are distributed in ten thousand affairs, they do not exceed the mind of any man. Because one (the philosopher Chu) separates them and another (Wang) unites them, it is inevitable that students should enter into the mistake of making them (mind and principles) separate things. The later scholars' misfortune of merely seeking to attain to the nature of his mind, while losing the principles of things, arises out of his ignorance that mind is the embodiment of principles（“此后世所以有专求本心，遂遗物理之患，正由不知心即理耳”）. He who seeks the principles of things outside the mind will inevitably become confused and unintelligent（“夫外心以求物理，是以有暗而不达之处”）. The philosopher Kao Tzu（告子）spoke of the external character of righteousness, and for that reason Mencius（孟子）said that he did not know what righteousness is. The mind is a unit. The feeling of sympathy of the entire mind is called benevolence (the highest virtue)（“仁”）. If one refers to the mind's getting what rightfully belongs to it, one speaks of righteousness（“义”）. When one refers to its order, one speaks of principles（“理”）. One should not seek either for the highest virtue or for righteousness outside the mind（“不可外心以求仁，不可外心以求义”）. Is the search for principles an exception to this? To seek for principles in external things implies separating knowledge and practice. The instruction of the sages, that knowledge and practice are united, implies seeking for principles within the mind. What doubt can you, my disciple, have regarding this?

来书云：“闻语学者乃谓即物穷理之说，亦是玩物丧志[语本伪《古文尚书•旅獒》：“玩人丧德，玩物丧志。”]；又取其厌繁就约，涵养本原数说标示学者，指为晚年定论[见《王文成公全书》卷三附《朱子晚年定论》。]，此亦恐非。”

Your letter says: “I have heard you say to students that the investigation of the principles of all things（“即物穷理之说”）with which we come into contact also means finding one's amusement in things and thereby ruining one's aims（‘玩物丧志’）. You take the philosopher Chu's sayings, such as disliking disorder and controlling it, and preserving and nourishing the source, and exhibit them to students, explaining that they are principles of his old age. May not this also be wrong?”

朱子所谓“格物”云者，在即物而穷其理也。即物穷理，是就事事物物上求其所谓定理者也。是以吾心而求理于事事物物之中，析“心”与“理”而为二矣。夫求理于事事物物者，如求孝之理于其亲之谓也。求孝之理于其亲，则孝之理其果在于吾之心邪？抑果在于亲之身邪？假而果在于亲之身，则亲没之后，吾心遂无孝之理欤(yú)？见孺子之入井，必有恻隐之理；是恻隐之理果在于孺子之身欤？抑在于吾心之良知欤？其或不可以从之于井欤？其或可以手而援之欤？是皆所谓理也，是果在于孺子之身欤？抑果出于吾心之良知欤？以是例之，万事万物之理，莫不皆然。……。

The saying of the philosopher Chu Tzu（朱子）regarding investigation of things is to be found in the expression, “We must investigate the principles of all things with which we come into contact（“即物而穷其理也”）.” This means that in all affairs and things the individual should seek for fundamental principles, and should use his mind in seeking these principles in affairs and things. Thereby mind and principles are separated. This seeking for fundamental principles in things and affairs is exemplified in seeking the principle of filial piety in one's parents. If a man seeks the principle of filial piety in the parents, is it, then, really in his own mind or is it in the person of his parents? If it is in the person of the parents, is it true that after the parents are dead the mind in consequence lacks the principle of filial piety? If one sees a child fall into a well, there must be sympathy(“见孺子之入井，必有恻隐之理”). Is this principle of commiseration present in the child or is it to be found in the intuitive faculty of the mind(“吾心之良知”)? Whether the individual is unable to follow the child and rescue it from the well, or seizes it with his hand and thus rescues it, this principle is involved. Is it, then, in the person of the child, or is it rather in the intuitive faculty of the mind?

夫析心与理而为二，此告子“义外”之说，孟子之所深辟也。务外遗内，博而寡要，吾子既已知之矣。是果何谓而然哉？谓之玩物丧志，尚犹以为不可欤？若鄙人所谓致知格物者，致吾心之良知于事事物物也。吾心之良知，即所谓天理也。致吾心良知之天理于事事物物，则事事物物皆得其理矣。致吾心之良知者，致知也。事事物物皆得其理者，格物也。是合心与理而为一者也。合心与理而为一，则凡区区前之所云，与朱子晚年之论，皆可以不言而喻矣！

What holds here is true with reference to the principles of all affairs and all things. Thus you may know the mistake of severing mind and principles, a severing which is in accordance with the philosopher Kaozi's (告子) sayings that righteousness is external(“义外之说”). This mistake Mencius fully exposed. You are familiar with the matter of devoting one's self to external things and thereby losing sight of the internal(“务外遗内”), as well as that of studying extensively but with meagre results(“博而寡要”). In what sense is this true? Would it seem improper to say that it implies finding amusement in things and thereby ruining one's aims? What I say about extending knowledge to the utmost through investigation of things means extending and developing my intuitive knowledge of good to the utmost on all affairs and things. The intuitive faculty and its knowledge of good are Heaven-given principles(“即所谓天理也”). If I extend and develop the Heaven-given principles of my intuitive faculty on affairs and things, then all affairs and things partake of Heaven-given principles(“致吾心良知之天理于事事物物也”). That extending the intuitive faculty of the mind to the utmost is extending knowledge to the utmost, and that the condition in which all things and affairs partake of these principles is to be identified with the investigation of things, means that mind and principles are one(“是合心与理而为一者也”). And if this is true, then what I have formerly said, and what the philosopher Chu formerly discussed, will be understood without further discussion.

来书云：“人之心体本无不明；而气拘(jū)物蔽鲜有不昏，非学问思辨以明天下之理，则善恶之机，真妄之辨，不能自觉；任情恣意，其害有不可胜言者矣。”

Your letter says, "In its original nature the mind is clear with reference to all things, but the passion-nature restrains it (changes it) and things obscure it, so that it inevitably becomes one-sided. Without study（"学"）, inquiry（"问"）, deliberation（"思"）, and discrimination（"辨"）, one cannot understand the principles of things, nor can the influences of good and evil（"善恶之机"）, and the discrimination between the true and the false（"真妄之辨"）be known of themselves. The evil inherent in following passions and fancies cannot be fully expressed in words."

此段大略似是而非，盖承沿旧说之弊，不可以不辨也。夫学、问、思、辨、行，皆所以为学，未有学而不行者也。如言学孝，则必服劳奉养，躬行孝道，然后谓之学，岂徒悬空口耳讲说，而遂可以谓之学孝乎？学射则必张弓挟矢，引满中的；学书则必伸纸执笔，操觚染翰[觚(gū)：古代用来写字的木简。翰：毛笔。]；尽天下之学无有不行而可以言学者，则学之始固已即是行矣。笃者敦实笃厚之意，已行矣，而敦笃其行，不息其功之谓尔。

What you have said in this section appears to be somewhat specious, but it is not really true. I must refute this defect of supporting and following the traditional sayings. Inquiry（"问"）, deliberation（"思"）, discrimination（"辨"）, and practice（"行"）are all to be considered as learning. Learning and practice always go together. For instance, if the individual says that he is learning filial piety（"孝"）, he will certainly bear the toil of his parents, take care of them, and himself walk in the path of filial piety. After that he may speak of learning filial piety. Can he who merely says that he is learning filial piety, therefore be said to be learning? He who learns archery must certainly take the bow and fit the arrow to the string, draw the bow and shoot. He who learns writing must certainly straighten the paper and take the pen, grasp the paper and dip the pen into the ink（"伸纸执笔，操觚染翰"）. In all learning of the Empire, there is nothing that can be called learning unless it is carried out in practice. Thus the beginning of learning is surely practice. The earnest one, being sincere and honest（"敦实笃厚"）, has already practiced his learning. Making his practice sincere and earnest, he does not cease from his work.

盖学之不能以无疑，则有问，问即学也，即行也；又不能无疑，则有思，思即学也，即行也；又不能无疑，则有辨，辨即学也，即行也。辨既明矣，思即慎矣，问即审矣，学既能矣，又从而不息其功焉，斯之谓笃行。非谓学、问、思、辨之后而始措之于行也。是故以求能其事而言谓之学；以求解其惑而言谓之问；以求通其说而言谓之思，以求精其察而言谓之辨；以求履其实而言谓之行：盖析其功而言则有五，合其事而言则一而已。此区区心理合一之体，知行并进之功，所以异于后世之说者，正在于是。

Since doubt must arise in connection with learning, inquiry is necessarily present. Making inquiry, the individual forthwith learns and practices（"问即学也，即行也"）. Since doubt arises there is deliberation. Deliberating, the individual learns and again practices. Being in doubt, he also begins to discriminate, and thus both learns and practices. When discrimination is clear, deliberation careful and sincere, inquiry discerning, learning competent and skillful, and application constant, practice is earnest(“斯之谓笃行”). It does not mean that after study, inquiry, deliberation, and discrimination, one first is ready to practice. For this reason I hold and say that seeking to be able to do anything is learning(“学”); seeking to dissipate any doubt connected therewith is inquiry(“问”); seeking to understand the underlying principles is deliberation(“思”); seeking to get at the essence is discrimination(“辨”); seeking to carry out its genuineness in action is practice(“行”). Any discussion of the situation that splits the task gives us these five stages. If the whole affair is united, it is one. This is the substance of my saying that mind and principles are one(“心理合一之体”); it is the task of mutually developing knowledge and practice. This is the real.

今吾子特举学、问、思、辨以穷天下之理，而不及笃行，是专以学、问、思、辨为知，而谓穷理为无行也已。天下岂有不行而学者邪？岂有不行而遂可谓之穷理者邪？明道云：“只穷理，便尽性至命。”故必仁极仁，而后谓之能穷仁之理；义极义，而后谓之能穷义之理。仁极仁则尽仁之性矣，义极义则尽义之性矣。学至于穷理至矣，而尚未措之于行，天下宁有是邪？是故知不行之不可以为学，则知不行之不可以为穷理矣；知不行之不可以为穷理，则知知行之合一并进，而不可以分为两节事矣。夫万事万物之理不外于吾心，而必曰穷天下之理，是殆以吾心之良知为未足，而必外求于天下之广，以裨补增益之[裨(bì)补：补充增添。]，是犹析心与理而为二也。夫学、问、思、辨、笃行之功，虽其困勉至于人一己百，而扩充之极，至于尽性知天，亦不过致吾心之良知而已。良知之外，岂复有加于毫末乎？今必曰穷天下之理，而不知反求诸其心，则凡所谓善恶之机，真妄之辨者，舍吾心之良知，亦将何所致其体察乎？

You have especially selected study, inquiry, deliberation, and discrimination as the method whereby the principles of all things are to be thoroughly investigated, but you fail to reach the point of earnest practice(“而不及笃行”). This means that you consider study, inquiry, deliberation, and discrimination as knowledge, but in this investigation of principles do not include practice. Is there a single instance in the Empire in which a person has learned without practice? Is there an instance in which there has been an actual investigation of principles without practice? Ming-tao says: “It is only by investigating principles most thoroughly that one exhausts his nature in attaining the decrees of Heaven(“只穷理，便尽性至命”).” After virtue has reached its highest development(“必仁极仁”), the individual may be said to be able to exhaust the principles of virtue in his investigation. After righteousness has reached its highest form(“义极义”), it may be said that he is able to exhaust in his investigation the principles of righteousness(“而后谓之能穷义之理”). When he has acquired the greatest development of virtue, he has exhausted that part of his nature which refers to virtue. Of righteousness the same holds true. Is there such a thing as that the individual has reached the point where he is able to investigate exhaustively the principles of things and yet does not practice them? For this reason, if knowledge of principles without practice cannot be considered learning, knowledge without practice cannot be considered an exhaustive investigation of principles. If knowledge without practice cannot be considered exhaustive investigation, then you may know that in the unity and mutual development of knowledge and practice no distinction can be made(“知不行之不可以为穷理，则知知行之合一并进，而不可以分为两节事矣”). The principles of things and affairs are not to be found external to the mind. If anyone says that it is insufficient to use the intuitive faculty(“良知”)in making an exhaustive investigation of the principles of things, and that it is necessary to seek externally in the Empire so as to supplement and strengthen this, he thereby splits mind and principles into two things. As for study, inquiry, deliberation, discrimination, and earnest practice, it is true that, though the individual in his stupidity and in his expenditure of effort uses a hundred efforts where another man succeeds by one, but nevertheless advances until he exhausts his nature in knowing Heaven, he is in reality doing nothing more than develop the intuitive faculty of his mind. Can anything further be added to the intuitive faculty? If he says that he is trying to investigate exhaustively the principles of things, and yet does not know that he must seek within his own mind, the influence of good and evil and the discrimination of the true and the false set aside the intuitive faculty. How, then, will he advance in his introspection ?

吾子所谓“气拘物蔽”者，拘此蔽此而已。今欲去此之蔽，不知致力于此，而欲以外求，是犹目之不明者，不务服药调理以治其目，而徒伥伥然求明于其外，明岂可以自外而得哉！任情恣意之害，亦以不能精察天理于此心之良知而已。此诚毫厘千里之谬者，不容于不辨，吾子毋谓其论之太刻也。

When you, my disciple, say that the passion-nature restrains the mind and things obscure it(“气拘物蔽”), you speak truly. If you wish to get rid of this obscuration and do not know how to use your strength to the utmost in this matter, but seek for relief in external things, your vision is not clear(“是犹目之不明者”). Instead of assisting with medicine and nursing your eyes in order to cure them, bewildered and undecided, you seek for relief in external things. Can you really effect the cure in this way? The injury resulting from following one’s passions and one’s fancies(“任情恣意之害”), is also due to the inability discriminately to investigate Heaven-given principles within the realm of the intuitive faculty(“精察天理于此心之良知而已”). This error, both small and great, I can clearly discriminate. Do not say that I have been too harsh in any discussion.

……良知良能，愚夫愚妇与圣人同，但惟圣人能致其良知，而愚夫愚妇不能致，此圣愚之所由分也。节目时变，圣人夫岂不知？ 但不专以此为学。而其所谓学者，正惟致其良知，以精察此心之天理，而与后世之学不同耳。

In the matter of intuitive knowledge of good and native ability to execute the good(“良知良能”), common simple men and women (“愚夫愚妇”)are like the sage. But the sage is able to extend his intuitive knowledge to the utmost(“能致其良知”), while common folks are not able to do so. It is from this point on that they differ. It is not that the sage knows the rites and the changes of circumstances(“节目时变”), but that he does not consider merely these as learning. What he means by learning consists simply in developing his intuitive knowledge in order to investigate minutely the natural laws of the mind. In this he differs from the learning of later scholars.

吾子未暇良知之致，而汲汲焉顾是之忧[汲汲焉：心情急切的样子]，此正求其难于明白者以为学之弊也。夫良知之于节目时变，犹规矩尺度之于方圆长短也。节目时变之不可预定，犹方圆长短之不可胜穷也。故规矩诚立，则不可欺以方圆，而天下之方圆不可胜用矣；尺度诚陈，则不可欺以长短，而天下之长短不可胜用矣；良知诚致，则不可欺以节目时变，而天下之节目时变不可胜应矣。毫厘千里之谬，不于吾心良知一念之微而察之，亦将何所用其学乎？是不以规矩而欲定天下之方圆，不以尺度而欲尽天下之长短，吾见其乖张谬戾，日劳而无成也已。

My disciple(“吾子”), you have no leisure for the development of your intuitive faculty, but with unremitting effort you are solicitous in caring for that which is correct. This is the evil of considering that learning consists in seeking that which is difficult to understand. The intuitive faculty is to changing circumstances (“节目时变”) as compasses and squares are to squares and circles, and measures are to length and shortness(“犹规矩尺度之于方圆长短也”). The changes in circumstances relative to paragraphs and sections (of the doctrine) cannot be determined beforehand, just as the size of the square or circle and the length or shortness cannot be perfectly estimated(“犹方圆长短之不可胜穷也”). But when the compasses and squares have been set(“规矩诚立”), there can be no deception regarding the size of the square and the circle. However, the squares and circles of the universe cannot all be used. When the rule and measure have been fixed(“尺度诚陈”), there can be no deception as to the length or shortness, but the lengths and shortnesses under Heaven cannot be exhausted. When the intuitive faculty has been completely developed(“良知诚致”), there can be no deception regarding its application to changing details. However, the changing details under Heaven cannot all be complied with. If both small and great errors(“毫厘千里之谬”) cannot be investigated in the recondite, abstruse thoughts of the intuitive faculty, how shall its learning be applied? If the individual does not use compasses and squares, and yet desires to determine squares and circles; if he does not use the measure, and yet desires to measure length, he in my estimation is unreasonable and perverse; he is daily laboring without completing his task.

吾子谓：“语孝于温凊定省，孰不知之”？[语本《礼记·曲礼》：“凡为人子之礼，冬温而夏凊，昏定而晨省。”]然而能致其知者鲜矣。若谓粗知温凊定省之仪节，而遂谓之能致其知，则凡知君之当仁者皆可谓之能致其仁之知，知臣之当忠者皆可谓之能致其忠之知，则天下孰非致知者耶？以是而言，可以知致知之必在于行，而不行之不可以为致知也明矣。知行合一之体，不益较然矣乎?

You say, "Who does not understand the filial piety involved in caring for the comfort of parents in winter and summer and in inquiring about their health both morning and evening?" And yet but few are able to extend their knowledge to the utmost（"能致其知者鲜矣"）at this point. If you mean that the individual roughly knows the ceremonial usages of caring for the comfort of parents both in winter and summer（"粗知温凊定省之仪节"）, and of inquiring about their health both morning and evening, and say that he is thus able to complete his intuitive knowledge, then whosoever knows what is meant by saying that the prince ought to be benevolent is able to extend his knowledge of benevolence, and whosoever knows what is meant by saying that the minister ought to be loyal is able to extend his knowledge of loyalty. Thus considered, who in the entire Empire does not extend his intuitive knowledge? This will serve to make clear that the extending of knowledge depends upon practicing（"知致知之必在于行"）, and that without the act there clearly can be no extending of knowledge. In the matter of unity of knowledge and practice, is it necessary to add more comparisons?

来书云："谓《大学》格物之说专求本心，犹可牵合；至于《六经》《四书》所载多闻多见[见《论语·述而》。]，前言往行[见《易·大畜卦》卦辞。]，好古敏求[见《论语·述而》。]，博学审问[见《中庸》。]，温故知新[见《论语·为政》。]，博学详说[见《孟子·离娄下》。]，好问好察[见《中庸》。]，是皆明白求于事为之际，资于论说之间者，用功节目固不容紊矣。"

Your letter says: "It would seem that the saying of *The Great Learning* (《大学》) regarding the investigation of things is probably in harmony with seeking the original character of the mind（'专求本心'）. But the following things from the *Six Classics*（《六经》）and *Four Books*（《四书》）should all be clearly sought within the limits of the books, to wit: hear much and see much（'多闻多见'）; what former sages have said should be carried out in practice（'前言往行'）; I am the one who is fond of antiquity, and earnest in seeking knowledge there（'好古敏求'）; extensive study of what is good and accurate inquiry about it（'博学审问'）; he cherishes his old knowledge and is continually acquiring new（'温故知新'）; in learning extensively and discussing minutely what is learned（'博学详说'）, the object of the superior man is that he may be able to go back and set forth in brief what is essential（'好问好察'）; he loved to question others and to study their words. Certainly confusion cannot be permitted in discussing the details of the rites and the order of the task."

格物之义，前已详悉；牵合之疑，想已不俟(sì)复解矣。至于多闻多见，乃孔子因子张之务外好高，徒欲以多闻多见为学，而不能求诸其心，以阙疑殆[阙疑：暂置不论。殆：疑。]，此其言行所以不免于尤悔，而所谓见闻者，适以资其务外好高而已。盖所以救子张多闻多见之病，而非以是教之为学也。夫子尝曰"盖有不知而作之者，我无是也[语见《论语·述而》。]。"是犹孟子"是非之心，人皆有之"之义也[语见《孟子·告子上》。]。

The idea involved in the investigation of things（"格物之义"）I have already thoroughly discussed. As for your doubt concerning the connection between this and devoting one's self to seeking the original nature of the mind, I judge that you will not need to wait until I have again explained it. Hearing much and seeing much was said by Confucius because Tzu-chang(子张) devoted himself to external things, loved superior position, and vainly considered learning to consist in hearing and seeing much. He was unable to seek within his own mind(“不能求诸其心”) in order to put aside the things regarding which he stood in doubt and which seemed perilous. Thus, both in his words and in his deeds, he was unable to avoid being blamable and having occasions for repentance. Moreover, the meaning of seeing and hearing much amounts to a dependence upon devotion to external things, and to love of lofty position. For that reason Confucius said this to rescue him from the error of depending upon hearing and seeing much, and not for the reason that he wished him to consider this as learning. The Master has said: "There may be those who act without knowing why. I do not do so." This has the same idea as the saying of Mencius that "all men have the mental capacity to distinguish between right and wrong."(“是非之心，人皆有之”)

此言正所以明德性之良知，非由于闻见耳。若曰“多闻择其善者而从之，多见而识之”，则是专求诸见闻之末，而已落在第二义矣，故曰：“知之次也”。夫以见闻之知为次，则所谓知之上者果安所指乎？是可以窥圣门致知用力之地矣。夫子谓子贡曰：“赐也，汝以予为多学而识之者欤？非也，予一以贯之[语见《论语·卫灵公》。]。”使诚在于多学而识，则夫子胡乃谬为是说以欺子贡者邪？“一以贯之”，非致其良知而何？《易》曰：“君子多识前言往行，以畜其德。[见《易·大畜卦》卦辞。]”夫以畜其德为心，则凡多识前言往行者，孰非畜德之事？此正知行合一之功矣。“好古敏求”者，好古人之学而敏求此心之理耳。

These sayings really have reference to understanding the intuitive knowledge of one's virtuous nature(“明德性之良知”), and not to hearing and seeing much. If anyone should refer to "hearing much and selecting what is good and following it; seeing much and keeping it in memory," this would imply a mere seeking for the result of seeing and hearing. It carries with it the second idea, and therefore the Master said that "this is the second style of knowledge." He thus considers the knowledge from seeing and hearing as the second type. What, then, is above this knowledge? Here you can have a peep at the place where the sage uses his effort in extending his knowledge. The Master said to Tzu-kung(子贡), "Ts'ze (sic), you think, I suppose, that I am one who learns many things and keeps them in memory? . . . No, I seek a unity all-pervading(“予一以贯之”)." If knowledge really depends upon learning much and remembering it, why did the Master mistakenly speak as he did? Was it in order to deceive Tzu-kung? If his seeking a unity all-pervading does not refer to extending his intuitive knowledge of good(“致其良知”), to what does it refer? *The Book of Changes*(《易经》) says: "The superior man remembers former sayings and virtuous practices in order to cultivate his virtue(“君子多识前言往行，以畜其德”)." Which of these do not contribute to cultivating virtue, if the individual uses them for this purpose? This surely is a task which implies a unification of knowledge and practice（“此正知行合一之功矣”）. Confucius says, “I am fond of antiquity and earnestly seek (knowledge there)（“好古敏求”）.” If he loved the learning of the ancients, he earnestly sought to know the principles of the mind.

心即理也；学者，学此心也；求者，求此心也。孟子云：“学问之道无他，求其放心而已矣。”非若后世广记博诵古人之言词，以为好古，而汲汲然惟以求功名利达之具于其外者也。“博学审问”，前言已尽。“温故知新”，朱子亦以温故属之尊德性矣。德性岂可以外求哉？惟夫知新必由于温故，而温故乃所以知新，则亦可以验知行之非两节矣。

Mind, I say, is just what is meant by principles（“心即理也”）. He who studies should study the mind and he who seeks should seek the mind. Mencius said, “The end of learning is nothing else but to seek for the lost mind（“求其放心”）.” This is not the same as when later generations consider fondness of antiquity to consist in extensively remembering and reciting the phrases of the ancients（“广记博诵古人之言辞”）. Moreover, with unremitting effort they seek for renown, gain, and advancement in that which is external. I have previously thoroughly discussed the matter of extensive study and careful inquiry（“博学审问”）. As regards cherishing old knowledge and yet continually acquiring new knowledge（“温故知新”）, the philosopher Chu Tzu（朱子）also held that the cherishing of the old referred to honoring one's virtuous nature. Is it possible to search for this virtuous nature outside the mind? Only if this continual acquiring of new knowledge proceeds from the cherishing of the old（“知新必由于温故”）, can one cherish the old and acquire the new（“温故乃所以知新”）. In this way you can also verify that knowledge and practice are not two things.

“博学而详说之”者，将以反说约也[见《孟子·离娄下》。]，若无反约之云，则博学详说者果何事邪？舜之“好问好察”，惟以用中而致其精一于道心耳。道心者，良知之谓也。君子之学，何尝离去事为而废论说？但其从事于事为论说者，要皆知行合一之功，正所以致其本心之良知；而非若世之徒事口耳谈说以为知者，分知行为两事，而果有节目先后之可言也。

As regards the saying of Mencius, “In learning extensively and discussing minutely what is learned（‘博学而详说之’）, the object is to go back and set forth in brief what is essential,” if, as he said, their virtue lies in opening the way to go back and set forth in brief what is essential, for what reason does he advocate them? Shun（舜）in loving to question others and to study their words（“好问好察”）used only the mean（“用中”）in governing his people, and extended his devotion to the essence of his mind in complete loyalty to the path. A mind loyal to the path of duty is what is meant by the intuitive faculty（“道心者，良知之谓也”）. When has the learning of the superior man absented itself from the affairs of life and discarded discussions? However, he who devotes himself to the affairs of life and to discussions should know that the unification of knowledge and practice involves developing the intuitive knowledge of his mind（“致其本心之良知”）. He should not be like the world, which considers vain speaking and hearing as learning, and which, by separating knowledge and practice, is able to discuss an order of first and last in this.

《传习录》(下篇)Instructions for Practical Living (Part III)[1]

本段讲圣人之知识也只是本体明了，只须识得一个天理，而不必于事事物物之枝节都去了解，以此照应前文所引孔子的话“吾道一以贯之。”此处阳明说明天地万物与人原是一体，其发窍最精处，是人心一点灵明。接着以个人的经验，论证朱子在外物上去“格物”的不对，最后落脚在“我的灵明便是天地鬼神的主宰。”阳明的观点，只好从境界论上去理解，若从认识论上看，其独断性是不言而喻的。

[Introduction] It is selected from Wang Yan-gming's *Instructions for Practical Living*. According to this paragraph, the original substance of a sage is clear only in itself, and he needs only to know the Principle of Nature rather than to search for the highest good in individual things, so as to respond to what Confucius said that "My doctrine is that of an all-pervading unity" which is in correspondence with quotes above. Here Yang-ming explains that the universe and man is originally in one, and the point at which this unity is manifested in its most refined and excellent form is the clear intelligence of the human mind. Then, with personal experience, he proves that Zhuzi is wrong to "investigate things" from outside, and finally settled on his statement that "My clear intelligence is the master of Heaven and Earth and spiritual beings".

黄以方问[黄以方：即黄直，字以方，金溪人，嘉靖进士，王守仁弟子。]：“先生格致之说，随时格物以致其知，则知是一节之知，非全体之知也。何以到得溥博如天，渊泉如渊地位[语本《礼记·中庸》。]？”

I asked, "Sir, according to your doctrine of investigation of things and the extension of knowledge, one should investigate things at any time in order to extend knowledge. If so, the knowledge extended is only a part and not the entirety(‘一节之知，非全体之知’). How can it reach the state described as ‘all embracing and extensive as heaven and deep and unceasingly springing as an abyss? ’"

先生曰：“人心是天渊。心之本体无所不该[该：同“赅”，包括一切。]，原是一个天。只为私欲障碍，则天之本体失了。心之理无穷尽，原是一个渊，只为私欲窒塞，则渊之本体失了。如今念念致良知，将此障碍窒塞一齐去尽，则本体已复，便是天渊了。”乃指天以示之曰：

---

[1] 中文选自郭齐勇主编：《中国古典哲学名著选读》，北京：人民出版社，2005 年。

Instructions for Practical Living and Other Neo-Confucian Writings by Wang Yang-ming, translated, with a note, by Wing-tsit Chan. New York and London;Columbia University Press, 1963.

“比如面前见天，是昭昭之天；四外见天，也只是昭昭之天。只为许多房子墙壁遮蔽，便不见天之全体。若撤去房子墙壁，总是一个天矣。不可道眼前天是昭昭之天，外面又不是昭昭之天也。于此便见一节之知，即全体之知；全体之知，即一节之知；总是一个本体。”

The Teacher said, “The human mind is heaven and it is the abyss. The original substance of the mind（“心之本体”）contains everything. In reality it is the whole heaven. Only because it is hidden by selfish desires is the original substance of heaven lost. The principle of the mind（“心之理”）is infinite. In reality it is the whole abyss. Only because it is obstructed by selfish desires is the original substance of the abyss lost. Now if one extends the innate knowledge in every thought and removes all these hindrances and obstacles, its original substance will be recovered and right then it will become both Heaven and abyss.” Thereupon he pointed to heaven, saying, “For instance, we see heaven in front of us. It is bright and clear heaven. If we see heaven outside the house, it is the same bright and clear heaven. Only because it is obscured by these many walls of the building do we not see heaven in its entirety. If we tear down the walls, we will see only one heaven. We should not say that what is in front of us is the bright and clear heaven but what is outside the house is not. From this we know that the knowledge of a part（“一节之知”）is the same as the knowledge of the whole, and the knowledge of the whole（“全体之知”）is the same as the knowledge of a part. All is but one original substance.”

问“知行合一”。先生曰：“此须识我立言宗旨。今人学问，只因知行分作两件，故有一念发动，虽是不善，然却未曾行，便不去禁止。我今说个知行合一，正要人晓得一念发动处，便即是行了。发动处有不善，就将这不善的年克倒了。须要彻根彻底，不使那一念不善潜伏在胸中。此是我立言宗旨。”

I asked about the unity of knowledge and action. The Teacher said, “You need to understand the basic purpose of my doctrine（“立言宗旨”）. In their learning people of today separate knowledge and action into two different things. Therefore, when a thought is aroused, although it is evil, they do not stop it because it has not been translated into action（“故有一念发动，虽是不善，然却未曾行，便不去禁止”）. I advocate the unity of knowledge and action precisely because I want people to understand that when a thought is aroused it is already action. If there is anything evil when the thought is aroused, one must overcome the evil thought. One must go to the root and go to the bottom and not allow the evil thought to lie latent in his mind. That is the basic purpose of my doctrine.”

“圣人无所不知，只是知个天理；无所不能，只是能个天理。圣人本体明白，故事事知个天理所在，便去尽个天理。不是本体明后，却于天下事物都便知得，便做得来也。天下事物，如名物度数、草木鸟兽之类，不胜其烦。圣人须是本体明了，亦何缘能尽知得？但不必知的，圣人自不消求知；其所当知的，圣人自能问人。如‘子入太庙，每事问’〔语见《论语·八佾》。〕之类，先儒谓‘虽知亦问，敬谨之至’〔见朱熹《论语集注》“每事问”注。〕。此说不可通。圣人于礼乐名物，不必尽知。然他知得一个天理，便自有许多节文度数出来。不知能问，亦即是天理节文所在。”

[The Teacher said,] “That the sage is omniscient(“圣人无所不知”) merely means that he knows the Principle of Nature and that he is omnipotent merely means that he is able to practice the Principle of Nature. The original substance of the mind of the sage is clear(“圣人须是本体明了”)and therefore in all things he knows where the Principle of Nature lies and forthwith carries it out to the utmost. It is not that after the original substance of his mind becomes clear he then knows all the things in the world and is able to carry all of them out. Things in the world, such as the names, varieties, and systems(“名物度数”), and plants and animals, are innumerable. Although the original substance of the sage is very clear, how can he know everything? What is not necessary to know, he does not have to seek to know. What he should know, he naturally asks others, like Confucius, who, ‘when he entered the grand temple, asked about everything. ’ A former scholar said that the fact that ‘although Confucius knew he still asked’ shows he was perfectly serious and careful. Such an interpretation is absurd. A sage does not have to know all the names and varieties of ceremonies and music. But since he knows the Principle of Nature, all measures, regulations, and details can be deduced from it. The fact that when he did not know he asked shows how the measure and pattern of the Principle of Nature operates.”

先生曰：“良知是造化的精灵。这些精灵，生天生地，成鬼成帝，皆从此出，真是与物无对。人若复得他完完全全，无少亏欠，自不觉手舞足蹈，不知天地间更有何乐可代。”

The Teacher said, “Innate knowledge(“良知”)is the spirit of creation(“精灵”). This spirit produces heaven and earth, spiritual beings, and the Lord. They all come from it. Truly nothing can be equal to this. If people can recover it in its totality without the least deficiency, they will surely be gesticulating with hands and feet. I don’t know if there is anything in the world happier than this.”

朱本思问[朱本思：王守仁弟子，名得之，靖江人，著有《参玄三语》、《庄子通义》等。]：“人有虚灵，方有良知。若草木瓦石之类，亦有良知否？”

Chu Pensi asked, “Man has innate knowledge because he possesses pure intelligence(“虚灵”). Have such things as plants and trees, tiles and stones innate knowledge also?”

先生曰：“人的良知，就是草木瓦石的良知。若草木瓦石无人的良知，不可以为草木瓦石矣。岂惟草木瓦石为然，天地无人的良知，亦不可为天地矣。盖天地万物与人原是一体，其发窍之最精处，是人心一点灵明。风、雨、露、雷、日、月、星、辰、禽、兽、草、木、山、川、土、石，与人原只一体。故五谷禽兽之类，皆可以养人；药石之类，皆可以疗疾：只为同此一气，故能相通耳。”

The Teacher said, “The innate knowledge of man is the same as that of plants and trees, tiles and stones. Without the innate knowledge inherent in man, there cannot be plants and trees, tiles and stones. This is not true of them only. Even Heaven and Earth cannot exist without the innate knowledge that is inherent in man. From at bottom Heaven, Earth, the myriad things, and man form one body(‘盖天地万物与人原是一体’). The point at which this unity is manifested in its most refined and excellent form is the clear intelligence of the human mind(‘其发窍之最精处，是人心一点灵明’). Wind, rain, dew, thunder, sun and moon, stars, animals and plants, mountains and rivers, earth and stones are essentially of one body with man. It is for this reason that such things as medicine and minerals can heal diseases. Since they share the same material force, they enter into one another."

先生游南镇，一友指岩中花树问曰："天下无心外之物，如此花树，在深山中自开自落，于我心亦何相关？"

The Teacher was roaming in Nanchen(南镇). A friend pointed to flowering trees on a cliff and said, "(You say) there is nothing under heaven external to the mind. These flowering trees on the high mountain blossom and drop their blossoms of themselves. What have they to do with my mind?"

先生曰："你未看此花时，此花与汝心同归于寂。你来看此花时，则此花颜色一时明白起来。便知此花不在你的心外。"

The Teacher said, "Before you look at these flowers, they and your mind are in the state of silent vacancy(‘同归于寂’). As you come to look at them, their colors at once show up clearly. From this you can know that these flowers are not external to your mind."

先生曰："众人只说格物要依晦翁[晦翁：朱子尊称。朱子，字晦庵。]，何曾把他的说去用？我着实曾用来。初年与钱友同论做圣贤，要格天下之物，如今安得这等大的力量？因指亭前竹子，令去格看。钱子早夜去穷格竹子的道理，竭其心思，至于三日，便致劳神成疾。当初说他这是精力不足，某因自去穷格。早夜不得其理，到七日，亦以劳思致疾。遂相与叹圣贤是做不得的，无他大力量去格物了。及在夷中三年[正德元年(1506)，王守仁因反对宦官刘谨，贬贵州龙场驿丞，次年起程，三年到任，五年后又迁升江西庐陵知县，龙场当时是少数民族地区，故称为夷中。]，颇见得此意思乃知天下之物本无可格者。其格物之功，只在身心上做，决然以圣人为人人可到，便自有担当了。这里意思，却要说与诸公知道。"

The Teacher said, "People merely say that in the investigation of things we must follow Chu Hsi(朱熹), but when have they carried it out in practice? I have carried it out earnestly and definitely. In my earlier years my friend Ch'ien(钱) and I discussed the idea that to become a sage or a worthy one must investigate all the things in the world. But how can a person have such tremendous energy? I therefore pointed to the bamboos in front of the pavilion and told him to investigate them and see. Day and night Mr. Chien (钱子)went ahead trying to investigate to the utmost the principles in the bamboos. He exhausted his mind and thoughts and on the third day he was tired out and took sick. At first I said that it was because his energy and strength was insufficient. Therefore, I myself went to try to investigate to the utmost. From morning till night, I was unable to find the principles of the bamboos. On the seventh day I also became sick because I thought too hard. In consequence we sighed to each other and said that it was impossible to be a sage or a worthy, for we do not have the tremendous energy to investigate things that they have. After I had lived among the barbarians(‘夷中’)for (almost) three years, I understood what all this meant and realized that there is really nothing in the things in the world to investigate, that the effort to investigate things is only to be carried out in and with reference to one's body and mind(‘其格物之功，只在身心上做’), and that if one firmly believes that everyone can become a sage, one will naturally be able to take up the task of investigating things. This idea, gentlemen, I must convey to you."

又问："心即理之说，程子云‘在物为理’，如何谓心即理？"

The disciple further asked about the theory that the mind is identical with principle and said, "Master Cheng(程颐先生)said, 'What is inherent in a thing is principle(‘在物为理’).' How can it be said that the mind is identical with principle?"

先生曰："在物为理，在字上当添一心字，此心在物则为理。如此心在事父则为孝，在事君则为忠之类。"

The Teacher said, "The word 'mind' should be added to the saying to mean that when the mind is engaged in a thing, there is principle(‘心在物则为理’). For example, when the mind is engaged in serving one's father, there is the principle of filial piety, and when the mind is engaged in serving the ruler, there is the principle of loyalty, and so forth."

先生因谓之曰："诸君要识得我立言宗旨。我如今说个心即理是如何，只为世人分心与理为二故，便有许多病痛。如五伯攘夷狄[五伯：指春秋时五霸，即齐桓公、晋文公、楚庄王、吴王阖闾、越王勾践。攘：排除、夺取，这里引申为征讨。]，尊周室，都是一个私心，便不当理。人却说他做得当理，只心有未纯，往往悦慕其所为，要来外面做得好看，却与心全不相干。分心与理为二，其流至于伯道之伪而不自知[伯道：霸道。]。故我说个心即理，要使知心理是一个，便来心上做工夫，不去袭义于外，便是王道之真。此我立言宗旨。"

Thereupon the Teacher said to the disciples, "You gentlemen must understand the basic purpose of my founding this doctrine(‘立言宗旨’). Why should I now declare that the mind is identical with principle? Simply because people of the world divide the mind and principle into two(‘分心与理为二’), thus giving rise to many defects and evils. For instance, the five powerful despots(五伯)drove out the barbarians and honored the House of Chou(‘尊周室’)all because of their selfishness, and therefore they were not in accord with principle. Some people say that they acted in accord with principle, but their minds did not completely become identified with the Principle of Nature. These people always admire the deeds of the powerful despots. They just want their deeds to look good on the outside and completely ignore the relationship to the mind. They divide the mind and principle into two and unwittingly drift into the insincerity which is characteristic of the way of despots(伯道). Therefore, I talk about the identification of the mind and principle so people will know that mind and principle are one and devote their efforts to the mind instead of accumulating individual acts of righteousness externally(‘不去袭义于外’). This is the essence of the kingly way(‘王道’)of moral principles. This is the basic purpose of my founding the doctrine."

问："人心与物同体，如吾身原是血气流通的，所以谓之同体。若于人便异体了。禽兽草木益远矣，则何谓之同体？"

I said, "The human mind and things form the same body. In the case of one's body, blood and the vital force in fact circulate through it and therefore we can say they form the same body. In the case of men, their bodies are different and differ even more from those of animals and plants. How can they be said to form the same body?"

先生曰："你只在感应之几上看，岂但禽兽草木，虽天地也与我同体的，鬼神也与我同体的。"请问。

The Teacher said, "Just look at the matter from the point of view of the subtle incipient activating force of their mutual influence and response. Not only animals and plants, but heaven and earth also, form the same body with me. Spiritual beings("鬼神")also form the same body with me." I asked the Teacher kindly to explain.

先生曰："你看这个天地中间，甚么是天地的心？"

The Teacher said, "Among the things under heaven and on earth, which do you consider to be the mind of Heaven and Earth?"

对曰："尝闻人是天地的心。"

"I have heard that 'Man is the mind of Heaven and Earth.'"

曰："人又甚么教做心？"

"How does man become mind?"

对曰："只是一个灵明。""可知充天塞地中间，只有这个灵明，人只为形体自间隔了。我的灵明，便是天地鬼神的主宰。天没有我的灵明，谁去仰他高？地没有我的灵明，谁去俯他深？鬼神没有我的灵明，谁去辨他吉凶灾祥？天地鬼神万物离却我的灵明，便没有天地鬼神万物了。我的灵明离却天地鬼神万物，亦没有我的灵明。如此，便是一气流通的，如何与他间隔得！"

"Clear intelligence(‘灵明’)and clear intelligence alone." "We know, then, in all that fills Heaven and Earth there is but this clear intelligence. It is only because of their physical forms and bodies(‘形体’)that men are separated. My clear intelligence is the master of Heaven and Earth and spiritual beings. If Heaven is deprived of my clear intelligence, who is going to look into its height? If Earth is deprived of my clear intelligence, who is going to look into its depth? If spiritual beings are deprived of my clear intelligence, who is going to distinguish their good and evil fortune or the calamities and blessings that they will bring? Separated from my clear intelligence, there will be no Heaven, Earth, spiritual beings, or myriad things, and separated from those, there will not be my clear intelligence. Thus they are all permeated with one material force(‘一气流通’). How can they be separated? ”

又问：“天地鬼神万物，千古见在，何没了我的灵明，便俱无了？”

I asked further, “Heaven, Earth, spiritual beings, and the myriad things have existed from great antiquity. Why should it be that if my clear intelligence is gone, they will all cease to exist?”

曰：“今看死的人，他这些精灵游散了，他的天地万物尚在何处？”

“Consider the dead man. His spirit has drifted away and dispersed. Where are his Heaven and Earth and myriad things?”

《大学问》Inquiry on *The Great Learning* [1]

该篇申言《大学》“明明德”之旨，在于恢复天地万物一体之本然而已。继而阐释“大人之学”缘何要“亲民”和“止于至善”。《大学问》是阳明的主要著作之一，收在《续篇》(见《全书》卷二十六)中，乃阳明弟子钱德洪所录。钱称：“《大学问》者，师门之教典也。”全文以问答的形式阐释《大学》的基本纲领，并批评朱子对《大学》的解释，贯穿王阳明的“心外无理”“万物一体”思想，是研究理学与心学之分歧的重要资料。

[Introduction] *Inquiry on The Great Learning* declares that the purpose of *The Great Learning* lies in “manifesting the clear character” and “regarding Heaven and Earth and the myriad things as one body. ” Then, he explains why “the learning of the Great Man” consists also in “loving the people” and “abiding in the highest good”. *Inquiry on The Great Learning* is one of Yang-ming’s master works, collected in the Sequel (see Volume 26), which was recorded by Qian Dehong, a disciple of Yang-ming. Qian commended “*Inquiry on The Great Learning* as a holy code of teaching practice.” Throughout the text, Yangming explains the

[1] 中文选自郭齐勇主编《中国古典哲学名著选读》，北京：人民出版社, 2005 年。

The Great Learning, selected from *Sources of Chinese Tradition: From Earliest Times to 1600* (Volume 1), translated by Bary, William Theodore De. Columbia University Press, 1999.

basic program of *The Great Learning* in the form of question and answer, and criticizes Zhuzi for his interpretation of *the Great Learning*. All in all, Yang-ming's thought like "There is no principle outside the mind" and "Heaven, Earth, and the myriad things are united into one " is running through the whole text, which provides a very important source for scholars to discriminate the differences between Neo-Confucianism and the concept of conscience.

"大学者，昔儒以为大人之学矣。敢问大人之学何以在于'明明德'乎？"

Question : "*The Great Learning* was considered by a former scholar (Chu Hsi)（'昔儒'）to be the learning of the great man. I venture to ask why the learning of the great man should consist in 'manifesting the clear character.（'明明德'）'"

阳明子曰："大人者，以天地万物为一体者也，其视天下犹一家，中国犹一人焉。若夫间形骸而分尔我者，小人矣。大人之能以天地万物为一体也，非意之也，其心之仁本若是，其与天地万物而为一也。岂惟大人，虽小人之心亦莫不然，彼顾自小之耳。是故见孺子之入井，而必有怵惕恻隐之心焉[怵惕：警惧。恻隐：痛而不忍。]，是其仁之与孺子而为一体也；孺子犹同类者也，见鸟兽之哀鸣觳觫[觳觫(hú sù)：恐惧颤抖貌。]，而必有不忍之心焉，是其仁之与鸟兽而为一体也；鸟兽犹有知觉者也，见草木之摧折而必有悯恤之心焉，是其仁之与草木而为一体也；草木犹有生意者也，见瓦石之毁坏而必有顾惜之心焉，是其仁之与瓦石而为一体也；是其一体之仁也，虽小人之心亦必有之。是乃根于天命之性，而自然灵昭不昧者也，是故谓之'明德'。小人之心既已分隔隘陋矣，而其一体之仁犹能不昧若此者，是其未动于欲，而未蔽于私之时也。及其动于欲，蔽于私，而利害相攻，忿怒相激，则将戕物圮类[圮(pǐ)：毁，绝。]，无所不为，其甚至有骨肉相残者，而一体之仁亡矣。是故苟无私欲之蔽，则虽小人之心，而其一体之仁犹大人也； 一有私欲之蔽，则虽大人之心，而其分隔隘陋犹小人矣。故夫为大人之学者，亦惟去其私欲之蔽，以自明其明德，复其天地万物一体之本然而已耳；非能于本体之外而有所增益之也。"

Master Wang said, "The great man regards Heaven and Earth and the myriad things as one body. He regards the world as one family and the country as one person. As to those who make a cleavage between objects and distinguish between the self and others, they are small men. That the great man can regard Heaven, Earth, and the myriad things as one body is not because he deliberately wants to do so, but because it is natural with the humane nature of his mind that he should form a unity with Heaven, Earth, and the myriad things. This is true not only of the great man. Even the mind of the small man is not different. Only he himself makes it small. Therefore, when he sees a child about to fall into a well, he cannot help a feeling of alarm and commiseration（'见孺子之入井，必怵惕恻隐之心'）. This shows that his humanity (*jen*) forms one body with the child. It may be objected that the child belongs to the same species (as he). Yet when he observes the pitiful cries and frightened appearance of birds and animals (about to be slaughtered), he cannot help feeling an 'inability to bear' their sufferings. This shows that his humanity forms one body with birds and animals. It may be objected that birds and animals are sentient beings (as he is). But when he sees plants broken and destroyed, he cannot help a feeling of pity. This shows that his humanity forms one body with plants. It may be said that plants are living things (as he is). Yet even when he sees tiles and stones shattered and crushed he cannot help a feeling of regret. This shows that his humanity forms one body with tiles and stones. This means that even the mind of the small man necessarily has the humanity that forms one body with all. Such a mind is rooted in his Heaven-endowed nature, and is naturally intelligent, clear, and not obscure. For this reason it is called the 'clear character.' Although the mind of the small man is divided and narrow（'小人之心既已分隔隘陋矣'）, yet his humanity that forms a unity can remain free from darkness like this. This is due to the fact that his mind has not yet been aroused by desires and blinded by selfishness. When it is aroused by desires and blinded by selfishness, compelled by the greed for gain and fear of harm, and stirred by anger, he will destroy things, kill members of his own species, and will do everything to the extreme, even to the slaughtering of his own brothers, and the humanity that forms a unity with all perishes. As soon as it is obscured by selfish desires, even the mind of the great man will be divided and narrow, like that of the small man. Thus the learning of the great man consists entirely in getting rid of the blindness of selfish desires in order by one's own efforts to make manifest his clear character, so that the original condition of the unity of Heaven, Earth, and the myriad things may be restored, that is all. Nothing can be added to this original nature from outside."

曰："然则何以在'亲民'乎？"

Qusetion: "Why, then, does the learning of the great man consist also in loving the people?"

曰："明明德者，立其天地万物一体之体也。亲民者，达其天地万物一体之用也。故明明德必在于亲民，而亲民乃所以明其明德也。是故亲吾之父，以及人之父，以及天下人之父，而后吾之仁实与吾之父、人之父与天下人之父而为一体矣；实与之为一体，而后孝之明德始明矣！亲吾之兄，以及人之兄、以及天下人之兄，而后吾之仁实与吾之兄、人之兄与天下人之兄而为一体矣；实与之为一体，而后弟之明德始明矣！君臣也，夫妇也，朋友也，以至于山川鬼神鸟兽草木也，莫不实有以亲之，以达吾一体之仁，然后吾之明德始无不明，而真能以天地万物为一体矣。夫是之谓明明德于天下，是之谓家齐国治而天下平，是之谓尽性。"

Answer: "To manifest the clear character（'明明德'）is to bring about the substance of the unity of Heaven, Earth, and the myriad things, whereas loving the people（'亲民'）is to put into universal operation of the function of the unity. Hence manifesting of the clear character must lie in loving the people, and loving the people is the way to manifest the clear character. Therefore, only when I love my father, the fathers of others, and the fathers of all men, can my humanity really form one body with my father, the fathers of others, and the fathers of all men. When it truly forms one body with them, then the clear character of filial piety will be manifested. Only when I love my brother, the brothers of others, and the brothers of all men can my humanity really form one body with my brother, the brothers of others, and the brothers of all men. When it truly forms one body with them, then the clear character of brotherly respect will be manifested. Everything from ruler, minister, husband, wife, and friends to mountains, rivers, heavenly and earthly spirits, birds, animals, and plants, all should be truly loved in order to realize my humanity that forms a unity, and then my clear character will be completely manifested, and I will really form one body with Heaven, Earth, and the myriad things. This is what is meant by 'manifesting the clear character throughout the empire.' This is what is meant by 'regulating the family, ' 'ordering the state, ' and 'pacifying the world.' This is what is meant by 'fully developing one's nature' . "

曰："然则又乌在其为'止至善'乎？"

Question: "Then why does the learning of the great man consist in 'abiding in the highest good?' "

曰："至善者，明德、亲民之极则也。天命之性，粹然至善，其灵昭不昧者，此其至善之发见，是乃明德之本体，而即所谓良知也。至善之发见，是而是焉，非而非焉，轻重厚薄，随感随应，变动不居，而亦莫不自有天然之中，是乃民彝物则之极［彝：常。民彝物则：民物的常则。］，而不容少有议拟增损于其间也。少有拟议增损于其间，则是私意小智，而非至善之谓矣。自非慎独之至，惟精惟一者，其孰能与于此乎？后之人惟其不知至善之在吾心，而用其私智以揣摸测度于其外，以为事事物物各有定理也，是以昧其是非之则，支离决裂，人欲肆而天理亡，明德、亲民之学遂大乱于天下。

Answer: "The highest good is the ultimate principle of manifesting character and loving people. The nature endowed in us by Heaven（'天命之性'）is pure and perfect. The fact that it is intelligent, clear, and not obscured is evidence of the emanation and revelation of the highest good. It is the original nature or the the clear character which is called innate knowledge(of the good)（'所谓良知也'）. As the highest good emanates and reveals itself, one will consider right as right and wrong as wrong. Things of greater or less importance and situations of grave or light character will be responded to as they act upon us. In all our changes and activities, we will entertain no preconceived attitude; in all this we will do nothing that is not natural. This is the normal nature of man and the principle of things. There can be no suggestion of adding to or subtracting anything from them. If any such suggestion is entertained, it means selfish purpose and shallow wisdom, and cannot be said to be the highest good. Naturally, how can anyone who does not watch over himself carefully when alone, and who has no refinement and singleness of mind, attain to such a state of perfection? Later generations fail to realize that the highest good is inherent in their own minds, but each in accordance with his own ideas gropes for it outside the mind, believing that every event and every object has its own definite principle（‘事事物物各有定理’）. For this reason the law of right and wrong is obscure; the mind becomes concerned with fragmentary and isolated details, the desires of man become rampant and the principle of Heaven is at an end. And thus the education for manifesting character and loving people is everywhere thrown into confusion."

“盖昔之人固有欲明其明德者矣，然惟不知止于至善，而骛其私心于过高[骛(wù)：追求。]，是以失之虚罔空寂[虚罔：虚无。]，而无有乎家国天下之施，则二氏之流是矣[二氏：指释老二氏，佛教讲空寂，老子讲虚无。]。固有欲亲其民者矣，然惟不知止于至善，而溺其私心于卑琐，是以失之权谋智术，而无有乎仁爱恻怛之诚[恻怛(dá)：怜悯。]，则五伯功利之徒是矣。是皆不知止于至善之过也。故止至善之于明德、亲民也，犹之规矩之于方圆也，尺度之于长短也，权衡之于轻重也。故方圆而不止于规矩，爽其则矣[爽：失。]；长短而不止于尺度，乖其剂矣[剂：指剂量。]；轻重而不止于权衡，失其准矣；明明德、亲民而不止于至善，亡其本矣。故止于至善以亲民，而明其明德，是之谓大人之学。”

"In the past, there have been people who wanted to manifest their clear character（‘欲明其明德矣’）, of course. But simply because they did not know how to abide in the highest good, but instead drove their own minds toward something too lofty, they thereby lost them in illusions, emptiness, and quietude（‘失之虚罔空寂’）, having nothing to do with the work of the family（‘家’）, the country（‘国’）, and the world（‘天下’）. Such are the followers of Buddhism and Taoism. There have been those who wanted to love their people, of course. But simply because they did not know how to abide in the highest good, but instead sank their own minds in base and trifling things（‘溺其私心于卑琐’）, they thereby lost them in scheming strategy and tricks, having neither the sincerity of humanity nor that of sympathy. Such are the followers of the Five Overlords (as opposed to true kings) and the pursuers of profit and gain（‘则五伯功利之徒是矣’）. All of these are due to a failure to know how to abide in the highest good. Therefore, abiding in the highest good is to manifesting character and loving people as the carpenter's square and compass（‘方园’）are to the square and the circle, or rule and measure to length, or balances and scales to weight. If the square and the circle do not abide by the compass and the carpenter's square, their standard will be wrong; if length does not abide by the rule and measure, its adjustment will be lost（‘长短而不止于尺度，乖其剂矣’）; if the weight does not abide by the balances, its exactness will be gone; and if manifesting clear character and loving people do not abide by the highest good, their foundation will disappear. Therefore, abiding in the highest good so as to love people and manifest the clear character is what it meant by the learning of the great man."

曰：“物有本末：先儒以明德为本，新民为末，两物而内外相对也。事有终始：先儒以知止为始，能得为终，一事而首尾相因也[先儒：指朱熹。]。如子之说，以新民为亲民，则本末之说亦有所未然与？”

曰：“终始之说，大略是矣。即以新民为亲民，而曰明德为本，亲民为末，其说亦未为不可，但不当分本末为两物耳。夫木之干，谓之本，木之梢，谓之末，惟其一物也，是以谓之本末。若曰两物，则既为两物矣，又何可以言本末乎？新民之意，既与亲民不同，则明德之功，自与新民为二。若知明明德以亲其民，而亲民以明其明德，则明德亲民焉可析而为两乎？先儒之说，是盖不知明德亲民之本为一事，而认以为两事，是以虽知本末之当为一物，而亦不得不分为两物也。”

曰：“古之欲明明德于天下者，以至于先修其身，以吾子明德亲民之说通之，亦既可得而知矣。敢问欲修其身，以至于致知在格物，其工夫次第又何如其用力与？”

曰：“此正详言明德、亲民、止至善之功也。盖身、心、意、知、物者，是其工夫所用之条理，虽亦各有其所，而其实只是一物。格、致、诚、正、修者，是其条理所用之工夫，虽亦皆有其名，而其实只是一事。何谓身心之形体？运用之谓也。何谓心身之灵明？主宰之谓也。何请修身？为善而去恶之谓也。吾身自能为善而去恶乎？必其灵明主宰者欲为善而去恶，然后其形体运用者始能为善而去恶也。故欲修其身者，必在于先正其心也。”[1]

曰：“‘知止而后有定，定而后能静，静而后能安，安而后能虑，虑而后能得’，其说何也？”

Question: “ ‘Only after knowing what to abide in can one be calm. Only after having achieved calm can one be tranquil. Only after having achieved tranquility can one have peaceful repose. Only after having peaceful repose can one begin to deliberate. Only after deliberation can the end be attained.’ How do you explain this? ”

曰：“人惟不知至善之在吾心，而求之于其外，以为事事物物皆有定理也，而求至善于事事物物之中，是以支离决裂，错杂纷纭，而莫知有一定之向。今焉既知至善之在吾心，而不假于外求，则志有定向，而无支离决裂、错杂纷纭之患矣。无支离决裂、错杂纷纭之患，则心不妄动而能静矣。心不妄动而能静，则其日用之间，从容闲暇而能安矣。能安，则凡一念之发，一事之感，其为至善乎？其非至善乎？吾心之良知自有以详审精察之，而能虑矣。能虑则择之无不精，处之无不当，而至善于是乎可得矣。”

Answer: “People fail to realize that the highest good is in their minds and seek it outside（‘求之于其外’）. As they believe that everything or every event（‘事事物物’）has its own definite principle, they search for the highest good in individual things（‘于事事物物之中’）. Consequently, the mind becomes fragmented and isolated（‘支离决裂’）; mixed and confused（‘错杂纷纭’）, it has no definite direction. Once it is realized that the highest good is in the mind and does not depend on any search outside（‘不假于外求’）, then the mind will have definite direction and there will be no danger of its becoming fragmented and isolated, mixed, or confused. When there is no such danger, the mind will not be foolishly perturbed but will be tranquil. Not being foolishly perturbed but tranquil, in its daily functioning it will be unhurried and at ease and will attain peaceful repose. Being in peaceful repose, wherever a thought arises or whenever an event acts upon it, the mind with its innate knowledge

[1] 以上三节问答被原译者省略或省译。——编者注。

(‘吾心之良知’)will thoroughly sift and carefully examine whether or not the thought or event is in accord with the highest good, and thus the mind can deliberate. With deliberation, every decision will be excellent and every act will be proper, and in this way the highest good will be attained."

“然心之本体则性也。性无不善，则心之本体本无不正也。何从而用其正之之功乎？盖心之本体本无不正，自其意念发动，而后有不正。故欲正其心者，必就其意念之所发而正之，凡其发一念而善也，好之真如好好色(hào hǎo sè)；发一念而恶也，恶之真如恶恶臭(wù è xiù)；则意无不诚，而心可正矣。”

"Now the original substance of the mind is man's nature. Human nature being universally good, the original substance of the mind is correct. How is it that any effort is required to rectify the mind? The reason is that, while the original substance of the mind is correct, incorrectness enters when one's thoughts begins to emanate and become active. Therefore, he who wishes to rectify his mind must rectify it in connection with the emanation of his thoughts and will. If, whenever a good thought emanates, he loves it as he loves beautiful colors(‘如好好色’), and whenever an evil thought emanates, he hates it as he hates bad odor (‘如恶恶臭’), then his will will always be sincere and the mind can be rectified."

“然意之所发，有善有恶，不有以明其善恶之分，亦将真妄错杂，虽欲诚之，不可得而诚矣。故欲诚其意者，必在于致知焉。致者，至也，如云丧致乎哀之致。《易》言，‘知至至之’，‘知至’者，知也；‘至之’者，致也。‘致知’云者，非若后儒所谓充广其知识之谓也，致吾心之良知焉耳。良知者，孟子所谓‘是非之心，人皆有之’者也。是非之心，不待虑而知，不待学而能，是故谓之良知。是乃天命之性，吾心之本体，自然灵昭明觉者也。”

"However, what emanates from the will may be good or evil, and unless there is a way to make a clear distinction between good and evil, there will be a confusion of truth and untruth(‘真妄错杂’). In that case, even if one wants to make his will sincere, he cannot do so. Therefore, he who wishes to make his will sincere must extend his knowledge. By extension it means to reach the limit. The word 'extension' is the same as that used in the saying, 'Mourning is to be carried to the utmost degree of grief.' In *The Book of Changes* it is said that 'Knowing the utmost, one should reach it.' 'Knowing the utmost' means knowledge and 'reaching it' means extension. Extension of knowledge is not what later scholars understand as enriching and widening knowledge. It means simply extending my innate knowledge of the good to the utmost(‘致吾心之良知焉耳’). This innate knowledge of the good is what Mencius meant when he said: 'The sense of right and wrong is common to all men'(‘是非之心，人皆有之’). The sense of right and wrong requires no deliberation to know, nor does it depend on learning to function. This is why it is called innate knowledge. It is my nature endowed by Heaven(‘是乃天命之性’), the original substance of my mind, naturally intelligent, clear, and understanding."

"凡意念之发，吾心之良知无有不自知者。其善与，惟吾心之良知自知之；其不善与，亦惟吾心之良知自知之；是皆无所与于他人者也。故虽小人之为不善，既已无所不至，然其见君子，则必厌然揜(pàn)其不善，而著其善者，是亦可以见其良知之有不容于自昧者也。今欲别善恶以诚其意，惟在致其良知之所知焉尔。何则？意念之发，吾心之良知既知其为善矣，使其不能诚有以好之，而复背而去之，则是以善为恶，而自昧其知善之良知矣。意念之所发，吾之良知既知其为不善矣，使其不能诚有以恶之，而复蹈而为之，则是以恶为善，而自昧其知恶之良知矣。若是，则虽曰知之，犹不知也，意其可得而诚乎！今于良知之善恶者，无不诚好而诚恶之，则不自欺其良知而意可诚也已。"

"Whenever a thought or a wish arises, my mind's faculty of innate knowledge itself also knows it. It has nothing to do with others. Therefore, although an inferior man（'小人'）may have done all manner of evil, when he sees a gentleman he will surely try to disguise this fact, concealing what is evil and displaying what is good in himself. This shows that innate knowledge of the good does not permit any self-deception（'是亦可以见其良知之有不容于自昧者也'）. Now the only way to distinguish good and evil in order to make the will sincere is to extend to the utmost the knowledge of the innate faculty（'致其良知之所知焉尔'）. Why is this? When (a good) thought or wish arises, the innate faculty of my mind already knows it to be evil. If I did not sincerely hate it but instead carried it out, I would be regarding evil as good and obscuring my innate faculty which knows evil. In such cases what is supposed to be knowledge is really ignorance. How then can the will be made sincere? If what the innate faculty knows to be good or evil is sincerely loved or hated, one's innate knowing faculty is not deceived and the will can be made sincere."

"然欲致其良知，亦岂影响恍惚而悬空无实之谓乎？是必实有其事矣。故致知必在于格物。物者，事也，凡意之所发必有其事，意所在之事谓之物。格者，正也，正其不正以归于正之谓也。正其不正者，去恶之谓也。归于正者，为善之谓也。夫是之谓格。《书》言'格于上下'，'格于文祖'，'格其非心'[引文见于《尚书・尧典》和《尚书・舜典》两篇。"格"：即"至"，作来到，到达解。"格其非心"：见于《尚书・冏命》篇，此"格"作"正"解。(说明：本篇点校，参考了吴光、钱明、董平、姚延福编校的《王阳明全集》一书。)]，格物之格实兼其义也。"

"Now, when one sets out to extend his innate knowledge to the utmost, does this mean something merely apparent, hazy, vacuous, and without substance（'影响恍惚而悬空无实之谓'）? No, it means something concrete. Therefore, the extension of knowledge must consist in the investigation of things（'格物'）. A thing is an event. For every emanation of the will there must be an event corresponding to it. The event to which the will is directed is a 'thing'. To investigate is to rectify（'格者，正也'）. It is to rectify that which is incorrect so as to return to its original correctness. To rectify that which is not correct is to remove evil, and to return to correctness is to do good. This is what is meant by investigation."

“良知所知之善，虽诚欲好之矣，苟不即其意之所在之物而实有以为之，则是物有未格，而好之之意犹为未诚也。良知所知之恶，虽诚欲恶之矣，苟不即其意之所在之物而实有以去之，则是物有未格，而恶之之意犹为未诚也。今焉于其良知所知之善者，即其意之所在之物而实为之，无有乎不尽。于其良知所知之恶者，即其意之所在之物而实去之，无有乎不尽。然后物无不格，而吾良知之所知者无有亏缺障蔽，而得以极其至矣。夫然后吾心快然无复余憾而自谦矣。夫然后意之所发者，始无自欺而可以谓之诚矣。故曰：‘物格而后知至，知至而后意诚，意诚而后心正，心正而后身修。’盖其功夫条理虽有先后次序之可言，而其体之惟一，实无先后次序之可分。其条理功夫虽无先后次序之可分，而其用之惟精，固有纤毫不可得而缺焉者。此格致诚正之说，所以阐尧舜之正传而为孔氏之心印也。”

“If one sincerely loves the good known by the innate faculty but does not in reality act on the thing to which the will is directed, it means that the thing has not been investigated and that the will to love it is not yet sincere. If one sincerely hates the evil known by the innate faculty but does not in reality repel the thing to which the will is directed, it means that the thing has not been investigated and that the will to hate it is not sincere. If within what is good as known by the innate faculty, one acts to the utmost degree on the thing to which the will is directed, and if within what is evil as known by the innate faculty, one really repels to the utmost degree the evil to which the will is directed, then everything will be investigated and what is known by one’s innate faculty will not be deficient or obscured but will extend to the utmost. Then the mind will be joyous in itself, happy and without regret, the emanation of the will will carry with it no self-deception and sincerity may be said to have been attained. Therefore, it is said: ‘When things are investigated, true knowledge is extended; when knowledge is extended, the will becomes sincere; when the will is sincere, the mind is rectified; and when the mind is rectified, the personal life is cultivated（‘心正而后身修’）.’ While the order of the tasks involves a sequence of first and last, in reality they are one and cannot be separated. At the same time, while the order and the tasks cannot be separated into first and last, their operation must be so refined as not to be wanting in the slightest degree. This is why the doctrine of investigation, extension, being sincere, and rectification is a correct exposition of the true heritage of (the sage-emperors) Yao and Shun and why it coincides with Confucius’own ideas.”

“是故圣人不治已病治未病，不治已乱治未乱，此之谓也。夫病已成而后药之，乱已成而后治之，譬犹渴而穿井，斗而铸锥，不亦晚乎。”

——《黄帝内经》《素问·四气调神大论》

中国经典双语阅读

《黄帝内经》（选）

Unit 8

《黄帝内经》（选）Selected from *The Yellow Emperor's Classic of Medicine*

［思想指要］《黄帝内经》又称《内经》，是中国最早的典籍之一，也是中国传统医学四大经典之首。相传为黄帝所作，因以为名。但后世较为公认此书最终成型于西汉，作者亦非一人，而是由中国黄老之学医家历代传承增补发展创作而来。作为“医学之宗”的《黄帝内经》，堪称是一部关于生命、认识生命、养护身体的百科全书。利用阴阳五行学说，对生命的形成、疾病的起因、心理现象和生理现象的关系，作了唯物主义和辩证法的说明。此书是黄老之学的代表性著作之一。

[Introduction] *The Yellow Emperor's Classic of Medicine*, also known as *The Classic of Internal Medicine,* is one of the earliest Chinese classics and the first of the four classics of traditional Chinese medicine. Legend has it that it was written by the Yellow Emperor (Huangdi), hence the name of *Huang Di Neijing*. However, it is generally recognized that the book was finally formed in the Western Han Dynasty. But it was supplemented and developed and innovated by generations of doctors who believed in Huang-Lao. According to *The Instructions for the Self-Cultivation and Practice* in *Huainanzi,* it was given the name of *the Yellow Emperor*, because it was intended to trace to and worship the source of medical treatment, whereby to explain the early development of Chinese medical culture. And it was neither written by one single person, nor completely formed once for all. *The Yellow Emperor's Classic of Medicine*, as a pioneering work of Chinese traditional medicine, is also an encyclopaedia about life, understanding life and preserving the body. In addition, Chinese ancient medicine fully absorbed the theory of *Yin and Yang* and the five elements which moved forward continually along with their integration with the unique path of medicine. Actually, the theory of *Yin and Yang* and the five elements are running throughout *The Yellow Emperor's Classic of Internal Medicine.* Accordingly, *The Yellow Emperor's Classic of Medicine* also embodies the spirit and cognition of Chinese traditional culture.

《灵兰秘典论》The Sacred Teachings [1]

本篇中，灵兰，即灵台兰室之简称，相传是古代帝王藏书之所。室之所以名兰，清代高士宗《素问直解》云："谓神灵相接，其气如兰。"秘典，珍重之辞，即秘藏之典籍。本文篇末有"藏灵兰之室，以传宝焉"之语，以强调所论内容的重要性，故篇名"灵兰秘典"。正如明代马莳《素问注证发微》云："黄帝乃择吉日良兆而藏灵兰之室以传宝焉，故名篇。"

[Introduction] In this essay, the two Chinese Characters of "*Ling Lan*" are the shortened form of Lingtai Orchid Room, which, according to the legend, is a library designated for ancient emperors to store books. While talking about the reason why "Lan" (Orchid) is used to name the room, Gao Shizong, a scholar in the Qing Dynasty, said in his *A Direct Explanation of Suwen*, "When the spirit and the soul is interconnected in the room, the pneuma exuded is like that of orchid". The "secret code" means what is said in it is the precious words, that is, the collected books of hidden treasures. At the end of this essay, there is a phrase like "What is preserved in room of orchids, is the treasure passed on from generation to generation", emphasizing the importance of its content, hence the name of "*Sacred Teachings of Linglan*". As Ma Shi in the Ming Dynasty said in his *Notes and Illuminations to Suwen* that "the Yellow Emperor chose a good omen of auspicious days and hid them in Lingtai Orchid Room for inheritance and protection, hence the name of this essay."

黄帝问曰：愿闻十二脏之相使[十二脏：指心、肝、脾、肺、肾、膻中、胆、胃、大肠、小肠、三焦、膀胱十二个脏器。相使：相互联系。]，贵贱何如[贵贱：主要与次要。]？

Huang Di(皇帝)asked Qi Bo(岐伯), "Can you please tell me the functions and the relationships of the twelve *zang fu*（'脏腑'）viscera and their meridians?"

岐伯对曰："悉乎哉问也！请遂言之。心者，君主之官也[官：职守。]，神明出焉。肺者，相傅之官[相傅：辅佐君主的宰相。相，为佐君者。傅：为教育太子及诸皇子者。]，治节(?)出焉。肝者，将军之官[将军：以将军比喻肝的易动而刚强之性。]，谋虑出焉。胆者，中正之官[中正：即中精，胆为清净之府，藏清汁。]，决断[决断：决定判断的能力。]出焉。膻中者[膻(dàn)中：心脏的外围组织，也叫心包。]，臣使之官[臣使：即内臣。因膻中贴近心，故为心的臣使。]，喜乐出焉。脾胃者，仓廪之官[仓廪：贮藏粮食的仓库。脾胃有受纳水谷和运化精微之能，故称"仓廪之官"。]，五味出焉。大肠者，传道之官[传道：转送运输。道，同"导"。]，变化出焉[变化：饮食消化、吸收、排泄的过程。]。小肠者，受盛之官[受盛：接受和容纳。]，化物出焉[化物：分别清浊，消化食物。]。肾者，作强之官[作强：作用强力，即指能力充实。]，伎巧出焉[伎巧：技巧。]。三

---

[1] 中文选自《黄帝内经》，北京：中华书局；2010 年。

The Sacred Teachings，Selected from *The Yellow Emperor's Classic of Medicine*：A New Translation of the Neijing Suwen with Commentary, translated by Maoshing Ni, Ph.D. Boston and London：Shambhala Publications, Inc., 2011.

焦者，决渎之官[决渎：通利水道。]，水道出焉。膀胱者，州都之官[州都：水液聚集的地方。]，津液藏焉，气化则能出矣[气化：气的运动而产生的生理变化。]。凡此十二官者，不得相失也，故主明则下安，以此养生则寿，殁世不殆，以为天下则大昌；主不明则十二官危，使道闭塞而不通[使道：十二宫相互联系的通道。]，形乃大伤，以此养生则殃，以为天下者，其宗大危。戒之戒之！”

Qi Bo replied, “Your question is very precise and I will try to answer you as precisely as you asked. The heart is the sovereign of all organs and represents the consciousness of one's being. It is responsible for intelligence, wisdom, and spiritual transformation. The lung is the advisor. It helps the heart in regulating the body's *qi*（‘气’）. The liver is like the general, courageous and smart. The gall bladder is like a judge for its power of discernment. The pericardium is like the court jester who makes the lung laugh, bringing forth joy. The stomach and spleen are like warehouses where one stores all the food and essences. They digest, absorb, and extract the food and nutrients. The large intestine is responsible for transportation of all turbidity. All waste products go through this organ. The small intestine receives the food that has been digested by the spleen and stomach and further extracts, absorbs, and distributes it throughout the body, all the while separating the pure from the turbid. The kidneys store the vitality and mobilize the four extremities. They also aid the memory, willpower, and coordination. The *sanjiao*（‘三焦者’）, or the three visceral cavities, promotes the transformation and transportation of water and fluids throughout the body. The bladder is where the water converges and where, after being catalyzed by the *qi*, it is eliminated. So these twelve *zang and fu* organs（‘十二官者’）must work together harmoniously, just like a kingdom.”

“However, the decision-making is the lung's job. If the spirit is clear, all the functions of the other organs will be normal. It is in this way that one's life is preserved and perpetuated, just as a country becomes prosperous when all its people are fulfilling their duties. If the spirit is disturbed and unclear, the other organs will not function properly. This creates damage. The pathways and roads along which the *qi*(气) flows will become blocked and health will suffer. The citizens of the kingdom will also suffer. These are the relationships of a kingdom.”

“至道在微，变化无穷，孰知其原？窘乎哉！消者瞿瞿[瞿瞿(jù)：惊恐]，孰知其要？闵闵之当，孰者为良？恍惚之数，生于毫厘，毫厘之数，起于度量，千之万之，可以益大，推之大之，其形乃制。”

Qi Bo continued, “The principles of healing and medicine in general are difficult to grasp because many changes occur in illness, and the healing process must adapt to that. It becomes difficult to know the root. The origin of illness can be so small and vague, in fact, so elusive, but the illness can still become substantial over time.”

黄帝曰：“善哉！余闻精光之道，大圣之业，而宣明大道。非斋戒择吉日，不敢受也。黄帝乃择吉日良兆，而藏灵兰之室，以传宝焉。”

As Qi Bo spoke of the subtlety and difficulty of medicine and healing, Huang Di exclaimed, "Aha! I finally understand the intricacies and the essence of healing. I cannot receive this treasure carelessly. I must pick the best day and time to receive and store this knowledge. I must put this in my secret chamber and preserve it and pass it down to future generations."

《五藏别论》Further Discourse on Five Zang Viscera [1]

《五藏别论》是战国时期创作的一篇散文，作者不详。别，另外的。本篇所论述有关脏腑的内容与其他篇章不同，自成一家之言，所以篇名为"五藏别论"。本篇着重讨论了奇恒之腑、传化之腑的概念、功能特点，以及五脏六腑的总体功能和各自功能特点。同时讨论了切寸口脉诊病的道理和诊断疾病的一般方法，并指出了信巫不信医的危害性。

[Introduction] The essay of *Further Discourse on the Five Zang Viscera* was written during the Warring States Period, whose author is unknown. "别" means something additional. This essay which differs in content from other chapters is related to the Five Zang Viscera, so it is called "Further Discourse on the Five *Zang* Viscera". Its theme focuses on the concept and functional characteristics of the extraordinary *fu* organs and the palaces of transportation, as well as the overall function of the viscera. At the same time, it discusses the principle of cunkou pulse diagnosis and the general method of disease diagnosis, and also points out the harm of believing in sorcery instead of believing in medicine.

黄帝问曰："余闻方士[方士：王冰"谓明悟方术之士也"。这里指医生。]，或以脑髓为脏，或以肠胃为脏，或以为腑。敢问更相反，皆自谓是。不知其道，愿闻其说。"

Huang Di asked, "I have heard from scholars the different explanations and classifications of the *zang*（'脏'）and *fu*（'腑'）organs. Some feel that the brain and marrow, the large intestine and the small intestine are *zang*（'藏'）. Others feel that these are *fu*（'腑'）. People all disagree. I would like to hear from you a clarification on the correct classification."

岐伯对曰："脑髓、骨、脉、胆、女子胞[女子胞：即子宫。]，此六者，地气之所生也，皆藏于阴而象于地，故藏而不泻，名曰奇恒之腑[奇恒之腑：异于一般的腑。]。夫胃、大肠、小肠、三焦、膀胱，此五者，天气之所生也，其气象天，故泻而不藏，此受五脏浊气，名曰传化之腑[传化之腑：指五腑，即胃、大肠、小肠、三焦、膀胱。]。此不能久留，输泻者也。魄门亦为六腑[魄门：即肛门。魄，通"粕"。王冰："魄门谓之肛门也。内通于肺，故曰魄门。"中医认为肺藏魄，肺与大肠相表里。]，使水谷不得久藏。所谓五脏者，藏精气而不泻也，故满而不能实。六腑者，传化物而不藏，故实而不能满也。水谷入口，则胃实

[1] 中文选自《黄帝内经》；北京：中华书局；2010 年，第 62-64 页。

Further Discourse on the Five Zang Viscera，selected from *The Yellow Emperor's Classic of Medicine*：*A New Translation of the Neijing Suwen with Commentary*, translated by Maoshing Ni, Ph.D.; Boston and London：Shambhala Publications, Inc., 2011.

而肠虚；食下，则肠实而胃虚，故曰实而不满。”

Qi Bo replied, “The brain, marrow, bones, blood vessels, gall bladder, and uterus are all born of the earthly *qi*. Similar to the earthly function, they store essence. So they are considered extraordinary *fu* organs. They are hollow containers that store substantial substances. On the other hand, the stomach, large and small intestines, *sanjiao*（‘三焦’）, and bladder are formed by the heavenly *qi*. Their function, like that of the heavenly circulation of continuous flow, is to transport rather than store. They receive the turbid *qi* from the five *zang*. Thus, they are named the palaces of transportation. They receive the food, water, and turbid *qi*, which cannot remain for long, and then transport such ‘acquired *jing*’（‘精’）to the five *zang* organs, and pass on the waste products. Even the *hunmen*（‘魄门’）, or rectum, works by eliminating, so that the waste does not become stored in the body. Such storage would be in opposition to the principles of the six *fu*, and disease would then manifest. Thus, the five *zang* organs store the essence of *jing*/essence *qi*. They do not transport. On the other hand, the six *fu* organs receive the food and digest, absorb, and transport it, passing it on. They are often full, but still do not store. Food enters the mouth and proceeds to the stomach. The stomach is now full, but the intestines are empty. The foodstuff passes downward, filling the intestines. Now the stomach is empty. That is why it is said that the six *fu* are full but never filled, and the five *zang* organs are filled but never full.”

黄帝曰：“气口何以独为五脏主[气口：诊脉部位，即掌后动脉部位。中医认为五脏六腑的脉气在此表现最为明显，故称气口，也叫“脉口”。又因诊脉部位距掌后横纹一寸，又称“寸口”。]？”

Huang Di further inquired, “From palpating the pulse at the radial position, how can one know the subtleties and conditions of the five *zang* organs? ”

岐伯曰：“胃者，水谷之海，六府之大源也。五味入口，藏于胃以养五藏气；气口亦太阴也，是以五脏六腑之气味，皆出于胃，变见于气口。故五气入鼻，藏于肺，肺有病，而鼻为之不利也。凡治病必察其下[下：指大小便。]，适其脉[适：调适，诊察。]，观其志意，与其病也。”

Qi Bo answered, “The stomach is the sea of nutrients, the fountain of the six *fu* organs. All foodstuff（‘五味’）enters the mouth and passes to the stomach. From here, the action of the spleen transforms the foodstuff into pure essence, which nourishes the five *zang* organs. The spleen, the foot *taiyin*（‘太阴’）, is responsible for the distribution of the *jing*（‘精’）and *ye*（‘液’）or body fluids. Its corresponding hand *taiyin* channel, the lung, is responsible for dispersing the *qi*. The *taiyyang*（‘太阳’）point, located on the hand *taiyin* channel, is the influential point for the pulses. It governs the pulses. Therefore, the five *zang* organs and six *fu* organs derive their *qi* and nutrition from the stomach. Their corresponding strengths are reflected in the pulses. At the same time, the five smells enter the nose and are stored in the heart and lung. These are really the five *qi* of environmental energy that we breathe in. If illness occurs in the heart or lung, it will manifest in the nose. In healing, one must inquire closely as to the state of the patient' s elimination, differentiate the pulse patterns, and observe accurately the patient's emotional, psychological, and spiritual states and other physical manifestations."

"拘于鬼神者，不可与言至德[至德：医学道理。]；恶于针石者，不可与言至巧[至巧：针石技巧。]；病不许治者，病必不治，治之无功矣。"

"If a patient is superstitious（'拘于鬼神者'）and does not believe in medicine, or if a patient refuses to be treated by acupuncture, or if a patient refuses any treatment, then no matter what the practitioner does, the patient will not get well. This is the evidence that healing actually comes from within."

《阴阳应象大论》The Manifestation of *Yin* and *Yang* from the Macrocosm to the Microcosm [1]

阴阳是我国哲学的一对范畴。作为抽象的哲学概念，阴阳主要代表相反相成的两种属性，用以说明自然界相互关联的事物之间及其内部对立统一的两个方面。古人认为，阴阳的运动变化，决定着事物的产生、发展、变化和消亡，是自然界的总规律。象，指形象、征象。应象，吴昆《素问吴注》："应乎天象，而配乎阴阳五行也。""阴阳应象"，即人体生命活动规律，与自然界四时五行阴阳的消长变化，其象相应的意思。正如马莳《素问注证发微》所云："此篇以天地之阴阳，万物之阴阳，合于人身之阴阳，其象相应。"本篇的内容，是取法于自然界阴阳五行之气的运动，以论人体脏腑阴阳五行之气变化的道理，因此以"阴阳应象"名篇。正如张志聪《素问集注》所云："此篇言天地水火、四时五行、寒热气味，合人之脏腑身形、清浊气血、表里上下，成象成形者，莫不合于阴阳之道。至于诊脉察色、治疗针砭，亦皆取法于阴阳，故曰《阴阳应象大论》。"

[Introduction] *Yin* and *Yang* are a couple of categories of the Chinese philosophy. As abstract concepts, *Yin* and *Yang* mainly represent two opposites and yet complementary attributes, which are used to describe two aspects of the unity of opposites between and within the interrelated things of nature. Ancient people believed that the interaction and change of *Yin* and *Yang* determined the generation, evolvement, change and extinction of things, which was the general law of nature. "Xiang"（"象"）refers to an image, a sign or a symptom. "*Ying Xiang*", said Wu Kun, a scholar of the Qing Dynasty, in his book entitled as *Wu's Notes to*

---

[1] 中文选自《黄帝内经》，北京：中华书局；2010 年。
The Manifestation of Yin and Yang from the Macrocosm to the Microcosm, selected from *The Yellow Emperor's Classic of Medicine: A New Translation of the Neijing Suwen with Commentary*, translated by Maoshing Ni, Ph.D.; Boston and Lordon: Shambhala Publications, Inc., 2011.

Neijing Suwen of Huang Di, means "corresponding to the motion and the change of the celestial phenomena and matching the Yin-Yang and the five elements", that is to say, the laws of life activities of the human body correspond to the ebb and flow of Yin-Yang along with the four seasons and the five elements in nature. As Ma Shi in the Ming Dynasty said in his *Notes and Illuminations To Suwen* that this article combines the Yin -Yang of Heaven and Earth, the Yin-Yang of all things, with the Yin -Yang of the human body." Based on the motion of *Qi* of Yin-Yang and the five elements in nature, it discusses the laws of the changes of the *Qi* of Yin-Yang and the five elements of the internal organs within the human body, hence the title of "*The Manifestation of Yin and Yang from the Macrocosm to the Microcosm.*"

黄帝曰："阴阳者，天地之道也，万物之纲纪[纲纪：纲领。总的为纲，分支为纪。]，变化之父母[变化之父母：万物生长变化的根源。父母，根源、起源。]，生杀之本始[生：生长。杀：杀伐，消亡。本始：根本。]，神明之府也[神明：变化不测谓之神，品物流行谓之明。推动万物生成和变化的力量称为神明。]，治病必求于本[本：根源，根本。这里指阴阳。]。故积阳为天，积阴为地。阴静阳躁，阳生阴长，阳杀阴藏。阳化气，阴成形[阳化气，阴成形：这里的气指能力、力量。形：指形体、物质。]，寒极生热，热极生寒。寒气生浊，热气生清。清气在下，则生飧泄[飧泄，音(sūn xiè)，中医病名。指大便泄泻清稀，并有不消化的食物残渣。]。浊气在上，则生䐜胀[䐜(chēn)胀：上腹部胀满。]。此阴阳反作，病之逆从也[逆：病的异常称逆证。从：病的正常称顺证。]。"

Huang Di said, "The law of *yin* and *yang* is the natural order of the universe, the foundation of all things（'万物之纲纪'）, mother of all changes, the root of life and death（'生杀之本始'）. In healing, one must grasp the root of the disharmony, which is always subject to the law of *yin* and *yang*. In the universe, the pure *yang qi* ascends to converge and form heaven, while the turbid *yin qi* descends and condenses to form the earth. *Yin* is passive and quiet, while the nature of *yang* is active and noisy. *Yang* is responsible for expanding and *yin* is responsible for contracting, becoming astringent, and consolidating. *Yang* is the energy, the vital force, the potential, while *yin* is the substance, the foundation, and the mother that gives rise to all this potential. Extreme heat or extreme cold will transform into its opposite. For example, on a hot day the heat will rise, causing condensation and eventually rain and therefore cold. Coldness produces turbid *yin*, heat produces the clear *yang*. If the clear *yang qi* descends instead of rising, problems such as diarrhea occur in the body. If the turbid *yin qi* becomes stuck at the top and fails to descend, there will be fullness and distension in the head. These conditions are imbalances of *yin and yang*."

"故清阳为天，浊阴为地。地气上为云，天气下为雨。雨出地气，云出天气。故清阳出上窍，浊阴出下窍。清阳发腠理[腠理(còu lǐ)，中医指皮肤等的纹理和皮下肌肉的空隙。]，浊阴走五藏。清阳实四支，浊阴归六府。"

"In nature, the clear *yang*（'清阳'）forms heaven and the turbid *yin qi*（'浊阴'）descends to form earth. The earthly *qi* evaporates to become the clouds, and when the clouds meet with the heavenly *qi*, rain is produced. Similarly, in the body, pure *yang qi* reaches the sensory orifices, allowing one to see, hear, smell, taste, feel, and decipher all information so that the *shen/ spirit* can remain clear and centered. The turbid *yin qi* descends to the lower orifices. The clear *yang qi* disperses over the surface of the body; the turbid *yin qi* flows and nourishes the five *zang* organs. The pure *yang qi* expands and strengthens the four extremities, and the turbid *yin qi* fills the six *fu* organs."

水为阴，火为阳。阳为气[气：指功能或活动能力。]，阴为味[味：泛指一切食物。]。味归形，形归气[形：指形体，包括脏腑、肌肉、血脉、筋骨、皮毛等。归：生成、滋养。]。气归精[气归精：真气化生精。]，精归化[精归化：精血充盛，又可化生真气。化，化生。]。精食气[精食(sì)气：精仰赖气化而成。食，仰求、给养或依赖。]，形食味[形食(sì)味：形体有赖食物的营养。]。化生精，气生形[化生精，气生形：气化、生化的作用，促进了精的生成，同时又充养了形体。]。味伤形，气伤精[味伤形，气伤精：味和气也能伤害人体的形和精。]。精化为气，气伤于味[精化为气，气伤于味：精可以化生气，产生功能，饮食五味失调也可以伤气，损伤功能。]。

"The elements of *fire* and *water* are categorized respectively into *yang* and *yin*, the fire being *yang* and the water being *yin*. The functional aspect of the body is *yang* and the nutritive or substantive aspect is *yin*. While food can be used to strengthen and nourish the body, the body' s ability to transform it is dependent on *qi*. The functional part of the *qi* is derived from the *jing/ essence*（'精'）. Food is refined into *jing/ essence*, which supports the *qi*, and the *qi* is required for both transformation and bodily functions. For this reason, when the diet is improper, the body may be injured, or if activities are excessive, *the jing/ essence qi* can be exhausted."

"阴味出下窍，阳气出上窍。味厚者为阴，薄为阴之阳。气厚者为阳，薄为阳之阴。味厚则泄，薄则通。气薄则发泄，厚则发热。壮火之气衰，少火之气壮，壮火食气，气食少火，壮火散气，少火生气。气味辛、甘发散为阳，酸、苦涌泄为阴。"

"Taste is a *yin* quality and has a descending nature, while *qi* is *yang* and rises to the upper orifices（'上窍'）. Heavy tastes are pure *yin*, light tastes are considered *yang* within *yin*. The heavier *qi* is pure *yang* in nature while the lighter *qi* is *yin* within *yang*. When taste or food is heavy and turbid, it may cause diarrhea, but the lighter, refined taste is able to circulate throughout the meridians. It is therefore advisable to eat simple, bland foods rather than rich ones. The lighter *qi* is expansive and has a tendency to disperse out of the body through the pores and orifices. The heavier, more substantial *qi* can assist the *yang* to produce fire in the body. If there is an excess of the *yang / fire*, it can damage the body's *yuan qi / source qi*, so it is advisable to avoid creating excess fire in the body. A taste is related to its energetic properties. The pungent and sweet tastes that have dispersing qualities are considered *yang*, while the sour and bitter tastes that have purging and eliminating qualities are considered *yin*."

"阴胜则阳病，阳胜则阴病。阳胜则热，阴胜则寒。重寒则热，重热则寒。寒伤形，热伤气。气伤痛，形伤肿。故先痛而后肿者，气伤形也；先肿而后痛者，形伤气也。风胜则动，热胜则肿，燥胜则干，寒胜则浮[浮：浮肿。]，湿胜则濡泻[濡泻：湿泻。指湿盛伤脾的泄泻]。"

"The *yin* and *yang* in the body should be in balance with one another. If the *yang qi* dominates, the *yin* will be deprived, and vice versa. Excess *yang* will manifest as febrile disease, whereas excess *yin* will manifest as cold disease. When *yang* is extreme, however, it can turn into cold disease, and vice versa. Cold can injure the physical body, and heat can damage the *qi* or energetic aspect of the body. When there is injury to the physical body there will be swelling, but if the *qi* level is damaged, it can cause pain because of the *qi* blockage. In an injury that has two aspects, such as swelling (*yin*) and pain (*yang*), treatment may consist of pungent herbs to disperse swelling and cooling herbs to subdue the pain. If a patient complains of pain first and swelling afterward, this means the *qi* level was injured first. But if a patient complains of swelling first followed by pain, the trauma occurred at the physical level initially."

Huang Di continued: "When the pathogenic wind comes like a storm, it can cause shaking. If fire burns excessively, there will be redness and swelling; if dryness is present, there will be withering; excess cold can result in swelling; and extreme dampness will lead to urinary problems and diarrhea."

“天有四时五行，以生长收藏，以生寒暑燥湿风。人有五藏化五气[五气：五脏之气，由五气而生五志，即喜怒悲忧恐。]，以生喜怒悲忧恐。故喜怒伤气，寒暑伤形；暴怒伤阴，暴喜伤阳。厥气上行[厥气：逆行之气]，满脉去形。喜怒不节，寒暑过度，生乃不固。故重阴必阳，重阳必阴。”故曰：“冬伤于寒，春必温病；春伤于风，夏生飧泄；夏伤于暑，秋必痎疟[痎疟(jiē nüè)，疟疾的通称。]；秋伤于湿，冬生咳嗽。”

"In nature, we have the four seasons and the five energetic transformations of wood(‘木’), fire(‘火’), earth(‘土’), metal(‘金’), and water(‘水’). Their changes and transformations produce cold, summer heat, dampness, dryness, and wind. The weather, in turn, affects every living creature in the natural world and forms the foundation for birth, growth, maturation, and death. In the human body there are the *zang* organs of the liver, heart, spleen, lung, and kidneys(‘五藏’). The *qi* of the five *zang* organs forms the five spirits(‘五气’)and gives rise to the five emotions(‘喜怒悲忧恐’). The spirit of the heart is known as the *shen*, which rules mental and creative functions. The spirit of the liver, the *hun*, rules the nervous system and gives rise to extrasensory perception. The spirit of the spleen, of *yi*, rules logic or reasoning power. The spirit of the lungs, or *po*, rules the animalistic instincts, physical strength and stamina. The spirit of the kidneys, the *zhi*, rules the will, drive, ambition, and survival instinct. Overindulgence in the five emotions—happiness, anger, sadness, worry or fear, and fright—can create imbalances. Emotions can injure the *qi,* while seasonal elements can attack the body. Sudden anger damages the *yin qi*; becoming easily excited or overjoyed will damage the yang *qi.* This causes the qi to rebel and rise up to the head, squeezing the *shen* out of the heart and allowing it to float away. Failing to regulate one's emotions can be likened to summer and winter failing to regulate each other, threatening life itself. If there is cold invasion in the winter, febrile disease will develop in the spring. An invasion by wind in the spring can result in digestive disturbances, food retention, and diarrhea in the summer. If there is an attack of summer heat during the summer, in the autumn there may be malaria. If dampness invades in the autumn, there will be coughing attacks in the winter. ”

黄帝曰：“余闻上古圣人，论理人形，列别脏腑[列别：分别，分辨。]；端络经脉[端络经脉：审察经脉的相互联系。端络，作动词解。]，会通六合[六合：四方上下为六合。另十二经脉的阴阳配合也称六合。这里包含这两个意思。联系自然界的四方上下六合来排比十二经脉的阴阳六合。]，各从其经；气穴所发，各有处名；谿谷属骨[谿谷：两山之间的夹道或流水道称“谷”。山间的河沟为“谿”，同“溪”。中医借用来指肌肉会聚之处。因肌肉会聚处肌腱交迭而形成凹陷似“谿谷”。属骨：骨相连之处。]，皆有所起；分部逆从，各有条理；四时阴阳，尽有经纪。外内之应，皆有表里，其信然乎？”

Huang Di then asked, “I have heard that in ancient times, persons educated in medicine emphasized the physical body by differentiating the *zang fu*, understood the distribution and function of the channels and collaterals, and gave names to the points of *qi*, or acupuncture points. In the muscles and spaces between the muscles and the joints can be found the points that connect the meridians. The meridians are further coupled as *yin/yang* pairs, called *liu he*（‘六合’）. Everything is distributed perfectly, corresponding to the *yin* and the *yang* and the four seasons in harmony with the universe（‘四时阴阳’）. Is what the ancient ones said accurate?”

岐伯对曰：“东方生风，风生木，木生酸，酸生肝，肝生筋，筋生心。肝主目。其在天为风，在地为木，在体为筋，在藏为肝，在色为苍，在音为角，在声为呼，在变动为握，在窍为目，在味为酸，在志为怒。怒伤肝，悲胜怒；风伤筋，燥胜风；酸伤筋，辛胜酸。”

Qi Bo answered, “With the arrival of spring the weather warms the earth. All plants begin to sprout and put forth green leaves, so the color associated with spring is green. Since most hits and trees are immature and unripe at this time, their taste is sour. This sour taste can strengthen the liver, and the liver can then nourish the tendons and muscular channels. The wood element of the liver can produce the fire element of the heart; thus, it is said that the tendons produce the heart. Liver connects with the eyes through its channels, and thus it is said that the upper orifice of the liver is the eyes. During spring the subtlety and vastness of the universe, the intelligence and intuition of the human being, the ability of the earth to produce the ten thousand things, the natural movement of the wind, and the upward motion of all plants, collectively produce the movement of the tendons, the color green, the shouting of the voice, the spasms and convulsions, the eyes, the sour taste, and the angry emotions. These are all associated with the liver, since the liver is responsible for maintaining the patency of the flow of energy, and its nature is movement and expansion. Anger can injure the liver, but sadness can relieve anger. When wind invades with dampness, it can injure the tendons, although dryness may eliminate the dampness and wind. Excessive consumption of sour foods can make the tendons flaccid, but this can be neutralized by the pungent taste.”

“南方生热，热生火，火生苦，苦生心，心生血，血生脾。心主舌。其在天为热，在地为火，在体为脉，在脏为心，在色为赤，在音为徵，在声为笑，在变动为忧，在窍为舌，在味为苦，在志为喜。喜伤心，恐胜喜；热伤气，寒胜热，苦伤气，咸胜苦。”

“In summer the weather is generally hot, and when there is extreme heat it produces fire, which can burn and char things, producing the bitter taste. Bitter-tasting substances can clear the heart. The heart governs the blood, the fire of the heart produces the earth, the heart opens to the tongue, and therefore subtle changes in the heart can be reflected in the tongue. The hot weather, the fire on the planet, the blood vessels, the color red, laughter, and joy are all related to the heart. The heart, or fire element, manifests emotionally as joy, but too much joy can cause a depletion of the heart *qi*. This can be counterbalanced by fear. Pathogenic *qi* can invade the heart via the pericardium, injuring heart *qi*. Cold and cooling herbs can be useful to counteract this condition. Consuming overly bitter foods can have a harmful effect on the heart *qi,* but salty foods can be used to balance the excess bitter.

“中央生湿，湿生土，土生甘，甘生脾，脾生肉，肉生肺。脾主口。其在天为湿，在地为土，在体为肉，在藏为脾，在色为黄，在音为宫，在声为歌，在变动为哕，在窍为口，在味为甘，在志为思。思伤脾，怒胜思；湿伤肉，风胜湿；甘伤肉，酸胜甘。”

“In the center we find dampness and humidity, which can nourish and lubricate the soil, preparing it to produce strong earth. During the season between summer and autumn, late summer, the hits ripen and turn yellow. When they ripen they taste sweet and can nourish the spleen *qi*. The spleen *qi* is then able to nourish the muscles and flesh. From the supple flesh and muscles the lungs are generated; these correspond to the metal element. The spleen opens to the mouth, and diseases of the spleen can enter through the mouth and will be reflected on the lips. On earth the weather correlation would be damp and humid conditions. The spleen manifests in the muscles and flesh; the color yellow is associated with the spleen, as is a singing, melodic voice. Pathologic conditions of turbidity indicate spleen imbalance. Melancholy and overworry will manifest. Excessive worry will deplete spleen *qi*, but anger can restrain this worry. Dampness can damage flesh and muscles, but wind can dry the damp. Too much sweet taste can injure the flesh by creating fat, but sour can neutralize the sweet.”

“西方生燥，燥生金，金生辛，辛生肺，肺生皮毛，皮毛生肾。肺主鼻。其在天为燥，在地为金，在体为皮毛，在脏为肺，在色为白，在音为商，在声为哭，在变动为咳，在窍为鼻，在味为辛，在志为忧。忧伤肺，喜胜忧；热伤皮毛，寒胜热；辛伤皮毛，苦胜辛。”

“In the western direction the deserts are rich in metal ores; the dry desert sands are white, and this dryness affects the lungs, skin, hair, and pores of the body. The sound of crying and the emotion of sadness and grief are associated with the metal element. The pungent taste can ventilate the lungs and open the pores. Extreme grief can injure the lungs, but may be counteracted by the emotion of happiness. Intense heat can damage the skin, hair, and lungs. In this case, coldness is required to control the pathogen. Excessive consumption of the pungent taste may injure the pores and skin, but this can be counteracted by the bitter taste."

"北方生寒，寒生水，水生咸，咸生肾，肾生骨髓，髓生肝。肾主耳。其在天为寒，在地为水，在体为骨，在脏为肾，在色为黑，在音为羽，在声为呻，在变动为栗，在窍为耳，在味为咸，在志为恐。恐伤肾，思胜恐；寒伤血，燥胜寒；咸伤血，甘胜咸。"

"In the northern direction there are vast snow-covered mountain ranges, and beyond, dark and cold seas whose ocean waters provide the salty taste. All of these conditions are connected with the kidney energy and enable it to develop strong, healthy bones and marrow. The kidneys are associated with the ears, the color black, fear and fright, and the sound of moaning. While fear and fright will damage the kidneys, understanding, logic, and rational thinking will enable one to defeat the fright. Coldness will slow down and stagnate the blood, but dryness will temper this harshness. Excesses of salty flavor can harm the blood, but the sweet flavor will neutralize it."

"故曰：'天地者，万物之上下也；阴阳者，血气之男女也[血气之男女：借用男女气血来说明阴阳的相对关系。]；左右者，阴阳之道路也[“左右者”两句：古人认为，阴气右行，阳气左行]；水火者，阴阳之征兆也[征兆：即是象征。]；阴阳者，万物之能始也[能(tāi)始：变化生成之开始。]。'故曰：'阴在内，阳之守也；阳在外，阴之使也。'"

"Therefore, Heaven and Earth, the masculine and feminine principles, the *qi* and the blood, all reflect the interplay of *yin* and *yang*. Water has the property of coldness, fire the property of heat. The interdependence of *yin* and *yang* is reflected in all things in the universe and cannot be separated."

帝曰："法阴阳奈何[法：取法，运用。]？"

Huang Di asked, "How would you apply the principle of *yin* and *yang* to the art of healing?"

岐伯曰："阳胜则身热，腠理(còu lǐ)闭，喘粗为之俯仰。汗不出而热，齿干以烦冤，腹满死。能冬不能夏[能：音义同“耐”。]。阴胜则身寒，汗出，身常清[清：同“凊”(qìng)，寒。]，数栗而寒，寒则厥，厥则腹满死，能夏不能冬。此阴阳更胜之变，病之形能也[能：通“态”。]。"

Qi Bo replied, "If the *yang qi* is in excess（'阳胜'）, the body will have fever, rapid breathing, tremors and shaking, dry throat and mouth, irritability, and abdominal distension. These signs are the precursors of death. When an excess of *yang qi* occurs in the winter, it is not as dangerous as in the summer, when environmental heat will rapidly worsen it. If the *yin qi* becomes excessive（'阴胜'）, the body will feel cold, and there will be clammy sweating, shivering, and convulsive spasms of the hands and feet. If the extremities are in spasm and the abdomen is swollen and distended, this will warn of death. During the summer it will be possible to recover, but in the winter it will be fatal. So we can see the manifestation of *yin* and *yang* in the process of disease."

帝曰："调此二者，奈何？"

Then Huang Di inquired, "What are the methods to balance *yin* and *yang*?"

岐伯曰："能知七损八益[七损：女子月事贵在时下。因女性以七年为生命节律变化周期。八益：男子精气贵在充满。因男性以八年为生命节律变化周期。（存疑，貌似有多重说法）]，则二者可调；不知用此，则早衰也。年四十，而阴气自半也，起居衰矣；年五十，体重，耳目不聪明矣；年六十，阴萎，气大衰，九窍不利，下虚上实，涕泣俱出矣。故曰：知之则强，不知则老，故同出而名异耳。智者察同，愚者察异["智者"两句：聪明人在未病之时注意养生。愚蠢的人，发病之后才知道调养。同，指健康。异，指疾病衰老。]。愚者不足，智者有余。有余则耳目聪明，身体轻强，老者复壮，壮者益治。是以圣人为无为之事，乐恬淡之能，从欲快志于虚无之守，故寿命无穷，与天地终，此圣人之治身也。"

Qi Bo answered, "If one understands the methods or *Tao* of maintaining health and the causes of depletion, then one can readily master the balance of *yin* and *yang* and stay healthy. Normally, by the age of forty, people have exhausted fifty percent of their *yin qi*, and their vitality is weakened. At the age of fifty, the body is heavy, the vision and the hearing deteriorated; by the age of sixty, the *yin qi* is further diminished, the kidneys drained; the sensory organs and the nine orifices, including the excretory organs, have all become functionally impaired. Conditions will manifest, such as prostatitis, vision loss, deficiency in the lower *jiao* (viscera cavity) and excess in the upper *jiao*, tearing, and nasal drainage problems. Thus, the body of one who understands the *Tao* will remain strong and healthy. The one who does not understand the *Tao* will age. One who is careless will often feel deficient, while one who knows will have an abundance of energy. Those who are knowledgeable have clear orifices, perceptions, hearing, vision, smell, and taste, and are light and strong. Even though their bodies are old, they can perform most of life's activities. Those who understand the principles of wholesome living tame their minds and prevent them from straying. They do not force anything upon themselves or others, are happy and content, tranquil and quiet, and can live indefinitely. These are the ancient methods of self-maintenance."

"天不足西北，故西北方阴也，而人右耳目不如左明也。地不满东南，故东南方阳也，而人左手足不如右强也。"

Qi Bo continued, "In the northwest direction the mountains are high and cold and are considered *yin*, while in the southwest the lowlands are hot and *yang* in nature. There is a correspondence between heaven and humankind. Just as there are inequalities in nature, such as hot and cold, high and low, so they also exist in people. In the body, the right ear is not as effective as the left, nor is the right eye as sharp as the left. However, the left hand and foot are not as coordinated as the right, in general."

黄帝曰："何以然？"

Huang Di asked, "What does this mean?"

岐伯曰："东方阳也，阳者其精并于上[并：聚合。]，并于上则上明而下虚，故使耳目聪明而手足不便也[便：便利，灵巧，自如。]。西方阴也，阴者其精并于下，并于下则下盛而上虚，故其耳目不聪明而手足便也。故俱感于邪，其在上则右甚，在下则左甚，此天地阴阳所不能全也，故邪居之。"

Qi Bo answered, "The east is the *yang* direction. The essence of *yang* circulates from the left, rises in the left, and the upper left side is full while the bottom left is deficient. The western direction is considered *yin*, and the essence of *yin* descends down the right side. Therefore, the lower right is full and the upper right is deficient. This is why we say the right eye and ear are not as strong as the left, and the left hand and foot are not as strong as the right. It is important to understand that the pathogen always attacks where there is deficiency. In human beings, the right upper and left lower are both deficient and therefore, vulnerable to pathogenic attacks. These are natural flaws that have been created."

"故天有精，地有形；天有八纪[八纪：立春、立夏、立秋、立冬、春分、秋分、夏至、冬至八个大节气。]，地有五里[五里：指东、南、西、北、中央五方。]。故能为万物之父母。清阳上天，浊阴归地。是故天地之动静，神明为之纲纪。故能以生长收藏，终而复始。惟贤人上配天以养头，下象地以养足，中傍人事以养五脏[人事：日常饮食和情志。]。天气通于肺，地气通于嗌[嗌(yì)：喉下之食管处，即咽。]，风气通于肝，雷气通于心，谷气通于脾[谷气：两山间通水之道路称"谷"。人体肌肉与肌肉之间也称"谷"。张志聪："谷气，山谷之通气也。"]，雨气通于肾。六经为川[六经：即太阳、阳明、少阳、太阴、少阴、厥阴，为气血运行的道路。张介宾："三阴三阳也。同流气血，故为人之川。"即是指十二经脉。]，肠胃为海，九窍为水注之气。以天地为之阴阳，人之汗，以天地之雨名之；人之气，以天地之疾风名之。暴气象雷[暴气：忿怒暴躁之气。]，逆气象阳[逆气象阳：比喻气之有升无降，有阳无阴。]。故治不法天之纪，不用地之理，则灾害至矣。"

"Heaven produces *qi*. Earth gives rise to form. Heaven regulates the four seasons. On earth the transformations of the five elements represent the interplay of *yin* and *yang*. *Yang* rises to produce heaven, while the turbid *yin* descends to form the earth. This movement helps create the rhythm of the seasons and the weather changes, enabling earthly things to manifest in the rhythm of birth in spring, growth in summer, consolidation in autumn, and storage in winter. Possessing this knowledge, people can coordinate their activities around these cycles and benefit by them, since human life is interconnected with its environment, heaven and earth. The heavenly *qi* travels through the lungs, and the earthly water and grains, or substantial *qi*, travels through the throat. The *qi* of the winds and trees connects with the liver, the thundering fire *qi* connects with the heart, the *qi* of the five grains from the earth connects with the spleen, and the rainwater *qi* connects to the kidneys. The movement and traveling of *qi* and blood in the six channels is like a river flowing; and the stomach and large intestine, which contain the fluids and food, are like the ocean. The nine orifices are like the spring where water gushes in and out. The *yin* and *yang* of the human body can thus be related to the phenomena of nature. The sweat from excess *yang* pours out like rain, the active *yang qi* moves like rapid wind, the anger of people is like the raging of thunder. Rebellious *qi* that rushes upward is like the blazing of fire.

Without understanding the metaphors present in nature and humans, one will not effectively avert or treat disease. In treatment, when one neglects to take the seasonal changes into consideration and fails to recognize the geography, the environment, the five elements and their transformations, one will miss the big picture and treatment will be unsuccessful."

"故邪风之至，疾如风雨，故善治者治皮毛，其次治肌肤，其次治筋脉，其次治六腑，其次治五脏。治五脏者，半死半生也。故天之邪气，感则害人五脏；水谷之寒热，感则害于六腑；地之湿气，感则害皮肉筋脉。"

"When the evil wind attacks people, it comes like a storm. We can map out its course of attack, beginning with the pores and skin, into the muscle layer, through the tendomuscular layer, into the vessels, and into the six *fu* and the five *zang* organs. A superior doctor arrests disease at the skin level and dispels it before it penetrates deeper. An inferior doctor treats illness after it passes the skin. If the pathogen is not stopped on the surface, it enters the muscle level and must be dispersed there. If it progresses and invades deep into the five *zang* organs, the prognosis for recovery is only fifty percent. The six exogenous pathogenic factors cause disharmonies in people by invading Lorn from the external to the internal and moving Lorn, the superficial level, deep into the *zang fu* organs. Improper diet mainly affects the six *fu* organs; pathogenic dampness will cause disruption to the skin, flesh, muscles, tendons, and vessels, and will stagnate at the joints."

"故善用针者，从阴引阳，从阳引阴[“从阴”两句：取阴经之穴，以治阳经之病；取阳经之穴以治阴经之病。]。以右治左，以左治右。以我知彼[以我知彼：用正常人与病人比较，来推测病变情况。我，指正常人。彼，指病人。]，以表知里，以观过与不及之理。见微得过，用之不殆。"

"A proficient acupuncturist(‘针灸师’) must understand the principle of external and internal, disease invading from outside to inside, inside to outside, and the connections and relationships between *yang* and *yin*, *qi* and blood, and the channels and collaterals. With this knowledge it is possible to direct the pathogen from the inside to the outside, to dispel it from the outside, or move it from the outside to the inside to be purged and eliminated. When disease is on the right side, treat the left, and when it is on the left, treat the right. Compare one's normalcy with others' abnormality. When observing the condition it is possible to see what is occurring on the inside from the symptoms on the outside. The progression of the condition, its severity and prognosis, can also be ascertained."

"善诊者，察色按脉，先别阴阳。审清浊，而知部分；视喘息[喘息：指呼吸的气息和动态。]，听音声，而知所苦；观权衡规矩[权衡规矩：指四时不同脉象，即春弦中规，夏洪中矩，秋毛中衡，冬沉中权。]，而知病所主；按尺寸[尺：尺肤。寸：寸口。]，观浮沉滑涩，而知病所生。以治无过，以诊则不失矣。"

"A doctor adept at diagnosis observes the patient's *shen*, complexion, facial color, and pulses. First, it must be determined whether the illness is *yin* or *yang*, then the facial colors will indicate the location of the disease, and finally the voice and breathing will confirm the nature of the suffering. When the abnormal pulse is compared to a normal one, it is possible to know if a pathogen is present. One must consider the variations of the normal pulses that are natural in each season. If the radial pulse at the most distal point on the wrist is floating or sinking, slippery or choppy, the cause of the imbalance will be known. Following this method, one will avoid mistakes."

故曰："病之始起也，可刺而已；其盛，可待衰而已。故因其轻而扬之[轻：病邪清浅，病在表。扬：用轻宣疏散方法驱邪外泄。]，因其重而减之[重：病邪重深，病在里。减之：以攻泻方法祛除病邪。]，因其衰而彰之[衰：正气衰弱。彰之：给予补益之剂。]。形不足者，温之以气；精不足者，补之以味。其高者，因而越之[越之：使用涌吐方法。]；其下者，引而竭之[引而竭之：使用通便方法。]；中满者[中满：胸腹胀满。]，泻之于内；其有邪者，渍形以为汗[渍形以为汗：即"清以为汗"，用辛凉解肌之法。]；其在皮者，汗而发之；其慓悍者，按而收之[其慓悍者，按而收之：病情发越太过，可用抑收法。]；其实者，散而泻之。审其阴阳，以别柔刚[柔刚：柔剂、刚剂。即药性平和或峻猛的药剂。]。阳病治阴，阴病治阳。定其血气，各守其乡，血实宜决之，气虚宜掣引之。"

"In the beginning stage of illness, while the pathogen is relatively superficial, acupuncture can be used effectively to open the surface and eliminate the pathogen. When the illness is at a raging stage, it is necessary to wait until the peak passes, then administer acupuncture for successful results. When the pathogenic factor is external and strong, one can retain the acupuncture needle longer and apply strong stimulation. This will weaken the pathogen and reinforce the *zheng* / antipathogenic *qi*, enabling it to eliminate the illness. When an illness is on the surface of the body, herbs that are pungent and diaphoretic can be used to disperse it. If the condition is excess and internal, purgative herbs are used to purge and eliminate it. If the *zheng* / antipathogenic *qi* is weakened, tonic herbs will fortify it. It is necessary to determine if the illness is due to *yang* or *yin* deficiency. If it is *yang* deficiency, warming herbs and *qi* tonics are appropriate, while in the case of *yin* deficiency, thicker, more nourishing *yin* and blood tonic herbs are indicated. The location of an illness will determine the treatment method. An illness located above the diaphragm and chest can be treated with emetics to induce vomiting, while an illness below the diaphragm and in the intestines can be purged. If it is in the middle, involving the stomach, then digestive and carminative herbs will be used. When the illness is in the skin, induce sweating to eliminate it, but if *zheng* / antipathogenic *qi* is weak, causing leakages such as diarrhea, astringent herbs will be helpful. If the *qi* is stuck, its movement can be restored through the use of carminative herbs; severe stagnation should be broken up with stronger herbs. Illness should be differentiated by the eight principles of *yin* or *yang*, internal or external, excess or deficiency, and hot or cold, so that the right method may be employed to counteract the condition and restore homeostasis. Acupuncture treatment can subdue the reckless movement of blood and *qi* and restore their natural and smooth flow. When a pathogen attacks the qi and blood, this is an excess condition. In this case acupuncture points can be used to induce bleeding and eliminate the pathogen. If there is a *qi* deficiency in a particular location or channel, the *qi* can be conducted or guided from other channels to supplement the weakness."

《六节藏象论》The Energetic Cycles of the Universe and Their Effects on Human Beings [1]

本篇先论天以六为节，后论藏象，故篇名叫“六节藏象论”。六节：节，次也，度也，这里有周期、循环的意思。古人以“甲子”纪天度，甲子一周为六十日，是为一节。每年三百六十日，分为六节。高士宗《素问直解》：“六节者，天以六为节。天气始于甲，地气始于子，子甲相合，六十日而甲子周，六六三百六十日，以成一岁。”藏象：此二字首见于本篇指脏腑居于体内，而形象表现于外，从外而知内，故名。藏(臓：脏)，藏也，指藏于体内的脏腑。象，征象、形象之意。唐代王冰注云：“象，谓气象也。言五脏虽隐而不见，然其气象性用，犹可以物类推之。”

[Introduction] This essay begins with dealing with the energetic six cycles of the universe, and later with the theory of visceral manifestation, so its title is called “The Energetic Cycles of the Universe and Their Effects on Human Beings.” The word “*Jie*” in “六节” means “section”, “period” or “degree”, here it has the meaning of “cycle” according to its context. Our forefathers used “*Jiazi*” to measure the degrees of the operation of the universe, that is, the cycle of one “*Jiazi*” is a measure of 60 days which is called a section of time. A year is of three hundred and sixty days, which is divided into six sections. Gao Shizong in the Qing Dynasty said in his *Straight Interpretation of Suwen* that “the so-called six-based section means that the Universe takes six as one section. The ‘*Qi*’ of the universe starts from ‘*Jia*’ and the ‘*Qi*’ of the earth starts from ‘*Zi*’. ‘*Zi*’ and ‘*Jia*’ are joined to form a cycle of 60 days, and 60 days times 6 cycles equals six sixty-day cycles or 360 days, hence tantamount to one year”. *Zang xiang*(“藏象”), which first appears in this essay, refers to the internal organs located in the body and manifested outside the body. The inside is known from the outside, hence the name of *Zang xiang*. *Zang* (viscera or internal organs) refers to the viscera hidden in the body. What is meant by *Xiang* is a sign with the meaning of an image. Wang Bing, a scholar in the Tang Dynasty, said that “*Xiang* is also known as the sign of *Qi*. Although the five *Zangs* are invisible, the functions and effects of their *Qi*-of-*Xiang* can be analogized.”

黄帝问曰：“余闻天以六六之节[六六：六十日为一甲子，是为一节。“六六”就是六个甲子。节：指腧穴，是人体气血交会出入的地方。以为天地：即人与天地相应。]，以成一岁，人以九九制会[九九制会：以九九之法，与天道会通。]，计人亦有三百六十

[1] 中文选自《黄帝内经》，北京：中华书局，2010 年。

The Energetic Cycles of the Universe and Their Effects on Human Being, selected from *The Yellow Emperor's Classic of Medicine: A New Translation of the Neijing Suwen with Commentary*, translated by Maoshing Ni, Ph.D.; Boston and London: Shambhala Publications, Inc., 2011.

五节，以为天地，久矣。不知其所谓也？”

Huang Di asked, “I have heard that in the heavenly realm, cycles of energy are composed of six sixty-day cycles, which create one year. On earth this is also measured by the nine continents and nine orifices, referred to as the ‘rule of nine.’ The combination of the six cycles and the rule of nine produces the three hundred and sixty-five days that make one year. There are three hundred and sixty-five energy points in the human body that are in concert with the philosophy with the human being as a microcosm of the macrocosmic universe. This kind of correspondence extrapolation has been in use for a long time; however, I am ignorant of its reasons.”

岐伯对曰：“昭乎哉问也！请遂言之。夫六六之节，九九制会者，所以正天之度，气之数也[数：一年二十四节气的常数。]。天度者[度：周天三百六十五度]，所以制日月之行也，气数者，所以纪化生之用也。天为阳，地为阴；日为阳，月为阴，行有分纪[行有分纪：日月是按照天体中所划分的区域和度数运行的。]，周有道理[周有道理：日月环周运行有一定的轨道。]。日行一度，月行十三度而有奇焉[“日行”两句：奇(jī)，余数。地球绕太阳公转一周(360 度)要 365 天，平均每天运行近似一度。古人认为地不动而日行，故曰日行一度。月亮绕地球运转一周，要 27.32 天，平均每日运行十三度有余(360 度÷27.32=13.18 度)，故曰“日行一度，月行十三度而有奇”]。故大小月三百六十五日而成岁，积气余而盈闰矣[积气余而盈闰矣：气，节气。闰，谓置闰，古历月份以朔望计算，每月平均得 29.5 日。节气以日行十五度来计，一年二十四节气，正合周天 365.25 度，一年十二个月共得 354 日，因此，月份常不足，节气常有余，余气积满二十九日左右，即置一闰月。故三年必有一闰月，约十九年间须置七个闰月，才能使节气与月份归于一致。]。立端于始[立端于始：立，确立。端，岁首。即冬至节。古历确定冬至节为一年节气的开始。]，表正于中[表正于中：以圭表测量日影的长短变形，计算日月的运度，来校正时令节气。表：即圭表，古代天文仪器之一。正，校正。]，推余于终，而天度毕矣。”

Qi Bo replied, “You have asked a very intelligent question. I will tell you everything about this. The six cycles and the rule of nine are used to measure the energy flow in the year and the degree of the travel of the sun and the moon in relation to the earth. The changes in heaven determine the birth and death of all things on earth. Heaven above is *yang* and earth below is *yin*. The sun travels during the day in the heaven and is *yang*. The moon travels in the evening and is *yin*. There is a regular rhythm of movement to the sun and the moon, and specific pathways that have been mapped out from ancient times. The earth makes a complete revolution around the sun in exactly one year, and it rotates exactly once before the sun in one day and one night. The moon moves a little more than thirteen degrees around the earth on a daily basis. Since ancient times, each month is determined by the waxing and waning of the moon. This is why we have ‘large months（‘大月’）’ and ‘small months（‘小月’）’ in the lunar calendar. To start one must accurately determine at the beginning of the year the commencement of the first cycle. This is done by planting a stick straight into the ground and measuring the shadows of the stick throughout the day and the year in relation to the sun. This will enable us to map out twenty-four solar terms accurately throughout the season.”

帝曰：“余已闻天度矣，愿闻气数何以合之？”

Huang Di said further, “Now I understand the measurements of Heaven. I would like to further understand the interactions between the measurement of heaven and the cycles of change that govern the earth which apply to human beings."

岐伯曰："天以六六为节，地以九九制会。天有十日[天有十日："天"指天干，天干有十，即甲、乙、丙、丁、戊、己、庚、辛、壬、癸。古以天干纪日，故曰"天有十日"。]，日六竟而周甲[日六竟而周甲：即十个天干与十二地支(子、丑、寅、卯、辰、巳、午、未、申、酉、戌、亥)相合，凡六十日为甲子一周，故称为周甲。]，甲六复而终岁，三百六十日法也。夫自古通天者，生之本，本于阴阳。其气九州、九窍，皆通乎天气。故其生五，其气三。三而成天，三而成地，三而成人，三而三之，合则为九，九分为九野[九野：九州之野。]，九野为九脏，故形脏四，神脏五[形脏四，神脏五：人身形脏指胃、大肠、小肠、膀胱。神脏指心、肝、脾、肺、肾五脏。即心藏神、肝藏魂、脾藏意、肺藏魄、肾藏志。]，合为九脏以应之也。"帝曰："余已闻六六九九之会也，夫子言积气盈闰，愿闻何谓气？请夫子发蒙解惑焉[发蒙解惑：启发蒙昧，解释疑惑。]！"岐伯曰："此上帝所秘，先师传之也。"帝曰："请遂闻之。"岐伯曰："五日谓之候[五日谓之候：五日称为一候。候，指气候。]，三候谓之气[三候谓之气：三候称为一个节气。气，指节气。]；六气谓之时，四时谓之岁。而各从其主治焉[各从其主治：治病就应顺从其当旺之气。主治，主管，当令。四时各有当令之主气，如木旺春、火旺夏等。]。五运相袭[五运相袭：五行运行之气，相互承袭。]，而皆治之；终期之日[期(jī)：周年。]，周而复始。时立气布[时立气布：一年之中分立四时，四时之中分布节气。]，如环无端，候亦同法。故曰：不知年之所加[年之所加：指各年主客气加临情况。]，气之盛衰，虚实之所起，不可以为工矣。"

Qi Bo answered, "Heaven is measured by the rules of six, and earth and human beings are governed by the rule of nine. The sages of ancient times carefully observed the heavens and noted their surroundings, and proposed a complex system, consisting of several subsystems to account for all possible variables, in the forecast of macrocosmic influence upon the world; especially the weather and the effects on people. The basic building blocks of this complex system utilize representative symbols of the ten heavenly stems and the twelve earthly branches, each symbol representing an aspect of the natural process of the universe. The combination of the stems and the branches produces a cycle of sixty which is applied to keeping track of time. Each year in the Chinese calendar is divided into twenty-four fortnightly segments called *jie qi*（'节气'）, or solar terms. Four terms equal sixty days and is called a bu or step. Six steps makes up a year. In a sixty-year cycle, there are all together one thousand and four hundred and forty solar terms. Since ancient times, one who understands this system would have mastery of all the processes in the universe, because everything that is living has an intimate association with this change in heavenly energy circulation. This is due to the interaction with heaven's *yang* and earth's *yin* and the *qi* to carry out the process of birth, growth, maturation, and death. The phases of the five elements and atmospheric influences in nature all have their peak flows during different times of the year. At a year's end, this begins over again. This continues in a cycle *ad infinitum*. Therefore, if a person does not grasp and understand the year's energy flow, the peaks and valleys of the *qi*, the excesses and deficiencies of the body, and the pathogens, that person does not qualify to become a doctor."

帝曰："五运之始，如环无端，其太过不及何如？"

Huang Di said, "Now I understand the energetic cycles throughout the seasons and within the five elements or phases. But I am still slightly baffled by the excesses and deficiencies during the process of energy transformation."

岐伯曰："五气更立[五气更立：木、火、土、金、水五运之气更替主时。]，各有所胜，盛虚之变，此其常也。"

Qi Bo replied, "All the changes and transformations through the five parts of the year—spring, summer, late summer, autumn, and winter—have their excesses and deficiencies. This is a normal process."

帝曰："平气何如？"

Huang Di asked, "How do you achieve balance or even flow between each season?"

岐伯曰："无过者也[无过：没有太过不及。]。"

Qi Bo replied, "It means neither extreme in weather patterns and hence the effect on people."

帝曰："太过不及奈何？"

Huang Di said, "Can you explain what constitutes an even cyclic flow?"

岐伯曰："在经有也[经：指古医经。]。"

Qi Bo answered, "This is recorded in the ancient books."

帝曰："何谓所胜？"

Huang Di asked, "What is meant by control or dominance of excessive energy?"

岐伯曰："春胜长夏，长夏胜冬，冬胜夏，夏胜秋，秋胜春，所谓得五行时之胜，各以气命其脏。"

Qi Bo replied, "This means when a seasonal attribute abnormally dominates during another season. For instance, spring controls late summer. Late summer controls winter. Winter controls summer. Summer controls autumn. And autumn controls spring. This is the control cycle in the transformation process of the five elemental phases. These abnormal occurrences in nature negatively affect the human body and its corresponding five *zang* organs. The wood element of spring corresponds to the liver, the summer element of fire corresponds to the heart; the late summer element of earth corresponds to the spleen, the autumn element of metal corresponds to the lungs, and the winter element of water corresponds to the kidneys."

帝曰："何以知其胜？"

Huang Di asked, "How do we predict when an element or season will control another, and what can we gain from this knowledge?"

岐伯曰："求其至也，皆归始春。未至而至[未至而至：前一"至"指时令，后一"至"指气候。"未至而至"，就是未到其时令而有其气候。]，此谓太过。则薄所不胜[薄：同"迫"，侵犯，伤害。]，而乘所胜也[乘：欺凌，凌侮。]，命曰气淫[气淫：气太过。]。至而不至，此谓不及。则所胜妄行，而所生受病，所不胜薄之也，命曰气迫。所谓求其至者，气至之时也，谨候其时，气可与期。失时反候，五治不分，邪僻内生[邪僻：不正之气。]，工不能禁也。"

Qi Bo answered, "In order to utilize the knowledge of the five elemental phases, one must first calculate the time of the arrival of the seasons and observe the normal and abnormal patterns. Generally, we would calculate from the first day of spring in the Chinese calendar. If the first day of spring has not arrived, but the weather or the atmospheric influence is warming, we consider this to be an excess of fire. This fire excess would then humiliate the water element and damage the normalcy of the season. It would further overcontrol the normal *qi* of metal. This is called *qi ying*, or reckless *qi*. In this case, disease of the kidneys and lungs would manifest. On the other hand, if the first day of the season has arrived, but the warming weather trend and the atmospheric influence have not arrived, this is considered to be fire deficiency. This fire deficiency is unable to control the original weather patterns and causes the originally controlled element to be unrestrained. Further, the water element would gain strength and cause the fire to be weakened. If the fire is weakened the earth cannot produce, and a disease pattern mirroring this imbalance will manifest. As a result of this deficiency the body or seasonal *qi* is invaded. This is called *qi po*, meaning suppression or deficient *qi*. Through careful observation of the time of the season and the arrival of the appropriate weather and cyclic patterns, we can understand and apply the knowledge of the transformation of the five elements. Thus, a doctor who does not understand or has misinterpreted the peaks and valleys of the cycles of nature will not understand the mechanism by which people get sick. That doctor will be ineffective in both the treatment and the prognosis of patients."

帝曰："有不袭[袭：承袭。本句意为：五行之气有不相承袭的吗]乎？"

Huang Di asked, "In this five-elemental circuit throughout the seasons, do normal changes and transformations ever not follow their proper order?"

岐伯曰："苍天之气，不得无常也。气之不袭，是谓非常，非常则变[本句：如果五行之气不按规律依次相承，就是反常的现象，反常就会使人发生病变]矣。"

Qi Bo answered, "In nature, the cyclic flow through the five seasons cannot afford to become disordered, because without order, injury and even death can occur."

帝曰："非常而变，奈何？"

Huang Di asked, "How then does it become abnormal and how does this manifest?"

岐伯曰："变至则病，所胜则微，所不胜则甚，因而重感于邪则死矣，故非其时则微，当其时则甚也。”

Qi Bo replied, “This abnormality of the five elemental phases circuit can cause illness in people. For example, if in spring we have the weather patterns of late summer, or dampness, this corresponds to wood controlling earth. This illness is considered to be mild, because it is one of the overcontrol. If in spring we find the dry, cool weather of fall, this becomes metal attacking wood. In this case the illness would be severe, because it results in a deficiency. If, at the same time, other pathogens come into play, there may be the possibility of death. When abnormal weather patterns occur in nature and are not invasive, the problem is light. When they are invasive or attacking, the illness can become quite severe.”

帝曰：“善！余闻气合而有形，因变以正名，天地之运，阴阳之化，其于万物，孰少孰多，可得闻乎？”

Huang Di said, “I have heard that all things in nature derive their form from the *qi* of Heaven and Earth. Because the *qi* of Heaven and Earth transforms and changes and is so variable, the forms of nature and living things are also variable. Can you further expound on this and the changes of *yin* and *yang*, Heaven and Earth, and the energetic phases of the environment and how these determine what will prosper and what will diminish?”

岐伯曰：“悉乎哉问也！天至广不可度，地至大不可量，大神灵问[大神灵问：所提问题是涉及天地阴阳、变化莫测、微妙难穷的大问题。大神灵，道理广泛深奥。]，请陈其方。草生五色，五色之变，不可胜视；草生五味，五味之美，不可胜极。嗜欲不同，各有所通。天食人以五气[天食(sì)人以五气：天供给人们五气。食，供给。五气，指五脏之气。]，地食人以五味。五气入鼻，藏于心肺，上使五色修明，音声能彰；五味入口，藏于肠胃，味有所藏，以养五气，气和而生[气和：五脏之气协调正常。生：生化机能。]，津液相成，神乃自生。”

Qi Bo said, “You have asked a very detailed question. Because of its vastness, the universe is difficult to measure. Your question is of tremendous depth. I do not think I can adequately detail my answer. But I can give you a generalization. In the plant kingdom there are the five colors. Within the five colors there are variations in tone. The plants have five flavors. Though distinct, there are also variations of the flavors. The five colors and five flavors correspond to and affect the five *zang* organs of the body. Heaven provides *yang* as *qi* and provides for people the five colors, while earth, being *yin* and substantial, provides people with five flavors. The five *qi*, or colors, can also be said to be absorbed through the nose as the five fragrances. These are stored in the heart and lungs. The heart is responsible for manifesting the facial colors and the lungs are responsible for producing sound. The five flavors enter through the mouth and are stored in the stomach and intestines. After the digestion and the absorption of nourishment, this *qi* is used to enhance the function of the five *zang* organs. The *qi* of the five *zang* organs combines with the *qi* of the five flavors to produce the *jin* and *ye* (body fluids), which lubricate and further fortify the body, marrow, and *jing* / essence. These naturally support a vigorous *shen* / spirit.”

帝曰："脏象何如[脏象：人体内脏机能活动表现于外的征象。脏，泛指体内的脏器。象，指内脏活动显现于外的各种生理和病理征象。]？"

Huang Di asked, "How do the functional aspects of the *zang* organs manifest outwardly?"

岐伯曰："心者，生之本，神之处也；其华在面，其充在血脉，为阳中之太阳，通于夏气。肺者，气之本，魄之处也[魄：人体的精神活动之一，表现为感觉和动作。]；其华在毛，其充在皮，为阳中之太阴，通于秋气。肾者，主蛰[蛰：虫类伏藏于土中。这里有闭藏的意思。]，封藏之本，精之处也；其华在发，其充在骨，为阴中之少阴，通于冬气。肝者，罢极之本[罢(pí)极：即四极、四肢。肝华在爪，充在筋，以生血气，所以为四肢(罢极)之本。罢，通"疲"。四肢过劳则疲软无力。]，魂之居也；其华在爪，其充在筋，以生血气，其味酸，其色苍，此为阳中之少阳，通于春气。脾者，仓廪之本，营之居也；其华在唇四白，其充在肌，此至阴之类，通于土气。胃、大肠、小肠、三焦、膀胱，名曰器，能化糟粕，转味而出入者也。凡十一脏取决于胆也。"

Qi Bo answered, "Heart is the root of life and the seat of *shen* or intelligence. It manifests its prosperity on the face, because of its function of keeping the blood vessels full. It is located above the diaphragm and is considered to be *yang*. Its element is fire. Therefore, it is called the *taiyang* of the *yang*. In the universal pattern flow it corresponds to the summer. The lungs, being the roots of the body's *qi*, dominate *qi*. They store *po*/courage. They manifest their abundance in the body hair, and their function is to maintain the fullness and suppleness of the skin. The lungs are the highest organs in the body, and their element is metal. They are considered the *taiyin* within the *yang*, and they correspond to autumn energy. The kidneys are the storage place of the true *yang* and the root of all storage in the body. They store the *jing*/essence *qi* of the five *zang* and six *fu* organs. They manifest their abundance and health in the head hair. Its effect is to fill the bones and marrow. Being a water element in the lower trunk, the kidneys are considered *yin*. They are called the *shaoyin* of the *yin* and correspond to the winter energy. The liver is the reservoir of stamina, storing the *hun* / intuition. It manifests in the nails, and functions in strengthening the tendons. It stores blood. The liver is in the *yin* location of the abdomen, but belongs to the *yang* element of wood. It is thus called the *shaoyang* of *yang*. It corresponds with the spring. The stomach, small intestine, large intestine, bladder, and *sanjiao* are also all receptors and storehouses of water and food. They are the producers of *ying* or nutritive *qi*. They absorb the essence from water and food, transport them properly, and eliminate waste and turbidity. They are able to transform the five flavors of food, and they manifest their health in the lips and mouth. They are responsible for keeping full the flesh and muscles. They are all located in the abdomen and are responsible for taking in and storing the turbid *yin* of the five flavors and substances. They collectively assist the functions of the spleen organ. They are considered to be extreme yin and correspond to late summer and the earth element. Therefore, we consider the spleen to be extreme *yin* with *yin*. The *zang* and *fu* organs that I have described are all dependent on the functions of the gall bladder and its decision-making. The gall bladder corresponds to spring, initiation, and decisiveness. When the gall bladder *qi* is properly ascended and dispersed, the other eleven organs can easily function in health and prosperity."

"故人迎一盛[盛：倍]，病在少阳，二盛病在太阳，三盛病在阳明，四盛已上为格阳。寸口一盛，病在厥阴，二盛病在少阴，三盛病在太阴，四盛以上为关阴。人迎与寸口俱盛四倍已上为关格，关格之脉赢，不能极于天地之精气，则死矣。"

"When the carotid pulse is twice as large as normal, the illness is in the beginning stage of heat and is located in *shaoyang*（'少阳'）. When it is three times as large, the illness is in the middle stage of heat and resides in *taiyang*（'太阳'）. When it is four times as large, the illness is in a severe stage of heat and is in *yangming*（'阳明'）. When it is five times as large, the *yang* has escaped to the outside. When the radial pulse is twice as large as normal, the illness is in the beginning stage of cold and is in *jueyin*（'厥阴'）. When it is three times as large, the illness is in mid-stage of cold and resides in *shaoyin*. When it is four times as large, the illness is in the severe stage of cold and is in *taiyin*（'太阴'）. When it is five times as large, the *yin* has collapsed. If both the carotid and radial pulses are five times larger than normal, this condition is called *guank*e（'关格'）or obstructed. This means that *yin* and *yang* have become extreme and stagnant, and collapse is imminent. The prenatal and postnatal *jing* /essence *qi* have become exhausted, and the eventual consequence is death."

《异法方宜论》On Measures for Treatment to Local Conditions [1]

《异法方宜论》是战国时期创作的一篇散文，作者不详。本篇首先分析五方地势、地形、地质、气候、物产等各自的特点，引出五方居民逐渐形成的不同的生活习惯和生活状况，在各自不同的地理环境和生活习惯的长期作用下，其体质也形成差异，所患的常见病、多发病亦不同，因而五方所发展起来的治疗方法也各具特色，体现了因地制宜的治疗原则。异法，指不同的治疗方法；方宜，谓地方环境各有所宜。本篇讨论了由于居住地区不同，人们受自然环境及生活条件的影响，形成了体质上的差异，因而产生的疾病有一定的区别，在治疗时必须采取不同的方法因地制宜的道理，故名。

[Introduction] The essay of *On Measures for Treatment to Local Conditions,* whose author is unknown, was created in the Warring States period. It first analyzes the characteristics of the topography, landform, geology, climate, products, etc., in the five directions of East, South, West, North and Middle, drawing forth the different living habits and living conditions gradually formed by residents of the five directions. Under the long-term effect of different

[1] 中文选自《黄帝内经》；北京：中华书局；2010 年。
On Measures for treanment to Local Conditions，selected from *The Yellow Emperor's Classic of Medicine*：*A New Translation of the Neijing Suwen with Commentary*, translated by Maoshing Ni, Ph.D.; Boston and London：Shambhala Publications, Inc., 2011.

geographical environment and living habits, their physical constitutions are also different, and the common diseases and the frequently-occurring diseases are also different. Therefore, the treatment methods developed in the five directions also have their own characteristics, reflecting the principle of treatment according to local conditions. "Yifa" refers to different methods of treatment for different diseases and "Fangyi" refers to the appropriate way of living in different local environment. This essay deals with the constitutional differences of people who live in different areas under the influence of natural environment and living conditions. Accordingly, the diseases that are caused have certain distinctions, and when being treated, appropriate measures of treatment must be administered according to local conditions. Hence the name of "Yifa" and "Fangyi".

黄帝曰：“医之治病也，一病而治各不同，皆愈，何也？”

Huang Di asked, "When doctors treat conditions, even though they may be illnesses of the same nature, they use different methods and techniques. But they all succeed. Why is this?"

岐伯对曰：“地势使然也[地势：指高低、燥湿等因素。]。故东方之域，天地之所始生也[始生：开始生发。取法春生之气。]，鱼盐之地。海滨傍水。其民食鱼而嗜咸，皆安其处，美其食。鱼者使人热中[热中：热邪滞留在肠胃里。因鱼性属火，多食使人热积于中，而痈发于外。]，盐者胜血[盐者胜血：盐味咸，咸能入血，多食则伤血。]。故其民皆黑色疏理，其病皆为痈疡[痈疡(yōng yáng)]。其治宜砭石[砭(biān)， 古代一种治病的石针]，故砭石者，亦从东方来。”

Qi Bo replied, "This is because of the differences or variables in geography, weather, lifestyle, and diet. For example, the east is the direction of the birth of Heaven and Earth. The weather there is mild, and it is close to the water. Many varieties of fish and salts can be found, so the local people eat many kinds of fish and like the salty flavor. But because they eat so much fish, which is considered a hot food, heat accumulates and stagnates in the body. They also eat too much salt, which dries, exhausts, and drains the blood. This is why people of the east often have dark skin. The commonly suffered illnesses are boils and carbuncles. The treatment of this disease often utilizes needles made of stone, which are thicker, and bleeding, which releases the heat. Thus, the method of stone needles comes from the east."

“西方者，金玉之域，沙石之处[沙石：即流沙，今称沙漠。]，天地之所收引也[收引：收敛引急，秋天的气象。]。其民陵居而多风[陵居：依山而居。]，水土刚强。其民不衣而褐荐[不衣：不穿丝绵。褐荐：用毛布为衣、细草为席的生活习惯。褐，毛布。荐，草席。]，华食而脂肥[华食：指吃鲜美酥酪、肉类食物。]，故邪不能伤其形体，其病生于内。其治宜毒药，故毒药者，亦从西方来[毒药：泛指治病的药物。]。”

"In the west, many mountains and plateaus and thousands of miles of desert produce a wide variety of metals or ores. This natural environment is similar to the season of autumn. It has an astringent, or conserving, nature. The natives here live naturally and simply by the mountains. They are not concerned about their clothing; they wear wool and sleep on straw mats. They eat food that is often heavy, such as meats and fatty milk and cheese products. Thus they are usually obese people. Externally they are not easily invaded, because they are strong. That is why their illnesses tend to be internal. So the treatment for them is herbal. It can be said, therefore, that herbal treatment comes from the west."

"北方者，天地所闭藏之域也。其地高陵居，风寒冰冽。其民乐野处而乳食[乐野处：乐于野外居住，即游牧生活。乳食：以牛羊乳为食品。]，脏寒生满病[脏寒生满病：内脏受寒，而发生胀满等疾病。]。其治宜灸焫[灸焫(ruò)：一种治疗方法，即用引燃的艾绒熏烤某些穴位和患处。]，故灸焫者，亦从北方来。"

"In the north we have high mountains. The majestic energy of solemn solitude is similar to the season of winter, where the atmosphere is one of calm and reserve. The weather is cold and snowy. Native people here are often nomadic and live amidst nature, exposed to the weather. Their diet also consists of meat and milk products. In this environment, their internal organs are often invaded by cold, and their conditions are excess and distended. The proper method of treating these conditions is moxibustion（'灸焫'）. It is therefore said that the method of moxibustion comes from the north."

"南方者，天地所长养[长养：南方的气候水土，适宜生长养育万物。]，阳之所盛处也。其地下[地下：地势低洼。]，水土弱[水土弱：水土卑湿。]，雾露之所聚也。其民嗜酸而食胕[胕：即"腐"字。经过发酵腐熟的食物。]，故其民皆致理而赤色[致理：肌肤密致。]，其病挛痹[挛痹：筋脉拘挛，麻木不仁。]。其治宜微针[微针：小针。]，故九针者，亦从南方来。"

"In the southern regions the weather is hot, and the *yang qi* is at its utmost. The geography consists of low mountains and valleys. Fog and mist often converge here. The local people like to eat sour and overly ripe foods, such as fruit. Their skin often shows redness. Conditions common in these areas are spasms, numbness, paralysis, *bi*/arthralgia syndrome, and *wei*/flaccidity syndrome. The correct treatment employs very fine needles. Thus, the art of the nine types of needles（'故九针者'）comes from the south. These are metal needles."

"中央者，其地平以湿，天地所以生万物也众["天地"句：中央之地，地势平坦，气候适宜，物产丰富。]。其民食杂而不劳[食杂：所食之物繁多]，故其病多痿厥寒热。其治宜导引按蹻[导引按蹻(qiāo)：古代保健和治病的方法，类似于气功和按摩。]，故导引按蹻者，亦从中央出也。"

"In the center are flatlands, which are often damp. Many varieties of foods abound, and living is peaceful. Conditions that manifest most are colds, influenza, cold and heat conditions, *wei*/flaccidity syndromes, and atrophy. One should utilize *Dao-in* exercise（'导引按蹻'）, manipulation, adjustment, *tuina*（'推拿'）, and massage（'按摩'）. It is said, therefore, that *Dao-in* exercise and manipulation come from the center of China（'亦从中央出也'）."

"故圣人杂合以治[杂合以治：综合各种疗法，用以治病。]，各得其所宜，故治所以异而病皆愈者，得病之情[得病之情：能够了解病情。]，知治之大体也。"

"A superior doctor is able to gather all techniques and use them either together or separately, to flexibly adapt to a changing environment, lifestyle, and geography, and to consider many variables in the treatment of a condition('各得其所宜'). Thus, it is understood that even though treatment methods are different, all can succeed in healing a condition. This is dependent on the ability of the doctor to consider all variables and select the proper principle of treatment."

《阴阳别论》Further Discussion on *Yin* and *Yang* [1]

本篇阴阳，系指脉象而言。别，另外、特殊的意思。由于本篇所论脉之阴阳，侧重于其在三阴三阳经病证诊断方面的意义，与其他篇所说的阴阳含义有所不同，故名《阴阳别论》。正如明代吴昆《素问吴注》云："此篇言阴阳与常论不同，自是一家议论，故曰别论。"

[Introduction]The essay of *Further Discussion on Yin and Yang* deals with the "Yin-Yang" from the pulse manifestation. "*Bie*" ("别") means what's more or what's special about it. Because its discourse on Yin-Yang of the pulse manifestation focuses on the significance in the diagnosis of menstrual diseases of three *Yin* and three *Yang*, it is different from the meaning of *Yin* and *Yang* dealt with in other essays, so it is entitled *Further Discussion on Yin and Yang.* Just as Wukun said in his book entitled as *Wu's Notes to Neijing Suwen of Huang Di* that "its remarks of *Yin* and *Yang* are unique and quite different from some other theories, hence, the name of *Further Discussion on Yin and Yang*".

黄帝问曰："人有四经十二从，何谓？"

Huang Di asked, "It is said that humans have four *jing*/pulses or four normally occurring pulses and twelve *cong*('十二从') or movements. What does this mean?"

岐伯对曰："四经应四时，十二从应十二月，十二月应十二脉。脉有阴阳，知阳者知阴，知阴者知阳。凡阳有五，五五二十五阳。所谓阴者，真脏[真脏：脉学名词。一种病情危重、难治，预后险恶的脉象。]也。见则为败，败必死也。所谓阳者，胃脘之阳也[所谓的阳脉，就是脉中反映有胃气，也就是具有从容和缓、柔和的脉]。别于阳者，知病处也，别于阴者，知生死之期。"

Qi Bo answered, "The four *jing* / pulses(四经) consist of the pulses of the four seasons, and the twelve movements correspond to the twelve channels, which in turn correspond to the twelve months of the year. Normally, in spring, the pulse is wiry, in summer it is flooding, in autumn it

---

[1] 中文选自《全本黄帝内经》，《线装经典》编委会编；昆明：云南教育出版社，2010 年。

Further Discussion on Yin and Yang, selected from *The Yellow Emperor's Classic of Medicine*: *A New Translation of the Neijing Suwen with Commentary*, translated by Maoshing Ni, Ph.D.; Boston and London: Shambhala Publications, Inc., 2011.

is floating, and in winter it is sinking. Additionally, in late summer, the pulse is normally moderate. These are normal signs reflecting the macrocosmic changes and are classified as *yang* pulses. The twelve movements reflect the *qi* flow in the various channels throughout the year. The hand *taiyin*/lung starts around February, the first month of the Chinese calendar. The hand *yangming*/large intestine occurs in March, the foot *yangming*/stomach in April, the foot *taiyin*/ spleen in May, the hand *shaoyin*/heart in June, the hand *taiyang*/small intestine in July, the foot *taiyang*/bladder in August, the foot *shaoyin*/kidney in September, the hand *jueyin*/pericardium in October, the hand *shaoyang/sanjiao* in November, the foot *shaoyang*/gall bladder in December, and the foot *jueyin*/liver in January. The five normally variable *yang* pulses due to season and the five individual pulses of the zang organs actually combine to make up twenty- five pulses. *Yang* pulses reflect the health of the stomach *qi*. A *yin* pulse that shows no stomach *qi* is called the pulse of *zhenzang*（‘真脏’）. *Zhenzang*, or decaying pulse, indicates that the stomach *qi* is drained and exhausted and the prognosis is usually death. Why? Because a *yin* pulse reflects absence of *yang* and thus absence of life activity. If you can distinguish the presence or absence of the stomach pulse, you can know where the disease is located and give the prognosis for life or death, and even know when death might occur."

"三阳在头，三阴在手，所谓一也。别于阳者，知病忌时；别于阴者，知死生之期。谨熟阴阳，无与众谋。所谓阴阳者，去者为阴，至者为阳；静者为阴，动者为阳；迟者为阴，数者为阳。凡持真脉之藏脉者，肝至悬绝急，十八日死；心至悬绝，九日死；肺至悬绝，十二日死；肾至悬绝，七日死；脾至悬绝，四日死。"

"The pulses of the three *yang* channels can be found next to the Adam's apple on the carotid artery, known as *ren ying* . The three *yin* pulses are detected at the radial artery on the wrist, which is called *guan kou*. Under healthy circumstances, the pulses of *ren ying* and *guan kou* should be identical and in harmony. We can also categorize each individual pulse. When the pulse arrives it is *yang*, and when it recedes it is *yin*. When the pulse is active it is *yang*, and when it is quiet it is *yin*. When the pulse is rapid it is *yang*. Rapid is defined as more than five beats per breath of the doctor. When the pulse is slow it is *yin*. *Yin* is defined as fewer than four beats per doctor's breath. Systolic is *yang*, and diastolic is *yin*. When the wave of the pulse goes up it is *yang*, and when it goes down it is *yin*. When *Yang* pulses are absent in a patient, the *yin* or the decaying pulse of the liver is like a thin thread on the verge of breaking, or like a tightly wound wire about to snap. The patient will die within eighteen days. If the decaying pulse of the heart is like a thin fragile thread, the patient will surely die in nine days. If this pulse is found in the lung pulse, the patient will not survive longer than twelve days. If it is found in the kidney pulse, the patient will die in seven days. If it is found in the spleen pulse, the patient will die in four days."

曰："二阳之病发心脾，有不得隐曲，女子不月；其传为风消，其传为息贲者[息贲(xī bì)：病名。指肺积。]，死不治。"

"Generally, disorders of the stomach and intestines affect the spleen and heart. People suffering from these imbalances have difficulty expressing their ills. In women, irregular menstruation or amenorrhea can occur. If illness lingers, emaciation will result. This is called *fengxiao*(‘风消’), dehydration and exhaustion caused by wind arising from heat. When rapid, shallow breathing occurs, with difficulty catching one's breath, or *xibi*(‘息贲’), it is considered incurable."

曰："三阳为病发寒热，下为痈肿，及为痿厥(wěi jué)，腨痟[腨(shuàn)，指小腿肚子；痟(yuān)：酸痛。]；其传为索泽，其传为癞疝(tuí shàn)。"

"Disease of the *taiyang* channel consists of symptoms such as fever and chills, skin lesions, boils, carbuncles, and swelling in the lower extremities. This disease may also manifest in weakness in the knees, cold and spasms with difficult movement, and soreness and pain in back of the thighs and calves. As the disease progresses and becomes chronic, it manifests as dryness of the shin, or it can cause swelling of the testicles or ovarian pain."

曰："一阳发病，少气，善咳，善泄；其传为心掣，其传为隔。二阳一阴发病，主惊骇，背痛，善噫，善欠，名曰风厥。二阴一阳发病，善胀、心满善气。三阴三阳发病，为偏枯萎易，四肢不举。"

"As it transfers to the *shao yang*(‘少阳’) channel, it manifests as susceptibility to cough, diarrhea, and low energy. If chronic, it can become pain in the chest due to heart deficiency or food retention with no appetite. *Yangming*(‘阳明’) and *jueyin*(‘厥阴’) disease will most often manifest as startling, anxiety, fright, and back pain with burping, hiccuping or yawning. This can lead to *Feng Jue*(‘风厥’), syncope due to wind. *Shaoyin* and *shaoyang* illnesses cause distension in the abdominal and epigastric areas. Then we have fullness, with possible nausea and vomiting, and also burping and hiccuping. When *taiyang* and *taiyin* illness occur together, we may see hemiplegia, *wei* condition or flaccidity, and weakness."

"鼓一阳曰钩，鼓一阴曰毛，鼓阳胜急曰弦，鼓阳至而绝曰石，阴阳相过曰溜。"

"But let us return to the pulses. When the pulse comes with force it is *yang*, and when it relaxes it is *yin*. When the pulse comes with much strength but then goes completely weak, this is called a flooding pulse. When the pulse arrives light and floating and slightly weak, we call it a floating pulse. A pulse that is full and tense, as if touching a string on the *pipa*(‘琵琶’), or Chinese guitar, is called wiry. When it is full but deep, that is, upon light pressure at the superficial level you don't feel much, but with strong pressure you feel it full, this is called a sinking pulse. A pulse that is neither too strong nor too weak, that comes and goes in a rhythmic fashion, flowing like a stream, is called a slippery or moderate pulse."

“阴争于内，阳扰于外，魄汗未藏，四逆而起，起则熏肺，使人喘鸣。阴之所生，和本曰和。是故刚与刚，阳气破散，阴气乃消亡。淖则刚柔不和，经气乃绝。”

“*Yin* and *Yang* are unbalanced when the *yin qi* is excessive and stagnant on the inside and the *yangqi* moves recklessly outward, with profuse sweating, cold extremities, dyspnea, and wheezing; this is dangerous because it involves the collapse of *yin* and *yang*. The transformation of *yin* depends on the normal balance of *yin* and *yang*. A gentle warming method is appropriate; if a harsh heating method is applied to counter the imbalance, the *yang qi* will be forced to escape, and the *yinqi* will follow it to oblivion. If the *yin qi* is abundant and excess, then cold and dampness will dominate and this will also stagnate blood and *qi,* causing death.”

“死阴之属，不过三日而死，生阳之属，不过四日而死。”

“There is a condition of dying *yin*（‘死阴’）in which the patient will not live beyond three days. An example of this can be illustrated with heart disease transferring to the lungs; in the control cycle of the five elements, this is fire dominating metal, resulting in dysfunction and subsequent death. In a condition of *yang* revival, the patient will recover within four days. *Yang* revival can be illustrated by liver disease transferring to the heart; wood creates fire, following the creative cycle of the five elemental phases, resulting in recovery.”

“所谓生阳死阴者，肝之心谓之生阳，心之肺谓之死阴，肺之肾谓之重阴，肾之脾谓之辟阴，死不治。”

“There are two other conditions: *zhong yin*, or heavy *yin*, in which lung disease transfers to the kidney; and *pi yin*（‘辟阴’）, or uncontrollable *yin*, in which kidney disease transfers to the spleen. Both are incurable. In *zhong yin*, metal creates water via the creation cycle, but is lacking *yang*, resulting in a negative outcome; hence, *zhong yin*. In *pi yin*, water humiliates earth, a reversal of the control cycle. The *yin* element is dominant and out of control; thus, the result is *pi yin*.”

“结阳者，肿四支。结阴者，便血一升，再结二升，三结三升。阴阳结斜，多阴少阳曰石水，少腹肿。二阳结，谓之消。三阳结，谓之隔。三阴结，谓之水。一阴一阳结，谓之喉痹。”

“When pathogens cause obstruction within the *yang* channels, edema occurs. When pathogens affect the *yin* channels, blood in the stools results. When both *yin* and *yang* channels are obstructed, but the *yin* channels are more severely affected, the lower abdomen will swell; this is called *shishui*（‘石水’）. Furthermore, when the stomach and large intestine channels are more seriously obstructed, a condition of *xiaoke*, or diabetic exhaustion syndrome, will occur. When the bladder and small intestine channels are more affected, obstructions of bowel and urine will occur. When the spleen and lung channels are affected, abdominal edema and distension occur. When the liver and gall bladder channels are affected, throat blockage, or *houbi*(喉痹), results."

"阴搏阳别，谓之有子。阴阳虚，肠澼死。阳加于阴，谓之汗。阴虚阳搏，谓之崩。"

"When examining the pulses, if one finds the *yin* pulses are distinctly different from the *yang* pulses, this indicates pregnancy. If both *yin* and *yang* pulses are deficient and the patient has dysentery, this indicates a grave prognosis. If the *yang* pulses are twice as strong as the *yin* pulses, the patient will sweat spontaneously. If the *yin* pulses are deficient and the *yang* pulses are excessively full, the indication is excess fire causing extravasation; in women, metrorrhagia will result."

"三阴俱搏，二十日夜半死；二阴俱搏，十三日夕时死；一阴俱搏，十日平旦死；三阳俱搏且鼓，三日死；三阴三阳俱搏，心腹满，发尽，不得隐曲，五日死；二阳俱搏，其病温，死不治，不过十日死。"

Abnormally full, the patient will not survive beyond the midnight of the twentieth day; if the heart and kidney pulses are abnormally full, the patient will not live past the evening of the thirteenth day; if the pericardium and liver pulses are abnormally full, the patient will not live longer than ten days; if the bladder and small intestine pulses are abnormally full, the patient will die within three days; if the stomach and large intestine pulses are abnormally full, particularly in febrile disease, the patient will not live beyond ten days. Finally, when all pulses are abnormally full, with epigastric and abdominal swelling or distension and obstruction of bowels and urine, the indication is that both *yin* and *yang qi* have reached the zenith of exhaustion. Consequently, the patient will not live beyond five days."

《阴阳离合论》The Interplay of *Yin* and *Yang* [1]

阴阳离合论出自《黄帝内经·素问》第六篇。阴阳，指阴经和阳经。离，分也；合，并也。本篇讨论阴阳离合之数的问题，故篇名《阴阳离合》。明朝马莳《素问注证发微》云："阴阳者，阴经阳经也。其义论离合之数，故名篇。"

[Introduction] *The Interplay of Yin and Yang* is the sixth article selected from *Neijing of Huang Di*. Here, *Yin* and *Yang* refer to Yin meridians and Yang meridians. "离"means "separation" and "合"means "integration ". It discusses the problems and integration of *Yin* and *Yang*, hence the name of *The Interplay of Yin and Yang*. Just as Ma Shi in the Ming Dynasty said, in his *Notes and Illuminations To Suwen,* that "What is so called the *Yin* and the *Yang* is

[1] 中文选自《全本黄帝内经》，《线装经典》编委会编；昆明：云南教育出版社，2010年。

The Interplay of Yin and Yang, selected from *The Yellow Emperor's Classic of Medicine: A New Translation of the Neijing Suwen with Commentary*, translated by Maoshing Ni, Ph.D.; Boston and London: Shambhala Publications, Inc., 2011.

what is called *Yin* meridians and *Yang* meridians. Its purpose is to deal with the *Shu* (number) in the separation and integration of *Yin* and *Yang*, hence the name of *The Interplay of Yin and Yang*."

黄帝问曰："余闻天为阳，地为阴，日为阳，月为阴，大小月三百六十日成一岁，人亦应之。今三阴三阳不应阴阳，其故何也？"

Huang Di said, "I understand that heaven and the sun are considered *yang*, and earth and the moon are considered *yin*. Because of the natural movement of heaven and earth and the sun and moon, we experience a change of long months and short months and go through three hundred and sixty days, which form one year in the Chinese calendar. The energy flow within the human body through the channels corresponds to this. Can you elaborate further?"

岐伯对曰："阴阳者，数之可十，推之可百，数之可千，推之可万，万之大不可胜数，然其要一也。天覆地载，万物方生，未出地者，命曰阴处，名曰阴中之阴；则出地者，命曰阴中之阳。阳予之正，阴为之主。故生因春，长因夏，收因秋，藏因冬。失常则天地四塞。阴阳之变，其在人者，亦数之可数。"

Qi Bo answered, "The reaches of heaven and earth and *yin* and *yang* are vast, and ultimately everything in the universe can be classified into the polarity of *yin* and *yang*. *Yin* and *yang* are not absolute, but their principle never changes. The law that governs does not falter, although everything around it changes according to the point of reference. For example, before the birth of all things and creatures above ground, the living potential resided in the place of *yin*. This is called *yin* with *yin*（'阴中之阴'）. Once it was born and appeared above ground, this phenomenon was called *yang* within *yin*（'阴中之阳'）. It was after birth or post-heaven that the *yang qi* enabled everything to grow. *Yin* provides form. *Yang* enables growth. Warmth of the spring gives rise to birth, the fire of the summer fuels rapid growth and development, the coolness of autumn matures all and provides harvest, and the coldness of winter forces inactivity and storing. This is the rhythmic change of nature. If the four seasons become disrupted, the weather becomes unpredictable and the energies of the universe will lose their normalcy. This principle also applies to the body."

帝曰："愿闻三阴三阳之离合也。"

Huang Di then said, "I wish to hear you expound on the separation and the union of the three *yang* ."

岐伯曰："圣人南面而立，前曰广明，后曰太冲。太冲之地，名曰少阴；少阴之上，名曰太阳。太阳根起于至阴，结于命门，名曰阴中之阳。中身而上，名曰广明；广明之下，名曰太阴；太阴之前，名曰阳明。阳明根起于厉兑，名曰阴中之阳。厥阴之表，名曰少阳。少阳根起于窍阴，名曰阴中之少阳。是故三之离合也：太阳为开，阳明为阖，少阳为枢。

三经者，不得相失也，搏而勿浮，命曰一阳。”

Qi Bo replied, “The sage stands facing south. In front of him is *guang ming*（‘广明’）or broad expanse, in back of him is *tai chong*（‘太冲’）or great fall. Traveling in this lower region of *tai chong* is a channel called *shaoyin* or minor *yin*. Above this is the *taiyang* or major *yang*/ bladder channel. The lower part of the *taiyang* / bladder channel begins at the outside of the small toe at the point *zhiyin*. The upper part connects with *jingming* in the face near the eyes. The *taiyang* / bladder channel is coupled with the *shaoyin*/kidney channel. The *taiyang*/bladder is lateral and exposed to the sun and is considered external. The *shaoyin* is medal and is in the shade and is considered internal. We call this *yang* within *yin*. Now let us take a look at the upper part of the body. The upper is *yang* and is called *guangming*. The lower is *yin* and is called *taiyin* or major *yin*. Anterior to the *taiyin* area is the *yangming* or moderate *yang*. The most distal point of the *yangming* / stomach channel ends on the tip of the second toe at the *lidui* point. Because the *yangming* is the exterior that is exposed to the sun, relative to the *taiyin*, it is also called *yang* within *yin*. The interior of the body is *yin*, just exterior to that which gives rise to the minor *yang*, as it is gradually exposed to the sun. This is called *shaoyang*, which is the pivot between the interior and the exterior. The *shaoyang*/gall bladder channel begins at the *zhuqiaoyin* point. *Jueyin* is the extreme of *yin* and the end of *yin*, and it gives birth to the beginning of *yang*. We call this *shaoyang* within *yin*. Now we should differentiate and summarize the three *yang* channels. *Taiyang* is on the surface, and its nature is open and expansive; it is the outside. The *yangming* is internal and its action is storing; thus it is the house. The *shaoyang*, which is between the internal and external, acts as a bridge and is considered the hinge between the interior and the exterior. The three *yang*, however, do not act separately, but rather in unison. So, collectively we call them one *yang*.”

帝曰：“愿闻三阴？”

Huang Di asked, “What about the separation and the union of the three *yin*?”

岐伯曰：“外者为阳，内者为阴。然则中为阴，其冲在下，名曰太阴，太阴根起于隐白，名曰阴中之阴。太阴之后，名曰少阴，少阴根起于涌泉，名曰阴中之少阴。少阴之前，名曰厥阴，厥阴根起于大敦，阴之绝阳，名曰阴之绝阴。是故三阴之离合也：太阴为开，厥阴为阖，少阴为枢。三经者，不得相失也，搏而勿沉，名曰一阴。阴阳雩(yú)重，重传为一周，气里形表而为相成也。”

Qi Bo replied, “The outside is *yang* and the inside *yin*; that has been established. What is inside consists of the three *yin*. The *taiyin* /spleen is medial and is in the shade. This channel begins on the side of the big toe at the point *yinbai*（‘隐白’）. It is called *yin* within *yin*. Behind the *taiyin* there is the *shaoyin*/kidney channel, which begins at the bottom of the foot at *yongchuan* point. It is considered the *shaoyin* within *yin*. Anterior to *shaoyin* we have *jueyin* or extreme *yin*. The *jueyin*/liver channel begins on the other side of the big toe at the point of *dadun*（'大敦'）. Surrounded and preceded by two *yin* channels, the *jueyin* is the most *yin* of the *yin* channels. Thus it is called *jueyin* of the *yin*, the extreme *yin*. In summary, we can say that the *taiyin* is the most superficial of the three *yin* channels, and its nature is expansive. The *jueyin* is the deepest inside of the *yin*. Its nature is that of storing and thus it is considered the house. The *shaoyin* is in between, and acts to connect and is considered the hinge or door. The three *yin* must also work in unison. Collectively, too, these are considered one *yin*. So you have one *yin* and one *yang*. The *qi* of the *yin* and of the *yang* move unobstructed throughout the entire body. This is because of the interplay of the *yin* and *yang* and the relationship of the exterior and interior."

僧肇乃“中国佛学史上第一个趋向于独立思考的人物”。

——韦政通《中国思想史·下卷》

Unit 9

《僧肇》（选）Selected from *Seng Chao*

［思想指要］僧肇（公元 *384*—公元 *414* 年），俗姓张，京兆人（今陕西西安），南北朝时期最重要的佛教哲学家之一，中国化佛教体系的奠基人。僧肇才华横溢，早年接触许多儒家典籍，尤其深受《道德经》《庄子》的吸引。后遁入佛门，成为鸠摩罗什的弟子，被鸠摩罗什誉为"中华解空第一人"，与僧融、僧睿、竺道生同为鸠摩罗什高足，被称为"四圣"。他从更彻底的大乘空宗理论出发，对佛教和玄学各派理论进行批判性总结，建立起自己的具有汉化色彩的中观学体系。著有《不真空论》《物不迁论》《般若无知论》等，收集在《肇论》一书中。这三篇著作着重论述了空与无、动与静、无知与有知、空间与时间的佛理关系。僧肇的哲学思想涉及本体论、方法论、认识论等方面，对以后佛教理论、中国佛教史、中国文化史都产生了重大而极其深远的影响。

[Introduction] Seng Zhao (384 A.D.—414 A.D.), with Zhang as his secular name, was born in Jing Zhao county (now Xi' an, Shaanxi) . He was one of the most important Buddhist philosophers in the period of the Southern and Northern dynasties and the founder of Sinicized Buddhism. Seng Zhao was very talented and had access to many Confucian classics in his early years, and he was especially attracted by *Dao De Jing* and *Zhuangzi*. After joining the Buddhist gate, he learned from Monk Kumarajiva and, together with Seng Rong, Seng Rui and Zhu Dao Sheng, was known as one of "the Four Saints". Kumarajiva praised him as "the first Chinese man to explain the theory of emptiness". He critically summarized a variety of theories of Buddhism and metaphysics from a more thorough standpoint of Mahayana Karmada, and finally set up his own theoretical system of Madhyamaka. He was the author of *No Vacuum Theory, On the Immovability of Things*(*Things Do Not Shift*), *On Prajna Ignorance*, etc., collected in the book entitled *Zhao Lun*. These three works mainly focus on Buddhist relations between emptiness and nothingness, motion and stillness, ignorance and knowledge, and space and time. The philosophical thoughts of Monk Seng Zhao involve the ontology, epistemology and methodology and *Zhao Lun* has a great and far-reaching influence on the development of later Buddhist theory and the history of Chinese Buddhism and culture.

《物不迁论》Things Do not Shift [1]

本篇着重论述了物不迁之旨，以破除世人对物迁的执着。僧肇发挥魏晋玄学家郭象“古今常存”“物各有性，性各有极”主张，指出物不相往来而事物“各性住于一世”之理，过去的事物并没有消灭，而现世的事物是独立存在的。其论旨背后则以佛教“刹那生灭”的理论为依据。所以才可以说“旋岚偃岳而常静”和“吾犹昔人非昔人”等话语。作者夸大了运动的间断性，否定其连续性。继之，因物不迁之理而论行业之不灭，因果报应之存在。《物不迁论》之旨趣，也在于论证此一目的。

[Introduction] The essay of *Things Do Not Shift* demonstrates the purport of “things without shift”, and then the necessity of removing the persistence of “things with shift”. Seng Zhao gives full play to Guo Xiang’s proposition that “past and now co-exist forever” and “everything has its own nature and each nature has its own attribute.” Actually, Seng Zhao claims that stillness should be sought in motion, and not separated from motion, even though it is still. He points out that things neither come nor go, instead everything is “in accordance with its primal nature and remains and lasts for one life”. That things of the past are not extinct, but that things of the present exist by themselves, behind each of them is the theory of “Instant Creation and Annihilation” of Buddhism. So it goes like the saying that “the raging storm that can uproot a huge mountain is always tranquil (at rest)” and that “I look like the man of the past but I am not him”. Obviously the author firstly exaggerates the discontinuity of movement and negates its extensibility. Secondly, because things do not move and the Karmic retribution is not extinguished, it is proved that the Karma exists. The purport in the article of *Things Do Not Shift* is to expound and prove this purpose.

夫生死交谢，寒暑迭迁，有物流动，人之常情。余则谓之不然，何者？《放光》云：“法无去来，无动转者[《放光》：指《放光般若经》。法：佛经的特殊概念，指一切的物质现象和精神现象。]。”寻夫不动之作[寻：推寻。不动之作：作，立说；此句是说佛经所宣扬的“不动”之旨。]，岂释动以求静[释：放弃，离开。]？必求静于诸动。必求静于诸动，故虽动而常静。不释动以求静，故虽静而不离动。然则动静未始异，而惑者不同。缘使真言滞於竞辨，宗途屈於好异，所以静躁之极未易言也[缘：于是，因而。宗途：根本的途径，通往真理的大道。]。何者？夫谈真则逆俗，顺俗则违真。违真则迷性而莫返，逆俗则言淡而无味。缘使中人未分于存亡，下士抚掌而弗顾[《老子》第 35 章：“道之出口，淡乎其无味。”第 41 章：“上士闻道，勤能行之；中士闻道，若存若亡；下士闻道，大笑之。”]，近而不可知者，其唯物性乎？然不能自已，聊复寄心于动静之际，岂曰必然？

[1] 中文选自郭齐勇主编：《中国古典哲学名著选读》，北京：人民出版社，2005 年。另：《肇论》三篇注释参考了任继愈《汉唐佛教思想论集》和中华书局出版的《中国哲学史教学资料汇编》。

Things Do not Shift, selected from *Chao Lun*（《肇论》）*: The Treatises of Seng-chao*, translated by Walter Liebenthal, Hong Kong: Hong Kong University Press, 1968.

That birth and death alternate, that winter and summer repeatedly succeed each other, and that all things move on like a current is an ordinary belief of men. But I think that it is not the case. Why? *The Fang-guang Jing* (《放光》, *Scripture of the Shedding of the Light of the Buddha*) says, "There is no dharma (thing) that goes or comes, or moves to change its position(“法无去来，无动转者”)." As we investigate the meaning of "immovability", does it mean to cast aside motion (activity) in order to seek rest (tranquility)? No, rest must be sought right in motion(“必求静于诸动”). As rest must be sought right in motion, therefore, there is eternal rest in spite of motion, and as motion is not to be cast aside in order to seek rest, therefore, although there is rest, it is never separated from motion. This being the case, motion and rest are from the beginning not different, but deluded people consider them to be dissimilar(“动静未始异，而惑者不同”). Consequently, the true words (of Buddhism) are obstructed by their competitive arguments and the orthodox path is deflected by their fondness of heterodoxy. Thus it is not easy to speak about the ultimate (relation) between rest and motion. Why? Because when one speaks the truth, he goes against the common folks; but if he follows them, he will violate the truth. When one violates the truth, he will be deluded about the (original) nature (of things) and will be forever lost; and when he goes against the common folks, his words will be insipid and tasteless. Consequently, when the average type of men (hear the truth) they half believe in it and half doubt it, and the lowest type of men clap their hands (and laugh heartily at it) and ignore it completely. (“缘使中人未分于存亡，下士抚掌而弗顾”) Indeed, the (original) nature of things is something near at hand but difficult to know. But I cannot help setting my mind on the relation between motion and rest. I dare not say that my ideas are necessarily true, but I shall try to discuss them.

试论之曰：《道行》云：“诸法本无所从来，去亦无所至[《道行》：指汉代支娄迦谶译的《道行般若经》。]。”《中观》云：“观方知彼去，去者不至方[《中观》：指鸠摩罗什译的《中论》。方：处所，此指去处。]。”斯皆即动而求静，以知物不迁明矣。夫人之所谓动者，以昔物不至今，故曰动而非静。我之所谓静者，亦以昔物不至今，故曰静而非动。动而非静，以其不来；静而非动，以其不去。然则所造未尝异，所见未尝同。逆之所谓塞，顺之所谓通。苟得其道，复何滞哉？伤夫！人情之惑也久矣。目对真而莫觉，既知往物而不来，而谓今物而可往。往物既不来，今物何所往？何则？求向物于向[向：从前，过去。]，于向未尝无；责向物于今[责：苛求。]，于今未尝有。於今未尝有，以明物不来，于向未尝无，故知物不去。复而求今，今亦不往。是谓昔物自在昔，不从今以至昔；今物自在今，不从昔以至今。故仲尼曰：“回也见新，交臂非故[见《庄子·田子方》中假托孔子对颜回说的一长段话。庄子原意是为了论说事物变化日新之理，僧肇却引这句话反过来证明“物不迁”。]。”如此，则物不相往来明矣。既无往返之微朕[朕：征兆。]，有何物而可动乎？然则旋岚偃岳而常静，江河竞注而不流，野马飘鼓而不动，日月历天而不周，复何怪哉[旋岚：猛风之名。偃岳：吹倒大山。野马：出自《庄子·逍遥游》，指游荡在大地上的尘埃灰土，形似野马奔跑，故以之名风。飘 鼓：飘荡飞扬。历天：经天，在天上运行。不周：不周行。]？

The *Dao-xing Jing* (《道行般若经》, *Scripture on Learning and Practicing the Way*) says, "In reality dharmas do not come from anywhere or go anywhere." *The Zhong Lun* (《中论》,

Treatise on the Middle Path) says, "From one's own point of view one knows that a thing has gone away, but what is (thought to have) gone does not arrive anywhere." Both of these show that rest must be sought right in motion. From this we know that it is clear that things do not shift. ("斯皆即动而求静，以知物不迁明矣") What other people mean by motion is that because things of the past (have gone away) and do not reach the present, therefore, they are said to have moved and are not at rest (continue to exist). What I mean by rest is that, similarly, because things of the past do not reach the present, therefore, they may be said to be at rest and have not moved. ("我之所谓静者，亦以昔物不至今，故曰静而非动") (Other people believe) things move but are not at rest because (past things) have not come down (continue to exist) to the present. (I believe) things are at rest and do not move because (past things) have not gone anywhere. Thus the situation (that past things have neither come to the present nor have gone anywhere) remains the same but our viewpoints are different ("所见未尝同"). People who go against (the truth) will call (that situation) a barrier but those who follow (the truth) will call it a passage. If one has found the right way, what is there to obstruct him? It is sad that people have been deluded in their views for such a long time. Truth is right before their eyes but they do not realize it. They already know that past things cannot come (to the present) but still maintain that present things can go (pass on). As past things cannot come (to the present), where do present things go? ("往物既不来，今物何所往？") Why? If we look for past things in the past, we find that they are never nonexistent in the past, but if we search for past things in the present, we find that they are never existent there. That they are never existent in the present shows that they never come; and that they are never nonexistent in the past shows that they do not go away from it. If we turn our attention to investigate the present, we know that the present, too, does not go (to the future). This means that past things by their very nature exist in the past and have not gone there from the present, and present things by their nature exist in the present and have not come here from the past. This is why Confucius said, "Hui (颜回), (every day) I see something new. (Although you and I have been associated with each other for a long time), in a single moment you are no longer the same as before." ("回也见新，交臂非故") Thus it is clear that (past) things do not come and (present) things do not go. As there is not even a subtle sign of going or returning, what thing can there be that can move? This being the case, the raging storm that uproots mountains is always tranquil (at rest), rivers rushing to the sea do not flow, the fleeting forces moving in all directions and pushing about do not move, and the sun and moon revolving in their orbits do not turn round. What is there to wonder about any more?

噫！圣人有言曰："人命逝速，速於川流[语意出自《大涅槃经•寿命品》。圣人：指释迦牟尼。]。"是以声闻悟非常以成道[声闻：指小根器的人，他们只有通过佛的亲自教诲才能觉悟大道。]，缘觉觉缘离以即真[缘觉：指中根器的人，通过观十二因缘法而领悟佛道。]。苟万动而非化，岂寻化以阶道[寻：寻求。阶：阶梯，这里作动词用，是进入、领悟的意思。]？复寻圣言，微隐难测。若动而静，似去而留。可以神会，难以事求。是以言去不必去，闲人之常想；称住不必住，释人之所谓往耳[闲：防止。释：消除。]。岂曰去而可遣，住而可留邪？故《成具》云：

“菩萨处计常之中，而演非常之教[《成具》：指汉代支曜译《成具光明定意经》。菩萨：菩提萨埵，梵文音译，意为“觉有情”、“发大心之心”。计常：执着事物常存不变。]。”《摩诃衍论》云：“诸法不动，无去来处[《摩诃衍论》：指鸠摩罗什译《大智度论》。]。”斯皆导达群方，两言一会，岂曰文殊而乖其致哉？ 是以言常而不住，称去而不迁。不迁故虽往而常静，不住故虽静而常往。虽静而常往，故往而弗迁；虽往而常静，故静而弗留矣。然则庄生之所以藏山[《庄子•大宗师》：“夫藏舟于壑，藏山于泽，谓之固矣。然而夜半有力者负之而走，昧者不知也。”]，仲尼之所以临川[《论语•子罕》：“子在川上曰：逝者如斯夫，不舍昼夜。”]，斯皆感往者之难留，岂曰排今而可往？是以观圣人心者，不同人之所见得也。何者？人则谓少壮同体，百龄一质。徒知年往，不觉形随。是以梵志出家[梵志：泛指出家人。]，白首而归，邻人见之曰：“昔人尚存乎？”梵志曰：“吾犹昔人，非昔人也。”邻人皆愕然，非其言也。所谓有力者负之而趋，昧者不觉，其斯之谓欤？是以如来因群情之所滞[如来：乘彼如实道，来化群生。]，则方言以辩惑乘莫二之真心[方言：不同之言，各种宣说。]，吐不一之殊教。乖而不可异者，其唯圣言乎！

Alas, the Sage has said, “Man’s life passes away quickly, more quickly than the stream current.” Therefore, by realizing the impermanence of things the Buddha’s ordinary disciples (śrāvaka, those who attain to their own salvation by hearing the Buddha’s teachings) attain enlightenment(“声闻悟非常以成道”), and the Buddhas-for-themselves (pratyekabuddha, who attain enlightenment by their own exertions), by realizing that the co-operating causes (*pratyaya*/*yuan*, which makes a thing a dependent being) can be removed, become identified with the truth(“缘觉觉缘离以即真”). If all motions (activities) of things are not changes, why should they seek after (the principle) of change in order to ascend the steps of enlightenment? (However), if we again investigate the saying of the Sage, we shall find its meaning to be subtle, hidden, and unfathomable. Things seem to move but are really at rest, and they seem to go away but really remain. (“若动而静，似去而留”) (Its meaning) can only be grasped by the spirit-like understanding and cannot be discovered in ordinary facts. (“可以神会，难以事求”) Therefore, when the Sage said that things go, he did not mean that they really go; he merely wanted to prevent ordinary thoughts. And when he said that things remain in the same state, he did not mean that they really remain; he merely wanted to discard what ordinary people call the passing (impermanence) of things. He did not mean to say that by going is meant something being sent away and by remaining something being retained. Therefore, the *Cheng-ju Jing* (《成具》, *Scripture on Producing and Completing the Light*) says, “The Bodhisattva, living in the midst of people who believe in permanence, propagates the doctrine of impermanence. And the *Mo-he-yan lun* (《摩诃衍论》, *Treatise of Great Wisdom*)says, “Dharmas do not move. They neither go anywhere nor come to anywhere.” All these are intended to lead the common folks to reach enlightenment. The two different sayings aim at the same thing. Shall we say that because they differ in language they are contradictory in the realm of truth(“岂曰文殊而乖其致哉”)? Although permanence is mentioned, it does not mean remaining in the same state; and although going is mentioned, it does not mean instability. Since Dharmas are not mutable, they are always at rest even though they have gone; and because they do not remain, they are always gone even though they are at rest. As they are always gone although at rest, they do not mutate while being gone; and as they are always at rest while they are gone, they do not remain while at rest. When Zhuangzi (庄子) said that (it is impossible to) hide a mountain (in a lake for at midnight a strong man may come and carry it away on his back) and when Confucius(仲尼) stood by the stream (and said, "Passing on like this, it never ceases, night and day."), both expressed the feeling that what is gone cannot be retained. Did they say that (things) can cast aside the present and pass on? Thus we see that the minds of the sages are different from the views of the common people("不同人之所见得也").

Why? They say that a man possesses the same body in youth and in old age and that the years pass on but do not realize that the body follows. A young ascetic (seeking *Nirvāṇa*) left his family and when his hair had turned white, returned home. When his neighbors saw him and asked, "Is the man of the past still living?" he replied, "I look like the man of the past but I am not he("吾犹昔人，非昔人也")". The neighbors were all startled and rejected his words. (When Zhuangzi) said that a strong man comes and carries it away on his back but an ignorant man does not know this, this is the meaning. Therefore, the *Tathāgata* (*rulai* / Buddha)(如来/佛陀), in accordance with the obstruction in the common people's views, speaks appropriate words to dispel their delusions. He exercises his true mind which transcends any duality and preaches various doctrines which need not be the same (but which vary according to circumstances). The words of the Sage are indeed conflicting but never different (from the Middle Path).

故谈真有不迁之称，导俗有流动之说，虽复千途异唱，会归同致矣。而征文者闻不迁[征文：死扣字眼。]，则谓昔物不至今；聆流动者，而谓今物可至昔。既曰古今，而欲迁之者何也？是以言往不必往，古今常存，以其不动。称去不必去，谓不从今至古，以其不来。不来故不驰骋于古今，不动故各性住于一世[各性住于一世：三世，过去世，现在世，未来世；指事物各自停留在它所在的那一刻。]。然则群籍殊文，百家异说，苟得其会，岂殊文之能惑哉？是以人之所谓住，我则言其去；人之所谓去，我则言其住。然则去住虽殊，其致一也。故经云："正言似反，谁当信者[经：指《普曜经》。]？"斯言有由矣。何者？人则求访于今，谓其不住；吾则求今于古，知其不去。今若至古，古应有今；古若至今，今应有古。今而无古，以知不来；古而无今，以知不去。若古不至今，今亦不至古，事各性住于一世，有何物而可去来？然则四象风驰，璇玑电卷[四象：春夏秋冬。璇玑：北斗星座的第二颗叫璇，第三颗叫玑。]，得意毫微，虽速而不转。是以如来功流万世而常存，道通百劫而弥固[劫：佛经认为世界经历了千万年毁灭一次，重新开始，这样的一个周期叫一劫。]。成山假就于好篑[篑(kuì)：古代的土筐。]，修途托至于初步[修途：长途。]，果以功业不可朽故也。功业不用朽，故虽在昔而不化，不化故不迁，不迁故则湛然明矣。故经云："三灾弥纶，而行业湛然[经：夺经，《长阿含经》有类似之语。三灾：佛教认为，到世界毁灭的末日，会发生水灾、火灾及风灾。行业：指人的所作所为及思想言论。佛教认为，人所造的业即使经历了三灾，也不会消除，会引起或善或恶的报应后果，使人永远陷入轮回的灾难；只有相信佛的教义，出家修行，才能免于因果报应。]。"信其言也。何者？果不俱因，因因而果。因因而果，因不昔灭。果不俱因，因不来今。不灭不来，则不迁之致明矣。复何惑于去留，踟蹰于动静之间者哉？然则乾坤倒覆，无谓不静；洪流滔天，无谓其动。苟能契神于即物[即物：当前事物。]，斯不远而可知矣。

Therefore, when he talks about truth, he speaks in terms of (things being) immutable; but when he wants to lead the ordinary folk, he talks in terms of (things) moving on like a current. Although there are a thousand paths and a variety of tunes (“千途异唱”), they all converge at the same point. However, people who rely on the letter, when they hear of immutability, believe that things of the past cannot reach the present; and when they hear of things moving on like a current, believe that things of the present can reach the past. Since they have already made the distinction of past and present, how can things pass on between them? To say that (things) have gone does not necessarily mean that they have gone away. Both the past and the present exist permanently because they do not move. To say that (things) go does not necessarily mean that they really go, for the past cannot be reached from the present, since (the past) does not come (to the present). As (things) do not come, there cannot be any shifting between past and present; and since they do not move, everything, in accordance with its primal nature, remains for one period of time. This being the case, although the various books differ in language and the many schools differ in theory, if we find out where they converge, how can different expressions delude us? (“然则群籍殊文，百家异说，苟得其会，岂殊文之能惑哉？”) What people call remaining, I call passing on; whereas what people call passing on, I call remaining. Although passing on and remaining are different, ultimately they are the same. This is why it is said in the scripture, “Straight words seem to be their opposite. Who will believe them?” (“正言似反，谁当信者？) There is reason for this saying. What shall we say? People seek the past in the present. (Since it is not found in the present), they say that it does not remain. I seek the present in the past. (Since it is not in the past), I know that it does not go anywhere. If the present passes on to the past, then there should be the present in the past. If the past reaches to the present, then there should be the present in the past. If the past reaches to the present, then there should be the past in the present. Since there is no past in the present, we know that it does not come, and since there is no present in the past, we know that it does not go. As neither does the past reach to the present nor does the present reach to the past, everything, according to its primal nature, remains for only one period of time. What thing is there to come and go? (“若古不至今，今亦不至古，事各性住于一世，有何物而可去来？”) This being the case, although the four seasons are as fleeting as the wind and although the polar star revolves with lightning speed, if we understand the least bit (that things do not shift), we will realize that, quick as they are, they do not shift. For the above reason, the merit of the *Tathāgata* (如来) continues for countless generations and exists permanently, and his truth remains firmer after having gone through a hundred aeons. The completion of a mountain lies in the first basket, and arriving at the destination of a long journey depends on the first step. (“成山假就于始篑，修途托至于初步”) The reason, surely, is that merit is immortal. Since merit is immortal, it does not change though it is in the past. Since it does not change, it is immutable. And since it is immutable, it is clear that (merit remains) tranquil. Therefore, the scripture says, “Although the three calamities (of fire, water, and wind) extend everywhere, the merit remains tranquil.” How true are these words! Why? The effect does not exist together with causes, because the effect is produced by the causes. Since the result is produced by the causes, the causes could not have been extinguished in the past. Since the result and the causes do not exist simultaneously, the causes do not come to the present. As they neither perish nor come to the present, the conclusion that they are immutable is clear. (“不灭不来，则不迁之致明矣”) Why should we be deluded about (things) going or remaining any more, or be undecided as to whether (things) move or are at rest(“踟蹰于动静之间者哉？”)? Thus even if heaven and earth turn upside down, it does not mean that they are in motion. If one’s spirit is harmonized with things as they are found(“契神于即物”), one can realize (the principle of the immutability of things) right where he is.

《不真空论》(Wu) Pu Chen-Kung Lun [1]

本篇在缘起论的基础上论证所谓物与虚、有与无的关系。就事物之有与无而言，有是假有，并非实有；无是对有的否定，而非绝无。事物是有与无的统一，必须以中道空观才能真实、全面了解事物的本相。名是事物之假号，因现象而起名，现象是刹那生灭，并非真实不变的；而事事物物真实不变的本性，对现象是超越的，它既肯定现象之假有，亦因其假有而说本体之真无。因此名与实是不相统一的，现象之名无当于超越之实。虽然实相有超越之义，但是万物的真实本性并不在万物之外，即万物之自身、即事物之立处，已包含所谓的真相：空之本性立于万物之中，离万物而无所谓空；反之，事物离其空性也无现象可言，真性亦是现象存在的根据。

[Introduction] *Pu Chen-Kung Lun* demonstrates the relationship between the so-called things and nothingness, and existence and non-existence on the basis of Prattyasamutpada. As things are taken into account in terms of existence and non-existence, existence is false existence rather than real existence. Nothingness is the negation of existence, but not absolute negation of nothingness itself. Things are the unity of existence and non-existence. Only by accepting the theory of emptiness and Madhyamapratipad can we truly and comprehensively understand the truth of things. Name is the pseudonym of things. Name is given to phenomenon. Phenomena are of instantaneous birth and death, which are not real and remain unchangeable. However, the true and unchanging nature behind everything transcends the phenomena, which affirms not only the false existence of phenomena, but also proves the absence of noumenon because of the false existence of the phenomena. Thus the name and entity are not unified, and the name of the phenomenon has no place in the transcendental

---

[1] 中文选自郭齐勇主编：《中国古典哲学名著选读》，北京：人民出版社，2005 年。

(*Wu*) *Pu Chen-Kung Lun*, selected from *Chao Lun*(《肇论》)*: The Treatises of Seng-chao*, translated by Walter Liebenthal, Hong Kong：Hong Kong University Press, 1968.

realm. Although entity enjoys the meaning of transcendence, the true nature of all things is not outside of all things, that is to say, everything itself or where they rest with, contains the so-called truth: the nature of emptiness is inherent in all things and, therefore, nothing is empty from everything. On the contrary, things which are devoid of the nature of emptiness are far from the so- called phenomenon, and the truth is the basis on which all things exist.

至虚无生者[至虚无生：极端虚寂，无生灭变化。]，盖是般若玄鉴之妙趣[般若(bō rě)：梵语音译，即智慧。玄鉴：玄妙的镜子。]，有物之宗极者也[宗极：最高、最后的本质。]。自非圣明特达，何能契神于有无之间哉[有无：诸法或有或无之理。]？是以至人通神心于无穷，穷所不能滞；极耳目於视听，声色所不能制者，岂不以其即万物之自虚[即万物之自虚：即，不舍不离；就万物自身而言本来就是不真实而虚假的，不必在万物之外另有一虚无的本体。]，故物不能累其神明者也？是以圣人乘真心而顺，则无滞而不通；审一气以观化[审：明确。一气：僧肇借用“一气”观念来阐明万物虽殊，其本质为一的道理。]，故所遇而顺适。无滞而不通，故能混杂致淳；所遇而顺适，故则触物而一。如此，则万象虽殊，而不能自异[万象虽殊，而不能自异：事物之象虽千差万别，但它们各自并没有不同的本质以相区别。]。不能自异，故知象非真象；象非真象故，则虽象而非象。

A perfect void where nothing grows (and decays), such is, perchance, the transcendent realm as it shows in the dark mirror of Prajfia(“般若波罗蜜”). Into it all that exists (and non-exists) is resolved. Who, not having the mental power of the Sage with which to penetrate to full understanding, can attain that power of vision in which ‘existence’ and ‘non-existence’ lose their meaning? (Only) the Perfect Being(“至人”) may let his mind go beyond the borders of finality, unhemmed by these borders, may send his eyes and ears beyond the limits of seeing and hearing (to regions) where eyes and ears cannot reach. Is it not just that perfect ‘voidness’(“虚”), in which all things are equal, which prevents the Cosmic Soul from being troubled by individual sorrows? Therefore, when the Sage uses his true understanding to follow the natural course, there is no obstacle which he does not transcend(“是以圣人乘真心而理顺，则无滞而不通”); because he views the transformations (of the universe) as all of one breath, he passes through, adapting himself to whatever he encounters. He transcends all the obstacles, hence he can reduce the turbid and the mixed to a state of clarity. He passes through whatever he encounters, he sees oneness behind each particular experience. This being so, although the various forms are different, they are not so in themselves(“万象虽殊，而不能自异”); not being distinct in themselves, it follows that the (multitude of apparent) forms is not true form; as that (multitude of) forms is not such, it is not form, although it (seems to be) form.

然则物我同根，是非一气，潜微幽隐，殆非群情之所尽[群情：有情众生。]。故顷尔谈论，至于虚宗，每有不同。夫以不同而适同，有何物而可同哉？故众论竞作，而性莫同焉[性：法性，事物的本性。]。何则？心无者，无心于万物，万物未尝无。此得在于神静，失在于物虚[“心无”指支愍度建立的心无宗的立教理论。得：可取之处。失：缺点，不足之处。]。即色者，明色不自色，故虽色而非色也[“即色”指支遁的即色论。色：佛教的基本概念之一，指与精神相对待的物质现象。]。夫言色者，但当色即色[当色即色：谓此当下之色就是色，而非色色才成其为色。在此基础之上，佛家认为色即是空。元康《肇论疏》：“林法师但知言色非自色，因缘而成，而不知色本是空，犹存假有也。”]，岂待色色而后为色哉？此直语色不自色，未领色之非色也。本无者，情尚于无多，触言以宾无，故非有，有即无，非无，无即无[“本无”指道安或竺法汰的本无论。]。寻夫立文之本旨者，直以非有非真有，非无非真无耳，何必非有无此有，非无无彼无？此直好无之谈，岂谓顺通事实，即物之情哉[僧肇主张非无非有的中道观，而本无论却偏好于无，所以批评本无论，说佛经中所说的非有，只是说万物缘生，并非真有；说非无，是不坏假相，并非绝无。如果把非有理解为绝无此有，非无理解为绝无彼无，这就不符合事物的本来情况了。]？

Thus all things and I spring from the same root. Whatever there is and whatever there is not is one in essence. Impalpable and darkly concealed, surely this is not a matter which an ordinary intellect can encompass. That is the reason why in the discussions of today, everybody has his own opinion, as soon as the subject of *sūnyatā*（“虚宗”）is touched upon. But if the undifferentiated is approached with the (preconceived idea of) difference, can anything be established as one ? Therefore, the disputations go on and on (trying to define the relation between the Two Worlds) and on that very reason they cannot establish their oneness.

Outline of the Schools

(The first school defines *sūnyatā* as) “emptiness of mind” hsin-wu（心無）.

(Tenet:) (*Sunyatii* means that) the mind (is “empty” when it) does not reflect things, though things (themselves) are never non-existent (“empty”).

(Criticism:) This is correct with regard to mind when it is calm (“empty”) (like that of) the Spirit, but it fails to understand (the true reason why) things are (called) “empty. ”

(The second school defines *sūnyatā* as) “emptiness” (*sūnya*) identical with matter (chi-se 即色).

(Tenet:) What does it mean to say that “emptiness” is identical with matter? Matter (as it is found) is not in itself matter. Therefore, though matter, it is not matter.

(Criticism:) Speaking of matter, (“emptiness”) is identical with matter, because where matter is there it is. There is no need to wait until it is taken for what in itself it is to justify the saying that it is identical with matter.

The opponent says correctly that matter (as it is found) is not in itself matter but he does not understand that matter (as it is found) is (itself) non-matter.

(The third school defines *sūnyatā* as) original “emptiness” (*pen-wu*)(本无).

(Tenet:) There are many who are fond of nothingness, so in all their talk they submit to it. Therefore, (when the *sutras*) deny that things exist (they understand that) they do not exist; when they deny that things do not exist (they understand) the same.

(Criticism:) If we look for the original meaning of these sentences, (we find that) ‘not existent’ means “not truly existent, ” that “not non-existent” means “not truly non-existent”. They do not deny that here may be something and there may be nothing (in the ordinary understanding).

How can this talk, so partial to the negations, be said to agree with the facts and to adequately describe the identity of things (with *sūnyatā*)?

夫以物物于物，则所物而可物；以物物非物，故虽物而非物。是以物不即名而就实，名不即物而履真[履真：践真，达到真。]。然则真谛独静于名教之外，岂曰文言之能辩哉[真谛：佛学概念，指最真实的道理，与“俗谛”相对。名教：名言概念。文言：巧饰之言。]？然不能杜默，聊复厝言以拟之[厝：同措。]。试论之曰：《摩诃衍论》云：“诸法亦非有相，亦非无相[《摩诃衍论》：此指《大智度论》。：诸法：佛教的基本概念，轨持义，包括心法与心所法，泛指一切物质的和精神的，存在的和不存在的事物。相：形相。]。”《中论》云：“诸法不有不无者，第一真谛也。”寻夫不有不无者，岂谓涤除万物，杜塞视听，寂寥虚豁，然后为真谛者乎？诚以即物顺通，故物莫之逆；即伪即真，故性莫之易。性莫之易，故虽无而有；物莫之逆，故虽有而无。虽有而无，所谓非有；虽无而有，所谓非无。如此，则非无物也，物非真物。物非真物，故于何而可物？故《经》云[《经》：指《维摩诘经•不二法门》。]：“色之性空，非色败空。”以明夫圣人之于物也，即万物之自虚，岂待宰割以求通哉[宰割：谓把色与空割裂开来。实际色与空只是事物的一体两面。]？是以寝疾有不真不谈，《超日》有即虚之称[《超日》：指《超日明三昧经》。经中有“不有寿，不保命”和地、水、火、风“四大皆空”的说法。]。然则三藏殊文，统之者一也[三藏：佛教经典经、律、论的统称。]。故《放光》云：“第一真谛无成无得，世俗谛故，便有成有得[《放光》：指《放光般若经》。就真理而言，万物毕竟空，所以无成无得；就世俗的道理来说，万物缘生，所以有成有得。]。”夫有得即是无得之伪号，无得即是有得之真名。真名故，虽真而非有；伪号故，虽伪而非无。是以言真未尝有，言伪未尝无。二言未始一，二理未始殊。故经云：“真谙俗谛，谓有异邪？”

If one calls “thing” what is a thing then what is called “thing” is (something) fit to be called “thing”; if one calls “thing” what is not a thing then though called “thing” it is still not a thing. Therefore, a thing called up by a name may not appear (as what it is expected to appear); a name calling up a thing may not lead to the real (thing). Therefore, the sphere of Truth (“真谛”) is beyond the noise of verbal teaching. How then can it be made a subject of discussion? Still I cannot remain silent. In spite of (what I have just said) I shall state my opinion and defend it.

The Mahāyāna sāstra (《摩诃衍论》) says, “Dharma either have the characteristics of existence nor those of non-existence”. The *Chung-lun* (《中论》) says, “Dharma are neither existent nor non-existent”. (These double negations define) *paramārtha satya* (“第一真谛”). These double negations (“不有不无”), do they imply that the thousand things must be blotted out, that the senses must be prevented from seeing and hearing (“杜塞视听”), that a state must be created which is soundless, substanceless, void like a gap in a mountain range, in order to produce the true state? Be assured that things represent no obstruction whenever one passes through them knowing that they are identical (with what is not a thing). (Understanding that) they are not true (when seen from one angle) but true (when seen from the other angle) (he will know that) essentially they are without sides.

Thus, being without sides, things, though in-existent, exist (as phenomena); Representing no obstructions, things, though (appearing to) exist, in-exist (in truth). In-existent (in truth), though they (appear to) exist, they are called different from (merely) existent things. (Appearing to) exist, though they in-exist (in truth), they are called different from the in-existent.

Now, things which do not (merely) in-exist, are not truly existent things. If they are not truly existent things, what else does there exist apt to be designated “thing”?

A *sūtra*（《契经》）says, "*Rūpa*（"色法"）is *sūnya* by nature not by destruction".（"色之性空，非色败空"）And thus the Buddha（"圣人"）conducts himself in relation to things: "empty" by nature exactly as things themselves, he passes through them not waiting until a path is cut out (for him).

This is why (*Vimalakirti*'s)(《维摩诘经 •问疾品》) sickness is explained as unreal, why *the Sūtra of the Samādhi Outstanding Sunshine*（《超日明三昧经》）says that (the four elements) are "empty. " But then, though the expressions in the *Tripitaka*（《三藏经》）vary, the leitmotif is only one. Therefore, the *Fang-kuang*（《放光》）says, "In the true state (*paramārtha*)（'真谛'）neither (Buddhahood,佛性) nor (*Nirvāna*, 涅槃) is attained, though in the world (*samvrti,* 三昧) they are attained. " Therefore, the term "attainment" is conventionally used to designate non-attainment; the term "non-attainment" is the true designation of attainment.

Using "true language" (attainment is called) in-existent though in truth (it is realized); using conventional language (attainment is called) not in-existent though it seems (to be realized). Or else, to say that in truth (it exists) implies that (in the world) it could never exist; to say that seemingly (it exists) excludes that (in the world) it could ever in-exist.

These two sentences are surely contradictory but, as surely, what they express is the same. This is confirmed by a sutra (in which the Bodhisattva is asked:) "Would you say that *paramārtha* and *laukika*（'真谛' / '俗谛'）are different?"

答曰："无异也。"此经直辩真谛以明非有，俗谛以明非无。岂以谛二而二于物哉[这是说，真谛和俗谛也是同一件事情的两个方面，尽管两个概念的名言不同，而其实质都是为了阐明非有非无的中道观。]？然则万物果有其所以不有，有其所以不无。有其所以不有，故虽有而非有。有其所以不无，故虽无而非无。虽无而非无，无者不绝虚；虽有而非有，有者非真有。若有不即真，无不夷迹，然则有无称异，其致一也。

Answers: "No. " This *sūtra*（"契经"）wants to say (what we have said just now, namely, that the same in the aspect of) *paramārtha*（"真谛"）is said not to exist and (in the aspect of) *laukika*（"世俗谛"）is said not to non-exist. It rejects the proposition that these two aspects are two different things. Surely, there is a reason why things are called in-existent, and also a reason why they are called not non-existent. For, in the first instance, though existent they in-exist; in the second instance, though in-existent they are not non-existent. For their "non-existence, " as negated in the second clause, does not imply "spontaneous non-existence" (as of what could never exist) and their 'existence, ' as negated in the first clause, does not imply "spontaneous existence" (as of what must always exist). Now, if "existence" does not imply "existence as of the universe which is " and "non-existence" does not imply "non-existence as of the universe before it came into being, " then these two terms, though different as terms, refer to the same item.

故童子叹曰："说法不有亦不无，以因缘故，诸法生[语出《维摩诘经•佛国品》。因缘：佛教用来论证万物产生和万物皆空的概念。主要条件叫因，辅助条件叫缘。]。”《璎珞经》云：“转法轮者，亦非有转，亦非无转，是谓转无所转[见《璎珞经》卷二十。法轮：轮是古代印度作战的轮状武器。佛经以此比喻佛教的威力可以摧毁世俗见，改变世界，因此把佛教的理论叫做法轮。转法轮：谓宣说、宣扬佛教的真理。]。”此乃众经之微言也。何者？谓物无邪，则邪见非惑；谓物有邪，则常见为得。以物非无，故邪见为惑；以物非有，故常见不得。然则非有非无者，信真谛之谈也。故《道行》云：“心亦不有亦不无[《道行》：指《道行般若经》。]。” 然者，夫有若真有，有自常有，岂待缘而后有哉？譬彼真无，无自常无，岂待缘而后无也？若有不能自有，待缘而后有者，故知有非真有。有非真有，虽有不可谓之有矣。不无者，夫无则湛然不动，可谓之无。万物若无，则不应起，起则非无。以明缘起，故不无也。故《摩诃衍论》云：“一切诸法，一切因缘，故应有。一切诸法，一切因缘，故不应有。一切无法，一切因缘，故应有。一切有法，一切因缘，故不应有。”寻此有无之言，岂直反论而已哉[反论：相反之论。]？若应有，即是有，不应言无；若应无，即是无，不应言有。言有是为假有，以明非无，借无以辨非有。此事一称二，其文有似不同；苟领其所同，则无异而不同。然则万法果有其所以不有，不可得而有；有其所以不无，不可得而无。何则？欲言其有，有非真生。欲言其无，事象既形[形：显露，露迹。]。象形不即无，非真非实有。然则不真空义，显於兹矣。故《放光》云：“诸法假号不真。”譬如幻化人，非无幻化人，幻化人非真人也[幻化人：魔术中的假人。]。

Therefore, (in the *Vimalakirti sūtra*) the young says with a sigh (of admiration), "(The Buddha) has said: the dharma neither are nor are not, they (simply) arise from causes and conditions".（“以因缘故，诸法生”）

The (Great) *Bodhisattva-keyura sūtra*（《璎珞经》）says, "When the Bodhisattva（“菩萨”）turns the Wheel-of-the-Law（“法轮”）, there is neither turning nor no turning". This means that (the Buddhas) turn the Wheel where there is nothing to be turned. That then is the subtle meaning of all the *sūtras*.（“此乃众经之微言也”）

What do you propose? That things are not? Then negativism would not be heretical. That things are? Then positivism would be orthodox. (Actually) because things are not simply nothing, negativism is a heresy; because things are not simply something, positivism is not orthodox. Then it is evident that these two negations describe Highest Truth (*paramārtha satya,* 真谛).

So *The Tao-hsing* (*Subhūti*)（《道行》）says, "Mind neither is existent nor non-existent". *The Chung-kuan*（《中观》）says, "Because the existence of things depends on causes and conditions, they are not existent; because they arise from these conditions, they are not non-existent. " The theory expounded (in the *sūtras*) is such. Why is it such?

Existence, if true, would imply self-sufficiency and permanency; it would not depend upon causation for its existence. Just so, non-existence, if true, would imply self-sufficiency and permanency; it would not depend upon causation for its non-existence. As what exists is not self-sufficient but depends upon causation for its existence, it is obvious that it is not truly existent. Not truly existent, though existent, it should not be called "existent. " But why is it called "not non-existent"? Whatever non-exists could be called "non-existent" only if, like the day before daybreak it were unaffected by mundane changes. If the ten thousand things were unaffected like that, they could not possibly rise (and decay). As they rise (and decay) they are "not non-existent". This is expressed in the (above) *sūtra*: "Because they rise from conditions they are not non-existent" .（"以明缘起，故不无也"）

The Mahāyāna sātra (摩诃衍那/大乘) says, "All dharma must be considered to exist because (though) dependent upon causation (they exist); all dharma cannot be considered to exist because (only) dependent upon causation (they exist). All non-existing dharma must be considered to exist, because (though *in modo negativo*) dependent upon causation they exist; all existing dharma cannot be considered to exist because (only) dependent upon causation they exist." These sentences, if properly understood, are more than simple inversions. For, if (in the preceding paragraph) "must be considered to exist" implied that (the non-existing dharma just) exist, (the Buddha could not have added that they) do not exist; if "cannot be considered to exist" implied that (the existing dharma just) non-exist, (he could not have said that they) exist. Saying that they exist he borrows the term "existence" to denote that they do not (just) non-exist; saying that they do not exist he borrows the term "non-existence" to denote that they do not (just) exist. One meaning; two words, language creates the difficulty. If one knows the reason why (that strange language is used), then all ambiguities disappear.

The ten thousand dharma looked at from one side do not exist, and therefore, they cannot be treated as existent, but looked at from the other side, they do not non-exist, and therefore, they cannot be treated as non-existent.

If you say they exist (I answer), (You may call it) existence but it is not true life. If you say: they do not exist (I answer): Phenomenal life has taken shape already. This is not just non-existing, (The ten thousand dharma) neither in truth exist nor just non-exist. This is the meaning of the title *Pu chen-kung lun* (of the *Treatise*)(《不真空论》).

Therefore, the *Fang-kuang*（《放光》）says, "All the dharma are symbols and are not real. They resemble a man produced by magic: this man is not non-existent, yet he is not a real man."

夫以名求物，物无当名之实。以物求名，名无得物之功。物无当名之实，非物也；名无得物之功，非名也。是以名不当实，实不当名。名实无当，万物安在？故《中观》云："物无彼此[《中观论•如来品》："诸法实相，无有此彼。"]。"而人以此为此，以彼为彼；彼亦以此为彼，以彼为此。此彼莫定乎一名，而惑者怀必然之志。然则彼此初非有，惑者初非无。既悟彼此之非有，有何物而可有哉？故知万物非真，假号久矣。是以《成具》立强名之文[《成具》：即《成具光明定意经》，经中说："是法无所有法故，强为其名。"]，园林托指马之况[园林：指庄子，庄子曾为漆园吏。托指马之况：典出《庄子•齐物论》中的一段话："以指喻指之非指，不若以非指喻指之非指也。以马喩马之非马，不若以非马喻马之非马也。天地一指也，万物一马也。"]。如此，则深远之言，于何而不在？是以圣人乘千化而不变、履万惑而常通者，以其即万物之自虚，不假虚而虚物也。故《经》云："甚奇，世尊！不动真际，为诸法立处[《经》：指《大品经》。世尊：佛教徒对释迦牟尼的尊称。真际：事物的真实本性。]。"非离真而立处，立处即真也。然则道远乎哉？触事而真。

圣远乎哉？体之即神。

If one searches for a thing using its name as a guide (he will discover that) where the name is found the thing is not found also. If one searches for a name using the thing (it names) as a guide (he will discover that) what the thing achieves the name does not also achieve. If the thing is not found where the name is found, it is the wrong thing; if the name does not achieve what the thing achieves, it is the wrong name. Thus, names do not correspond with facts and facts do not correspond with names. Now, if names and facts do not correspond with each other, how are the ten thousand things to be found (with the help of ordinary language) ?

Therefore, the *Chung-kuan*(《中观》) says, "Things are not this or that. But someone (in the position of this) makes this a this and that a that, while (in the position of that) he makes this a that and that a this. "

This and that do not denote only one kind of thing, but ignorant people believe that (these words) have a definite significance. It follows that this and that at first do not exist, while ignorant people believe that (even) at first they may not non-exist. Once one has recognized the non-existence of this and that, what else could there be whose existence he would be willing to assert? So we know, things are not real, they are just symbols.

That is why the *Ch'eng-chü* (《成具》) maintains that names are artificially applied to things, and *Yüan-lin*("园林") uses the similes of the finger and the horse. So, profound doctrines may be found anywhere.

The Sage, who rides the thousand (waves) of becoming, yet remains unchanged; he falls into a thousand errors but emerges from all of them. Why? Because he knows that *sūnyatā*("空") is the very nature of phenomenal life and does not misunderstand this term as meaning absence of existence.

Therefore, a sūtra says, "Marvellous, World-honoured One! Unchanging Reality (*bhūtakoti,* 实相) is the realm where all dharma are assigned their places." Not outside of Reality are they placed. Where they are placed (in the world) that indeed is Reality. This being so, is *Tao* far away? This life of ours is Reality. Is the Sage far away? Recognize him as in truth he is, and you are the (cosmic) Spirit.

《般若无知论》Pan-Jo Wu-Chin Lun [1]

本篇着重论述了般若之体用，认为其体非有非无，虚不失照，用即寂，寂即用，并从无知与有知的角度对般若之性作了深入探讨。般若无知无相、无状无名，但其照用无所不知而曰一切知。真般若，清净如虚空，无知无见，无作无缘，亦

[1] 中文选自郭齐勇主编：《中国古典哲学名著选读》，北京：人民出版社，2005 年。

Pan-Jo Wu-Chin Lun，selected from *Chao Lun*(《肇论》)：*The Treatises of Seng-chao*, translated by Walter Liebenthal, Hong Kong：Hong Kong University Press, 1968.

无生无灭；而以所知性空、清净称美般若者，则依然不识般若之体。般若无明无说，超越有、无，既非“有”的存在亦非“无”的存在，体(虚)不舍其(照)，作用亦不离其本体；用即寂，寂即用，用寂一体，同出而异名。在体用、知与所知之辨的基础上，僧肇分析了般若与真谛之间的关系。般若是能知，五蕴是所知，所知的五蕴，乃缘起之物；但真谛无相，非所知，非缘起，故以般若观真谛，乃是一种直观、自觉，是对所知的了断。般若与真谛，言用即同而异，言寂即异而同。在《般若无知论》中，僧肇还着力区分了他所谓的真智与惑智。

[Introduction] The essay of *Pan-Jo Wu-Chin Lun* deals with the substance and the use of *Prajñã*. It is believed that its substance is neither existent nor non-existent; though void, it does not fail to shine; it is neither visible nor describable. Seng Zhao makes a deep discussion on the nature of *Prajñã* from the angle of uncognitive and cognitive cognition. *Prajñã* is without knowledge and phase, without shape and name, but its light is known by knowing everything. Though Prajñã, as the highest wisdom, is of no cognition, no reality, no shape and no name, it is a mirror which reflects no less than the Whole. True *Prajñã*, as pure as emptiness, is of no cognition, no sight, no action, no involvement, and no life or death. But he who is called *Prajñã* by the understanding of the empty spirit and original purity and blank essence is still ignorant of the substance of *Prajñã*. *Prajñã*, which is unenlightened and speechless, transcends being and non-being, neither existing as “being” nor as “non-being”; though void in its substance, it never gives up its enlightenment and its use is never separated from its nouma. Use is silence and silence is use, that is, use and silence are united as a whole, each of which comes out of one with different names. On the basis of the argument between the substance and the knowledge, the cognizable and the cognized, Seng Zhao analyzes the relationship between *Prajñã* and the truth. *Prajñã* cognizes and the five skandhas are what who cognizes. The five skandhas who know are derivated from the relationship of things. But Z*hen Di* (truth) does not manifests itself as phenomena, the cognized and anything arising from conditions (*pratitya-samutpanna*), and therefore, viewed from the perspective of *Prajñã*, *Zhen Di* (truth) is a kind of intuition, consciousness, and a break of knowledge. *Prajñã* and truth are the same with difference in terms of its use, and it is the difference with the same in terms of silence. In the Prajñã theory of ignorance (*Pan-Jo Wu-Chin Lun*), Seng Zhao has also sought to make a distinction between what he calls true wisdom and what he calls false wisdom.

夫般若虚玄者[般若(bō rě)：梵语音译，，是佛教所说的真智慧。]，盖是三乘之宗极也[三乘：三乘说法有多种，这里是指大乘之三乘。一声闻乘，又云小乘，速则三生，迟则六十劫间修空法，终于现世闻如来之声教，而悟四谛之理，以证阿罗汉者。二缘觉乘，又云中乘，辟支佛乘，速则四生，迟则百劫间修空法，于其最后之生不依如来之声教，感飞花落叶之外缘，而自觉十二因缘之理，以证辟支佛果者。三大乘，又云菩萨乘，三无数劫间修六度之行，更于百劫间植三十二相福因，以证无上菩提者，或以羊鹿牛三车譬之，或以象马兔三兽比之。是为大乘之三乘。]，诚真一之无差。然异端之论，纷然久矣。有天竺沙门鸠摩罗什者，少践大方[沙门：音译，有息心、静志，勤修佛道，勤修息烦恼之义。大方：大道。]，研几斯趣，独拔于言象之表，妙契于希夷之境，齐异学于迦夷[迦夷：地名，迦夷罗之略，佛之生国。]，扬淳风于东扇，将爰烛殊方而匿耀凉土者[爰：同援。殊方：异地，它国。凉土：西凉国。鸠摩罗什来后秦长安之前曾在西凉国姑臧居留十八年。]，所以道不虚应，应必有由矣[应：应缘而生，应缘而弘播。]。弘始三年，岁次星纪[弘始：后秦姚兴年号；三年，即公元 401 年。星纪：是指岁星处于丑位。弘始三年正当丑年，所以说“岁次星纪”。]，秦乘人国之谋，举师以来之。意也，北天之运数其然也[意：我想，我推测，我认为。北天之运，数其然也：中国古代以北斗星为天极，天人之象受斗星之运数支配，僧肇亦借用传统信仰来盛赞鸠摩罗什弘道 中华的佛事，甚合天意。]。大秦天王者，道契百王之端，德洽千载之下，游刃万机，弘道终日，信季俗苍生之所天，释迦遗法之所仗也。时乃集义学沙门五百余人于逍遥观[逍遥观：逍遥观是一所宫殿，在逍遥园中。后秦姚兴所建，供翻译佛教经典和授学之用。]，躬执秦文，与什公参定方等。其所开拓者，岂谓当时之益？乃累劫之津梁矣！余以短乏，会厕嘉会，以为上闻异要，始于时也[短乏：才疏学浅。会厕：有幸侧身于，有幸参与。上闻：与中闻、下闻相对，谓深契佛理也。时：此时。]。然则圣智幽微，深隐难测，无相无名，乃非言象之所得。为试罔象其怀[罔象：典出《庄子•天地》。“罔象”与“象”相对，指无用心于象，不执着于言象。]，寄之狂言耳，岂曰圣心而可辨哉？

Prajñã(“般若”), void and dark(“虚玄”), is, perchance, the far starting-point of the Three Vehicles(“三乘”). Being cosmic Reality, she is certainly not definable as something, yet attempts to define her as having always been numerous. The Indian *Sramana Kumārajīva*(天竺沙门鸠摩罗什) as a small boy ventured into the vast field of the *Mahāyāna*(“大乘”), desiring to get to the root of things. He alone could grasp (the essence) beyond the “words and symbols”, and mysteriously found himself on “the plane unaccessible to the senses”. He reconciled the divergent doctrines in *Kapilavastu*(迦夷); he fanned the pure breeze (of the Law) to the East. Willing to carry his candle further, he (was forced to) hide his light in the country of *Liang*(凉国). *Tao* (“道”) does not work without design; when it works there is a purpose. In the third year of *Hung-shih*(弘始三年), the cyclical sign of which was *hsingchi* (A.D. 401)(“岁次星纪”), the ruler of *Chin*(秦王) used (*Lü Lung*'s) readiness to surrender to send an army in order to bring (*Kumãrajīva*) to *Changan*). Thus a prophecy concerning the fate of the North came true. The Divine King of *Ta Ch'in*(大秦天王), he whose piety (*tao*) surpasses that of the Hundred Kings (of Antiquity), whose achievements (*te*) will make happy a thousand generations to come, skillfully attends to his thousand duties, spreading the *Tao* (Dharma) all the day. Surely he is to the people of the third period what Heaven is to creatures, the support of the Dharma left by *Sākyamuni*(释迦牟尼佛).

(After *Kumãrajīva*'s arrival in *Chang-an*) the King gathered more than five hundred students (of Buddhism) in the Hall of the *Hsiao-yao garden*(“逍遥观”) (where they attended to translation work). Personally interested in the Chinese version, he took part when the *Vaipulya sutras* (《方等经》) were being edited by *Kumãrajīva*(鸠摩罗什). The knowledge which, in this way, he made available, will be helpful not only to the present generation, but (will serve) as a ford and bridge (across the Ocean of Becoming) in *kalpas*(《仪轨经》) to come.

Though inexperienced and slow, I was admitted to this fortunate assembly and thus finally heard the message so new and important. Truly, the wisdom of the Sages is obscure and subtle, deeply concealed and difficult to plumb; shapeless and nameless, it cannot be expressed in words and symbols. Should I (behave like the Yellow Emperor who) employ “Ignorance” (to find the pearl after "Learning" had searched in vain) and in my inadequate language tell of it? How dare I say that the Mind of the Sage can be described? (Nevertheless) I shall try.

试论之曰：《放光》云："般若无所有相，无生灭相[《放光般若经》卷十四："佛言般若波罗蜜如虚空相，亦非相，亦不作相。"]。"《道行》云："般若无所知，无所见[《道行般若经》卷一："何所是菩萨般若波罗蜜，当何从说菩萨都不可得见，亦不可知处。"]。"此辨智照之用，而曰无相无知者，何耶？果有无相之知，不知之照，明矣。何者？夫有所知，则有所不知。以圣心无知，故无所不知。不知之知，乃曰一切知[“有所知”，指普通之知。普通之知总是有局限的，不能穷尽一切事物，所以“有所知，则有所不知”。圣人之知与普通之知不同，可以说是无知；但这种无知之知不受任何的局限，能知一切事物，所以又无所不知。“不知之知”是证悟本体所得到的圣知，叫做一切知。]。故《经》云："圣心无所知，无所不知[《思益梵天所问经》卷一："如来坐道场时，唯得虚妄颠倒所起烦恼，毕竟性空。以无所得，故得；以无所知，故知。"]。"信矣！是以圣人虚其心而实其照，终日知而未尝知也。故能默耀韬光，虚心玄鉴，闭智塞聪，而独觉冥冥者矣。然则智有穷幽之鉴，而无知焉；神有应会之用，而无虑焉。神无虑，故能独王于世表[世表：世外。]；智无知，故能玄照于事外。智虽事外，未始无事；神虽世表，终日域中[元康《肇论疏》："虽云圣智玄照事外，即色知空也，非谓离色有空也。虽云圣神自在于世间之表，非谓不化众生，终日在域中应化也。"]。所以俯仰顺化，应接无穷，无幽不察，而无照功。斯则无知之所知，圣神之所会也。然其为物也，实而不有，虚而不无，存而不可论者[《庄子•齐物论》："六合之外，圣人存而不论；六合之内，圣人论而不议。"]，其唯圣智乎！何者？欲言其有，无状无名；欲言其无，圣以之灵。圣以之灵，故虚不失照；无状无名，故照不失虚。照不失虚，故混而不渝；虚不失照，故动以接粗[粗：指外物、外境。]。是以圣知之用，未始暂废；求之形相，未暂可得。故《宝积》曰："以无心意而现行"[《宝积》：即《维摩诘经》。其卷一："始在佛树力降魔，得甘露灭觉成道，以无心意而现行。"]。《放光》云："不动等觉而建立诸法[《放光般若经》卷二十："凡夫声闻辟支佛于等正觉，亦复不动。"]。"所以圣迹万端，其致一而已矣。是以般若可虚而照，真谛可亡而知，万动可即而静，圣应可无而为。期则不知而自知，不为而自为矣。复何知哉？复何为哉？

The Fang-kuang（《放光》）says, " Prajñã is not a thing among things; it is not a thing which is born and dies." *The Tao-hsing*（《道行》）says, "There is nothing that *Prajñã* cognizes, nothing that she sees." These quotations describe the act of (Cosmic) Manifestation (*chao* /照) which is characteristic of (Cosmic) Cognition (*chih*/知). They say that (in this act) no things are perceived and no cognitive act is performed. What does this mean? Evidently, there exists a kind of cognition which is not (related to) an object, a vision which is not cognitive.

(In the following syllogism it is proved that such Cognition is possible.) Where things are cognized other things are not cognized.

As the Mind of the Sage（"圣心"）is free from things cognized, it is (also free from things not cognized). (Such) uncognitive cognition is called omniscience. Therefore, a *sūtra* say, "The Mind of the Sage cognizes nothing (and therefore) nothing is cognized (by him). " So it is. Therefore, the Sage, "his mind empty (of single events), his vision filled with the universe, " is always and yet never cognizant. He dims his radiance, covers his light, and yet, in a mind that is void, mirrors the invisible. He conceals his wisdom, hides his intelligence, and yet he alone is aware of what goes on beneath the surface (of things).

Prajñã and Shen:

(*Prajñã:*) (In the mirror of her mind) Prajñã reflects what is totally concealed (from our eyes), yet does so without cognition (of objects).

(*Shen*:) Responding (to our needs) the Spirit acts, yet his action is uninterested.

(*Shen*:) Sovereignly he rules the world regardless of what happens to us in the historical process.

(*Prajñã*:) Yet it is this life which she manifests.

(*Shen*:) Yet it is our life which he "unceasingly directs."

Therefore, whether he looks upward (to the supramundane) or downward (to the mundane sphere), the Sage remains in harmony with the cosmic changes and helps wherever he is needed. There is nothing so hidden that it is overlooked but this reflection is not purposive observation. This then is what is found in Cognition which does not cognize, in the Response called forth in the spirit of the Sage.

What kind of thing can (*Prajñã*) be?

Though full of things she does not exist (as a thing exists). Though void she does not non-exist (as a thing may non-exist). *Prajñã* is there and yet defies all qualifications. Such is the Vision of the Sage.

Cosmic life (*Prajñã*), how it exists?

Neither can its existence be asserted because it is nothing visible, nothing describable; Nor can its non-existence be asserted because the Sage manifests himself thereby. He manifests himself thereby. Though void it does not fail to shine. It is nothing visible, nothing describable. Though shining it remains void. As it is void, "the phenomenal chaos does not impair its stillness". As it shines it leads the blind (beings to their destinies). And that is the reason why the Sage never ceases to be active and why, nevertheless, an individual feature (in the field of his Vision) is never discovered. Therefore, Ratnakiita says, "Without conscious intention (a Bodhisattva) appears and acts." *The Fang-kuang* says, "Without moving (the Buddha), in sambodhi, assigns the dharma to their places." So the footprints of the Sage are a thousandfold, all leading to the same end.

That is why *Prajñã* (Truth), though sightless, still sees; why the True State, though not an object, is still seen; why the Thousand Changes (go on) and still all is calm; why the Sage does not act and still responds. So, here we are confronted with the cognition which needs no object to cognize, with action which has nothing on which to act. Now, what cognition, what action are they?

难曰：夫圣人真心独朗，物物斯照，应接无方，动与事会。物物斯照，故知无所遗；动与事会，故会不失机。会不失机，故必有会于可会；知无所遗，故必有知于可知。必有知于可知，故圣不虚知；必有会于可会，故圣不虚会。既知既会，而曰无知无会者，何耶？若夫忘知遗会者，则是圣人无私于知会，以成其私耳[《庄子•天道》：“夫兼爱，不迹迂乎！无私焉，乃私耳。”]。

斯可谓不自有其知，安得无知哉？

DISCUSSION OF THE SUBJECT

First Objection

OPPONENT: (You have said:) The mind of the Sage, (containing) the True State of Things, in its own lonely light, reflects every single thing. He leads them forsaking none, he moves with the changing situations.

ARGUMENT: If every single thing is reflected, there must be cognition (so perfect indeed that) no thing remains unnoticed. If he moves with the changing situations, no situation claiming his action is overlooked. If no situation is overlooked, there must be situations to which he responds. If no thing remains unnoticed, there must be cognizable things (in his mind). If there are cognizable things, the mind of the Sage cannot be free from objects. If there are situations to which he responds, his response is not without design.

Now, if the Sage cognizes and responds, what do you mean by denying him both qualities? (I shall try to answer this question on your behalf.) Saying that the Sage is free from cognition and response, you may mean: it is for no personal end that the Sage cognizes and responds. "So all his personal ends are fulfilled." Or, differently formulated: you may not maintain that he does not cognize but that he does not cognize for his own selfish reasons. Is that so?

答曰：夫圣人功高二仪而不仁[二仪：阴阳二仪。《易·系辞》：“一阴一阳之谓道。”]，明逾日月而弥昏，岂曰木石瞽其怀[瞽(gǔ)：眼睛瞎，这里是蒙塞的意思。]，其于无知而已哉？诚以异于人者神明，故不可以事相求之耳。子意欲令圣人不自有其知，而圣人未尝不有知。无乃乖于圣心，失于文旨者乎？何者？《经》云：“真般若者，清净如虚空，无知无见，无作无缘[《大品般若经》卷六：“说摩诃衍与空等，如虚空无见无闻，无觉无识。”]。”斯则知自无知矣，岂待返照然后无知哉[返照：返离照用。即前文“忘知遗会”之意。]？若有知性空而称净者，则不辨于惑智。三毒四倒皆亦清净[三毒：贪、嗔、痴。四倒：作者认为，人们对于佛教关于涅槃(常、乐、我、净)神秘境界抱有错误的态度，或以为这四种神秘境界不存在，或以为不具有这四种性质，称做“四倒”。]，有何独尊净于般若？若以所知美般若，所知非般若。所知自常净，故般若未尝净，亦无缘致净，叹于般若。然经云般若清净者，将无以般若体性真净，本无惑取之知。本无惑取之知，不可以知名哉？岂唯无知名无知，知自无知矣。是以圣人以无知之般若，照彼无相之真谛。真谛无兔马之遗，般若无不穷之鉴[昙无谶译《优婆塞戒经》卷一：“如恒河水，三兽俱渡，兔、马、香象。兔不至底，浮水而过；马或至底，或不至底；象 则尽底。恒河水即是十二因缘也。声闻渡时，犹如彼兔。缘觉渡时，犹如彼马。如来渡时，犹如香象。”又参见《大般涅槃经》。]。所以会而不差，当而无是，寂泊无知，而无不知者矣。

Answer: The Sage's bounties are spread over Heaven and Earth, though no sympathy is shown (in any individual case). His light, brighter than the sun and the moon, is all the darker for that. How could I say that he is blind like wood and stone, that he is simply lacking cognition? Surely, his divine intelligence is different from the human, so it cannot be found in the patterns of daily life.

You propose as a solution that "it is for no personal end" that the Sage cognizes, whereas cognition could not be denied to him. Your criticism shows that you misunderstand the nature of the Sage's mind, and also that you err about the meaning of the scriptures. For there is a sutra which says, "*Prajñã*, existing in truth, is pure like the empty space. There is nothing that she cognizes, perceives, by which she is provoked or stimulated. Such a cognition is in itself non-cognition. It need not to be terminated in order to be not."

You may object: Though (*Prajñã*) is cognizant, yet (in the *sutra*, *Prajñã*) is called pure, i.e. non-cognizant, because she is empty in herself. (If so, I answer: ）In this case (*Prajñã*) could not be distinguished from Illusion. (Everything is empty in itself.) Even the Three Poisons（"三毒"）and the Four Basic Errors（"四倒"）would be pure. What then is superior in *Prajñã*?

You may further object: (*Prajñã*) is to be praised on account of (the purity of her) contents (the True State of things).

If so, I answer: It is not possible to draw conclusions about *Prajñã* from the contents of (*Prajñã*). (These are two different things.) Even though (*Prajñã*'s) contents are absolutely pure, she need not therefore be pure. Thus the purity of her contents is no reason for praising *Prajfia*.

Conclusion: Where the Sūfra says: "*Prajñã* is pure" (and thereby denies cognition to her), that can only mean that *Prajñã* as cosmic (purity) is real and pure, and (therefore) is essentially free from ignorance perceiving (objects). That cognition free from perceiving (objects) cannot be called cognition (in the ordinary sense of the word). Thus, if (I said) "not cognizant", (I did not mean that) *Prajñã* is not cognizant (in the ordinary sense of the phrase) but that (*Prajfia*'s) cognition is in itself free from cognition.

That is why the Sage by means of *Prajñã* free from cognition reflects Truth which is free from contents. Truth is not like the hare and the horse which (are limited in size and therefore) fail (to reach to the depth of the stream like the elephant). *Prajñã* is a mirror which reflects no less than the whole. Therefore, (*Prajfia*) responds (to want) without erring (among those wanting). (*Prajfia*) is full (of things) though to her no (things) exists. Silent, withdrawn, (*Prajñã*) cognizes not and yet there is nothing that is not cognized by her.

夫物无以自通，故立名以通物。物虽非名，果有可名之物当于此名矣。是以即名求物，物不能隐。而论云圣心无知，又云无所不知。意谓无知未尝知，知未尝无知，斯则名教之所通，立言之本意也。然论者欲一于圣心，异于文旨，寻文求实，未见其当。何者？若知得于圣心，无知无所辨；若无知得于圣心，知亦无所辨。若二都无得，无所复论哉[问难者认为，知就是知，无知就是无知，如果说圣心有知，就不应该说无知；如果说圣心无知，就不应该说有知。如果二者都不恰当，无论怎么说也是多余的。]！

Second Objection

Opponent: Things cannot cause themselves to be found. Therefore, they are given names which lead to their finding. Though things are different from names, there certainly are things which are nameable and which agree with their names. That is the reason why things cannot hide whenever called by the right name. But you said that "the Mind of the Sage is not cognizant" and also that "there is nothing not cognized by him". Now, the first sentence means that "there is no cognition at all" and the second that "there is no absence of cognition at all".

(You must keep to your definitions.) This is a rule which we are taught by logic; it is the essential condition of all argument.

You want us (to believe that) the Mind of the Sage is one while you give us (two) contradictory descriptions of it. Those who expect to be led to the actual facts by your descriptions will look in vain for correspondence (between these two).

Why? If the "cognizant" qualifies the Mind of the Sage, the "non-cognizant" would not be (the proper word) for its definition and vice versa. If both (words) are unfit for this purpose, then there is no point in continuing our argument.

答曰：经云般若义者，无名无说，非有非无，非实非虚。虚不失照，照不失虚，斯则无名之法，故非言所能言也。言虽不能言，然非言无以传。是以圣人终日言，而未尝言也[《庄子•寓言》："言无言；终身言，未尝言；终身不言，未尝不言。"]。今试为子狂言辨之。夫圣心者，微妙无相，不可为有；用之弥勤，不可为无。不可为无，故圣智存焉；不可为有，故名教绝焉。是以言知不为知，欲以通其鉴[鉴：照用。]；不知非不知，欲以辨其相[相：体相。]。辨相不为无，通鉴不为有。非有，故知而无知；非无，故无知而知。是以知即无知，无知即知。无以言异，而异於圣心也。

Answer: A *sūtra* says: "*Prajñā* is unnameable, undefinable, not existent not non-existent, not real not unreal." Though void she does not fail to shine, though shining she remains void. (*Prajñā*) is a dharma which cannot be defined and is therefore unsuitable for use as a subject of argument. Yet speech is necessary if (my message) is to be handed down. And that is the reason why sages speak all the time without speaking. So I (too) shall discuss (*Prajñā*) for your benefit using words which are (inevitably) inadequate.

The mind of the sage: It fades into the transcendent (whenever we search for it): it cannot be assumed to exist; restlessly exhibiting (what it contains): it cannot be assumed not to exist. It cannot non-exist; it is a fact—the Vision of the Sage. It cannot exist; definitions fail to describe it. Therefore, the word cognition (as used here) does not imply cognition (in the ordinary sense); it is meant to confront (the reader with the problem of) its manifestation. Nor does the word non-cognition (as used here) imply non-cognition (in the ordinary sense); it is meant to hint at the contents of (that manifestation, which are not such as are ordinarily cognized). Still, contents are contents and not nothing though his manifestation is not a something. Thus, (the Vision of the Sage) not existent, though cognition, is not cognition, not non-existent, though not cognition, is cognition. Or else, in this case, cognition is just non-cognition and vice versa, and you are wrong to say that the two contradictory attributes imply a split in the Mind of the Sage.

难曰：夫真谛深玄，非智不测。圣智之能，在兹而显。故《经》云："不得般若，不见真谛[《大智度论》卷十八："解脱涅槃道，皆从般若得。"]。"真谛则般若之缘也[缘：指所缘虑的境。]。以缘求智，智则知矣[智：指般若。知：指普通之知。]。

Third Objection

Opponent: Truth is so deeply concealed that only in the Vision of the Sage is it discovered.

The power of his Vision is proved just by this fact (that he sees Truth). Therefore, a *sūtra* says: "Who has not obtained *Prajñā* cannot see Truth." So Truth is object of *Prajñā* and one may, from the existence of this object, infer that Cognition（"智"）is cognition（"知"）.

答曰：以缘求智，智非知也。何者？《放光》云："不缘色生识，是名不见色[《放光般若经》卷十一《问相品》："须菩提问佛，言：'世尊，云何不见五阴为世间导？''须菩提，不以五阴因缘起识者，是为不见五阴。'"五阴：即五蕴，色、受、想、行、识五法之名。元康《肇论疏》："五阴无相，故云清静；般若无知，故云清净也。"]。"又云："五阴清净，故般若清净。"般若即能知也，五阴即所知也。所知即缘也。夫知与所知，相与而有，相与而无。相与而无，故物莫之有，相与而有，故物莫之无。物莫之无，故为缘之所起；物莫之有，故则缘所不能生。缘所不能生，故照缘而非知；为缘之所起，故知缘相因而生。是以知与无知，生于所知矣[这句包含这样的意思：所知不同，而有知与无知之分。]。何者？夫智以知所知，取相故名知。真谛自无相，真智何由知？所以然者，夫所知非所知，所知生于知。所知既生知，知亦生所知。所知既相生，相生即缘法。缘法故非真，非真故非真谛也。故《中观》云："物从因缘有，故不真；不从因缘有，故即真[《中论》卷四《观四谛品》："众因缘生法，我说即是无，亦为是假名，亦是中道义。"]。"今真谛曰真，真则非缘。真非缘，故无物从缘而生也[这句是说，真谛非缘，因而世间无物能以真谛为缘而生起的。]。故《经》云："不见有法，无缘而生[见《般若经》。这句仍是论般若智与真诗的关系，真智不见有法，则真谛不由缘生。]。"是以真智观真谛，未尝取所知。智不取所知，此智何由知？然智非无知，但真谛非所知，故真智亦非知。而子欲以缘求智。故以智为知緣自非缘。于何而求知？

Answer: One may, from the existence of an object, infer that Cognition is not cognition（"以缘求智，智非知也"）. Why? *The Fangkuang*（《放光》）says, "If such consciousness(*vijñāna,* the intellectual function of consciousness) appears and it is unconditioned by *rūpa*(色), it is said not to perceive *rūpa.*" The same *sūtra* says, "(in the absolute aspect) the five skandha（"五阴"或"五蕴"）are pure (unconditioned). (Therefore) *Prajñā* is pure (unconditioned). " (*Demonstrandi causa*) let us assume that *Prajñā* cognizes and the five skandha is what who cognizes. Then, what she so cognizes would be an object.

(Proposition:) Cognition("能知") and the object cognized("所知") can (only) both exist together or both together not exist. If (both) do not exist, then there are no things; if (both) exist, then things exist and nothing else. (It follows that) where things exist and nothing else, whatever there is is of the conditioned kind; where no things exist, whatever there is is not of the conditioned kind. What cannot be brought about by conditions is "object" of (Cosmic) Manifestation and not object of a cognition; What is brought about by conditions is caused to arise by the cooperation of cognition and its object (*pratitya-samutpanna* /因缘).

Conclusion: Whether or not cognition arises depends on the kind of (object) cognized.

SECOND ARGUMENT

Now Cognition. Supposing that it cognized what is cognized and (in this way) acquired a distinct (impression of the object) (*laksanam prāpnoti*) it might be called cognition. Truth is by nature free from distinctive features (*laksanam*). What (impression) could True Cognition（"真知"）acquire (and be polluted) by in order to be cognitive? On the same reasoning we might say that objects are not (in themselves) objects; objects are produced by cognition. While an object produces a cognition, the cognition produces the object. So, the object arises in dependence (*pratītya-samutpanna*/因缘) and therefore it is a conditioned dharma (samskrta). As conditioned it is not a true (dharma). As such, it is not Truth (*paramārtha* /真谛). Therefore, it is said in the *Chung-kuan*(《中观》): "Because things arise from causes and conditions they are not true. What does not arise from causes and conditions is true". The very name (*paramārtha*) implies that Truth cannot be an object. Not being an object, it is not a "thing" of the kind which rise from (causes and) conditions. Therefore, it is said in a sutra: "A dharma which exists (*saddharma* /法) and has not arisen from conditions is not to be found."

Conclusion: True Cognition seeing Truth never perceives an object. On what reasoning could such a Cognition be called cognition? Still, Cognition does not imply absence of cognition. We simply deny that True Cognition is cognition because Truth is not an object (without asserting the opposite). You said that from the existence of an object (Truth) we may infer that Cognition is cognition. As in this case the object is not an object, on what will you base your inference?

难曰：论云不取者，为无知故不取？为知然后不取耶？若无知故不取，圣人则冥若夜游，不辨缁素之异耶？若知然后不取，知则异于不取矣[不取：指上文所说的"真智观真谛，未尝取所知。"问难者认为，如果说本来无知故不取，圣人就一无所知，和在黑夜中行走不分黑白的情形一样。如果说知然后不取，这就不是真的不取了。]。

Fourth Objection

(Opponent:) You have said, "*Prajñã* does not perceive objects." Do you mean that she does not cognize and therefore does not perceive, and that she cognizes but thereafter does not perceive? In the first case the Sage would be blind like a traveller in the night who cannot distinguish black from white; in the second case (the problem of) cognition and (that of) non-perception (must be considered) separately.

答曰：非无知故不取，又非知然后不取。知即不取，故能不取而知。

Answer: Both alternatives are wrong. Her cognition is identical with non-perception. Thus she is able not to perceive and yet to cognize.

难曰：论云不取者，诚以圣心不物于物，故无惑取也。无取则无是，无是则无当。谁当圣心，而云圣心无所不知耶？

Fifth Objection

Opponent (tries another explanation of) the sentence: (*Prajñã*) does not perceive (objects). Then you probably mean that the Mind of the Sage does not take things to be and therefore does not harbour the wrong idea (that things exist and are desirable). As (the Sage) does not harbour this wrong idea, (things) do not exist to him. If they do not exist (in his Mind), it cannot be (full of things). If so, what else fills the Mind of the Sage? Nevertheless you have said that there is nothing not cognized by the Sage.

答曰：然，无是无当者。夫无当则物无不当，无是则物无不是。物无不是，故是而无是；物无不当，故当而无当。故《经》云："尽见诸法，而无所见[《放光般若经》卷二："菩萨作是行般若波罗蜜，于诸法无所见。……一切诸法悉现。]。"

Answer: You are right to say that (things) do not exist to him, that (his Mind) cannot be (full of things). (I say:) Though (his Mind) is empty (of things), (all things) are (in his Mind); though (things) do not exist to him, (all things) exist to him. Though (all things) exist to him, existing they do not exist. Though (all things) are (in his Mind), (they are not there). Therefore, a *Sutra* says, "The Bodhi (菩提) sees all the dharma and yet no thing is seen."

难曰：圣心非不能是，诚以无是可是，虽无是可是，故当是于无是矣。是以经云真谛无相，故般若无知者，诚以般若无有有相之知。若以无相为无相，有何累于真谛耶？

Sixth Objection

(Opponent:) The Mind of the Sage cannot be completely free from things. It may be that there is no thing (occupying his mind) still what is not a thing might serve as a thing. The scriptures say, "Truth has no distinct features, so *Prajñã* does not cognize." This means that *Prajñã* cognizes nothing which has distinct features. If (now we would take it to mean that *Prajñã*) cognizes what has no distinct features, we need no longer worry about *Prajñã*.

答曰：圣人无无相也。何者？若以无相为无相，无相即为相。舍有而之无，譬犹逃峰而赴壑，俱不免于患矣[僧肇认为真谛的无相并不是一种独立的存在者，若如此则仍是一种有相，不免错误。]。是以至人处有而不有，居无而不无，虽不取于有无，然亦不舍于有无。所以和光尘劳[尘劳：犹烦恼。]，周旋五趣[五趣：又称五道，即地狱、饿鬼、畜生、人、天。]，寂然而往，泊尔而来，恬淡无为而无不为。

Answer: (The Mind of) the Sage is not what has no distinct features. If we interpret as you propose, then what has no distinct features would mean something that has (just that) distinct feature (of having no distinct feature). Rejecting the positive and turning to the negative instead, he would be behaving like one who, in order to avoid peaks, walks into the mountain-torrent. In either case he cannot avoid disaster. Therefore, the Cosmic Man ("至人") takes his stand on the positive without asserting it (one-sidedly) ("处有而不有"); he takes his stand on the negative also without asserting it (one-sidedly); though he does not hold on to either of them, he also does not let one go. Therefore, "adapting his brilliance to the dust of daily life" he wanders through the Five Planes of Existence ("周旋五趣"). Noiseless he goes, unnoticed he comes, not mingled in life and yet everywhere present.

难曰：圣心虽无知，然其应会之道不差。是以可应者应之，不可应者存之。然则圣心有时而生，有时而灭，可得然乎？

Seventh Objection

(Opponent:) You maintain that the Sage, though not cognizant, responding to (our needs), never discriminates. Therefore, when there is an occasion to respond he responds, when there is none he spares himself. His Mind is sometimes awake sometimes not. Is that the right way to put it?

答曰：生灭者，生灭心也。圣人无心，生灭焉起？然非无心，但是无心心耳。又，非不应，但是不应应耳。是以圣人应会之道，则信若四时之质；直以虚无为体，斯不可得而生，不可得而灭也。

Answer: Rise and decay are states of mind (citta/心). As the Sage has no mind, how can these states originate? Still, he has a Mind, though a Mind which is not a mind (filled with single facts). And he makes responses, though not responses which are responses (to single demands). Therefore, *the Way* (*Tao*) of the Sage, understanding (our needs) and responding to them, resembles the law (which makes) the four seasons (come and go). As there is no substantial core (in this process, such as might undergo changes) the *Way* of the Sage does not (like a thing) rise and decay.

难曰：圣智之无，惑智之无，俱无生灭，何以异之？

Eighth Objection

(Opponent:) Non-cognition of the Sage and non-cognition of ignorant people have this in common that they do not (like normal cognition) arise and decay. If so, how do you propose to discriminate between them? (Both are non-cognitions.)

答曰：圣智之无者，无知；惑智之无者，知无[这句是说圣智之无，乃是指圣智的本体虚寂，而本无所知也；惑智之无，乃是惑者有知，认为其知可无，非就般若的本体而言也。]。其无虽同，所以无者异也。何者？夫圣心虚静，无知可无，可曰无知，非谓知无。惑智有知，故有知可无，可谓知无，非曰无知也。无知即般若之无也，知无即真谛之无也[这句是说“无知”是般若的本性，“知无”则是般若之发用，直觉真谛之无也。惑者直接把“知无”等同于圣智自身，则是不正确的。]。是以般若之与真谛，言用即同而异，言寂即异而同。同故无心于彼此，异故不失于照功。是以辨同者同于异，辨异者异于同，斯则不可得而异，不可得而同也。何者？内有独鉴之明，外有万法之实。万法虽实，然非照不得。内外相与以成其照功，此则圣所不能同，用也。内虽照而无知，外虽实而无相，内外寂然，相与俱无，此则圣所不能异，寂也。是以《经》云“诸法不异”者[《般若波罗蜜经》卷二十二：“诸法无相，非一相，非异相。”]，岂曰续凫(fú)截鹤[《庄子•骈拇》：“凫胫虽短，续之则忧；鹤胫虽长，断之则悲。”]，夷岳盈壑，然后无异哉？诚以不异于异，故虽异而不异也。故《经》云：“甚奇世尊，于无异法中而说诸法异[《摩诃般若波罗蜜多经》卷二十三：“云何无异法中而分别说异相。”]。”又云：“般若与诸法，亦不一相，亦不异相[《摩诃般若波罗蜜多经》卷二十二：“诸法无相，非一相，非异相。”]。”信矣！

Answer: In the case of the Sage, non-cognition means absence of (normal) cognition (*wu-chih* /“无知”); in the case of ignorant people it means non-cognition of what is (true) (*chih-wu*)(“知无”). Though in both cases cognition is said to be not (*wu* / “无”) the reason why (this is said) is not the same. The Mind of the Sage is blank and tranquil. It contains no cognition (and therefore also none) which could be said to be not true. So I call it *wu-chih.* (Normal) cognition contains cognition which we might say is not (true). So I call it *chih-wu*（“知无”）. (The same might be expressed as follows:) *Wu-chih* refers to *Prajñã* not cognizant (of Illusion), *chih-wu* refers to Truth not cognized (by the ignorant).

PRAJÑÃ AND TURTH

(Their relation is describable only in two seemingly contradictory, depending on whether we regard the internal power of that relation as unfolded or as infolded.) If we regard it as unfolded, both (members) seem to separate though (actually) they remain in union. If we regard it as infolded, they seem to be in union though (actually) they remain separate. In the aspect of union, the Cosmic Mind contains no individual things. In the aspect of separation, (the cosmic contents) are fully displayed in the light (of the Cosmic Mind). Therefore, what we consider as single is double and what we consider as double is a two-sided unity. That, well understood, is neither single nor double.

(The relation regarded as unfolded) In the (cosmic) centre the Mirror shines. Nothing else is there. At the periphery the "ten thousand dharma" are (waiting). They are there (waiting to be called into being). Surely, this could never take place if (the Mirror) did not shine. Within (the light) and without (all things) co-operate and thereby produce (World) manifestation. Thus, dividing their union, the Sage manifests himself.

(The relation, regarded as infolded,) within (the Mirror,) radiates. But (in the light) no things are perceptible. Without (all things) are (waiting though) not (yet) individualized. Within and without (the cosmos) is calm. Co-operation has ceased. Thus, restoring the union, the Sage withdraws into silence. Therefore, a *Sūtra* says, "Dharma do not differ (from each other). Does it tell us to stretch the legs of the duck and cut short those of the crane? " to pull down the mountains and fill up the valleys in order to smooth out life? If only you can understand that the diverse is of the relative order, then it loses its diversity. Therefore, a *Sūtra* says, "Marvelous, World-honoured One, taking your stand in oneness you say that the dharma vary." It also says, "*Prajñã* and the dharma are neither one nor two." This we may believe.

难曰：论云言用则异，言寂则同，未详般若之内，则有用寂之异乎？

Ninth Objection

(Opponent:) You have said (of *Prajñã* and Truth) that "they separate in the active state, they unite in the passive state." Do you mean to say that *Prajñã* could be either in one or the other of two states?

答曰：用即寂，寂即用。用寂体一，同出而异名，更无无用之寂而主于用也。是以智弥昧，照逾明；神弥静，应逾动。岂曰明昧动静之异哉？故《成具》云：“不为而过为。”[《成具》：《成具光明定意经》。]《宝积》曰：“无心无识，无不觉知[《维摩经》卷上：“己无心意无受行，而悉摧伏诸外道。”受：

苦受、乐受、不苦不乐受。(说明：《肇论》三篇注释参阅了任继愈《汉唐佛教思想论集》和中华书局《中国哲学史教学资料汇编》(魏晋南北朝)等书。)]。”斯则穷神尽智，极象外之谈也。即之明文，圣心可知矣。

Answer: These states are two aspects of the same state; they do not occur in isolation. “Springing from one root they are given different names.” There is no passive state produced by inactivity of an active one. Thus, the more Cognition fades, the brighter shines the Light (of *Prajñã*); the calmer the Spirit becomes, the more vividly he moves. How can it be said that light and darkness, motion and rest, are different states (in *Prajñã*)? *The Cheng-chu*（《成具》）says, “(The Bodhisattva/菩萨) not acting, acts untiringly.” And *Ratnakuta*（《宝积》）says, “Neither mind nor consciousness are required (of the Buddha-mind) to be intuitively cognizant.” These words refer to the World-spirit and his perfect wisdom, to things utterly beyond our reach. Interpreting them in the spirit of the Middle Path one should know the Mind of the Sage.

“他主张佛性人人皆有，创顿悟成佛说，一方面使繁琐的佛教简易化，一方面使印度传入的佛教中国化。因此，他被视为禅宗的真正创始人，亦是真正的中国佛教的始祖。”

——毛泽东谈六祖慧能：见王凡东平著《我在不寻常年代的特别经历》，中共党史出版社，2006 年。

中国经典双语阅读

慧能《坛经》（选）

Unit 10

慧能《坛经》(选) Selected from Hui Neng's Altar Scriptures[1]

[思想指要]慧能(公元 638—公元 713 年)，一作惠能，俗姓卢，生于唐岭南东道新州(今广东新兴县)，接受黄梅东山寺禅宗五祖弘忍密传衣法南归，成为禅宗六祖。由慧能开创的南派禅宗强调“明心见性”“直指人心”“见性成佛”“担水劈柴，皆能悟道”，对中国佛教及佛教文化具有深远影响。禅宗由汉地佛教宗派之一，安史之乱后迅速发展成为东亚地区主要的宗教和文化力量。慧能是佛教中国化的完成者。他的思想，集中地体现在《坛经》一书中。

[Introduction] Huineng (638 A.D.—713 A.D.) was born in Xinzhou County of East Lingnan (now Xinxing County of Guangdong Province). He accepted the tantra given by Hong Ren, the fifth Patriach of Chan Budhism at Huangmei Dongshan Temple and then went back to the South of China. Huineng was a seminal figure in the history of Chinese Buddhism. He is called the "Sixth Patriarch" of the Chan or the meditation tradition, which is better known as "Zen" in Japan. After Huineng, the Sect of Chan had great development and evolution, and produced the so-called Five Schools and Seven Sects. The South Sect of the Chan Buddhism, initiated by Huineng, insists on the practice of "understanding the mind and seeing the insight of the nature, " "seeing the nature of one's mind directly, " "becoming a Buddha instantly, " and "attaining to one's enlightenment in carrying water and chopping wood." The practice of the Chan is a provincial Chinese version of Buddhism, but after An-Shi Rebellion it rapidly rose to become a major religious and cultural force throughout the East Asia. Huineng is the actual completer of the sinicization of Buddhism. His thoughts are intensively reflected in the book of *the Altar Scriptures*.

---

[1] 中文选自《中国古典哲学名著选读》，郭齐勇主编，北京：人民出版社，2005 年。

Prajñā，selected from *The Sixth Patriarch's Dharma Jewel Platform Sutra With the Commentary of Tripitaka Master Hua,* edited by Martin Verhoeven, Ph.D, University of Wisconsin and trans., by Buddhist Text Translation Society, Burlingame, California, 2001.

《般若品》Prajna

本篇所选《坛经》之《般若品》，是慧能应请在韶州大梵寺讲修行大般若波罗蜜(大智慧到彼岸)的记录整理稿。慧能认为修行大般若波罗蜜法门，须以心行，不在口念，口念心行，则心口相应，因为本性是佛，离性无别佛。修行，首先是心量广大，犹如虚空，但不执着空。而世人妙性本空，自性真空，一真一切真，无有一法可得。做到心无滞碍，去住自由。其次，不论何时何地，都能念念不愚，常行智慧，做到口念心行。所谓般若即是智慧心。最后能解离生灭，于一切法不取不舍，即是见性成佛道。慧能提出了凡夫即佛、烦恼即菩提的思想，特别强调一念之觉否与成佛的关系。随后慧能着重论述了“顿教”的内涵。第一，众生皆有般若之智，与大智人本无差别。第二修行有小根器与大根器之别，若识自性，不执外修，一悟即成佛。圣与愚、佛与众生的区别只在于一念之悟否，若悟，众生是佛，不悟，佛即众生。第三识自本心。若识本心，即本解脱，若得解脱，即是般若三昧。这就是所谓明心见性、顿悟成佛的南宗禅宗思想，它对前此的修行道路来说，是一场革命。

[Introduction] This essay is selected from *Prajñã* of *the Altar Scriptures*, which is a record of Huineng's teachings on Great Prajñã Parami (from Great Wisdom to the Other World) while he was invited by the Great Buddhist Temple of Shao County. Huineng believes that, to master the initial approach to practise the Great Prajñã Parami, one must act with his heart, not with his mouth; and speak both with his mouth and act with his heart; then your heart and your mouth correspond to each other, because the nature is Buddha and there is no difference between Buddha and the nature. In practice of Buddhism, first of all, one's mind must be vast and wide as emptiness, but it does not cling to emptiness. Huineng first proposes that “All Buddha-lands are ultimately the same as empty space. The wonderful nature of worldly people is originally empty. The true emptiness of the self-nature is also like this.” And “One truth is all truth”. To set your mind free from everything, you can go and come freely. Second, everywhere and at all times, while one thought comes after another thought, one should remain undeluded and practice wisdom constantly; when the mouth recites and the mind practices, then mind and mouth are in mutual accord. This is *Prajñã* which is also called the mind of wisdom. Finally, to free yourself from the trouble of birth and death, neither grasping nor rejecting all dharma, you are to see your own nature and realize the Buddha Way. At the same time, Huineng proposes that common people are Buddhas and affliction is Bodhi, especially emphasizing the relationship between a stroke of mindfulness and becoming Buddha. Then Huineng emphasizes the connotation of “Sudden Teaching”: first, all living beings have the wisdom of *Prajñã*, no different from that of people of great wisdom and superior faculties. Secondly, practice of

Prajñã is differentiated by the small root apparatus and the big root apparatus. If one knows his own nature and does not adhere to external practice, he will become Buddha once he understands it. The difference, between saints and fools, Buddhas and all common people, lies only in whether they are enlightened at one thought. If they are enlightened, all common people are Buddhas, and if they are not, Buddhas are all common people. The third is the recognition of your original mind: if you recognize your original mind, your original mind is originally liberated. If you reach the attainment of liberation, you will attain to the Prajñã Samadhi. This is the thought of the Chan which insists on seeing one's nature by the light of one's intelligence and attaining to buddhahood in the way of sudden enlightenment. The Chan, initiated by Huineng, was a revolution for the way of Buddhistic practice.

次日，韦使君请益[韦使君：韦璩，时任韶州刺史。请益：指之前受过传教，现在再问之前没有问完的问题。]。师升座，告大众曰：总净心念摩诃般若波罗蜜多[摩诃般若波罗蜜多：摩诃是大，般若是智慧，波罗蜜多是到彼岸，合起来意思是大智慧到彼岸。]。复云：善知识，菩提般若之智，世人本自有之，只缘心迷，不能自悟，须假大善知识，示导见性[示导：引导启发。见性：见佛性。佛性，觉体。]。当知愚人智人，佛性本无差别，只缘迷悟不同，所以有愚有智。吾今为说摩诃般若波罗蜜法，使汝等各得智慧，志心谛听[志心：专心。]，吾为汝说。善知识，世人终日口念般若，不识自性般若，犹如说食不饱[说食不饱：口头上说食物的名称，但不能充饥。]。口但说空，万劫不得见性[劫：意译是远大时节，指世界一成一毁的周期。]，终无有益。善知识，摩诃般若波罗蜜是梵语，此言大智慧到彼岸。此须心行，不在口念，口念心不行，如幻如化，如露如电。口念心行，则心口相应，本性是佛，离性无别佛。

Sutra: The following day, at the invitation of Magistrate Wei(韦使君), the Master took his seat and said to the great assembly, "All of you purify your minds and think about Maha Prajñã Paramita(摩诃般若波罗蜜多)." He then said, "Good Knowing Advisors, (“善知识”) the wisdom of Bodhi(“菩提”) and Prajna (“般若”) is originally possessed by worldly people themselves." It is only because their minds are confused that they are unable to enlighten themselves and must rely on a great Good Knowing Advisor who can lead them to see their Buddha-nature(“见性”). You should know that the Buddha-nature of stupid and wise people is basically not different. It is only because confusion and enlightenment are different that some are stupid and some are wise. I will now explain for you the *Maha Prajñã Paramita Dharma*(摩诃般若波罗蜜法) in order that each of you may become wise. Pay careful attention, and I will explain it to you. "Good Knowing Advisors, worldly people recite 'Prajñã' with their mouths all day long and yet do not recognize the Prajñã of their self-nature(“自性般若”). Just as talking about food will not make you full, so, too, if you only speak of emptiness you will not see your own nature in ten thousand ages. In the end you will not have obtained any benefit." "Good Knowing Advisors, Maha Prajñã Paramita is a *Sanskrit* (梵语) word which means 'great wisdom which has arrived at the other shore.' It must be practiced in the mind, and not just recited in words. When the mouth recites and the mind does not practice, it is like an illusion, a transformation, dew drops, or lightning. However, when the mouth recites and the mind practices, then mind and mouth are in mutual accord. One's own original nature is Buddha; apart from the nature there is no other Buddha."

何名摩诃？摩诃是大，心量广大，犹如虚空，无有边畔，亦无方圆大小，亦非青黄赤白，亦无上下长短，亦无瞋无喜[瞋：瞋恨，是三毒之一。]，无是无非，无善无恶，无有头尾。诸佛刹土[刹土：刹，梵语差多罗之略译，意思是土田，梵汉双举，故名刹土。]，尽同虚空。世人妙性本空，无有一法可得，自性真空，亦复如是。善知识，莫闻吾说空便即著空[著空：执著于空。]，第一莫著空，若空心静坐，即著无记空[无记：佛教从宗教道德性质的角度把事物分为三类，善性、恶性和无记性。无记性是不属于善或恶的中性。]。善知识，世界虚空，能含万物色像，日月星宿，山河大地，泉源溪涧，草木丛林，恶人善人，恶法善法，天堂地狱，一切大海，须弥诸山[须弥：须弥山，佛经中神话传说的山名，意译为妙高。]，总在空中，世人性空，亦复如是。善知识，自性能含万法是大，万法在诸人性中，若见一切人恶之与善尽皆不取不舍，亦不染著[染著：沾染执着。]，心如虚空，名之为大，故曰摩诃。善知识，迷人口说，智者心行。又有迷人，空心静坐，百无所思，自称为大，此一辈人，不可与语，为邪见故[为邪见故：因为他们心中邪见太多。]。

Sutra: "What is meant by *Maha*? *Maha* means 'great'. The capacity of the mind is vast and great like empty space, and has no boundaries. It is not square or round, great or small. Neither is it blue, yellow, red or white. It is not above or below, or long or short. It is without anger, without joy, without right, without wrong, without good, without evil, and it has no head or tail." All Buddha-lands are ultimately the same as empty space. The wonderful nature of worldly people is originally empty, and there is not a single dharma which can be obtained. The true emptiness of the self-nature is also like this. "Good Knowing Advisors, do not listen to my explanation of emptiness and then become attached to emptiness. The most important thing is to avoid becoming attached to emptiness. If you sit still with an empty mind you will become attached to undifferentiated emptiness."

Sutra: "Good Knowing Advisors, the emptiness of the universe is able to contain the forms and shapes of the ten thousand things: the sun, moon, and stars; the mountains, rivers, and the great earth; the fountains, springs, streams, torrents, grasses, trees, thickets, and forests; good and bad people, good and bad dharmas（'善法恶法'）, the heavens and the hells, all the great seas, Sumeru and all mountains（须弥诸山）—all are contained within emptiness. The emptiness of the nature of worldly men is also like this." "Good Knowing Advisors, the ability of one's own nature to contain the ten thousand dharmas（'万法'）is what is meant by 'great.' The myriad dharmas are within the nature of all people（'诸人性'）. If you regard all people, the bad as well as the good, without grasping or rejecting, without producing a defiling attachment, your mind will be like empty space. Therefore, it is said to be 'great Maha.' "

Sutra: "Good Knowing Advisors, the mouth of the confused person speaks, but the mind of the wise person practices. There are deluded men who sit still with empty minds, vainly thinking of nothing and declaring that to be something great. One should not speak with these people because of their deviant views."

善知识，心量[心量：佛教语。集起万有的精神现象的总称。]广大，遍周法界[遍周：周遍，指全部通达。法界：界是种类之意，凡属于法一类的叫法界。法界，有时指现象界的全体，有时又指现象界的本质。遍周法界：意思是普遍于现象界的一切事物。]，用即了了分明，应用便知一切，一切即一，一即一切，去来自由，心体无滞，即是般若。善知识，一切般若智，皆从自性而生，不从外入，莫错用意，名为真性自用。一真一切真，心量大事，不行小道，口莫终日说空，心中不修此行，恰似凡人，自称国王，终不可得，非吾弟子。

"Good Knowing Advisors, the capacity of the mind is vast and great, encompassing the Dharma realm. Its function is to understand clearly and distinctly. Its correct function is to know all. All is one; one is all. Coming and going freely, the mind's substance is unobstructed. That is *Prajñã*." "Good Knowing Advisors, all *Prajñã* wisdom is produced from one's own nature; it does not enter from the outside. Using the intellect correctly is called the natural function of one's true nature. One truth is all truth. The mind has the capacity for great things, and is not meant for practicing petty ways. Do not talk about emptiness with your mouth all day and in your mind fail to cultivate the conduct that you talk of. That would be like a common person calling himself the king of a country, which cannot be. People like that are not my disciples."

善知识，何名般若？般若者，唐言智慧也[唐言：唐，唐朝国号；唐言，即华语、汉语。]。一切处所，一切时中[时中：时间]，念念不愚，常行智慧，即是般若行。一念愚即般若绝，一念智即般若生。世人愚迷，不见般若，口说般若，心中常愚，常自言我修般若，念念说空，不识真空。般若无形相，智慧心即是，若作如是解，即名般若智。

Sutra: "Good Knowing Advisors, what is meant by '*Prajñã*?' *Prajñã* in our language means wisdom. Everywhere and at all times（'一切处所，一切时中'）, in thought after thought, remain undeluded and practice wisdom constantly; that is *Prajñã* conduct（'般若行'）. *Prajñã* is cut off by a single deluded thought. By one wise thought, *Prajñã* is produced. Worldly men, deluded and confused, do not see *Prajñã*. They speak of it with their mouths, but their minds are always deluded. They constantly say of themselves, 'I cultivate *Prajñã*!' and though they continually speak of emptiness, they are unaware of true emptiness. *Prajñã*, without form or mark, is just the wisdom mind. If thus explained, just this is *Prajñã* wisdom."

何名波罗蜜？此是西国语，唐言到彼岸，解义离生灭。著境生灭起[境：有情众生所认识且与其相对待的现象界。]，如水有波浪，即名为此岸；离境无生灭，如水常通流，即名为彼岸，故号波罗蜜。

Sutra: "What is meant by *Paramita*(波罗蜜)? It is a *Sanskrit*(梵语/西国语) word which in our language means 'arrived at the other shore,'（'彼岸'）and is explained as 'apart from production and extinction.' When one is attached to states of being, production and extinction arise like waves on water. That is what is meant by 'this shore.'（'此岸'）To be apart from states of being, with no production or extinction, is to be like freely flowing water. That is what is meant by 'the other shore.' Therefore, it is called '*Paramita*.' "

善知识，迷人口念，当念之时，有妄有非。念念若行，是名真性，悟此法者，是般若法；修此行者，是般若行。不修即凡，一念修行，自身等佛。善知识，凡夫即佛，烦恼即菩提。前念迷即凡夫，后念悟即佛；前念著境即烦恼，后念离境即菩提。善知识，摩诃般若波罗蜜最尊最上最第一，无住无往亦无来，三世[三世诸佛：指出现于三世之一切佛。三世指现在世、过去世、未来世。]诸佛从中出，当用大智慧打破五蕴烦恼尘劳[五蕴：蕴是积集的意思。指构成我们的存在以至周围环境的五种要素的集合。这五种要素是色(物质，人的形体)、受(感受作用)、想(想像，心中浮现的形象，或表象作用)、行(精神与物质现象的生起和变化活动，意志、意欲冲动)、识(精神作用的主体，或指识别作用，主要是意识)。尘劳：佛教徒指世俗事务的烦恼。《圆觉疏钞》：“尘是六尘，劳谓劳倦，由尘成劳，故云尘劳”。]，如此修行，定成佛道，变三毒为戒定慧[三毒：贪、嗔、痴。]。

Sutra: “Good Knowing Advisors, deluded people recite with their mouths, but while they recite they live in falsehood and in error. When there is practice in every thought, that is the true nature. You should understand this dharma, which is the *Prajñã* dharma; and cultivate this conduct, which is the *Prajñã* conduct. Not to cultivate is to be a common person, but in a single thought of cultivation, you are equal to the Buddhas.” “Good Knowing Advisors, common people are Buddhas and affliction is *Bodhi*(菩提). Past thoughts（‘前念’）deluded are the thoughts of a common person. Future thoughts（‘后念’）enlightened are the thoughts of a Buddha. Past thoughts attached to states of being are afflictions, and future thoughts separate from states of being are *Bodhi*.” “Good Knowing Advisors, *Maha Prajñã Paramita*(摩诃般若波罗蜜) is the most honored, the most supreme, the foremost. It does not stay; it does not come or go. All Buddhas of the three periods of time（‘三世诸佛’）emerge from it. You should use great wisdom to destroy affliction, defilement, and the five *skandhic* heaps（‘五蕴’）. With such cultivation as that you will certainly realize the Buddha Way（‘佛道’）, transforming the three poisons（‘三毒’）into morality, concentration, and wisdom（‘戒’ ‘定’ ‘慧’）.”

善知识，我此法门，从一般若生八万四千智慧。何以故？为世人有八万四千尘劳，若无尘劳，智慧常现，不离自性。悟此法者，即是无念，无忆无著，不起诳妄，用自真如性，以智慧观照。于一切法，不取不舍，即是见性成佛道。

Sutra: “Good Knowing Advisors, my Dharma-door produces 84,000 wisdoms from the one Prajñã. Why? Because worldly people have 84,000 kinds of defilement（‘尘劳’）. In the absence of defilement, wisdom is always present, since it is not separate from the self-nature（‘自性’）. Understand that this dharma is just no-thought（‘无念’）, no remembrance（‘无忆’）, non-attachment（‘无著’）, and the non-production of falsehood and error. Use your own true-suchness nature（‘用自真如性’）, and, by means of wisdom, contemplate and illuminate all dharmas without grasping or rejecting them. That is to see one’s own nature and realize the Buddha Way.”

善知识，若欲入甚深法界，及般若三昧者[三昧：梵语，又云“三摩地”、“三摩提”，有“正定”、“等持”等含义。这里是“甚深”、“究竟”的意思。]，须修般若行，持诵《金刚般若经》，即得见性，当知此经功德，无量无边，经中分明赞叹，莫能具说。此法门是最上乘，为大智人说，为上根人说。小根小智人闻，心生不信。何以故？醬如(譬如之误？)天龙下雨于阎浮提[阎浮提：新译“赡部洲”。佛教传说，以“须弥山”为中心，东、南、西、北分四大洲“东胜神洲”“南赡部洲”“西牛贺洲”“北俱卢洲”。“南赡部洲”，即我们所处的这个世界。]，城邑聚落，悉皆漂流，如漂草叶；若雨大海，不增不灭。若大乘人，若最上乘人，闻说《金刚经》，心开悟解，故知本性自有般若之智，自用智慧，常观照故，不假文字。譬如雨水，不从无有，元是龙能兴致，令一切众生，一切草木，有情无情，悉皆蒙润，百川众流，却入大海，合为一体，众生本性般若之智，亦复如是。

Sutra: "Good Knowing Advisors, if you wish to enter the extremely deep Dharma realm and the *Prajnasamadhi*(‘般若三昧’), you must cultivate the practice of *Prajñã*. Hold and recite *The Diamond Prajñã Sutra*(《金刚般若经》) and that way you will see your own nature. You should know that the merit and virtue of this *Sutra* is immeasurable, unbounded, and indescribable, as the *Sutra* text itself clearly states. This Dharma-door is the Superior Vehicle(‘最上乘’), taught for people of great wisdom and superior faculties(‘上根人’). When people of limited faculties and wisdom(‘小根小智’) hear it, their minds give rise to doubt. Why is that? Take for example the rain which the heavenly dragons shower on Jambudvipa(‘阎浮提’). Cities and villages drift about in the flood like thorns and leaves. But if the rain falls on the great sea, its waters neither increase nor decrease. If people of the Great Vehicle(‘大乘人’), the Most Superior Vehicle, hear *The Diamond Sutra*(《金刚经》), their minds open up, awaken, and understand. They then know that their original nature itself possesses the wisdom of Prajñã. Because they themselves use this wisdom constantly to contemplate and illuminate, they do not rely on written words. Take for example the rain water. It does not come from the sky. The truth is that the dragons cause it to fall in order that all living beings, all plants and trees, all those with feeling and those without feeling may receive its moisture. In a hundred streams it flows into the great sea and there unites in one substance. The wisdom of the *Prajñã* of the original nature of living beings acts the same way."

善知识，小根之人闻此顿教[顿教：顿，顿悟，与渐修相对。]，犹如草木，根性小者，若被大雨，悉皆自倒，不能增长，小根之人，亦复如是。元有般若之智，与大智人更无差别，因何闻法不自开悟？缘邪见障重，烦恼根深。犹如大云覆盖于日，不得风吹，日光不现。般若之智亦无大小，为一切众生自心迷悟不同，迷心外见，修行觅佛，未悟自性，即是小根。若开悟顿教，不执外修，但于自心常起正见，烦恼尘劳，常不能染，即是见性。善知识，内外不住，去来自由，能除执心，通达无碍，能修此行，与《般若经》本无差别[《般若经》：即《般若波罗蜜经》。《般若经》说“空”，慧能说“有”(佛性)。]。

Sutra: "Good Knowing Advisors, when people of limited faculties hear this Sudden Teaching(‘顿教’), they are like the plants and trees with shallow roots which, washed away by the great rain, are unable to grow. But at the same time, the *Prajñã* wisdom which people of limited faculties possess is fundamentally no different from the *Prajñã* that men of great wisdom possess. Hearing this Dharma, why do they not become enlightened? It is because the obstacle of their deviant views is a formidable one and the root of their afflictions is deep. It is like when thick clouds cover the sun: if the wind does not blow, the sunlight will not be visible. *Prajñã* wisdom is itself neither great nor small. Living beings differ because their own minds are either confused or enlightened. Those of confused mind look outwardly to cultivate in search of the Buddha. Not having awakened to their self-nature yet, they have small roots. When you become enlightened to the Sudden Teaching（‘若开悟顿教’）, you do not grasp onto the cultivation of external things. When your own mind constantly gives rise to right views, afflictions and defilement can never stain you. That is what is meant by seeing your own nature（‘见性’）.” “Good Knowing Advisors, the ability to cultivate the conduct of not dwelling inwardly or outwardly, of coming and going freely（‘通达无碍’）, of casting away the grasping mind, and of unobstructed penetration, is basically no different from *The Prajñã Sutra*（《般若经》）.”

善知识，一切修多罗及诸文字[修多罗：梵文音译。佛教经典按内容分为经、律、论三藏，修多罗即经。]，大小二乘，十二部经[十二部经：按体裁指契经、重颂、讽颂、因缘、本事、本生、阿毗达摩、譬喻、论议、自说、方广、授记等。一般指佛经的全部著作的意思]，皆因人置[由于人的需要而施设。]，因智慧性，方能建立，若无世人，一切万法本自不有，故知万法本自人兴。一切经书，因人说有，缘其人中有愚有智，愚为小人，智为大人。愚者问于智人，智者与愚人说法，愚人忽然悟解心开，即与智人无别。

Sutra: “Good Knowing Advisors, all *Sutras* and writings of the Great and Small Vehicles（‘大小二乘’）, the twelve divisions of *Sutras*, have been devised because of people and established because of the nature of wisdom. If there were no people the ten thousand dharmas would not exist. Therefore, you should know that all dharmas are originally postulated because of people, and all *Sutras* are spoken for their sakes.” “Some people are deluded and some are wise; the deluded are small people（‘愚为小人’）and the wise are great people（‘智为大人’）. The deluded question the wise and the wise teach Dharma to the deluded. When the deluded people suddenly awaken and understand, their minds open to enlightenment and they are no longer different from the wise.”

善知识，不悟即佛是众生，一念悟时，众生是佛。故知万法尽在自心，何不从自心中，顿见真如本性[真如：佛教语。指永恒存在的实体、实性。亦即宇宙万有的本体。]。《菩萨戒经》云[《菩萨戒经》：姚秦的鸠摩罗什曾译出《梵网经·卢遮那佛说菩萨心地戒品》第十，後来别录为一卷，以便持诵，台祖智者名之为《菩萨戒经》。]：“我本元自性清净，若识自心见性，皆成佛道。”《净名经》云：“即时豁然，还得本心[《净名经》：即《维摩经》。此语见《维摩经·弟子品》第三。]”。

“Good Knowing Advisors, unenlightened, the Buddha is a living being. At the time of a single enlightened thought, the living being is a Buddha. Therefore, you should know that the ten thousand dharmas exist totally within your own mind. Why don’t you, from within your own mind, suddenly see the true suchness of your original nature（‘顿见真如本性’）?” *The Bodhisattva-shila Sutra*（《菩萨戒经》）says, “Our fundamental self-nature is clear and pure.” If we recognize our own mind and see the nature, we shall all perfect the Buddha Way. *The Vimalakirti Nirdesha Sutra*（《净名经》）says, “Just then, suddenly regain your original mind.”

善知识，我于忍和尚处[忍和尚：指禅宗五祖弘忍大师。湖北黄梅人，开东山法门，门下弟子有神秀、慧能等人。一说禅宗真正的创始人是弘忍。]，一闻言下便悟，顿见真如本性。是以将此教法流行，令学道者顿悟菩提，各自观心，自见本性。若自不悟，须觅大善知识，解最上乘法者，直示正路，是善知识有大因缘，所谓化导令得见性。一切善法，因善知识能发起故。三世诸佛、十二部经，在人性中本自具有。不能自悟，须求善知识，指示方见；若自悟者，不假外求，若一向执谓须他善知识望得解脱者，无有是处。何以故？自心内有知识自悟。若起邪迷，妄念颠倒，外善知识虽有教授，救不可得。若起正真般若观照，一刹那间，妄念俱灭；若识自性，一悟即至佛地。

"Good Knowing Advisors, when I was with the High Master Jen(忍和尚), I was enlightened as soon as I heard his words, and suddenly saw the true suchness of my own original nature（'一闻言下便悟'）. That is why I am spreading this method of teaching which leads students of the Way to become enlightened suddenly to Bodhi as each contemplates his own mind and sees his own original nature." "If you are unable to enlighten yourself, you must seek out a great Good Knowing Advisor, one who understands the Dharma of the Most Superior Vehicle and who will direct you to the right road." "Such a Good Knowing Advisor possesses great karmic conditions, which is to say that he will transform you and guide you and lead you to see your nature. It is because of the Good Knowing Advisor that all wholesome Dharmas can arise. All the Buddhas of the three periods of time（'三世诸佛'）, and the twelve divisions of *Sutra* texts as well（'十二部经'）, exist within the nature of people, originally complete within them. If you are unable to enlighten yourself, you should seek out the instruction of a Good Knowing Advisor who will lead you to see your nature." "If you are one who enlightens himself, you need not seek a teacher outside（'不假外求'）. If you insist that it is necessary to seek a Good Knowing Advisor in the hope of obtaining liberation, you are mistaken. Why? Within your own mind there is self-enlightenment which is a Knowing Advisor. "But if you give rise to deviant confusion, false thoughts, and perversions, although a Good Knowing Advisor external to you instructs you, he cannot save you." "If you give rise to genuine *Prajñã* contemplation and illumination（'般若观照'）, in the space of an instant all false thoughts are extinguished. If you recognize your self-nature, in a single moment of enlightenment you will arrive at the stage of a Buddha."

善知识，智慧观照，内外明彻，识自本心。若识本心，即本解脱，若得解脱，即是般若三昧。般若三昧，即是无念。何名无念？知见一切法，心不染著，是为无念。用即遍一切处，亦不著一切处，但净本心，使六识出六门，于六尘中无染无杂[六识，即眼、耳、鼻、舌、身、意六识。又称"六贼"。六门：即眼、耳、鼻、舌、身、意六根。"六识"从"六门"走出，故称为"门"。六尘：即色、声、香、味、触、法。以能"染污""本性"，所以称为"尘"。]，来去自由，通用无滞，即是般若三昧[三昧：佛教语。梵文音译。又译"三摩地"。意译为"正定"。指屏除杂念，心不散乱，专注一境。]，自在解脱，名无念行。若百物不思，当令念绝，即是法缚，即名边见[边见：五见之一，指片面极端的错误见解。]。善知识，悟无念法者，万法尽通；悟无念法者，见诸佛境界；悟无念法者，至佛地位。

Sutra: "Good Knowing Advisors, when you contemplate and illuminate with the wisdom which brightly penetrates within and without, you recognize your original mind. 'The recognition of your original mind（'若识本心'）is the original liberation. The attainment of liberation is the *Prajñā Samadhi*（'般若三昧'）, is no-thought（'无念'）.' What is meant by 'no-thought?' No-thought means to view all dharmas（'一切法/万法'）with a mind undefiled by attachment. The function pervades all places but is nowhere attached. Merely purify your original mind and cause the six consciousnesses to go out of the six gates, to be undefiled and unmixed among the six objects, to come and go freely and to penetrate without obstruction. That is the *Prajñā Samadhi* and freedom and liberation, and it is called the practice of 'no-thought.' 'Not thinking of the hundred things and constantly causing your thought to be cut off is called Dharma bondage and is an extremist view.' " "Good Knowing Advisors, one who awakens to the no-thought dharma completely penetrates the ten thousand dharmas; one who awakens to the no-thought dharma sees all Buddha realms; one who awakens to the no-thought dharma arrives at the Buddha position."

善知识，后代得吾法者，将此顿教法门，于同见同行，发愿受持[发愿：许发誓愿。"受持：佛教语。指领受在心，持久不忘。]，如事佛故，终身而不退者，定入圣位。然须传授从上以来默传分付，不得匿其正法；若不同见同行，在别法中，不得传付，损彼前人，究竟无益。恐愚人不解，谤此法门，百劫千生，断佛种性。善知识，吾有一无相颂，各须诵取，在家出家，但依此修。若不自修，惟记吾言，亦无有益。听吾颂曰：

Sutra: "Good Knowing Advisors, those of future generations who obtain my Dharma should take up this Sudden Teaching Dharma door（'顿教法门'）and with those of like views and like practice they should vow to receive and uphold it as if serving the Buddhas. To the end of their lives they should not retreat, and they will certainly enter the holy position. In this way it should be transmitted from generation to generation. It is silently transmitted. Do not hide away the orthodox Dharma（'正法'）and do not transmit it to those of different views and different practice who believe in other teachings, since it will harm them and ultimately be of no benefit." "I fear that deluded people may misunderstand and slander this Dharma-door（'法门'）, and will cut off their nature which possesses the seed of Buddhahood（'佛性'）for hundreds of ages and thousands of lifetimes." Good Knowing Advisors, I have a verse of no-mark which you should all recite. Those at home and those who have left home（"在家出家"）should cultivate according to it. If you do not cultivate it, memorizing it will be of no use. Listen to my verse:

说通及心通，如日处虚空；唯传见性法，出世破邪宗。
法即无顿渐，迷悟有迟疾；只此见性门，愚人不可悉。
说即虽万般，合理还归一；烦恼暗宅中，常须生慧日。
邪来烦恼至，正来烦恼除；邪正俱不用，清净至无余。
菩提本自性，起心即是妄；净心在妄中，但正无三障。

世人若修道，一切尽不妨；常自见己过，与道即相当。
色类自有道，各不相妨恼；离道别觅道，终身不见道。
波波度一生，到头还自懊；欲得见真道，行正即是道。
自若无道心，暗行不见道；若真修道人，不见世间过。
若见他人非，自非却是左；他非我不非，我非自有过。
但自却非心，打除烦恼破；憎爱不关心，长伸两脚卧。
欲拟化他人，自须有方便；勿令彼有疑，即是自性现。
佛法在世间，不离世间觉；离世觅菩提，恰如求兔角。
正见名出世，邪见名世间；邪正尽打却，菩提性宛然。
此颂是顿教，亦名大法船；迷闻经累劫，悟则刹那间。

With speech and mind both understood,
Like the sun whose place is in space,
Just spread the 'seeing-the-nature way'
Appear in the world to destroy false doctrines.

Dharma is neither sudden nor gradual,
Delusion and awakening are slow and quick,
But deluded people cannot comprehend
This Dharma-door of seeing-the-nature.

Although it is said in ten thousand ways,
United, the principles return to one;
In the dark dwelling of defilements,
Always produce the sunlight of wisdom.

The deviant comes and affliction arrives,
The right comes and affliction goes.
The false and true are both cast aside,
In clear purity the state of no residue is attained.

Bodhi is the original self-nature,
Giving rise to a thought is wrong.
The pure mind is within the false,
Only the right is without the three obstructions.

If people in the world practice the Way,
They are not hindered by anything.
By constantly seeing their own transgressions,
They are in accord with the Way.

Each kind of form has its own way

Without hindering one another;
Leaving the Way to seek another way
To the end of life is not to see the Way.

A frantic passage through a life,
Will bring regret when it comes to its end.
Should you wish for a vision of the true Way,
Right practice is the Way.

If you don't have a mind for the Way,
You walk in darkness blind to the Way;
If you truly walk the Way,
You are blind to the faults of the world.

If you attend to others' faults,
Your fault-finding itself is wrong;
Others' faults I do not treat as wrong;
My faults are my own transgressions.

Simply cast out the mind that finds fault,
Once cast away, troubles are gone;
When hate and love don't block the mind,
Stretch out both legs and then lie down.

If you hope and intend to transform others,
You must perfect expedient means.
Don't cause them to have doubts,
And then their self-nature will appear.

The Buddhadharma is here in the world;
Enlightenment is not apart from the world.
To search for Bodhi apart from the world
Is like looking for a hare with horns.

Right views are transcendental;
Deviant views are all mundane.
Deviant and right completely destroyed:
The Bodhi nature appears spontaneously.

This verse is the Sudden Teaching,
Also called the great Dharma boat.
Hear in confusion, pass through ages,
In an instant's space, enlightenment.

师复曰：今于大梵寺说此顿教[大梵寺：在韶州，慧能生前宣讲《坛经》主要内容的场所。]，普愿法界众生言下见法成佛。时韦使君与官僚道俗，闻师所说，无不省悟，一时作礼，皆叹善哉！何期岭南有佛出世！

Sutra: The Master said further, "In the Ta-Fan Temple(大梵寺) I have just now spoken the Sudden Teaching(‘顿教’), making the universal vow that all living beings of the Dharma-realm(‘法界众生’) will see their nature and realize Buddhahood as they hear these words." Then among Magistrate Wei and the officials, Taoists and lay people who heard what the Master said, there were none who did not awaken. Together they made obeisance and exclaimed with delight, "Good indeed! Who would have thought that in Lingnan a Buddha would appear in the world?"

《定慧品》(选) Selected from *Concentration and Wisdom* [1]

本篇阐明禅学以定慧为本，“定慧一体”的思想，其特点是以无念为宗，无相为本，强调真如本性恒常自在的一面。定是慧体，慧是定用，二者是一不是二，即慧之时定在慧，即定之时慧在定。无念、无相，强调的是不要执着外物、外境的一面，离境物、离念相才能自识本心本性。关于念与真如的关系，本篇认为真如本性为体，念为真如之用。真如自性起念，故恒常自在。

[Introduction] This article, selected from *Concentration and Wisdom*, illustrates the idea that Zen Buddhism takes concentration and wisdom as its foundation and that "concentration and wisdom are two in one", which is characterized by no-thought as its doctrine, no-mark as its substance, and no-dwelling as its basis, emphasizing the aspect of the True Suchness Self-Nature. Concentration (“定”)is the substance of wisdom and wisdom(“慧”)is the instrument of the substance. They are one, but not two. They are two, but in one. "Where there is wisdom, concentration is in the wisdom. Where there is concentration, wisdom is in the concentration." To say no-thought and no-mark, it means that one should not cling to something outside. Only by freeing oneself out of the worldly things can one realize his true nature. As for the relationship between the thought and the true suchness, this article holds that the nature of the true suchness is the substance and that the thought is the use of the true suchness. The True Suchness Self-Nature gives rise to thought, therefore, your true nature is eternally independent.

师示众云：善知识，我此法门，以定慧为本，大众勿迷。言定慧别，定慧一体，不是二。定是慧体，慧是定用[智慧是禅定的作用。]，即慧之时定在慧，即定之时慧在定，若识此义，

[1] 中文选自郭齐勇主编：《中国古典哲学名著选读》，北京：人民出版社，2005 年。
Concentration and Wisdom(*IV*), selected from *The Sixth Patriarch's Dharma Jewel Platform Sutra with the Commentary of Tripitaka Master Hua*, edited by Martin Verhoeven, Ph.D, University of Wisconsin and trans. by Buddhist Text Translation Society, Burlingame, California, 2001.

即是定慧等学[等：等同，相合不二。]。诸学道人，莫言先定发慧，先慧发定，各别，作此见者，法有二相。口说善语，心中不善，空有定慧，定慧不等。若心口俱善，内外一如，定慧即等。自悟修行，不在于诤[诤，同“争”，争论]，若诤先后，即同迷人。不断胜负，却增我法，不离四相[四相：相，形相。所谓“四相”，说有多种，这里的“四相”当指：一、异、非一非异、亦一亦异；或者是我、人、众生、寿者。佛教认为“凡所有相，皆是虚妄”，应远离“四相”。]。善知识，定慧犹如何等[等：类。]？犹如灯光，有灯即光，无灯即暗，灯是光之体，光是灯之用，名虽有二，体本同一。此定慧法，亦复如是。

Sutra: The Master instructed the assembly: “Good Knowing Advisors, this Dharma-door（‘法门’）of mine has concentration（‘定’）and wisdom（‘慧’）as its foundation. Great assembly, do not be confused and say that concentration and wisdom are different. Concentration and wisdom are one substance, not two. Concentration is the substance of wisdom, and wisdom is the function of concentration. Where there is wisdom, concentration is in the wisdom. Where there is concentration, wisdom is in the concentration. If you understand this principle, you understand the balanced study of concentration and wisdom.” “Students of the Way（‘诸学道人’）, do not say that first there is concentration, which produces wisdom, or that first there is wisdom, which produces concentration, do not say that the two are different.” To hold this view implies a duality of dharma（‘法有二相’）. If your speech is good, but your mind is not, then concentration and wisdom are useless because they are not equal. If mind and speech are both good, the inner and outer are alike（‘内外一如’）, and concentration and wisdom are equal. “Self-enlightenment, cultivation, and practice are not a matter for debate. If you debate which comes first, then you are like a confused man who does not cut off ideas of victory and defeat, but magnifies the notion of self and dharmas, and does not disassociate himself from the four marks（‘四相’）.” “Good Knowing Advisors, what are concentration and wisdom like? They are like a lamp and its light. With the lamp, there is light. Without the lamp, there is darkness. The lamp is the substance of the light and the light is the function of the lamp. Although there are two names, there is one fundamental substance. The dharma of concentration and wisdom is also thus.”

师示众云：善知识，一行三昧者[一行三昧：传统的解释是说专于一行，修习正定。慧能的解释不同，注意分别。]，于一切处行住坐卧，常行一直心是也[直心：真心，真如，佛性。]。《净名经》云：“直心是道场，直心是净土[《净名经》：即《维摩经》。]”。莫心行谄曲，口但说直。口说一行三昧，不行直心。但行直心，于一切法勿有执著。迷人著法相，执一行三昧，直言常坐不动，妄不起心，即是一行三昧。作此解者，即同无情，却是障道因缘[因缘：佛教语。佛教谓使事物生起、变化和坏灭的主要条件为因，辅助条件为缘。]。善知识，道须通流，何以却滞？心不住法，道即通流。心若住法，名为自缚。若言常坐不动是，只如舍利弗，宴坐林中，却被维摩诘诃[《维摩经·弟子品第三》：“尔时长者维摩诘自念寝疾于床，世尊大大慈，宁不垂愍？佛知其意，即告舍利弗：‘汝行诣维摩诘问疾。’舍利弗问佛言：‘世尊！我不堪诣彼问疾。所以者何？忆念我昔曾于林中宴坐树下，时维摩诘来谓我言唯！舍利弗，不必是坐为宴坐也。夫宴坐者，不于三界现身意，是为宴坐。若能如是坐者，佛所印可、时我、世尊，闻说是语，默然而止，不能加报。故我不往诣彼问疾。’”]。善知识，又有人教坐，看心观静，不动不起，从此置功，迷人不会，便执成颠。如此者众，如是相教，故知大错。

Sutra: The Master instructed the assembly: “Good Knowing Advisors, the Single Conduct Samadhi(‘一行三昧者’) is the constant practice of maintaining a direct, straightforward mind in all places, whether one is walking, standing, sitting, or lying down. As the *Vimalakirti Sutra* (《净名经》) says, ‘The straight mind is the Bodhimandala(‘道场’); the straight mind is the Pure Land(‘净土’).’ Do not speak of straightness with the mouth only, while the mind and practice are crooked, nor speak of the Single Conduct Samadhi(‘三昧’) without maintaining a straight mind. Simply practice keeping a straight mind and have no attachment to any dharma.” “The confused person is attached to the marks of dharmas, while holding to the Single Conduct Samadhi and saying, ‘I sit unmoving and falseness does not arise in my mind. That is the Single Conduct Samadhi.’ Such an interpretation serves to make him insensate and obstructs the causes and conditions for attaining the Way.” “Good Knowing Advisors, the Way must penetrate and flow. How can it be impeded? If the mind does not dwell in dharmas, the Way will penetrate and flow. The mind that dwells in dharmas is in self-bondage. To say that sitting unmoving is correct is to be like Shariputra(舍利弗) who sat quietly in the forest but was scolded by *Vimalakirti*(维摩诘).” “Good Knowing Advisors, there are those who teach people to sit looking at the mind and contemplating stillness, without moving or arising. They claim that it has merit. Confused men, not understanding, easily become attached and go insane. There are many such people. Therefore, you should know that teaching of this kind is a great error.”

师示众云：善知识，本来正教，无有顿渐。人性自有利钝，迷人渐修，悟人顿契，自识本心，自见本性，即无差别，所以立顿渐之假名。善知识，我此法门，从上以来，先立无念为宗，无相为体，无住为本。无相者，于相而离相[离：远离，不计较、不执著的意思。相：事相。]；无念者，于念而无念[于念无念：于体念“真如本性”的正念上，远离杂念、妄念。]；无住者，人之本性，于世间善恶好丑，乃至冤之与亲，言语触刺欺争之时，并将为空，不思酬害[酬：回报。]，念念之中，不思前境。若前念今念后念，念念相续不断，名为系缚。于诸法上，念念不住，即无缚也。此是以无住为本。善知识，外离一切相，名为无相。能离于相，则法体清净，此是以无相为体。善知识，于诸境上，心不染，曰无念。于自念上，常离诸境，不于境上生心。若只百物不思，念尽除却，一念绝即死，别处受生，是为大错。学道者思之，若不识法意，自错犹可，更劝他人，自迷不见，又谤佛经，所以立无念为宗。善知识，云何立无念为宗？只缘口说见性，迷人于境上有念，念上便起邪见，一切尘劳妄想[尘劳：犹烦恼。尘，谓情尘、尘垢；“劳”，谓劳累、烦扰。]，从此而生。自性本无一法可得，若有所得，妄说祸福，即是尘劳邪见，故此法门立无念为宗。善知识，无者无何事，念者念何物？无者无二相无诸尘劳之心；念者念真如本性，真如即是念之体，念即是真如之用。真如自性起念，非眼耳鼻舌能念，真如有性，所以起念，真如若无，眼耳色声当时即坏。善知识，真如自性起念，六根虽有见闻觉知，不染万境，而真性常自在，故《经》云：“能善分别诸法相，于第一义而不动[二相：生灭、有无、空有、人我、是非、染净、内外等等。二相必将障蔽“真如本性”，故称这种烦恼妄见为“尘劳”。]”。

Sutra: The Master instructed the assembly: “Good Knowing Advisors, the right teaching is basically without a division into ‘sudden’(‘顿’)and ‘gradual’(‘渐’).People’s natures themselves are sharp（‘利’）or dull（‘顿’）. When the confused person（‘迷人’）who gradually cultivates and the enlightened person（‘悟人’）who suddenly connects each recognize the original mind（‘本心’）and see the original nature（‘本性’）, they are no different. Therefore, the terms sudden and gradual are shown to be false names.” “Good Knowing Advisors, this Dharma-door of mine, from the past onwards, has been established from the first with no-thought as its doctrine, no-mark（‘无相’）as its substance, and no-dwelling as its basis. No-mark means to be apart from marks while in the midst of marks. No thought means to be without thought while in the midst of thought. No-dwelling is the basic nature of human beings. In the world of good and evil, attractiveness and ugliness, friendliness and hostility, when faced with language which is offensive, critical, or argumentative, you should treat it all as empty and have no thought of revenge. In every thought, do not think of former states. If past, present, and future thoughts succeed one another without interruption, it is bondage. Not to dwell in dharmas from thought to thought is to be free from bondage. That is to take no-dwelling as the basis.” “Good Knowing Advisors, to be separated from all outward marks is called ‘no-mark.’ The ability to be separate from marks is the purity of the Dharma’s substance. It is to take no-mark as the substance.” “Good Knowing Advisors, the non-defilement of the mind in all states is called ‘no-thought.’ In your thoughts you should always be separated from states; do not give rise to thought about them. If you merely do not think of the hundred things, and so completely rid yourself of thought, then as the last thought ceases, you die and undergo rebirth in another place. That is a great mistake, of which students of the Way should take heed. To misinterpret the Dharma and make a mistake yourself might be acceptable, but to exhort others to do the same is unacceptable. In your own confusion you do not see, and, moreover you slander the Buddha’s Sutras. Therefore, no-thought is established as the doctrine.” “Good Knowing Advisors, why is no-thought established as the doctrine? Because there are confused people who speak of seeing their own nature, and yet they produce thought with regard to states. Their thoughts cause deviant views to arise, and from that all defilement and false thinking are created. Originally, not one single dharma can be obtained in the self-nature. If there is something to attain, or false talk of misfortune and blessing, that is just defilement and deviant views. Therefore, this Dharma-door establishes no-thought as its doctrine.” “Good Knowing Advisors, ‘No’ means no what? ‘Thought’ means thought of what? ‘No’ means no two marks, no thought of defilement. ‘Thought’ means thought of the original nature of True Suchness（‘真如’）. True Suchness is the substance of thought and thought is the function of True Suchness. The True Suchness self-nature（‘真如自性’）gives rise to thought. It is not the eye, ear, nose, or tongue which can think. The True Suchness possesses a nature and therefore gives rise to thought. Without True Suchness, the eye, ear, forms, and sounds immediately go bad.” “Good Knowing Advisors, the True Suchness self-nature gives rise to thought, and the six faculties（‘六根’）, although they see, hear, feel, and know, are not defiled by the ten thousand states. Your true nature is eternally independent. Therefore, the *Vimalakirti Sutra* says, ‘If one is well able to discriminate all dharma marks, then, in the primary meaning, one does not move.’ ”

“诚既勇兮又以武，终刚强兮不可凌。身既死兮神以灵，魂魄毅兮为鬼雄。”

——屈原《离骚》

中国经典双语阅读

屈原（选）

Unit 11

屈原（选）Selected from Qu Yuan [1]

［思想指要］屈原（约公元前 *343*— 约公元前 *278* 年）是中国古代最伟大的诗人之一。他极富独创性和想象力的诗歌对中国早期诗歌产生了巨大的影响。其代表作品《离骚》《天问》《九歌》等都收集在《楚辞》中。《楚辞》由西汉时期刘向编辑，收有屈原、宋玉、景差等人的作品。因其作品具有楚地的文学样式、方言声韵、风土人情色彩，故名《楚辞》。《楚辞》不仅保存了不少楚地民歌、民谣、巫歌的形式与风格，而且保存了中国上古以来丰富的神话与传说。其中，《天问》表达了作者对天、地、人，对自然、人类的求索与追问的精神。

[Introduction] Qu Yuan (about 343 B.C.—278 B.C.), born in Zigui of Danyang in the state of Chu[Now Yichang, Hubei Province], was one of the greatest poets of ancient China. He is highly valued for his original and imaginative verse in early Chinese poetry. His representative works include *Lisao*, *Tianwen*, *Nine Songs*, and etc., which are collected in *Chuci*. *Chuci,* edited by Liu Xiang, in Xihan Dynasty, contains the works written by Qu Yuan, Song Yu, Jing Chà, and other poets. His works were named *Chuci* because their literary style, dialect, sound meter, and native color are characteristic of the region of Chu. *Chuci* has not only preserved many forms and styles of folk songs, ballads and witch songs of the state of Chu, but also preserved the rich myths of ancient China, among which *Tianwen* expresses the author's spirit of searching and inquiring for the heaven, the earth and the human beings, and even for the evolution of the natural and human history.

《离骚》On Encountering Trouble

《离骚》是中国古代最长的抒情诗，全诗 *373* 行，近 *2500* 字。此诗以诗人

---

[1] 中文选自郭齐勇主编：《中国古典哲学名著选读》，北京：人民出版社，2005 年。

On Encountering Trouble，selected from *The Songs of the South and Anthology of Ancient Chinese Poems by Qu Yuan and Other Poets*, trans. by David Hawks, Penguin Classics, 1985.

自述身世、美德、遭遇、心志为中心。前半篇反复倾诉诗人对楚国命运和人民生活的关心，表达革新政治的愿望，和坚持理想、虽逢灾厄也绝不与邪恶势力妥协的意志；后半篇通过诗人神游天界、追求理想的实现和失败后欲以身殉志的陈述，反映出诗人热爱祖国和人民的思想感情。全诗运用美人香草的比喻、大量的神话传说和丰富的想象，形成绚烂的文采和宏伟的结构，表现出积极的浪漫主义精神，并开创了中国文学史上的“骚体”诗歌形式，对后世文学创作产生了深远影响。

[Introduction] *Lisao,* composed of 373 lines, nearly 2,500 words, is thought to be the longest lyric poem or romantically and politically lyric poem in ancient China. *Lisao* centers on the poet's self-narration of his life, his experience, his virtues and his ambitions. In the first half of the poem, the poet repeatedly voices his earnest concern for the fate of the state of Chu and the life of its people, expresses his intense desire to reform politics, and adheres to his noble ideals and vows not to compromise with evil forces in spite of his personal adversity. In the latter part, through the description of his wandering in Heaven, his frustration in pursuit of the ideals and therefore wanting to sacrifice his life to his motherland, the poet expresses his love for his country and its people. The whole poem, full of metaphors and imagination, such as using a vanilla of beauty as a vivid metaphor, and many myths and legends, forms a gorgeous literary style and magnificent structure, manifests the poet's positive romantic spirit and feelings, and creates the poetic form of "Saoti" in the history of Chinese literature, and accordingly has initiated a tradition of Romanticism in Chinese literature and has exerted a profound influence on later literary creation.

帝高阳之苗裔(yì)兮，朕皇考曰伯庸。
摄提贞于孟陬(zōu)兮，惟庚寅吾以降(hóng)。
皇览揆(kuí)余于初度兮，肇(zhào)锡余以嘉名；
名余曰正则兮，字余曰灵均。

1 Scion of the high lord Gao Yang,
Bo Yong was my father's name.
When She Ti pointed to the first month of the year,
On the day *geng-yin* I passed from the womb.
My father, seeing the aspect of my nativity,
Took omens to give me an auspicious name.
The name he gave me was True Exemplar;
The title he gave me was Divine Balance.

纷吾既有此内美兮，又重(chóng)之以修能(tài)。
扈(hù)江离与辟(pì)芷(zhǐ)兮，纫秋兰以为佩。

汩(yù)余若将不及兮，恐年岁之不吾与。
朝搴(qiān)阰(pí)之木兰兮，夕揽洲之宿莽。

9 Having from birth this inward beauty,
I added to it fair outward adornment:
I dressed in selinea and shady angelica,
And twined autumn orchids to make a garland.
Swiftly I sped as in fearful pursuit,
Afraid Time would race on and leave me behind.
In the morning I gathered the angelica on the mountains;
In the evening I plucked the sedges of the islets.

日月忽其不淹兮，春与秋其代序;
惟草木之零落兮，恐美人之迟暮。
不抚壮而弃秽兮，何不改乎此度?
乘骐(qí)骥(jì)以驰骋(chěng)兮，来吾道夫先路!

17 The days and months hurried on, never delaying;
Springs and autumns sped by in endless alternation:
And I thought how the trees and flowers were fading and falling,
And feared that my Fairest's beauty would fade too.
Gather the flower of youth and cast out the impure!
Why will you not change the error of your ways?
I have harnessed brave coursers for you to gallop forth with:
Come, let me go before and show you the way!

昔三后之纯粹兮，固众芳之所在;
杂申椒与菌桂兮，岂维纫夫蕙(huì)茝(chǎi)?
彼尧舜之耿介兮，既遵道而得路。
何桀纣之猖披兮，夫唯捷径以窘(jiǒng)步。

25 The three kings of old were most pure and perfect:
Then indeed fragrant flowers had their proper place.
They brought together pepper and cinnamon;
All the most-prized blossoms were woven in their garlands.
Glorious and great were those two, Yao and Shun,
Because they had kept their feet on the right path.
And how great was the folly of Jie and Zhou,
Who hastened by crooked paths, and so came to grief.

惟夫党人之偷乐兮，路幽昧以险隘

岂余身之惮(dàn)殃兮，恐皇舆之败绩！
忽奔走以先后兮，及前王之踵武。
荃(quán)不察余之中情兮，反信谗而齌(jì)怒。

33 The fools enjoy their careless pleasure,
But their way is dark and leads to danger.
I have no fear for the peril of my own person,
But only lest the chariot of my lord should be dashed.
I hurried about your chariot in attendance,
Leading you in the tracks of the kings of old.
But the Fragrant One refused to examine my true feelings:
He lent ear instead to slander, and raged against me.

余固知謇謇(jiǎn)之为患兮，忍而不能舍也。
指九天以为正兮，夫唯灵修之故也！
初既与余成言兮，后悔遁而有他。
余既不难夫离别兮，伤灵修之数(shuò)化。

41 How well I know that loyalty brings disaster;
Yet I will endure: I cannot give it up.
I called on the ninefold heaven to be my witness,
And all for the sake of the Fair One, and no other.
There once was a time when he spoke with me in frankness;
But then he repented and was of another mind.
I do not care, on my own count, about this divorcement,
But it grieves me to find the Fair One so inconstant.

余既滋兰之九畹兮，又树蕙之百亩。
畦(qí)留夷与揭车兮，杂杜衡与芳芷。
冀枝叶之峻茂兮，愿竢(sì)时乎吾将刈(yì)。
虽萎绝其亦何伤兮，哀众芳之芜(wú)秽(huì)。

49 I had tended many an acre of orchids,
And planted a hundred rods of melilotus;
I had raised sweet lichens and the cart-halting flower,
And as arums mingled with fragrant angelica,
And hoped that when leaf and stem were in their full prime,
When the time had come, I could reap a fine harvest.
Though famine should pinch me, it is a small matter;
But I grieve that all my blossoms should waste in rank weeds.

众皆竞进以贪婪兮，凭不厌乎求索。
羌内恕己以量人兮，各兴心而嫉妒。
忽驰骛以追逐兮，非余心之所急。
老冉冉其将至兮，恐修名之不立。

57 All others press forward in greed and gluttony,
No surfeit satiating their demands:
Forgiving themselves, but harshly judging others;
Each fretting his heart away in envy and malice.
Madly they rush in the covetous chase,
But not after that which my heart sets store by.
For old age comes creeping and soon will be upon me,
And I fear I shall not leave behind an enduring name.

朝饮木兰之坠露兮，夕餐秋菊之落英。
苟余情其信姱(kuā)以练要兮，长颇(kǎn)颔(hàn)亦何伤。
掔(qiān)木根以结茝(chǎi)兮，贯薜荔之落蕊。
矫菌桂以纫蕙兮，索胡绳之𫄨𫄨(xǐ xǐ)。

65 In the mornings I drank the dew that fell from the magnolia;
At evening ate the petals that dropped from chrysanthemums.
If only my mind can be truly beautiful,
It matters nothing that I often faint for famine.
I pulled up roots to bind the valerian
And thread the castor plant's fallen clusters with;
I trimmed sprays of cassia for plaiting melilotus,
And knotted the lithe, light trails of ivy.

謇(jiǎn)吾法夫前修兮，非世俗之所服。
虽不周于今之人兮，愿依彭咸之遗则！
长太息以掩涕兮，哀民生之多艰。
余虽好修姱以鞿(jī)羁(jī)兮，謇朝谇(suì)而夕替。

73 I take my fashion from the good men of old:
A garb unlike that which the rude world cares for;
Though it may not accord with present-day manners,
I will follow the pattern that Peng Xian has left.
Heaving a long sigh, I brush away my tears,
Sad that man's life should be so beset with hardship.
Though goodness and beauty were my bit and bridle,
I was slandered in the morning and cast off that same evening.

既替余以蕙(huì)纕(xiāng)兮，又申之以揽茝。
亦余心之所善兮，虽九死其犹未悔！
怨灵修之浩荡兮，终不察夫民心。
众女嫉余之蛾眉兮；谣诼(zhuó)谓余以善淫。
81 Yet, though cast off, I would wear my orchid girdle;
I would pluck some angelicas to add to its beauty;
For this it is that my heart takes most delight in,
And though I died nine times, I should not regret it.
What I regret is the Fair One's waywardness,
That never once stops to ask what is in men's minds.
All your ladies were jealous of my delicate beauty;
In their spiteful chattering they said I was a wanton.

固时俗之工巧兮，偭(miǎn)规矩而改错。
背绳墨以追曲兮，竞周容以为度。
忳郁邑余侘(chà)傺兮，吾独穷困乎此时也。
宁溘(kè)死以流亡兮，余不忍为此态也！
89 Truly this generation are cunning artificers,
From square and compass turn their eyes and change the true measurement,
Disregard the ruled line to follow their crooked fancies;
To emulate in flattery is their only rule.
But I am sick and sad at heart and stand irresolute:
I alone am at a loss in this generation.
Yet I would rather quickly die and meet dissolution,
Before I ever would consent to ape their behaviour.

鸷(zhì)鸟之不群兮，自前世而固然。
何方圜(yuán)之能周兮，夫孰异道而相安！
屈心而抑志兮，忍尤而攘(rǎng)诟(gòu)。
伏清白以死直兮，固前圣之所厚！
97 Eagles do not flock like birds of lesser species;
So it has ever been since the olden time.
How can the round and square ever fit together?
How can different ways of life ever be reconciled?
Yet humbling one's spirit and curbing one's pride,
Bearing blame humbly and enduring insults,
But keeping pure and spotless and dying in righteousness:
Such conduct was greatly prized by the wise men of old.

悔相道之不察兮，延伫乎吾将反。
回朕车以复路兮，及行迷之未远。
步余马于兰皋(gāo)兮，驰椒丘且焉止息。
进不入以离尤兮，退将复修吾初服。

105 Repenting, therefore, that I had not conned the way more closely,
I halted, intending to turn back again—
To turn about my chariot and retrace my road
Before I had advanced too far along the path of folly.
I walked my horses through the marsh's orchid-covered margin;
I galloped to the hill of pepper-trees and rested there.
I could not go in to him for fear of meeting trouble,
And so, retired, I would once more fashion my former raiment.

制芰(jì)荷以为衣兮，集芙蓉以为裳。
不吾知其亦已兮，苟余情其信芳。
高余冠之岌岌兮，长余佩之陆离。
芳与泽其杂糅兮，唯昭质其犹未亏。

113 I made a coat of lotus and water-chestnut leaves,
And gathered lotus petals to make myself a skirt.
I will no longer care that no one understands me,
As long as I can keep the sweet fragrance of my mind.
Higher still the hat now that towered on my head,
And longer the girdle that dangled from my waist.
Fragrance and foul mingle in confusion,
But my inner brightness has remained undimmed.

忽反顾以游目兮，将往观乎四荒。
佩缤纷其繁饰兮，芳菲菲其弥章。
民生各有所乐兮，余独好修以为常。
虽体解吾犹未变兮，岂余心之可惩！

121 Suddenly I turned back and let my eyes wander.
I resolved to go and visit all the world's quarters.
My garland's crowded blossoms, mixed in fair confusion,
Wafted the sweetness of their fragrance far and wide.
All men have something in their lives that gives them pleasure:
With me the love of beauty is my constant joy.
I could not change this, even if my body were dismembered;
For how could dismemberment ever hurt my mind?

女媭(xū)之婵媛兮，申申其詈(lì)予。
曰鲧(gǔn)婞(xìng)直以亡身兮，终然殀(yāo)乎羽之野。
汝何博謇(jiǎn)而好修兮，纷独有此姱节。
薋(cí)菉(lù)葹(shī)以盈室兮，判独离而不服。

129 My Nü Xu was fearful and clung to me imploringly,
Lifting her voice up in expostulation:
Gun in his stubbornness took no thought for his life,
And perished, as a result, on the moor of Feather Mountain.
Why be so lofty, with your passion for purity?
Why must you alone have such delicate adornment?
Thorns, king-grass, curly-ear hold the place of power:
But you must stand apart and not speak them fair.

众不可户说(shuì)兮，孰云察余之中情？
世并举而好朋兮，夫何茕(qióng)独而不予听？
依前圣以节中兮，喟凭心而历兹。
济沅湘以南征兮，就重华而陈词。

137 You cannot go from door to door convincing everybody;
No one can say, “See, look into my mind!”
Others band together and like to have companions:
Why must you be so aloof? Why not heed my counsel?
But I look to the wise men of old for my guidance.
So sighing, with a full heart, I bore her upbraidings,
And crossing the Yuan and Xiang, I journeyed southwards,
Till I came to where Chong Hua was and made my plaint to him.

启九辩与九歌兮，夏康娱以自纵。
不顾难以图后兮，五子用失乎家巷。
羿淫游以佚(yì)畋(tián)兮，又好射夫封狐。
固乱流其鲜终兮，浞(zhuó)又贪夫厥家。

145 Singing the Nine Songs and dancing the Nine Changes,
Qi of Xia made revelry and knew no restraint,
Taking no thought for the troubles that would follow:
And so his five sons fell out, brother against brother.
Yi loved idle roaming and hunting to distraction,
And took delight in shooting at the mighty foxes.
But foolish dissipation has seldom a good end:
And Han Zhuo covetously took his master’s wife.

浇(ào)身被服强圉(yǔ)兮，纵欲而不忍。
日康娱以自忘兮，厥首用夫颠陨。
夏桀(jié)之常违兮，乃遂焉而逢殃。
后辛之菹(zū)醢(hǎi)兮，殷宗用而不长。

153 Zhuo's son, Ao, put on his strong armour
And wreaked his wild will without any restraint.
The days passed in pleasure; far he forgot himself,
Till his head came tumbling down from his shoulders.
Jie of Xia all his days was a king most unnatural,
And so he came finally to meet with calamity.
Zhòu cut up and salted the bodies of his ministers;
And so the days were numbered of the House of Yin.

汤禹俨而祗敬兮，周论道而莫差。
举贤而授能兮，循绳墨而不颇。
皇天无私阿兮，览民德焉错辅。
夫维圣哲以茂行兮，苟得用此下土。

161 Tang of Shang and Yu of Xia were reverent and respectful;
The House of Zhou chose the true way without error,
Raising up the virtuous and able men to government,
Following the straight line without fear or favour.
High God in Heaven knows no partiality;
He looks for the virtuous and makes them his ministers.
For only the wise and good can ever flourish,
If it is given them to possess the earth.

瞻前而顾后兮，相(xiàng)观民之计极。
夫孰非义而可用兮，孰非善而可服？
阽(diàn)余身而危死兮，览余初其犹未悔。
不量凿(zuó)而正枘(ruì)兮，固前修以菹(zū)醢(hǎi)。

169 I have looked back into the past and forward to later ages,
Examining the outcomes of men's different designs.
Where is the unrighteous man who could be trusted?
Where is the wicked man whose service could be used?
Though I stand at the pit's mouth and death yawns before me,
I still feel no regret at the course I have chosen.
Straightening the handle, regardless of the socket's shape:
For that crime the good men of old were hacked in pieces.

曾歔(xū)欷(xī)余郁邑兮，哀朕时之不当。
揽茹蕙以掩涕兮，沾余襟之浪浪。
跪敷衽(rèn)以陈辞兮，耿吾既得此中正，
驷玉虬(qiú)以乘鷖(yī)兮，溘(kè)埃风余上征。

177 Many a heavy sigh I heaved in my despair,
Grieving that I was born in such an unlucky time.
I plucked soft lotus petals to wipe my welling tears
That fell down in rivers and wet my coat front.
I knelt on my outspread skirts and poured my plaint out,
And the righteousness within me was clearly manifest.
I yoked a team of jade dragons to a phoenix-figured car
And waited for the wind to come, to soar up on my journey.

朝发轫(rèn)于苍梧兮，夕余至乎县圃。
欲少留此灵琐兮，日忽忽其将暮。
吾令羲和弭节兮，望崦(yān)嵫(zī)而勿迫。
路曼曼其修远兮，吾将上下而求索。

185 I started out in the morning on my way from Cang-wu;
By evening I had arrived at the Hanging Garden.
I wanted to stay a while in those fairy precincts,
But the swift-moving sun was dipping to the west.
I ordered Xi He to stay the sun-steeds' gallop,
To stand over Yan-zi mountain and not go in;
For the road was so far and so distant was my journey,
And I wanted to go up and down, seeking my heart's desire.

饮余马于咸池兮，总余辔乎扶桑。
折若木以拂日兮，聊逍遥以相羊。
前望舒使先驱兮，后飞廉使奔属(zhǔ)。
鸾皇为余先戒兮，雷师告余以未具。

193 I watered my dragon steeds at the Pool of Heaven,
And tied their reins up to the Fu-sang tree.
I broke a sprig of the Ruo tree to strike the sun with:
First I would roam a little for my enjoyment.
I sent Wang Shu ahead to ride before me;
The Wind God went behind as my outrider;
The Bird of Heaven gave notice of my comings;
The Thunder God warned me when all was not ready.

吾令凤鸟飞腾兮，继之以日夜。
飘风屯其相离兮，帅云霓而来御。
纷总总其离合兮，斑陆离其上下。
吾令帝阍(hūn)开关兮，倚阊(chāng)阖(hé)而望予。

201 I caused my phoenixes to mount on their pinions
And fly ever onward by night and by day.
The whirlwinds gathered and came out to meet me,
Leading clouds and rainbows, to give me welcome.
In wild confusion, now joined and now parted,
Upwards and downwards rushed the glittering train.
I asked Heaven' s porter to open up for me;
But he leant across Heaven' s gate and eyed me churlishly.

时暧暧(ài ài)其将罢兮，结幽兰而延伫。
世混浊而不分兮，好蔽美而嫉妒。
朝吾将济于白水兮，登阆(láng)风而緤(xiè)马。
忽反顾以流涕兮，哀高丘之无女。

209 The day was getting dark and drawing to its close.
Knotting orchids, I waited in indecision.
The muddy, impure world, so undiscriminating,
Seeks always to hide beauty, out of jealousy.
I decided when morning came to cross the White Water,
And climbed the peak of Lang-feng, and there tied up my steeds.
Then I looked about me and suddenly burst out weeping,
Because on that high hill there was no fair lady.

溘(kè)吾游此春宫兮，折琼枝以继佩。
及荣华之未落兮，相下女之可诒(yí)。
吾令丰隆乘云兮，求宓(fú)妃之所在。
解佩纕以结言兮，吾令謇(jiǎn)修以为理。

217 Here I am, suddenly, in this House of Spring.
I have broken off a jasper branch to add to my girdle.
Before the jasper flowers have shed their bright petals,
I shall look for a maiden below to give it to.
So I made Feng-long ride off on a cloud
To seek out the dwelling-place of the lady Fu-fei.
I took off my girdle as a pledge of my suit to her,
And ordered Lame Beauty to be the go-between.

纷总总其离合兮，忽纬(wěi)繣(huà)其难迁。
夕归次于穷石兮，朝濯发乎洧(wěi)盘。
保厥美以骄傲兮，日康娱以淫游。
虽信美而无礼兮，来违弃而改求。
225 Many were the hurried meetings and partings:
All wills and caprices, she was hard to woo.
In the evenings she went to lodge in the Qiong-shi mountain;
In the mornings she washed her hair in the Wei-pan stream.
With proud disdain she guarded her beauty,
Passing each day in idle, wanton pleasures.
Though fair she may be, she lacks all seemliness:
Come! I'll have none of her; let us search elsewhere!

览相观于四极兮，周流乎天余乃下。
望瑶台之偃(yǎn)蹇(jiǎn)兮，见有娀(sōng)之佚女。
吾令鸩(zhèn)为媒兮，鸩告余以不好。
雄鸠之鸣逝兮，余犹恶其佻(tiāo)巧。
233 I looked all around over the earth's four quarters,
Circling the heavens till at last I alighted.
I gazed on a jade tower' s glittering splendour
And spied the lovely daughter of the Lord of Song.
I sent off the magpie to pay my court to her,
But the magpie told me that my suit had gone amiss.
The magpie flew off with noisy chatterings.
I hate him for an idle, knavish fellow.

心犹豫而狐疑兮，欲自适而不可。
凤皇既受诒兮，恐高辛之先我。
欲远集而无所止兮，聊浮游以逍遥。
及少(shào)康之未家兮，留有虞(yú)之二姚。
241 My mind was irresolute and havering;
I wanted to go, and yet I could not.
Already the phoenix had taken his present,
And I feared that Gao Xin would get there before me.
I wanted to go far away, but had nowhere to go to:
Where could I wander to look for amusement?
Before they were married to Prince Shao Kang,
Lord Yu's two daughters were there for the wooing.

理弱而媒拙兮，恐导言之不固。
世混浊而嫉贤兮，好蔽美而称恶。
闺中既以邃(suì)远兮，哲王又不寤(wù)。
怀朕情而不发兮，余焉能忍与此终古！

249 But my pleader was weak and my matchmaker stupid,
And I feared that this suit, too, would not be successful.
For the world is impure and envious of the able,
Eager to hide men's good and make much of their ill.
Deep in the palace, unapproachable,
The wise king slumbers and will not be awakened.
That the thoughts in my breast should all go unuttered—
How can I endure this until I end my days?

索藑(qiòng)茅以筳(tíng)篿(zhuān)兮，命灵氛为余占之。
曰：两美其必合兮，孰信修而慕之？
思九州之博大兮，岂唯是其有女(rǔ)？
曰：勉远逝而无狐疑兮，孰求美而释女？

257 I searched for the holy plant and twigs of bamboo,
And ordered Lin g Fen to make divination for me.
He said, 'Beauty is always bound to find its mate,
Who that was truly fair was ever without lovers?
Think of the vastness of the wide world:
Here is not the only place where you can find your lady.
Go farther afield,' he said, 'and do not be faint-hearted.
What woman seeking handsome mate could ever refuse you?'

何所独无芳草兮，尔何怀乎故宇？
世幽昧以昡(xuàn)曜(yào)兮，孰云察余之善恶？
民好恶(wù)不同兮，惟此党人其独异。
户服艾以盈要兮，谓幽兰其不可佩。

265 What place on earth does not boast some fragrant flower?
Why need you always cleave to your old home?
The world today is blinded with its own folly:
You cannot make people see the virtue inside you.
Most people's loathings and likings are different,
Only these men here are not as others are;
For they wear mugwort and cram their waistbands with it,
But the lovely valley orchid they deem unfit to wear.

览察草木其犹未得兮，岂珵(chéng)美之能当？
苏粪壤以充帏兮，谓申椒其不芳。
欲从灵氛之吉占兮，心犹豫而狐疑。
巫咸将夕降兮，怀椒糈(xǔ)而要之。

273 Since beauty of flower, then, and of shrub escapes them,
What chance has a rarest jewel of gaining recognition?
They gather up muck to stuff their perfume bags with;
The spicy pepper-plant they say has got no scent at all.
I wanted to follow Ling Fen's auspicious oracle,
But I faltered and could not make my mind up.
I heard that Wu Xian was descending in the evening,
So I lay in wait with offerings of peppered rice-balls.

百神翳(yi)其备降兮，九疑缤其并迎。
皇剡剡其扬灵兮，告余以吉故。
曰：勉升降以上下兮，求矩矱(yuē)之所同。
汤禹俨而求合兮，挚咎(gāo)繇(yáo)而能调。

281 The spirits came like a dense cloud descending,
And the host of Doubting Mountain came crowding to meet him.
His godhead was manifested by a blaze of radiance,
And he addressed me in these auspicious words:
To and fro in the earth you must everywhere wander,
Seeking one whose thoughts are of your own measure.
Tang and Yu sought sincerely for the right helpers;
So Yi Yin and Gao Yao worked well with their princes.

苟中情其好修兮，又何必用夫行媒。
说(yuè)操筑于傅岩兮，武丁用而不疑。
吕望之鼓刀兮，遭周文而得举。
宁戚之讴歌兮，齐桓闻以该辅。

289 As long as your soul within is beautiful,
What need have you of a matchmaker?
Yue laboured as a builder, pounding earth at Fu-yan,
Yet Wu Ding employed him without a second thought.
Lü Wang wielded the butcher's knife at Zhao-ge,
But King Wen met him and raised him up on high.
Ning Qi sang as he fed his ox at evening;
Duke Huan of Qi heard him and took him as his minister.

及年岁之未晏兮，时亦犹其未央。
恐鹈(tí)鴂(jué)之先鸣兮，使夫百草为之不芳。
何琼佩之偃(yǎn)蹇(jiǎn)兮，众薆(ài)然而蔽之。
惟此党人之不谅兮，恐嫉妒而折之。

297 Gather the flower of youth before it is too late,
While the good season is still not yet over.
Beware lest the shrike sound his note before the equinox,
Causing all the flowers to lose their fine fragrance.
How splendid the glitter of my jasper girdle!
But the crowd make a dark screen, masking its beauty.
And I fear that my enemies, who never can be trusted,
Will break it out of spiteful jealousy.

时缤纷其变易兮，又何可以淹留。
兰芷变而不芳兮，荃蕙化而为茅。
何昔日之芳草兮，今直为此萧艾也？
岂其有他故兮，莫好修之害也。

305 The age is disordered in a tumult of changing,
How can I tarry much longer among them?
Orchid and iris have lost all their fragrance;
Flag and melilotus have changed into straw.
Why have all the fragrant flowers of days gone by
Now all transformed themselves into worthless mugwort?
What other reason can there be for this
But that they all have no more care for beauty?

余以兰为可恃兮，羌无实而容长。
委厥美以从俗兮，苟得列乎众芳。
椒专佞以慢慆(tāo)兮，榝(shā)又欲充夫佩帏。
既干进而务入兮，又何芳之能祗(zhī)。

313 I thought that orchid was one to be trusted,
But he proved a sham, bent only on pleasing his masters.
He overcame his goodness and conformed to evil counsels:
He no more deserves to rank with fragrant flowers.
Pepper is all wagging tongue and lives only for slander;
And even stinking dogwood seeks to fill a perfume bag.
Since they only seek advancement and labour for position,
What fragrance have they deserving our respect?

固时俗之流从兮，又孰能无变化？
览椒兰其若兹兮，又况揭车与江离。
惟兹佩之可贵兮，委厥美而历兹。
芳菲菲而难亏兮，芬至今犹未沫(mò)！

321 Since, then, the world's way is to drift the way the tide runs,
Who can stay the same and not change with all the rest?
Seeing the behaviour of orchid and pepper-flower,
What can be expected of cart-halt and selinea?
They have cast off their beauty and come to this:
Only my garland is left to treasure.
Its penetrating perfume does not easily desert it,
And even to this day its fragrance has not faded.

和调(diào)度以自娱兮，聊浮游而求女。
及余饰之方壮兮，周流观乎上下。
灵氛既告余以吉占兮，历吉日乎吾将行。
折琼枝以为羞兮，精琼靡(mí)以为粻(zhāng)。

329 I will follow my natural bent and please myself;
I will go off wandering to look for a lady.
While my adornment is in its pristine beauty
I will travel around looking both high and low.
Since Ling Fen had given me a favourable oracle,
I picked an auspicious day to start my journey on.
I broke a branch of jasper to take for my meat,
And ground fine jasper meal for my journey's provisions.

为余驾飞龙兮，杂瑶象以为车。
何离心之可同兮，吾将远逝以自疏。
邅(zhān)吾道夫昆仑兮，路修远以周流。
扬云霓之晻(ǎn)蔼兮，鸣玉鸾之啾(jiū)啾(jiū)。

337 Harness winged dragons to be my coursers;
Let my chariot be of fine work of jade and ivory!
How can I live with men whose hearts are strangers to me?
I am going a far journey to be away from them.
I took the way that led towards the Kun-lun Mountain:
Along, long road with many a turning in it.
The cloud-embroidered banner flapped its great shade above us;
And the jingling jade yoke-bells tinkled merrily.

朝发轫于天津兮，夕余至乎西极。
凤皇翼其承旂兮，高翱翔之翼翼。
忽吾行此流沙兮，遵赤水而容与。
麾(huī)蛟龙使梁津兮，诏西皇使涉予。

345 I set off at morning from the Ford of Heaven;
At evening I came to the world's western end.
Phoenixes followed me, bearing up my pennants,
Soaring high aloft with majestic wing-beats.
See, I have come to the Desert of Moving Sands!
Warily I drove along the banks of the Red Water,
Then, beckoning the water-dragons to make a bridge for me,
I summoned the God of the West to take me over.

路修远以多艰兮，腾众车使径待。
路不周以左转兮，指西海以为期。
屯余车其千乘兮，齐玉轪(dài)而并驰。
驾八龙之婉婉兮，载云旗之委(wēi)蛇(yí)。

353 So long the road had been and full of difficulties,
I sent word to my escort to take another route,
To wheel around leftwards, skirting Bu-zhou Mountain:
On the shore of the Western Sea we would reassemble.
When we had mustered there, all thousand chariots,
Jade hub to jade hub we galloped on abreast.
My eight dragon steeds flew on with writhing undulations,
My cloud-embroidered banners flapped on the wind.

抑志而弭(mǐ)节兮，神高驰之邈(miǎo)邈。
奏《九歌》而舞《韶(sháo)》兮，聊假日以媮(yú)乐。
陟(zhì)升皇之赫戏兮，忽临睨(nì)夫旧乡。
仆夫悲余马怀兮，蜷(quán)局顾而不行。

361 In vain I tried to curb them, to slacken the swift pace:
The spirits soared high up, far into the distance.
We played the Nine Songs and danced the Shao Dances,
Borrowing the time to make a holiday.
But when I had ascended the splendour of the heavens,
I suddenly caught a glimpse below of my old home.
My groom's heart was heavy and the horses for longing,
Arched their heads back and refused to go on.

乱曰：已矣哉！
国无人莫我知兮，又何怀乎故都？
既莫足与为美政兮，吾将从彭咸之所居！
369 LUAN: Enough! There are no true men in the state: no one understands me.
Why should I cleave to the city of my birth?
Since none is worthy to work with in making good government,
I shall go and join Peng Xian in the place where he abides.

《天问》Tianwen (Heavenly Questions)[1]

《天问》是屈原创作的一首长诗。该诗首先是问天，继而问地，问人，问阴阳之合和。作者不满于关于天地开辟的神话传说，以怀疑的态度，探索的精神，考问宇宙的起源及其形成、生命与生民的起源、天体的构造、上古人与动物的产生、洪水传说、自然现象以及上古、唐虞、三代古史传说等。从中可以看出，中国古代关于宇宙自然与人类生命起源的看法，与西方人的“创世纪”有很大的不同。本篇对自然史观、人类史观、天文学、天道性命观均有独到的见解。全诗通篇是对天地、自然和人世等一切事物现象的发问，内容奇绝，显示出作者沉潜多思、思想活跃、想象丰富的个性，表现出超卓非凡的学识和惊人的艺术才华，被誉为是“千古万古至奇之作”。

[Introduction] *Tianwen,* a long poem written by Qu Yuan, first starts with asking the sky, then the earth, then the people, then the motion and union of *Yin* and *Yang*. The poet is dissatisfied with the myths and legends about the creation of heaven and earth (the oneness and the split of heaven and earth). With the skeptical attitude and the spirit of exploration, he critically interrogates the origin of the universe and the origin of life and people, the generation of ancient people and the animals, the flood myth, the natural phenomena, the union between *Yin* and *Yang*, and even the Ancient Times (Three Sovereigns and Five Emperors), Tang Yu (Tang Yao and Yu Shun), the Three Generations(the dynasties of Xia, Shang and Zhou). It can be seen that the version of ancient Chinese on the origin of the universe and the human life is very different from the Western version of genesis. *Tianwen* manifests its author's unique views on natural history, human history, astronomy, universe and human life. The whole poem is an inquiry into the universe, earth, nature and human life, which shows the author's deep thinking, active imagination, extraordinary knowledge and amazing artistic talent. Accordingly, it is regarded as "an extraordinary work of all ages. "

---

[1] 中文选自郭齐勇主编：《中国古典哲学名著选读》，北京：人民出版社，2005。
Tianwen (*'Heavenly Questions'*)，selected from *The Songs of The South*: *An Ancient Chinese Anthology of Poem by Qu Yuan and Other Poets*, trans. by David Hawkes, Penguin Classics, 1985.

1. 曰：遂古之初，谁传道之[遂：往也。初：始也。传道：世世所传说往古之事也。]？上下未形，何由考之[上下：天地。未形：指天地、上下尚未形成。考：考察。]？

2. 冥昭瞢闇，谁能极之[冥：幽也。昭：明也。瞢闇(méng àn)：隐晦不明，极：穷。]？冯翼惟像，何以识之[冯翼(píng yì)：大气饱满蓬勃的 样子。惟：语气助词。像：仿佛。]？

3. 明明暗暗，惟时何为[明明暗暗：指昼夜。惟时：其时的意思。]？阴阳三合，何本何化[阴阳三合：《春秋谷梁传·庄公三年》：“独阴不生，独阳不生，独天不生：三合然后生。”化：阴阳变化。]？

4. 圜则九重，孰营度之[圜(yuán)：今通圆，指天宇。九重：即下文的九天。营度：进行测量。]？惟兹何功，孰初作之[功：功效。]？

5. 斡维焉系，天极焉加[斡(wò)维：指天体旋转维系之处。天极：天体中央最高点，相当于运转中轴之顶端。]？八柱何当，东南何亏[八柱。传说中天宇的八根柱子。亏：短缺。]？

6. 九天之际，安放安属[九天：九重天宇。]？隅隈多有，谁知其数[隅隈(yú wèi)：拐角。隅，角也：隈，曲。]？

7. 天何所沓，十二焉分[沓：重合。十二：指十二辰。古代天文学上将黄道均分为十二等分，也就是十二星次。]？日月安属，列星安陈[属：聚会。列星：指环列于周天的二十八宿。陈：列。]？

8.出自汤谷，次于蒙汜[汤(yáng)谷：太阳升起的地方。蒙汜(sì)：太阳落下去的地方。]？自明及晦，所行几里[晦：暗。]？

9. 夜光何德，死则又育[夜光：月亮。德：品德、品质。育：生长、培养。]？厥利维何，而顾菟在腹[厥(jué)：其，指月。维：语气助词。顾：看。菟：同兔。腹：怀抱。]？

10. 女歧无合，夫焉取九子[女歧：神祇名，无夫而生九子。九子：指二十八宿之尾宿。]？伯强何处，惠气安在[伯强：指二十八宿之箕宿。闻一多《天问释天》有详论。惠气：春日阳和之气。东方苍 龙七宿主春令，尾箕二宿居东北方时，角宿适在东南：东方七宿正当其位，乃春日载阳、惠风和畅之时也。]？

11. 何阖而晦，何开而明[阖(hé)：闭也。与开对文，均指天门。]？角宿未旦，曜灵安藏[角宿：东方七宿之首，二十八宿之长。曜(yào)灵：日也。王逸《章句》曰：“言东方未明旦之时，日安藏其精光乎?”]？

1. Who passed down the story of the far-off, ancient beginning of things? How can we be sure what it was like before the sky above and the earth below had taken shape?

2. Since none could penetrate that murk when darkness and light were yet undivided, how do we know about the chaos of insubstantial forms?

3. What manner of things are the darkness and light? How did *Yin* and *Yang* come together, and how could they originate and transform all things that are by their commingling?

4. Whose compass measured out the nine-fold heavens? Whose work was this, and how did he accomplish it?

5. Where were the circling cords fastened, and where was the sky's pole fixed? Where did the Eight Pillars meet the sky, and why were they too short for it in the south-east?

6. Where do the nine fields of heaven extend to and where do they join each other? The ins and outs of their edges must be very many: who knows their number?

7. How does heaven coordinate its motions? Where are the Twelve Houses divided? How do the sun and the moon hold to their courses and the fixed stars keep their places?

8. Setting out from the Gulf of Brightness and going to rest in the Vale of Murk, from the dawn until the time of darkness, how many miles is the journey?

9. What is the peculiar virtue of the moon, the Brightness of the Night, which causes it to grow once more after its death? Of what advantage is it to keep a toad in its belly?

10. How did the Mother Star get her nine children without a union?

11. Where is Lord Bluster, the Wind Star, and where does the warm wind live?

12. 不任汩鸿，师何以尚之[汩(gǔ)：治也。鸿：洪水。师：众人。尚：崇。]？佥曰何忧，何不课而行之[佥：咸，皆。课：试。]？

13. 鸱龟曳衔，鲧何听焉[鸱：鸱鸺(chī xiū)，猫头鹰一类的鸟。曳(yè)衔：牵引衔接。听：听从。]？顺欲成功，帝何刑焉[顺：依计而行。帝：《天问》中的“帝”字均指天帝。刑：杀。]？

14. 永遏在羽山，夫何三年不施[永：长。遏：遏止。羽山：地名。施：陈尸或毁坏。]？伯禹愎鲧，夫何以变化[愎(bì)：刚愎、摔直。以愎称鲧，实称道之也。]？

15. 纂就前绪，遂成考功[纂：同缵，《说文》曰：“继也”。就：就原有的基础而有以形成的意思。绪：端也。考：父死称考。]。何续初继业，而厥谋不同[言禹承鲧志，终于完成了治水大业，在办法上又有什么不同呢？]？

16.洪泉极深，何以窴之[泉：不断涌流的水。窴(tián)：同填，塞也。此指“息壤”事。]？地方九则，何以坟之[则：指天下被有次序地划分为九州。则，一本作州。坟：坟起，水边高起之地曰坟。]？

17. 河海应龙，何尽何历[应龙：有鳞曰蛟龙，有翼曰应龙。历：过也。王逸《章句》云：“或曰：禹治洪水时，有神龙以尾画地，导水所注当决者，因而治之也。”]？焉有虬龙，负熊以游[虬(qiú)龙：无角之龙。熊：指鲧死后化为黄熊。《左传•昭公七年》：“子产曰：‘昔尧殛鲧于羽山，其神化为黄熊，以人于羽渊。’”据林庚先生《天问论笺》，“焉有虬龙”句，应由原王逸《章句》第四十八句，改为此处。因为这两句均涉及龙，而且均问及有关鲧禹治水的传说。]？

18. 鲧何所营？禹何所成？康回冯怒，地何故以东南倾[康：充盛貌。回：雷声回荡貌。冯(píng)怒：形容雷震。《春秋传》曰：“震电冯怒。”]？

19. 九州安错？川谷何洿[九州。据《尚书•禹贡》，九州指冀州、兖州、青州、徐州、扬州、荆州、豫州、梁州、雍州。错：置、分布。洿(hù)：深也。]？东流不溢，孰知其故？

20. 东西南北，其修孰多[东西：指大地横的宽度。南北：指大地纵的长度。修：长也。]？南北顺隳，其衍几何[隳(tuǒ)：同椭，狭而长。衍：曼衍。]？

12. What is it whose closing causes the dark and whose opening causes the light? Where does the Bright God hide before the Horn proclaims the dawning of the day?

13. When the bird-turtles linked together, how did Gun follow their sign? And if he accomplished the work according to his will, why did the high lord punish him?

14. Long he lay cast off on Feather Mountain: why for three whole years did he not rot? When Lord Gun brought forth Yu from his belly, how was he transformed?

15. Yu inherited the same tradition and carried on the work of his father. If he continued the work already begun, in what way was his plan a different one?

16. How did he fill the flood waters up where they were most deep? How did he set bounds to the Nine Lands?

17. What did the winged dragon trace on the ground? Where did the seas and rivers flow?

18. What did Gun plan and what did Yu accomplish? Why, when the Wicked One was enraged, did the earth sink down towards the south-east?

19. Why are the lands of the earth dry and the river valleys wet? They flow eastwards without ever getting exhausted: who knows the cause of this?

20. What are the distances from east to west and from south to north? From north to south the earth is longer and narrower. What is the difference between its length and breadth?

21. 昆仑县圃，其凥安在[昆仑：山名，在西北，元气之所出也。其巅为县圃，上通于天也。县，音玄，一作玄。凥(jū)：古居字，一作尻，音考，平声。]？增城九重，其高几里[增城：层城，九重之城。]？

22. 四方之门，其谁从焉[从：自。]？西北辟启，何气通焉[气：天地之间的元气。]？

23. 日安不到？烛龙何照[烛龙：古代传说中照亮幽冥的神。]？羲和之未扬，若华何光[羲和：古代传说中御日车的神。扬：起。若华：西极若木的赤花。]？

24. 何所冬暖？何所夏寒[冬暖、夏寒：言东南和暖、西北高寒的传说。]？焉有石林？何兽能言[石林：此本南方楚图画而难问之也。]？

25. 雄虺九首，儵忽焉在[虺(huī)：毒蛇。儵(shù)忽：儵，同倏，倏息，迅速神疾。]？何所不死？长人何守[不死：《括地志》曰："有不死之国"。《吕氏春秋·求人篇》载：(禹)"南至交阯孙朴续樠之国，丹粟漆树，沸水飘飘，九阳之山，羽人裸民之处，不死之乡。"长人：(招魂》曰："魂兮归来东方不可以托些，长人千仞惟魂是索些。"据林庚先生说，长人属东南方炎热地带的传说。何守：守卫不死之所。]？

26. 靡蓱九衢，枲华安居[靡蓱(píng)：一作萍，蘼萍浮草。九衢(qú)：九出的意思。枲(xǐ)华：未详。]？一蛇吞象，厥大何如[一蛇吞象：《山海经·海内南经》"巴蛇食象，三岁而出其骨；君子服之无心腹之疾，其为蛇青黄赤黑，一曰黑蛇青首。"]？

27. 黑水玄趾，三危安在[黑水、玄趾、三危均为《山海经》中想象的事物或地方，近于南海。]？延年不死？寿何所止？

28. 鲮鱼何所？鬿(qí)堆焉处[鲮(líng)鱼：王逸曰："绞鲤也，有四足，出南方。"《山海经·海内北经》："鲮鱼，人面手足鱼身。"鬿堆：鬿，一作魁。堆为雀，鬿堆，即魁雀。《山海经》："有鸟焉，其状如鸡而白首，鼠足而虎爪，其名曰魅雀，亦食人。"]？羿焉彃日？乌焉解羽[彃(bì)：射。乌：《大荒东经》曰："大荒之中有山名曰孽摇頵羝，上有扶木柱三百里，其叶如芥。有谷曰温源谷。汤谷上有扶木，一日方至，一日方出，皆载于乌。"解羽：羽毛散落。此指载日之乌被射落。]？

21. Where is Kun-lun with its Hanging Garden? How many miles high are its nine-fold walls?

22. Who goes through the gates in its four sides? When the north-east one opens, what wind is it that passes through?

23. What land does the sun not shine on and how does the Torch Dragon light it? Why are the *Ruo* flowers bright before Xihe is stirring?

24. What place is warm in winter? What place is cold in summer? Where is the stone forest? What beast can talk?

25. Where are the hornless dragons which carry bears on their backs for sport? Where is the great serpent with nine heads and where is the *Shu Hu*? Where is it that people do not age? Where do giants live?

26. Where is the nine-branched weed? Where is the flower of the Great Hemp? How does the snake that can swallow an elephant digest its bones?

27. Where is the Black Water that dyes the feet, and where is the Mountain of Three Perils? The folk there put death off for many years: what is the limit of their age?

28. Where does the man-fish live? Where is the Monster Bird? When *Yi* shot down the suns, why did the ravens shed their feathers?

29. 禹之力献功，降省下土四方[力献功：指禹治理洪水，献功于天帝。降省下土：省(xǐng)，视察。此指禹奉了天帝之命，下降到人间来视察洪水后的九州情况。]。焉得彼嵞山女，而通之于台桑[嵞(tú)山：即涂山，在淮水东南岸。通：私通幽会。台桑：禹与涂山氏女幽会的地方。]？

30. 闵妃匹合，厥身是继[闵妃：涂山氏女；闵，伤心思念的意思；妃：配偶的意思。匹合：指“通之于台桑”的私通幽会。厥身是继：有了后代。]。胡维嗜不同味，而快鼌饱[嗜味不同：并不情投意合。鼌(zhāo)饱：一时的满足。鼌同“朝”，本义为旦，早晨。]？

31. 启代益作后，卒然离蠥[启：夏后启。益：后益。卒然：终然。离蠥(niè)：遭忧。]。何启惟忧，而能拘是达[能拘是达：能从困境中摆脱出来。]？

32. 皆归射鞫，而无害厥躬[射：射猎。鞫：养，此指畜牧。厥躬：其身，指后益。]。何后益作革，而禹播降[作革：更新、改进。播降：指禹之降生启。]？

33. 启棘宾商，九辩九歌[棘：戟。商：疑为帝；宾，或以为嫔。九辩九歌：古代舞乐之名。]；何勤子屠母，而死分竟地[勤子：劳苦的孩子，指启。屠母：屠，分裂，指涂山氏女生启时已化为石。竟：终。死分竟地：指最后的归宿。]？

34. 帝降夷羿，革孽夏民[夷羿：东夷的后羿。革孽夏民：革除夏民族百姓的忧患。]；胡射夫河伯，而妻彼雒嫔[河伯：河洛一带的土著部族；伯同霸，说明这一部族在黄河一带的势力。雒嫔(luò pín)：洛妃。]？

35. 冯珧利决，封狶是射[冯(píng)：满。珧(yáo)：弓。决。搬指，指箭。封狶(xī)：即封豕。《方言》：“猪，南楚谓之狶。”]；何献蒸肉之膏，而后帝不若[蒸肉之膏：这里指祭飨于天帝的祭品。后帝不若：后不若于帝。若，顺。后指后羿。帝指天帝。]？

36. 浞娶纯狐，眩妻爰谋[浞(zhuó)：寒浞，后羿的宰相。纯狐：姓氏。]；何羿之射革，而交吞揆之[射革：形容后羿的勇力善射。揆(kuí))：算计。交吞揆之：里应外合，算计后羿。]？

29. Yu laboured with all his might. He came down and looked on the earth below. How did he get that maid of *Tu-shan* and lie with her in *Tai-sang*?

30. The lady became his mate and her body had issue. How came they to have appetite for the same dish when they sated their hunger with the morning food of love?

31. Qi supplanted *Yi* and made himself lord, but later met with mishap. How did *Qi* fall into trouble, and how did he succeed in warding it off ?

32. All gave him their allegiance and did no harm to his person. How is it that *Yi* lost lordship and *Yu*' s seed was continued?

33. Qi was many times the guest of God in heaven and brought back the Nine Changes and the Nine Songs. Why, if he was so good a son, did he kill his mother, and why were his lands divided up after his death?

34. God sent down Lord *Yi* to overcome the calamities of the people below. Why then did he shoot the River Lord and take to wife that Lady of the *Luo*?

35. With his trusty bow and good thumb-ring he shot the Great Swine. Why, when he offered the fat of its flesh cooked as a sacrifice, was the Lord God displeased?

36. Zhuo took the Black Fox to wife, and that Dark Woman plotted with him. How was *Yi*'s body boiled, and how did they conspire to have him eaten?

37. 阻穷西征，岩何越焉[穷：阻，阻截；穷：有穷氏，后羿率领的部落。]？化为黄熊，巫何活焉[黄熊：鲧的传说。]？

38. 咸播秬黍，莆雚是营[秬黍(jù shǔ)：泛指粮食。莆雚(pú guàn)：泛指水草。]？何由并投，而鲧疾修盈[并投：都向四处投奔。修盈：长、满。]？

39. 白蜺婴茀，胡为此堂[白蜺(ní)：白霓。这里形容衣裳。婴茀(fú)：古代妇女的首饰。此堂：指 后羿珍藏良药之堂。]？安得夫良药，不能固臧[良药：：指不死药。]？

40. 天式从横，阳离爰死[式：法式，即常规。从(zōng)横：横竖分明或无往不在的意思。阳离爰死：失去了元气就成了死尸。]；大鸟何鸣，夫焉丧厥体[大鸟何鸣：指羿的尸体化为大鸟飞鸣而去。]？

42. 蓱号起雨，何以兴之[蓱(píng)：屏翳。《广雅》："雨师为之荓翳。"号：呼唤。兴：引，发作。这里指兴云起雨。]？撰体胁鹿，何以膺之[撰：造。胁：两膀也。这里指指鹿两膀生翅体现鸟形。膺：承也，向也。有响应的意思。]？

43. 鳌戴山抃，何以安之[鳌(áo)：大龟。戴：负荷。抃(biàn)：拍手。安：静也。安然平稳的意思。]？释舟陵行，何以迁之？

44. 惟浇在户，何求于嫂[浇：传说中的寒浞之子。]？何少康逐犬，而颠陨厥首[少康：夏后启的曾孙，夏王朝中兴之主。逐：追踪。颠陨厥首：被砍掉了头。]？

45. 女歧缝裳，而馆同爰(yuán)止[女歧：浇嫂。馆同爰止：同居同宿。]；何颠易厥首，而亲以逢殆[颠易：被杀。易：代。指代浇被害。]？

46. 汤谋易旅，何以厚之[汤：浇字之误。易旅：换上新甲。]？覆舟斟寻，何道取之[覆舟：覆，反也；舟，船也。斟寻：国名。]？

37. On that westward journey from *Zu* to *Qiong-shi* how did *Yi* cross the heights? And when Gun turned into a brown bear, how did the shamans bring him back to life?

38. Both sowed the black millet, and the rushlands became a place of husbandry. Why, if each made the same sowing, did Gun alone reap a harvest of infamy?

39. What is the halo of white light doing in this hall? Where did *Yi* get that goodly herb, and why could he not keep it?

41. The heaven-made pattern embraces all, and when the *yang*-spirit leaves, death ensues. Why did the great birds cry? How did they lose their substance?

42. When *Ping* summons up the rain, how does he raise it? When those different parts were assembled and joined on to a deer, how were they fitted into shape?

43. When the Great Turtle walks along with an island on his back, how does he keep it steady? When the Strong Man made the boat move over dry land, how did he lift it?

44. When *Jiao* was in *Hu*, what did he want with his sister-in-law? How did *Shao Kang* go hunting with his dogs and bring his head tumbling down?

45. Nü Qi sewed *Jiao*' s lower garment for him, and he lodged with her in her house. How did her head fall from her body and she herself meet the end that was meant for him?

46. When the Strong Man prepared his warriors for battle, with what did he strengthen them? When he overturned the boat of the Lord of *Zhen-xun*, by what means did he take it?

47. 桀伐蒙山，何所得焉[桀：夏王朝最后一位国王。蒙山：地名或国名。]？妺嬉何肆？汤何殛焉[妺嬉：桀妻。殛：诛杀。]？

48. 舜闵在家，父何以鳏[舜：舜帝]？尧不姚告，二女何亲？

49. 厥萌在初，何所亿焉[萌：萌发。亿：度，一本作意。]？璜台十成，谁所极焉[璜：近似玉的美石。成：重。极：穷尽，这里是达到的意思。]？

50. 登立为帝，孰道尚之[登立为帝：登而立之为帝。]？女娲有体，孰制匠之[女娲：《说文》：“娲，古之神圣女，化万物者也。”]？

51. 舜服厥弟，终然为害。何肆犬豕，而厥身不危败[豕，一本作体 。厥身：犬豕之体]？

52. 吴获迄古，南岳是止[吴：族名 。迄古：终古。南岳：衡山。是止：“终古之所居”。]。孰期去斯，得两男子[去斯：离开这里。两男子：太伯、仲雍两兄弟。]。

53. 缘鹄饰玉，后帝是飨[缘：因。饰玉：鼎。后帝是飨：即后于帝是飨。]。何承谋夏桀，终以灭丧[承谋：继续辅佑，指天帝辅佑夏王朝直到夏桀。]？

54. 帝乃降观，下逢伊挚[帝：天帝。降观：天帝到人间察访。伊挚：伊尹，挚是他的名。]；何条放致罚，而黎服大说[条：鸣条，地名。致罚：《商书•汤誓》：“致天之罚。”黎：众人。]？

47. What did *Jie* get when he attacked *Meng-shan*? How did *Mo Xi* bewitch him, and how did *Tang* kill him?

48. If *Shun* had a wife in his house, how could he be a bachelor? How could *Yao*'s two daughters be married to him if he did not tell his family?

49. Who built the ten-storeyed tower of jade? Who foresaw it all in the beginning, when the first signs appeared?

50. By what law was *Nü Wa* raised up to become high lord? By what means did she fashion the different creatures?

51. *Shun* served his brother, but his brother still did him evil. Why, when he behaved worse than a brute beast to *Shun*, did *Shun*'s brother come to no harm?

52. Fleeing from *Gu Gong,* they possessed *Wu* and stayed in *Nan-yue*. Who would have thought to find the two princes in that place?

53. From a bird-shaped vessel embellished with jade the high lord was feasted. How did he receive counsel for *Jie of Xia*'s overthrow, so that at the last he destroyed him?

54. The high lord came down and looked about, and there he met *Yi Zhi*. How did he bring about *Jie*'s chastisement, so that the people were mightily rejoiced?

55. 简狄在台，喾何宜[简狄：有娀氏女。传说因玄鸟而生契，为商之始祖。台：简狄所居住的高台。喾(kù)：传说中的高辛氏。]？玄鸟致贻，女何喜[贻：赠。指玄鸟遗卵。]？

56. 该秉季德，厥父是臧[该：即殷主亥。季：亥之父。臧(zāng)：善。]；胡终弊于有扈，牧夫牛羊[弊：通毙。有扈：浇国名也。]？

57. 干协时舞，何以怀之[干：盾。此指干戚舞。协：和。]？平胁曼肤，何以肥之[胁：胸前。曼：柔润的意思。]？

58. 有扈牧竖，云何而逢[牧竖：牧童]？击床先出，其命何从[击床：刺杀。先出：走脱。]？

59. 恒秉季德，焉得夫朴牛[恒：亥的弟弟。王亥为有易所杀，王恒便又继承了季的事业。朴牛：《山海经》作“仆牛”，即“服牛”。]？何往营班禄，不但还来[班禄：班，颁布；禄，禄爵。]？

60. 昏微遵迹，有狄不宁[微：上甲微，王亥之子。遵迹：遵循行迹。有狄：有易之误。]；何繁鸟萃棘，负子肆情[繁鸟萃棘：指战场上勇士丛集，耀武扬威。负子：上甲微。肆情：纵兵逞豪情。]？

61. 眩弟并淫，危害厥兄[眩弟：指上甲微诸弟作乱。不止一弟，故云“并淫”。]；何变化以作诈，后嗣而逢长[逢长：迎来了发展。]？

55. When *Jian Di* was in the tower, how did *Ku* favour her? When the swallow brought his gift, why was the maiden glad?

56. *Hai* inherited *Ji*'s prowess. His father was a goodly man. Why did he end by losing his oxen and sheep in *You-yi*?

57. How did he win her heart by dancing with shield and plumes, and how did she of the smooth sides and lovely skin become his paramour?

58. What did *You-yi*'s herdsmen say when they found them? When they struck the bed, he had already left the chamber: how did he meet his fate?

59. *Heng,* too, inherited *Ji* prowess. How did he get back those oxherds and oxen? How did he go about there dispensing gifts, but not return empty-handed?

60. Dark *Wei* followed in his brothers' footsteps and the Lord of *You-yi* was stirred against him. Why, when the birds flocked together, did she forsake her own son and give herself to him?

61. The Dark Man lay with her adulterously and destroyed his elder brother. Why, after such falsehood and treachery, was it given to his posterity to flourish?

62. 成汤东巡，有莘爰极[有莘：国名，在伊水一带。]；何乞彼小臣，而吉妃是得[乞彼小臣：小臣，媵臣，指伊尹。吉妃：指成汤自有莘国迎娶之妃。]？

63. 水滨之木，得彼小子[水滨：指伊水之滨。]；夫何恶之，媵(yìng)有莘之妇？

64. 汤出重泉，夫何罪尤[重泉：地名，传说汤曾被夏桀囚在这里。]？不胜心伐帝，夫谁使挑之[伐：称美。挑，一作桃。]？

65. 会朝争盟，何践吾期[会朝：诸侯之师会集于甲子之朝的意思。争盟：争赴盟誓。指诸侯争赴武王伐纣之盟。]？苍鸟群飞，孰使萃之[苍鸟群飞：形容诸侯大军云集。孰使萃之：指得天之集命，姜尚指挥众军。]？

66. 列击纣躬，叔旦不嘉[列：指周武王等戮纣王尸体。叔旦：周公，武王之弟，名旦。不嘉：不赞成。]。何亲揆发，定周之命以咨嗟[揆(kuí)：揆度；发：调兵。此指武王亲自调度，终于一举灭纣。]？

67. 授殷天下，其位安施？反成乃亡，其罪伊何？

68. 争遣伐器，何以行之[伐器：攻伐之器。]？并驱击翼，何以将之？

69. 昭后成游，南土爰底[爰：于。底：至。]；厥利惟何，逢彼白雉[逢：迎。]？

70. 穆王巧梅，何为周流[穆王：周穆王。梅：贪。]?环理天下，夫何索求？

62. *Tang* the Successful travelled to the east and came to *You-xin*. How did he come to ask for that bondsman and win a goodly queen?

63. From the tree by the water's edge they got that little child. Why did they so hate him that they sent him away with the lady of *You-xin*?

64. *Tang* came out of *Chong-quan*: for what crime was he shut up there? Who provoked him to march with impatient heart against his lord king?

65. On the morning of the first day we took our oath. How did we all arrive on time? When the grey geese came flocking together, at whose summons did they gather?

66. When *Zhòu*'s body was beheaded and mutilated, why was *Shu Dan* unhappy? When on his own he planned to make the dominion of *Zhou* secure, why did King *Fa* sigh?

67. For what kingly virtue did Heaven bestow *Yin*'s empire on him, and for what sin was it taken from him so soon after he had achieved it?

68. How were the princes able to make rebellion when all the weapons of war had been handed in? And how did *Shu Dan* lead his armies to smite them on both their flanks?

69. Lord *Zhao* did much travelling. What did it profit him to meet that white rhinoceros when he went to the South Land?

70. King *Mu* was a breeder of horses. For what reason did he roam about? What was he looking for when he made his circuit of the earth?

71. 妖夫曳炫，何号于市[妖：怪。号：呼。]？周幽谁诛，焉得夫褒姒[褒姒：周幽王后。]？

72. 天命反侧，何罚何佑？齐桓九会，卒然身杀[齐桓九会：言齐桓公任管仲，九合诸侯，一匡天下。卒：终。]。

73. 彼王纣之躬，孰使乱惑？何恶辅弼，谗谄是服？

74. 比干何逆，而抑沉之[比干：纣叔父。谏纣，纣怒，乃杀之剖其心。]？雷开阿顺，而赐封之[雷开：佞人，阿顺于纣。]？

75. 何圣人之一德，卒其异方[圣人：周文王。卒：终。]？梅伯受醢，箕子佯狂[梅伯：《吕氏春秋·行论篇》："昔者纣为无道，杀梅伯而醢之，醢(hǎi)：将人剁成肉酱。箕子：纣的叔父，比干被杀，箕子惧，乃佯狂为奴，终被纣所囚。]。

76. 稷惟元子，帝何竺之[稷：后稷。元子：始子。竺(zhú)：厚也。]？投之于冰上，鸟何燠之[燠(yù)：焐暖的意思。]？

77. 何冯弓挟矢，殊能将之[冯(píng)弓：满弓、张弓。殊能：绝能。将之：统帅之。]？既敬帝切激，何逢长之[敬帝切激：指后稷祭祀天帝的殷切。]？

78. 伯昌号衰，秉鞭作牧[伯昌：周文王，名昌，殷纣时为西伯。号衰：号令于殷之衰世。秉鞭作牧：执政而为一方之长。]；何令彻彼岐社，命有殷国[彻：通。岐：岐周。社：土地神社，指社稷。]？

71. When the witches were tied up together, what was it that was crying in the market-place? Whom was You of *Zhou* punishing when he got that *Bao Si*?

72. Huan of *Qi* nine times assembled the vassals, yet in the end his body was destroyed. Heaven in its dispensations veers first to one side and then to the other. Why did it first favour him and then afterwards punish him?

73. Who was it that led *King Zhou* into folly? Why did he hate his ministers and let flatterers and backbiters serve him?

74. How had *Bi Gan* offended that he should be suppressed, and how had *Lei Kai* found favour to be given a fief?

75. Mei Bo was sliced and salted, but *Ji Zi* feigned madness. Why is it that wise men whose virtue is the same yet act in different ways?

76. King Millet was his firstborn: why did the high lord treat him so cruelly? When he was left out on the ice, how did the birds keep him warm?

77. Drawing his bow to the full and grasping the arrow, how did he become a war-leader? After giving the high lord so great a shock, how did he come to have a glorious future?

78. Lord *Chang* abandoned his own title and consented to be a shepherd of the marches for King *Zhou*. Why then did he remove his altars from *Qi* and claim heaven mandate to supplant *Yin*?

79. 迁藏就岐，何能依[迁藏：暗迁。依：依存。]？殷有惑妇，何所讥[讥：刺怨。]？

80. 受赐兹醢(hǎi)，西伯上告[受赐兹醢：指纣王以文王长子肉做的羹赐文王。]。何亲就上帝罚，殷之命以不救[罚：纣所受天之罚。]？

81. 师望在肆，昌何识[师望：姜太公。]？鼓刀扬声，后何喜[鼓刀：传说吕望在遇到文王之前曾在屠肆操刀。后：指文王。]？

82. 武发杀殷，何所悒[杀：攻克。悒(yì)：忧虑。]？载尸集战，何所急[尸：木主。《史记•周本纪》："为文王木主，载以军车中。"]？

83. 伯林雉经(zhì jīng)，惟其何故[伯林：地名或林名，待考。雉经：自缢。这里指管叔。]？何感天抑地，夫谁畏惧[感天抑地：感天动地。]？

84. 皇天集命，惟何戒之[集命：成命，授予天下的意思。]？受礼天下，又使至代之[受礼：受天子之礼。言王者既已修行礼义，受天命而有天下，为什么又使异姓取而代之？]。

85. 初汤臣挚，后兹承辅[臣挚：伊尹，名挚。]，何卒官汤，尊食宗绪[卒：终。绪：业。官汤：相汤。尊食：庙食。]？

86. 勋阖梦生，少离散亡[勋：功也。阖：吴王阖闾也。]，何壮武厉，能流厥严[壮：大。此句言吴王阖庐少小散亡，为什么能够壮大厉其勇武，流其威严呢？]？

87. 彭铿斟雉，帝何飨(xiǎng)[彭铿：彭祖。斟：勺也。]？受寿永多，夫何久长？

89. 中央共牧，后何怒[中央：周之中央，渭水流域一带。共牧：指秦先民与周民族共同放牧于渭水一带。]？蜂蛾微命，力何固[蜂蛾微命：指秦民族当时寄居于周民族势力范围之内，十分弱小，有如蜂蛾。]？

79. When *Tai* packed up his possessions and moved to *Qi*, how did he get the people to follow him? *Yin* had a woman of guile: what protests did he hear?

80. When *Zhòu* bestowed that flesh on him, the Lord of the West declared it to heaven. Why did *Zhòu* invite God's chastisement, so that the dominion of *Yin* could not be saved?

81. When *Wang* the Counsellor was in the market, how did *Chang* know him? When he struck with his knife and the sound rang out, why was the king pleased?

82. When *Wu* set out to kill *Yin*, why was he grieved? He went into battle carrying his father's corpse: why was he in such a hurry?

83. Why did *Bo Lin* hang himself? When heaven was moved by his death to afflict the earth, who was so afraid?

84. When High God in heaven confers His mandate, how does He give notice of it? When He has bestowed dominion over the world on one, why does He take it away and give it to another?

85. At first *Tang* made *Zhi* his servant, but afterwards he made him his counsellor. How did *Zhi* end by becoming *Tang*'s minister, and after his death share in the sacrifices of the royal ancestors?

86. He the Valiant was the grandson of *Meng*. When he was young he was an outcast. How did he make strong his might, so that he could spread his authority abroad?

87. What happened when *Peng Keng* offered the pheasant' s broth to the high lord? After enjoying so long a life, why did he still have regrets?

89. When the lords of the centre ruled together, why was the lord king angry? Wasps and ants have a mean fate: how could their power be enduring?

90. 惊女采薇，鹿何祐[鹿：指飞廉。]？北至回水，萃何喜[回水：指汾水在临汾附近一段分而复合的大迂回。萃：聚集。]？

91. 兄有噬(shì)犬，弟何欲[兄：指秦民族先人非子。噬：发语词。犬：犬丘。弟：非子之异母弟，名成。]？易之以百两，卒无禄[易之：指周孝王没有答应封成为犬丘之主，而让他去出使西戎。百两：指车，即百辆。无禄：指非子之弟出使西戎，终无爵禄。]。

92. 薄暮雷电，归何忧[归何忧：指楚灵王因内乱而无家可归。]？厥严不奉，帝何求[厥严不奉：指楚灵王失去了王位的尊严。帝何求：指天帝舍弃了灵王而出来一个更为无道的平王，究竟是为什么呢？]。

93. 伏匿穴处，爰何云[伏匿穴处：指楚昭王因吴师将入郢都，出逃东渡汉江，先后伏匿于云梦、郧、随的故事。]？荆勋作师，夫何长[荆勋作师：自楚庄王以来，以五霸之强，称雄南方。]？

94. 悟过改更，我又何言[悟过：指昭王代父受过，深有所悟。]？吴光争国，久余是胜[争国：指吴公子光杀王僚争得吴国王位。久余是胜：久是胜余，余指楚国。]。

95. 何环闾穿社，以及丘陵[闾：闾里。社：里社。此句王逸《章句》本作“何环穿自闾社丘陵爰出子文”，据林庚《天问论笺》改]？是淫是荡，爰出子文[是淫是荡：指令尹子文之母。]？

96. 吾告堵敖以不长[吾：据闻一多《楚辞校补》，当为“语”。语告：诉说的意思 。堵敖：楚文王之子，楚成王之兄。]，何诫上自予，忠名弥彰[诫：王逸《章句》本作“试 ”。自予：据林庚《天问论笺》，当为“自”纾，即“自毁其家以纾国难”，也就是子文之所以忠名弥彰的缘故。(本篇释文参考了王逸章句本、林庚《天问论笺》、闻一多《楚辞校补》及陈子展《楚辞直解》等。)]？

90. When the maiden warned the brothers not to pick ferns, how did the deer come to their aid? When they came north to the whirling water, why were they glad to be in That at place?

91. The elder brother had a hunting-dog. Why did the younger brother desire it? The elder bestowed a hundred chariots on him, yet he ended by losing all his substance.

93. Towards evening there was thunder and lightning. Why was the lady sad? The high lord did not reveal his majesty. What was he seeking?

93. What was the king's sorrow when he lay in hiding and lived in caves? What did we say when he awoke to the error of his ways? When *Jing* was glorious in war, how came we to be the leaders?

94. But when *Guang* of *Wu* seized power, why were we so long defeated?

95. Round the village they went and through the altars until they came to the holy mounds. How came *Zi Wen* to be the fruit of such wantonness?

96. Du Ao did not reign for long. How is it that though he murdered his lord and seized kingship for himself, yet the fame of his loyalty spread through out the world?

“文变染乎世情，兴废系乎时序。”

——南朝·梁 刘勰《文心雕龙》

中国经典双语阅读

刘勰《文心雕龙》（选）

Unit 12

刘勰《文心雕龙》(选)

Selected from Liu Xie's *Wen Xin Diao Long*[1]

[思想指要]刘勰(约公元465—公元520年),字彦和,生活于南北朝时期的南朝梁代,京口(今镇江)人。他所写《文心雕龙》一书,奠定了他在中国文学批评史上作为文学理论家、文学批评家的地位。全书共10卷,50篇(原书分上、下部,各25篇),以孔子美学思想为基础,兼采道家,认为道是文学的本源,圣人是文人学习的楷模,而"经书"是文章的典范。他把作家创作个性的形成归结为"才""气""学""习"四个方面。《文心雕龙》还系统论述了文学的形式和内容、继承和革新的关系,又在探索研究文学创作构思的过程中,强调指出了艺术思维活动的具体形象性这一基本特征,并初步提出了艺术创作中的形象思维问题,对文学的艺术本质及其特征有较自觉的认识,开研究文学形象思维的先河。《文心雕龙》全面总结了齐梁时代以前的美学成果,细致地探索和论述了文学的审美本质及其创造、鉴赏的美学规律。

[Introduction] Liuxie (465A.D.—520 A.D.), born in Jingkou (now Zhenjiang, Jiangsu Province), lived in the Liang Generation of the Southern Dynasties during the period of the Southern and Northern Dynasties. *Wen Xin Diao Long* established his position as a literary theorist and critic in the history of Chinese literary criticism. It consists of 10 volumes and 50 articles (25 each in the first and second parts). Based on the aesthetic principles of Confucianism and Taoism, Liuxie holds that "Tao" is the ontological source of literary creation, the sage is the exemplar that later scholars should hold by admiration, and the "Confucius Canon" is the ethic model that all writings are supposed to follow. He attributed the construction of writers' creative personality to the Four Aspects of "Talent", "Qi", "Insight" and

[1] 中文选自《文心雕龙注释》，刘勰著，周振甫注，北京：人民文学出版社，1981年。

Wind and Bone, selected from *Readings in Chinese Literary Thought,* written and translated by Stephen Owen, Harvard University, Cambridge, Massachusetts, 1992.

"Learning". In *Wen Xin Diao Long*, he also thoroughly discusses the relationship between the form and the theme of literature, and the relation between the inheritance and innovation of literature. And when exploring and researching the conception of literary creation, he emphasizes the basic trait of the image-thinking and initially comes up with the problem of image thinking in artistic creation. Liuxie pioneers the investigation of image thinking in literary creation for his more strong consciousness of the artistic nature and the characteristics of literature. In a word, *Wen Xin Diao Long* comprehensively outlines the aesthetic achievements before the Qi and Liang dynasties, and meticulously explains the aesthetic essence and the laws of literary creation and appreciation.

《风骨》Wind and Bone

本节所选《风骨》篇的“风骨”一词，原是用于汉魏以来品评人物的词语，指人物的风神骨相。刘勰借用这一用语来论述文学作品的基本要求。其中“风”是对作品情感内容方面的美学要求，“骨”是对作品语言文辞方面的美学要求。“风骨”即要求内容富有感染力，语言刚健挺拔。黄侃《文心雕龙札记》：“风即文意，骨即文辞。”黄侃学生范文澜在其《文心雕龙注》也指出：“风即文意，骨即文辞，黄先生论之详矣。窃复阐明其意曰：辞之端直者谓之辞，而肥辞繁杂亦谓之辞，惟前者始得文骨之辞，肥辞不与焉。”郭绍虞《中国历代文论选》：“风骨是思想性和艺术性的统一体，它的基本特征，在于明朗刚健，遒劲而有力，和‘索莫乏气’‘瘠义肥辞’的文学是冰炭不相容的。”总之，风骨，就是健康的内容与生动有力的语言形式的统一。

[Introduction] *Feng Gu* is the twenty-eighth article of *WenXin Diao Long*. "Wind and Bone" was originally used to evaluate characters since the period of Han and Wei Dynasties, referring to the elegant bearing and bodily constitution of characters. Liuxie used this term to discuss the basic requirements for literary creation. Respectively speaking, the word of "wind" is the aesthetic requirement for emotional content of works and the word of "bone" is an aesthetic requirement for the language of the works. To put "Feng" and "Gu" together, it means that the literary creation should be appealing in its content and should be vigorously artistic and mentally penetrating in its language. Huang Kan, a modern scholar, said in his *Reading Notes on WenXin Diaolong*, "Wind refers to the literary meaning and bone refers to the literary phrases. " Fan Wenlan, a student of Huang Kan, also pointed out in his *Notes on WenXin Diaolong* that "Mr. Huang's discourse is clearly detailed that 'wind refers to literary meaning and bone to literary phrases. ' But I want to clarify their meanings again, that is, the phrases with straightforwardness means the diction, while the phrases with fatty words also mean the diction, but the former refers to the phrases with literary bones, the phrases with fatty words are not encouraged". Guo Shaoyu said in his *Selected Literary Theories of the Past Dynasties in China,* "what is insisted on by *Feng Gu* lies in the unity of thought and art. And its basic feature is of being clear and energetic, vigorous and powerful, which is incompatible with the literary style of "being dull, lifeless, lacking *qi*" and of the phrasing fat, which is indiscriminately mixed and lacking all governing coherence — then we see no evidence of bone". In short, wind and bone is the unity of healthy content and the vivid form.

诗总六义，风冠其首，斯乃化感之本源，志气之符契也[这里先讲"风"的来源，本于《诗经》中的国风。《毛诗序》："风，风也，教也，风以动之，教以化之。"化感：即教化。风有教化作用。]。是以怊怅述情，必始乎风[怊怅(chāo chàng)：犹惆怅。始乎：始于。]；沈吟铺辞，莫先于骨。故辞之待骨，如体之树骸，情之含风，犹形之包气[沈吟：沉吟，低声吟味。铺辞：陈辞，作文。骨是对文辞的美学要求。辞之待骨，如体之树骸：骸是骨架。体不是骨架，但有了骨架才能直立；辞不是骨，但有了骨才显得有力。骨要求文辞的端直。情之含风，犹形之包气：形体没有气，就死了；抒情没有风，就感动不了人。形不是气，但有气才活；情不是风，但有风才动人。]。结言端直，则文骨成焉；意气骏爽，则文风清焉[端直：正直。语言正直构成文骨，正直和意义有关，说明骨同意义相关。《附会》："必以情志为神明，事义为骨髓，辞采为肌肤。"因此骨不是作品的思想，而是情志，骨是事义，就是《事类》里讲的引事引言。但风骨的骨是对引事引言的美学要求，即端直。骏爽：快利，意气快利产生风。]。若丰藻克赡，风骨不飞，则振采失鲜，负声无力[赡(shàn)：丰富。这里讲缺乏风骨的毛病。没有骨，则振采失鲜，用字浮泛，辞藻不鲜明；没有风，则负声无力，结响凝滞。风像人有气，是活的，没有风，辞藻都死了。骨像体的骨架，没有骨架，辞藻像软骨病立不起来。]。是以缀虑裁篇，务盈守气，刚健既实，辉光乃新，其为文用，譬征鸟之使翼也[缀(zhuì)虑裁篇：运思谋篇。务盈守气：务必充实守气。守气指生气，《左传》昭公十一年，叔向说："单子其将死乎?……无守气矣。"生气兼指风骨，生气勃勃则"辉光乃新"，即有风；又"刚健笃实"，即有骨。有了风骨像鹰隼的奋飞。《易·大畜》："刚健笃实，辉光日新。"《礼记·月 ·令》："季冬之月，征鸟厉疾。"征鸟，指鹰隼等猛禽。]。

The Book of Songs (《诗经》) encompasses "Six Principles("六义")," of which "wind"(风, the "Airs" section) is the first. This is the original source of stirring (感) and transformation (化), and it is the counterpart of intent (志) and *qi*(气). The transformation of the disconsolate feelings (情) always begins with wind; but nothing has priority over bone's disposing the words (辞), as one intones them thoughtfully. The way in which the words depend upon bone is like the way in which the skeleton is set in the (human) form (体). And the quality of wind contained in the affections is like the way our shape holds *qi* within it. When words are put together straight through, then the bone of writing (文一骨) is complete therein; when concept (意) and are swift and vigorous, then the wind of writing (文一风) is born therein. If a piece of writing is abundantly supplied with elegant phrasing, but lacks wind and bone to fly, then it loses all luster when it shows its coloration (采) and lacks the force to carry any resonance. Thus in composing one's reflections and in cutting a piece to pattern, it is essential to conserve a plenitude of *qi*. Only when its firm strength has become solid (实) will its radiance be fresh. We may compare its (wind and bone) function in literature to the way in which a bird of prey uses its wings.

故练于骨者，析辞必精；深乎风者，述情必显。捶字坚而难移，结响凝而不滞，此风骨之力也[这里讲锻炼风骨，练骨要求用字扎实而不能移动，避免浮泛。练风要求声韵凝定而不板滞，凝定指抒情确切，不滞指抒情生动，才能述情必显。]。

若瘠义肥辞，繁杂失统，则无骨之徵也；思不环周，[索莫]牵课乏气，则无风之验也[失统：失掉统绪，没有条理。索莫：杨注：“莫”，黄校云：元作 “课”。何焯云：“疑是‘牵课’。”按作“牵课”是，“索”即“牵”之误。《养气》 “非牵课才外也。”《宋书·孝武帝纪》(大明二年诏)：“勿使牵课虚悬。”“牵课”犹今言勉强。]。

One who has refined the bone of the work must keep to the essentials in argument; one who has attained depth in wind must transmit the affections clearly. In the first case, the words have been pounded so firmly that they cannot be moved; in the second case, the resonance will be knit fixedly and not get bogged down—this is the force of wind and bone. If the truth（义）are emaciated but the phrasing fat—a profusion indiscriminately mixed and lacking all governing coherence — then we see no evidence of bone. If the thought（思）does not go full circle — dull, lifeless, lacking *qi* — then we see no evidence of wind.

昔潘勗锡魏，思摹经典，群才韬笔，乃其骨髓峻(jǔn)也[潘勖(xù)锡魏：见《诏策》注[26]。思摹经典：文思摹仿经典。韬(tāo)笔：藏笔。骨髓峻：事义为骨髓，即用经典中的辞义来写，故以为高。]；相如赋仙，气号凌云，蔚为辞宗，乃其风力遒也[《史记·司马相如传》：“相如既奏大人之颂，天子大说(悦)，飘飘有凌云之气，似游天地之间意。”赋仙：指作《大人赋》。蔚：蔚然，状文彩富。遒(qiú)：劲；风力遒劲。]。能鉴斯要，可以定文，兹术或违，无务繁采。故魏文称“文以气为主，气之清浊有体，不可力强而致[曹丕《典论·论文》：“文以气为主，气之清浊有体，不可力强而致。譬诸音乐，曲度虽均，节奏同检，至于引气不齐，巧拙有素，虽在父兄，不能以移子弟。”气指才气。曹丕认为才气有清浊，本于天性，不是可以用力达到的。这是宣传天才决定论，参看《体性》的说明。]。”故其论孔融，则云“体气高妙”。论徐干，则云 “时有齐气”；论刘桢，则云“有逸气”[《典论·论文》：“孔融体气高妙，有过人者。”又：“徐干时有齐气。”齐气，齐俗文气舒缓。曹丕《与吴质书》：“公干(刘桢字)有逸气，但未遒耳。”逸气，气高超。]。公干亦云：“孔氏卓卓，信含异气，笔墨之性，殆不可胜叫[刘桢的话已散失。信含异气：确实含有特异的气，这个气也指才气。笔墨之性，殆不可胜：文字几乎不够表达他的才气。]。”并重气之旨也。夫翚翟备色而翾翥百步，肌丰而力沈也；鹰隼乏采而翰飞戾天，骨劲而气猛也[翚(huī 灰)翟(zhái)备色：《说文》：“雉五采备曰翚。”又：“翟，山雉尾长者。”翻翥(xuān zhù宣注)：小飞，指飞不高。肌丰力沉：肌肉丰满，气力不足。翰飞戾天：高飞至天，见《诗··小雅·小宛》。]。文章才力，有似于此。若风骨乏采，则鸷集翰林；采乏风骨，则雉窜文囿：唯藻耀而高翔，固文[笔]章之鸣凤也[翰林：文翰之林；文囿(yòu)：文章苑囿。都指文学园地。藻耀高翔：有文彩的照耀，又有风骨而能高飞。笔，孙云：“御览乍章。”]。

Long ago when Pan Xu（潘勗）wrote [on behalf of the Han Emperor（汉帝）] a Grant of Honor for the Duke of Wei［Cao Cao/（曹操）], his literary thought aspired to emulate the Classical canons, and all other persons of talent hid their writing brushes: this was due to the excellence of bone and marrow in his work. When Si-ma Xiang-ru（司马相如）wrote his poetic exposition on the immortal［“The Poetic Exposition on the Great Man（《大人赋》),” presented to Han Wu-di（汉武帝）]，people declared that his *qi* passed up over the clouds, and they found splendor in his mastery of language（辞）; this was the firmness of the force of wind in his work. If a person sees the essential points clearly here, he can perfect his writing; but should he stray from this technique, there’s nothing to be gained from lush coloration（采）. For this reason, Cao Pi（曹丕）claimed, ‘‘In literature *qi* is the dominant factor. *Qi* has its nonnative forms—clear and murky. It is not to be brought by force.” Thus when he discussed Kong Rong（孔融）, he said that his “form and *qi* are lofty and subtle.” And when he discussed Xu

Gan(徐干), he said that "at times he shows languid *qi*. In discussing Liu Zhen(刘桢), Cao Pi says that he has "an untrammeled *qi*." and Liu Zhen himself said, "Kong Rong is superlative and truly has an unusual *qi* within him; it would hardly be possible to surpass him in the nature of his brushwork. All of them laid stress on the significance of *qi*. The pheasant has a full complement of colors, but it can flutter only a hundred paces — its force gives out because its flesh is fat. A falcon lacks bright colors, but it flies high, to the very heavens — its bone is sturdy and its *qi* is fierce. The force of talent in literary works bears resemblance to these examples. If wind and bone lack bright coloration, we have a bird of prey roosting in the forest of letters. And if bright color lack wind and bone, we have a pheasant hiding away in the literary garden. Only with glittering rhetoric and high soaring do we really have a singing phoenix in writing.

若夫熔铸经典之范，翔集子史之术，洞晓情变，曲昭文体，然后能孚甲新意，雕画奇辞[熔铸经典之范：按照经典的典范来创作。熔铸犹创作。翔集子史之术：采择子史的技巧。翔集，鸟飞回翔而后停下，指审察采择。洞晓情变：通晓情伪变化。曲昭文体：曲折详尽地明白各种文体。孚(莩) 甲：萌芽，指开始产生。雕画：犹修饰。]。昭体故意新而不乱，晓变故辞奇而不黩[意新而不乱：根据新意选择恰当的体式来写，不会选错，所以不乱。辞奇而不黩：自铸奇辞，不会滥用辞语。黩(dú)，滥。]。若骨采未圆，风辞未练，而跨略旧规，驰骛新作，虽获巧意，危败亦多[骨采未圆、风辞未练：这是互文，即风骨没有成熟，辞采没有精练。跨略旧规、驰骛(wù)新作：抛弃旧的规范，追逐新作。]。岂空结奇字，纰缪而成经[矣]乎[矣，范注："矣字疑当作乎。"]。周书云："辞尚体要，弗惟好异。"[《周书》的话，见《徵圣》]盖防文滥也。然文术多门，各适所好，明者弗授，学者弗师；于是习华随侈，流遁忘反。若能确乎正式，使文明以健，则风清骨峻，篇体光华[确乎正式：坚定地建立正确的体式，指具有风骨的风格。文明以健：文明指风清，文健指骨峻。]。能研诸虑，何远之有哉[《论语·子罕》："未之思也，夫何远之有(有何远)！"]！

When one casts and molds according to the model of the Classics, or soars and roosts among the techniques of the thinkers and historians, then one will comprehend the mutations of the affections (情—变), and one will have revealed the forms of literature (文—体) in their minute particulars. Only then can one cause fresh concepts (意) to sprout; only then can one carve out and paint wondrous phrasing (辞). Having the forms revealed means that concepts will be fresh but not in disarray; comprehending the mutations means that phrasing will be wondrous without getting muddy. But if bone and coloration are not fully perfected, if wind and phrasing are not polished, and a writer strides proudly over all former rules to go rushing after fresh creations — in such cases, even though one may attain some clever concept, danger and ruin usually follow. A hollow construction of strange words, full of error, cannot become a Classic. *The Book of Documents* (《周书》) says, "In diction value embodying the essentials, do not develop a passion for (mere) difference." This is to prevent excess in literature.

There are many ways into the techniques of literature, and each person suits his own preferences. Those who understand are not taught; those who study have no teachers. Therefore, one who becomes habituated to glitter and goes off into excels will drift away and never return. But if one can become firm in the proper models and make his writing bright [明, "showing comprehension and manifestly comprehensible"] and firm, then the wind will be clear, and the bone, splendid; and the form of the piece will shimmer. Accomplishment will not be far to anyone who works at these considerations.

赞曰：情与气偕，辞共体并。文明以健，珪璋乃骋[情与气偕：情不能离气，要靠风来使情显气盛。辞共体并：辞不能离体，要靠骨来树立。有风就文采鲜明，有骨就刚健。珪璋(guī zhāng)：喻美好的文才，如“珪璋挺其惠心，英华秀其清气。”骋(chěng)：指文才驰骋。]。蔚彼风力，严此骨鲠。才锋峻立，符采克炳[骨鲠(gěng)：指骨力。符采克炳：情文能够照耀。]。

Supporting Verse: When affections and *qi* are joined together, / When phrasing goes together with form, / The writing is bright and firm. / A fine piece of jade is presented. / The force of wind is rich, / The boniness is stern. /Talent's spearhead stands high, /And matching coloration gleams.

《神思》Spirit and Thought [1]

《神思》是《文心雕龙》的第二十六篇，主要探讨艺术构思问题。《神思》篇是刘勰创作论的总纲。本篇从物与情、物与言和情与言三种关系的角度，概括地提出了他的基本主张和要求。《神思》是古代文论中比较全面而系统论述艺术构思的一篇重要文献。它所提出的“神与物游”的构思活动，初步总结了形象思维的基本特点。他认为作家的精神活动和万物的形象相结合，从而构成作品的各种内容。外界事物以它们不同的形貌来打动作家，作家内心就根据一定的法则而产生相应的活动；然后推敲作品的音节，运用比兴的方法。刘勰认为，倘能掌握构思的法则，创作一定能够成功。

[Introduction] *Shensi* (*Spirit Thought*), the twenty-sixth article of *Wen Xin Diao Long*, mainly discusses the problem of artistic conception. *Shensi* is the general outline of Liu Xie's creative theory. He puts forward his basic propositions and requirements from the perspective of the relationship between things and feelings, things and words, and feelings and words. *Shensi*, as an important document in ancient literary theory, comprehensively and systematically deals with the artistic conception. The idea that "mind wanders together with things" proposed in this essay preliminarily summarizes the basic characteristics of imaginal thinking. He believes that the writer's spiritual activities are combined with the images of all things, thus constituting various contents of the writers' works. When things from the outside move the writers with their different shapes, he will produce corresponding images according to certain creative rules in his mind. Then he will carefully consider the words and phrases of the work, using the method of analogy and

---

[1] 中文选自《文心雕龙注释》，刘勰著，周振甫注. 北京：人民文学出版社，1981 年。

Spirit and Thought, selected from *Readings in Chinese Literary Thought,* written and translated by Stephen Owen, Harvard University, Cambridge, Massachusetts, 1992.

imagination. In Liu Xie's view, if one can master the essentials of literary conception, he will be successful.

古人云："形在江海之上，心存魏阙之下。"神思之谓也[《庄子·让王》："中山公子牟(魏公子，名牟，封在中山)谓瞻子曰：'身在江海之上，心居乎魏阙(朝廷)之下，奈何？'"指身隐居而心想利禄，这里借指心思不受空间限制。魏阙，挂象魏(法令)的阙。宫前有两台，中缺，有通道，称阙；象魏，象，即法；魏，状高。神思：变化不测的思想。]。文之思也，其神远矣。故寂然凝虑，思接千载，悄焉动容，视通万里；吟咏之间，吐纳珠玉之声，眉睫之前，卷舒风云之色：其思理之致乎[其神远矣：指精神活动不受时空限制，思接千载是想到千载以前，视通万里是好象看到万里以外。吟咏时发珠玉声，眉睫前现风云色，形容声调的美好和景物的变化壮丽。]？

Long ago someone spoke of "the physical form's being by the rivers and lakes, but the mind's remaining at the foot of the palace towers of Wei." This is what is meant by spirit thought (神一思). And spirit goes far indeed in the thought that occurs in writing (文). When we silently focus our concerns, thought may reach to a thousand years in the past; and as our countenance stirs ever so gently, our vision may cross (通) ten thousand leagues. The sounds of pearls and jade are given forth while chanting and singing; right before our eyelashes, the color (色) of windblown clouds unfurls. This is accomplished by the basic principle of thought (思一理).

故思理为妙，神与物游，神居胸臆，而志气统其关键；物沿耳目，而辞令管其枢机[神与物游：精神活动和外物相接触。神居胸臆：古人认为心是精神活动的主宰，所以说居胸臆。志气统其关键：精神活动的关键由志和气来统辖。《孟子·公孙丑》上："夫志，气之帅也；气，体之充也。"精神活动由意志作统帅，配合着气势。如理直气壮，理直是志，气壮是气。辞令管其枢机：外物通过耳目的观察，用语言来表达，关键在运用语言上。枢，门臼；机，弩的机件，比喻关键。《易·系辞》上："言行，君子之枢机。"枢机，制动之主。]。枢机方通，则物无隐貌；关键将塞，则神有遁心[枢机方通：语言表达这一关打通了，外物的形貌就无法隐遁。关键将塞：志和气受到阻塞，如心愁身病，对外物视而不见，听而不闻。神有遁心：精神不集中，心不在焉。]。

When the basic principle of thought is at its most subtle, the spirit wanders with things. The spirit dwells in the breast; intent (志) and *qi* control the bolt to its gate (to let it out). Things come in through the ear and eye; in this, language controls the hinge and trigger. When hinge and trigger permit passage, no things have hidden appearance; when the bolt to the gate is closed, then spirit is concealed.

是以陶钧文思，贵在虚静，疏瀹五藏，澡雪精神[陶钧文思：酝酿文思。陶，瓦器；钧，制瓦器用的圆转器；陶钧，犹盖象的经营构造。贵在虚静：虚，不主观；静，不躁动。有了主观偏见，不容易看到外物的真相；心情躁动，不容易进行细致观察；所以要虚静。疏瀹(yuè 越)：疏通。澡雪：洗雪，洗净。五藏：五脏，指性情。要虚静，就要对心情进行疏导洗雪，除去急躁等，这是疏导；清洗主观偏见，这是澡雪，《庄子·知北游》："老聃曰：'汝齐(斋)戒疏瀹而(汝)心，澡雪而精神。'"]；积学以储宝，酌理以富才，研阅以穷照，驯致以[怿]绎辞[积学：心虚了可以容纳，积累学问。酌理：心静了可以辨别是非，斟酌事理。研阅：周密地观察、体会。阅，阅历。穷照：彻底观照，深入探索。驯致：顺着自然酝酿文思。驯，顺；致，达到。绎辞：抽出文辞；绎，抽出头绪。怿，一作绎。]；然后使玄解之宰，寻声律而定墨；独照之匠，窥意象而运斤：此盖驭文之首术，谋篇之大端[玄解之宰：深通事物奥秘者。独照之匠：有独特感受者。称宰是主宰，称匠指匠人。《庄子·人间世》："古者谓是帝之 县(悬)解。"释文："县，音玄。"又《天道》：轮扁(制轮匠人名扁)说："斲轮 (砍制车轮)徐则甘而不固(砍慢了，就省劲，但轮子不牢固)，疾则苦而不入(砍快了，就费力，但砍不深)，不徐不疾，得之于手而应于心，口不能言，有数(技巧)存焉于其间。"因技巧说不出，只有独自领会，所以称独照。运斤：

《庄子· 徐无鬼》："郢人垩(白土)慢(漫，染)其鼻端，若蝇翼，使匠石斲之。匠石运斤(斧)成风，听而斲之，尽垩而鼻不伤。"]。

Thus in shaping and turning [as on a potter's wheel] literary thought（文*—思*), the most important thing is emptiness and stillness within. Dredge clear the inner organs and wash the spirit pure. A mass learning to build a treasure house; consult principle（理*）to enrich talent; investigate and experience to know all that spears (literally "exhaust what shines"]; guide it along to spin the words out. Only then can the butcher, who cuts things apart mysteriously, set the pattern according to the rules of sound; and the uniquely discerning carpenter wield his ax with his eye to the concept—image（意—象). This is the foremost technique in directing the course of *wen*, the major point for planning a piece.

夫神思方运，万涂竞萌，规矩虚位，刻镂无形；登山则情满于山，观海则意溢于海，我才之多少，将与风云而并驱矣[万涂竞萌：文思开始酝酿，各种各样的念头争着萌生。规矩虚位：开始萌生的许多念头并不都能进入作品，这时还没形成一个主题，就文思说，还是虚位、无形。对于这些念头要依照写作的规矩来衡量，再加修饰刻镂。]。

When spirit thought is set in motion, ten thousand paths sprout before it; rules and regulations are still hollow positions; and the cutting or carving as yet has no form. If one climbs a mountain, one's affection(情）are filled by the mountain; if one contemplates the sea, one's concepts（意）are brought to brimming over by the sea. And, according to measured talent in the self, one may speed off together with the wind and clouds.

方其搦翰，气倍辞前；暨乎篇成，半折心始。何则？意翻空而易奇，言徵(zhēng)实而难巧也[搦(nuò)诺翰：执笔。暨：及。半折心始：开始觉得有很多可写，写成时却比开始想的打了个对折。这是因为：一，原来想的有很多不能进入作品。二，凭空想容易觉得奇妙。用语言来表达，中间有个距离。]。是以意授于思，言授于意，密则无际，疏则千里[意指意象，思指神思，言指语言文辞。神思构成意象，意象产生文辞。这三者的结合有疏有密。有时神与物游，心境交融，作者所想到的就是一个完整的意象，用语言恰好地表达出来，思、意、言密切结合，不烦绳削而自合，即密则无际。有时作者想得很多，到形成意象时，比原来想的已经有了很大改变；用语言表达时，又经反覆哆改，对意象又有很大改变，甚至没有意象，写不出来，即疏则千里]；或理在方寸，而求之域表，或义在咫尺，而思隔山河：是以秉心养术，无务苦虑，含章司契，不必劳情也[这里讲神思、意匠、言辞的疏则千里。神思同外界境物接触，从神思方面说，有了触发，引起情理，这就构成意匠，要是没有触发，引不起情理，就象远在外国，苦思不得，忽然触发了，原来就在心头眼底。理指情理，方寸指心头眼底。从境物方面说，要从境物中看出意义，才构成意匠。这个意义就在境物中找，可是没有找到时，就象隔着山河那样遥远，找到时，近得很，就在眼前的境物中。义指意义。咫尺指近。思就是想，想找这个意义。秉心：用心。在没有触发情理时，不用苦思力索，等有了触发再写，这是就神思方面说。含章：指境物，《原道》："俯察含章。" 司契：意义就在境物中找，所以境物是主管这种契合的，在没有契合时，不必劳情去求索，这是就境物方面说的。]。

Whenever a person grasps the writing brush, the *qi* is doubled even before the words come. But when a piece is complete it goes no further than half of that with which the mind began. Why is this? When concepts soar the empty sky, they easily become wondrous; but it is hard to be artful by giving them substantial（实）expression in words. Thus concept（意）is received from thought（思), and language in turn is received from concept. These (language and concept) may be so close that there is no boundary between them, or so remote that they seem a thousand leagues from one another. Sometimes the principle（理）lies within the speck of mind, yet one seeks it far beyond the world; sometimes a truth（义）is only a foot away, but thought goes beyond mountains and rivers in pursuit of it. Thus if one grasps the mind and nourishes its technique, it will not be the requisite to brood painfully. If you retain the design within and retain control of the creditor' s half of the contract (司一契), you need not force the affections to suffer.

《体性》Nature and Form [1]

《体性》是《文心雕龙》的第二十七篇，从作品风格(“体”)和作者性格(“性”)的关系来论述文学作品的风格特色。刘勰以征圣、宗经的观点来强调或贬低某种风格，这给他的风格论带来一定局限。但在理论上，他正确地总结了风格形成的主要原因，明确了风格和个性的关系，强调后天学习的重要，这对中国古代文学风格论的建立和发展，都是有益的。

[Introduction]*Ti Xing* (Nature and Form), the twenty-seventh article of *Wen Xin Diao Long,* mainly discusses the style and personal characteristics of literary works from the relationship between the style (“Ti”) of works and the author's character (“Xing”). Liuxie emphasizes or belittles a certain style from the viewpoint of following the sages and worshiping the canon, which has brought certain limitations to his theory of style. But theoretically, he correctly summarizes the main reasons for the formation of style, clarifies the relationship between style and personality, and emphasizes the necessity of acquired learning, which is beneficial to the establishment and development of the style theory of ancient China.

夫情动而言形，理发而文见，盖沿隐以至显，因内而符外者也[隐显：情和理没有表达出来前是含蕴在内的，是隐的；用言和文表达出来后是表现在外的，是显的。表现在外的文辞也是作者性情的自然流露。这就把文辞的体貌和作者的性情结合起来了。文见：文现。]。

When the affections (情) are stirred, language gives them (external) form (形); when inherent principle (理) comes forth, pattern (文) is manifest. We follow a course from what is latent and arrive at the manifest. According to what lies within, there is correlation to what lies without.

然才有庸俊，气有刚柔，学有浅深，习有雅郑，并情性所铄，陶染所凝，是以笔区云谲，文苑波诡者矣[情性所铄(shuò)，陶染所凝：作者的才气，是他的性情所形成的；作者的学问和习气，是他所受的文化教养和环境影响所形成的。这里从文辞的本貌和作者的性情的关系，推求出才、气、学、习来。习，习惯、习俗、习气。雅郑：雅正和淫靡；雅本指周王朝的标准音乐，郑本指郑国的靡靡之音。笔区、文苑：指文学园地。云谲波诡：作品像云彩和波纹的变幻多端。扬雄《甘泉赋》：“于是大厦云谲波诡。”]。故辞理庸俊，莫能翻其才；风趣刚柔，宁或改其气；事义浅深，未闻乖其学；体式雅郑，鲜有反其习：各师成心，其异如面[从才有庸俊，构成理有庸俊。辞理即文理，有平庸的，有卓越的，这是才决定的。从气有刚柔，构成风有刚柔。《风骨》：“情之含风，犹形之包气。”风趣

[1] 中文选自《文心雕龙注释》，刘勰著，周振甫注，北京：人民文学出版社，1981年。
Nature and Form, selected from *Readings in Chinese Literary Thought,* written and translated by Stephen Owen, Harvard University, Cambridge, Massachusetts, 1992.

指文情说的，情有刚柔。学有浅深，形成事义的浅深。事义即《知音》中的“五观事义”，即文中引证的事类，这同学问有关。从习有雅郑里形成体式的雅郑，指体制格调的正淫，跟习染有关。师：效法。成心：犹个性。各师成心：各人依据个性写作。《庄子·齐物论》：“夫随其成心而师之，谁独且无师乎?”成心本指偏见、成见，这里借用。《左传》襄公三十一年：“人心之不同，如其面焉。”]。

But talent（才）varies between mediocrity and excellence; *Qi* varies between the firm and the yielding; learning varies between the shallow and the profound; practice (or “habit”) varies between the crude and the gracious. These all are smelted in the forge by one’s nature and disposition（性一情）, and fused by how a person has been shaped and influenced. Thus, there are extraordinary cloud shapes in the realm of the writing brush, and in the garden of letters, strange waves.

But no one can countervail against the measure of talent evidenced in the mediocrity or excellence of the principles（理）or the use of language（辞）, No one can alter the quality of *qi* in the firm or yielding disposition of someone’s manner（风一趣）. I’ve never heard of anyone running contrary to the degree of learning apparent in the shallowness or profundity of (knowledge of) events and truths（义）. Few reverse habits of crudeness or grace in form（体）. Each person takes as his master his mind as it has been fully formed, and these are as different as faces.

若总其归涂，则数穷八体[八体：八种风格。]：一曰典雅，二曰远奥，三曰精约，四曰显附，五曰繁缛，六曰壮丽，七曰新奇，八曰轻靡。典雅者，熔式经诰，方轨儒门者也[熔式经诰：取法经典；熔，培化；式，以为法式；诰，如《尚书·大诰》等。方轨儒门：依傍儒家立论。方轨，两车并行，指依傍、遵照。]。远奥者，[馥]复采典文，经理玄宗者也[馥，当作复。复采典文：辞采丰富，文义深远。典，指常道。经理玄宗：按照道家立论；经理，指意匠经营；玄宗，指道家学说，以玄谈为宗。]。精约者，核字省句，剖析毫厘者也[精约：精练，即短小精悍。核字：衡量用字，要同情事相称。省句：删去多馀的话。]。显附者，辞直义畅，切理厌心者也[辞直：文辞不曲折隐晦。义畅：意义畅达。切理：切合事理。厌心：心里感到满足，心服。厌，同餍，满足。]。繁缛者，博喻酿采，炜烨枝派者也[博喻酿采：广博的譬喻构成文采纷披。炜烨枝派：枝条流派都有光彩。炜烨，状光彩。]。壮丽者，高论宏裁，卓烁异采者也[高论宏裁：理论高，识见广。宏，大；裁，断，指识见。卓烁异采：文彩照耀而突出。卓异，突出；烁，光耀。]。新奇者，摈古竞今，危侧趣诡者也[摈古竞今：抛弃古制，竞创今体。危侧趣(趋)诡：在危险的侧径上走向怪异。]。轻靡者，浮文弱植，缥缈附俗者也[浮文弱植：文字浮靡，内容无力。弱植，指不能自立。缥缈附俗：虚浮不切实而依附俗说。]。故雅与奇反，奥与显殊，繁与约舛，壮与轻乖，文辞根叶，苑囿其中矣[雅是正，奇是不正；奥是深隐，显是明显；繁是繁丰，约是简约；壮是壮实，轻是轻浮：所以相反。苑囿：文学园地，转指被范围在其中说，文章从根干到枝叶，都被范围在这个园地里。]。

If we can generalize about the paths followed, we find that the number（数）is complete in eight normative forms: *dian-ya*, decorous (or “having the quality of canonical writing”) and dignified; *yuan-ao*, obscure and far-reaching; *jing-yue*, terse and essential; *xian-fu*, obvious and consecutive; *fan-ru*, lush and profuse; *zhuang-li*, vigorous and lovely; *xin-qi*, novel and unusual; *qing-mi*, light and delicate. The decorous and dignified form is one that takes its mold from the Classics and Pronouncements and rides in company with the Confucian school. The obscure and far-reaching form is one whose bright colors（采）are covered over, whose writing is decorous, and one that devotes itself to the mysterious doctrines, the terse and essential form is one that examines every word and reflects on each line, making discriminations by the finest measures.

The obvious and consecutive form is one in which the language is direct and where the truths (义) are spread out before us, satisfying the mind by adherence to natural principle (理). The lush and profuse form is one with broad implications (喻) in its variegated colors, whose branches and tributaries sparkle and gleam. The vigorous and lovely form is one whose lofty discourses and grand judgments have superlative flash and rare color. The novel and unusual form is one that rejects the old and rushes instead after what is modern; off-balance, it shows delight in the bizarre. The light and delicate form is one whose insubstantial ornament(文) is not securely planted, whose airy vagueness is close to the common taste. We see that the dignified is set in opposition to the unusual; the obscure differs from the obvious; the lush and terse are at odds; the vigorous and light go against one another. Such is the root and leaf of literature (文一辞), and the garden of letters contains them all.

若夫八体屡迁，功以学成，才力居中，肇自血气；气以实志，志以定言，吐纳英华，莫非情性[才力、血气，情性：风格的成就，由于才力；才力从血气来，血气充实意志，意志决定语言。古代希腊学者把人的气质分为四种：一，胆汁质；二、多血质；三、神经质；四、粘液质。说由于四种气质的不同，对情绪的强弱和发生的迟速各有不同，也是用气质来说明情性的。]。

These eight forms often shift, in each is accomplished by learning. The force of one's talent (才一力) is located within and begins with *qi* in the blood; *qi* solidifies (or "actualizes," 实) that upon which one is intent (志); and that upon which one is intent determines language. The splendor that is given forth in this process is always a person's affections and nature (性一情)

是以贾生俊发，故文洁而体清[俊发：指才气卓越，所以文洁体清。《史记·贾谊列传》：“每诏令议下，诸老先生不能言，贾生尽为之对。”这是才气卓越之证。]；长卿傲诞，故理侈而辞溢[傲诞：骄傲夸诞，所以文章浮侈溢美。《史记·司马相如列传》：“是(这)时卓王孙有女文君新寡，好音，故相如……以琴心挑之。……相如……买一酒舍酤(卖)酒，而令文君当垆。相如自著犊鼻裈（像牛鼻的裤，即裤叉)，与保庸(佣人)杂作。”这就是傲诞，不拘守礼法。又传赞：“相如虽多虚辞滥说，然其要归，引之节俭。”虚滥即侈溢。]；子云沉寂，故志隐而味深[沉寂：性情沉静，所以志隐而味深。由于沉所以深。《汉书· 扬雄传》默而好深湛(沉)之思，清静亡(无)为，少耆(嗜)欲。”传赞说：“今扬子之书，文义至深。”]；子政简易，故趣昭而事博[简易：不讲究繁重礼节，平易近人，所以文章志趣明白，广引事例。昭：明。《汉书·刘向传》：“向为人简易无威仪。”传中载刘向章奏列举事例，明白切至。]；孟坚雅懿，故裁密而思靡[雅懿：雅正美好。裁密思靡：体裁绵密思想细致。《后汉书·班固传》：“博贯(通)载籍，九流百家之言无不穷究。”传论说：“固文赡而事详。若固之序事，不激诡，不抑抗(激，扬；诡，怪；抑，退；抗，进；指抑扬褒贬恰当)，赡而不秽(芜杂)，详而有体。”雅懿和赡博结合，所以裁密思靡。]；平子淹通，故虑周而藻密[淹通：博通；淹，淹盖，指博洽。虑周藻密：思虑周详，文藻绵密。《后汉书·张衡传》：“通五经，贯六艺，虽才高于世，而无骄尚之情。” 传论说：“故智思引渊(深)微。”由于博通，所以文章详密。]；仲宣躁锐，故颖出而才果[锐，当作竞。躁竞：急躁而好争胜。颖出才果：锋铓毕露，才思勇决。果，果敢，指勇决。]；公干气褊，故言壮而情骇[气褊：气度窄。言壮情骇：语言壮厉，情思惊人。]；嗣宗俶傥(tì tǎng)，故响逸而调远[俶傥：同倜傥，不羁，指不受礼法拘束。响逸调远：如《咏怀》诗格调高而含意深远。《晋书·阮籍传》：“任性不羁。”“发言玄远，口不臧否（褒贬)人物。”]；叔夜俊侠，故兴高而采烈[俊侠：英俊有侠气。兴高采烈：旨趣高超，辞采激烈。]；安仁轻敏，故锋发而韵流[轻敏：轻薄而敏慧。锋发韵流：锋铓发露，才华外露。]；士衡矜重，故情繁而辞隐[矜重：庄重，守礼仪。情繁辞隐：情思繁富，文辞含蓄。]：触类以推，表里必符；岂非自然之恒资，才气之大略哉[表里：外内，内指情性，外指风格，两者必然符合。自然恒资、 才气大略：上文指作家的风格，是作家的恒资所自然形成，是作家才气的大概表现。恒资：恒久不变的资质，指性情。]！

Jia Yi came forth grandly; thus his writing（文）was terse and its form（体）lucid. Sima Xiang-ru was proud and brash, thus in natural principle（理）he was extravagant and in diction（辞）excessive. Yang Xiong was brooding and still, thus his intent（志）was latent and the flavor（味）deep, Liu Xiang was plain and simple, thus his interest（趣）was patent and the (factual) matters（事）were extensive. Ban Gu was dignified and virtuous, thus his cutting to pattern was careful and his thought attained the delicate points. Zhang Heng was profound and comprehensive（通）, thus his considerations were all-encompassing and his rhetoric dense. Wang Can was rash and competitive, thus his work was sharp-witted and his talent daring. Xu Gan's *qi* was narrowly focused, thus his words were vigorous and his sentiments（情）were startling. Ruan Ji was unrestrained; thus the resonance of his work was aloof and tone far away. Xi Kang was bold and heroic, thus his being stirred（兴）was lofty and the colors（采）blazing. Pan Yue was airy and clever, thus the pointedness of hid works was in the open, and his rhymes were diffuse. Lu Ji was grave and serious, thus his sentiments（情）are richly complex and the language（辞）cryptic. Investigating each by his kind, we see that outside and inside necessarily correspond. What else can this be other than the constant endowment of Nature（自一然）, the general case of the operations of talent and *qi*.

夫才有天资，学慎始习，斲梓染丝，功在初化，器成彩定，难可翻移[有，当作由。]。故童子雕琢，必先雅制，沿根讨叶，思转自圆，八体虽殊，会通合数，得其环中，则辐辏相成[雕琢：指习作。先雅制：先学习正确的体制。沿根讨叶，思转自圆：必先雅制是根本，这里指根据自己的个性来学习与之相应的风格。再学习其他风格是讨叶。这样，文思自然圆转，可以根据不同内容来运用不同风格。各种风格虽然不同，懂得会通合法。合数：合法，合于运用各种风格的方法。得到适应个性的风格，其他各种风格就起到辅佐相成的作用。刘勰讲的风格有作品的风格，即八体；有作家的风格，即适应个性的。环中指后者，通会是指前者。不过他既认为新奇、轻靡有缺点，又要会通八体就有矛盾，大概他所指八体是泛指各体，不包括有缺点的在内。环中：《庄子·则阳》：“冉相氏得其环中以随成。”辐辏：车轮的直木凑聚在轮中心的毂上，毂正居中与辐构成车轮。]。故宜摹体以定习，因性以练才，文之司南，用此道也[摹体定习：指摹仿各体的风格说的，所以说“习有雅郑”，要崇雅绌郑。因性练才：根据各自的情性来锻炼文才。文之司南：学文的指南针。司南：《韩非子·有度》：“故先王立司南以端朝夕。”]。

Talent is endowed by Heaven, but in learning, we must take care of early practice: as in carving *zi* wood or dying silk, success resides in the initial transformation（化）. When a vessel is formed or a color is set, it is hard to alter or reverse it. Thus when a child learns to carve, he must first learn dignified（雅）construction. Following the roots, we reach the leaves; and the revolutions of thoughts achieve a perfect circle. Though the eight forms differ, there is a way of merging them that comprehends all. If you attain the center of the ring, all the spokes meet there to make the wheel. Thus it is fitting that one imitate normative forms in order to fix practice; then, according to individuating nature, he refines his talent. The compass of *wen* points along this path.

赞曰：才性异区，文辞繁诡[异区：指才性不同。繁诡：指风格的多样和诡异。辞，黄云：“冯本校作体。”]。辞为肤根，志实骨髓[肤根：杨注：“肤根”实不可解。《辨骚》：“观其骨鲠所树，肌肤所附。”《附会》：“事义为骨髓，辞采为肌肤。”正以“肌肤”与“骨髓”或“骨鲠”对。“肤根”作“肌肤”始合。]。雅丽黼黻(fǔ fú)，淫巧朱紫[黼黻：见《章表》注[30]，指文章的雅丽。朱紫：杨注：按此与《诠赋》“组织之品朱紫定势，《定势》“宫商朱紫”之“朱紫”，皆仅就其不同之色言，非关正色与间色也。范注改“朱”为“青”，青亦正色。]。习亦凝真，功沿渐靡[习亦凝真：摹体定习的习也可以形成真正的风格。功沿渐靡：培养的功效要逐渐磨冶。靡，通磨。]。

Supporting Verse

Talents with individual natures have differing realms,
The forms of literature are profuse and various.
The words used are skin and sinew.
Intent is solid bone and marrow.
Patterned ritual robes have dignity and beauty;
Vermilion and purple are a corrupting artfulness;
Yet practice may firmly set what is genuine,
And form that true accomplishment gradually follows.

“群贤毕至，少长咸集。”

——晋 · 王羲之《兰亭集序》

中国经典双语阅读

王羲之《兰亭集序》

Unit 13

王羲之《兰亭集序》

Wang Xizhi: Prologue of the Collection of Poems Composed at the Orchid Pavilion[1]

[思想指要]王羲之(公元 303—公元 361 年)，字逸少，号澹斋，原籍琅琊临沂(今属山东临沂)人。东晋时期著名书法家，有“书圣”之称。他的代表作《兰亭集序》被誉为“天下第一行书”。该序记载了晋穆帝永和九年(353 年)农历三月初三，王羲之在会稽山阴的兰亭(今绍兴城外的兰渚山下)，与名流高士谢安、孙绰等四十一人举行风雅集会。与会者临流赋诗，各抒怀抱，抄录成集，并推举此次聚会的召集人王羲之写一序文，即《兰亭集序》。作为中国古代书法史上最具有号召力的经典作品，《兰亭集序》集书、文一体，文墨俱佳，彼此相得益彰，在千百年的历史过程中不断地被传承。对中国广大书法爱好者而言，《兰亭集序》是不可或缺的法本。

[Introduction] Wang Xizhi (303 A.D.—361 A. D.), born in Linyi of Langya (now Lingyi County, Shandong Province), was a famous calligrapher in the Eastern Jin dynasty, known as the “the Sage of Calligraphy”. His masterpiece *A Preface of Collection of Poems Composed at the Orchid Pavilion* is praised as “King of Light Running Hand in Chinese calligraphy history”. This preface records that Wang Xizhi held elegant gatherings with 41 celebrities such as Xie An and Sun Chuo in Lanting (now, at the foot of Lanzhu Mountain outside Shaoxing City) on the third day of Lunar March in the ninth year of Yonghe (353 A.D.) in the reign of Jinmu Emperor. Participants were required to improvise poems, each expressing their innermost feelings, which were transcribed into a collection, and Wang Xizhi, the convenor of the

---

[1] 中文选自《古文观止》，吴楚材、吴调侯选，北京：中华书局，1959 年。
Prologue of the Collection of Poems Composed at the Orchid Pavilion, selected from《古文观止精选(汉英对照)》，罗经国译，北京：外语教学与研究出版社，2005 年。

gathering, was recommended to write a preface to this collection, hence this essay of *A Preface to Collection of Poems Composed at the Orchid Pavilion.* And this preface also depicts the scene of drinking wine along with the running stream that winds like a belt , shining in the bright sun. It was said that Emperor Taizong of the Tang Dynasty highly praised him. He himself wrote the biography of Wang Xizhi in the historical record of *Jin Shu* and eulogized his calligraphy as “perfect” and proposed its copies distributed among His officials. As one of the most appealing classics in the history of ancient Chinese calligraphy, *A Preface of the Collection of Poems Composed at the Orchid Pavilion* has been passed on for thousands of years because of its excellent calligraphy, broad-minded writing and overflowing and unrestrained sentiment. It is an indispensable model for its phrasing and calligraphy to the vast majority of Chinese calligraphy enthusiasts.

永和九年，岁在癸丑，暮春之初，会于会稽山阴之兰亭，修禊事也[永和：东晋皇帝司马聃(晋穆帝)的年号，从公元345—356年共12年。修禊(xì)事也：(为了做)禊礼这件事。古代习俗，于阴历三月上旬的巳日(魏以后定为三月三日)，人们群聚于水滨嬉戏洗濯，以祓除不祥和求福。实际上这是古人的一种游春活动。]。群贤毕至，少长咸集。此地有崇山峻岭，茂林修竹；又有清流激湍，映带左右，引以为流觞曲水，列坐其次[流觞(shāng)曲(qū)水：用漆器酒杯盛酒，放入弯曲的水道中任其飘流，杯停在某人面前，某人就引杯饮酒。这是古人一种劝酒取乐的方式。流，使动用法。曲水，引水环曲为渠，以流酒杯。]。虽无丝竹管弦之盛，一觞一咏，亦足以畅叙幽情。是日也，天朗气清，惠风和畅，仰观宇宙之大，俯察品类之盛，所以游目骋怀，足以极视听之娱，信可乐也。

At the beginning of the late spring in the ninth year of Yonghe(“永和”), that is, the year of Guichou (“癸丑”)according to the Chines lunar calendar, a group of learned scholars, old and young(“少长咸集”), are gathered at the Orchid Pavilion in the *Shanyin* County of *Kuaiji* Prefecture to celebrate the festival of Xiuxi(“修禊”). Here are high mountains and lofty ridges which are overgrown with tall bamboo groves and dense forests. A clear stream with a rapidly running current that winds like a belt, shining in the bright sun, is ideal for floating wine vessels. We sit by the water in proper order, sipping wine and composing poems. Though lacking musical accompaniment, each of us is inclined to pour forth his innermost feelings. It is a fine day. The sky is clear and the breeze is gentle. Looking upward, we see the great expanse of the universe. Looking downward, we see the great variety of living things. Then we look around as far as the eyes can see and feel elated, enjoying ourselves to the utmost both visually and aurally. What a delightful experience it is!

夫人之相与，俯仰一世，或取诸怀抱，悟言一室之内[夫人之相与，俯仰一世：人与人相交往，很快便度过一生。夫，句首发语词。相与，相处、相交往。俯仰，表示时间的短暂。]；或因寄所托，放浪形骸之外。虽趣舍万殊，静躁不同，当其欣于所遇，暂得于己，快然自足，不知老之将至[快然自足：感到高兴和满足。不知老之将至：(竟)不知道衰老将要到来。语出《论语·述而》：“其为人也，发愤忘食，乐以忘忧，不知老之将至云尔。”]。及其所之既倦，情随事迁，感慨系之矣。向之所欣，俯仰之间，已为陈迹，犹不能不以之兴怀。况修短随化，终期于尽[以之兴怀：因之引起心中的感触。以，因。之，指“向之所欣……以为陈迹”。兴，发生、引起。修短随化：寿命长短听凭自然造化。化，自然。]。古人云：“死生亦大矣。”[死生亦大矣：死生是一件大事啊。语出《庄子·德充符》。]岂不痛哉。

When friends get together, time flies quickly as if a lifetime were spent in the twinkling of an eye. Some engage in intimate conversations in the room, baring their hearts to each other; others identify themselves with what they like and abandon themselves to unrestrained joy. Though people may differ in their choices or temperaments, they invariably find temporary contentment, when they come upon something that delights them. They are so happy that they even forget they will be old soon. However, one's taste changes and soon one is bored with that one once liked. Then one cannot help but sigh deeply with emotion. It saddens me to think that the happiness we are enjoying at this moment will be a bygone thing at another moment, not to mention that we are subject to the natural law and that we will eventually perish. The wise man in ancient times said, "The problem of life and death is a matter of vital importance." Isn't it depressing to think of that?

每览昔人兴感之由，若合一契，未尝不临文嗟悼(jiē dào)，不能喻之于怀[契：符契，古代的一种信物。在符契上刻上字，剖而为二，各执一半，作为凭证。临文嗟(jiē)悼：读古人文章时叹息哀伤。临，面对。]。固知一死生为虚诞，齐彭殇为妄作[一死生，齐彭殇：都是庄子的看法。出自《齐物论》。]。后之视今，亦犹今之视昔，悲夫。故列叙时人，录其所述，虽世殊事异，所以兴怀，其致一也[列叙时人：一个一个记下当时与会的人。录其所述：录下他们作的诗。]。后之览者，亦将有感于斯文[后之览者：后世的读者。斯文：这次集会的诗文。]。

I have noticed whatever stirred up the emotions and feelings in the ancients also calls forth the same emotions and feelings in me, as if the ancients and I were the two halves of a deed. I have been perplexed as to why the writings of the ancients always make me sigh with grief, though I know that it is absurd to identify life with death and long life with early death. Alas! Our descendants will look upon us just as we look upon our forefathers. So I am listing the names of the people present at this gathering and the poems they have composed. Though times will change and things will be different in the future, the cause of their emotions and feelings will be the same as ours. I hope future readers would empathize with this writing of mine.

中国经典双语阅读

诸葛亮（选）

“非学无以广才，非志无以成学。”

——三国·诸葛亮《诫子书》

Unit 14

诸葛亮（选）Selected from Zhuge Liang

《前出师表》The First Memorial to the Throne Before Setting Off For War [1]

[思想指要]蜀汉章武元年（公元 221 年），刘备称帝，诸葛亮为丞相。蜀汉建兴元年（公元 223 年），刘备病死，生前将刘禅托付给诸葛亮。此后，诸葛亮实行了一系列政治和经济措施，使蜀汉境内呈现兴旺景象。为了实现全国统一，诸葛亮在平息南方叛乱之后，于建兴五年（公元 227 年）决定北上伐魏，拟夺取魏都长安，临行之前上书后主，即这篇《出师表》。此文以议论为主，融以叙事和抒情，语言率真质朴，感情恳切忠贞。全篇文字从作者肺腑中流出，析理透辟，真情充溢，感人至深。《出师表》感情充沛的特点和所表达的忠君爱国之情是一脉相通的，率直质朴的语言形式与文章的思想内容相得益彰。

[Introduction] In 221 A.D., the Year of Zhangwu which was the Reign Title of Liu Bei, during the Three Kingdoms period, Liu Bei proclaimed himself the Emperor of the State of Shu and Zhuge Liang was appointed the prime minister. In 223 A.D., the first year of Jianxing of the Kingdom of Shu Han (221 A.D.—263A.D.), Liu Bei fell ill and entrusted Zhuge Liang on his death bed with the duty of assisting Liu Chan in governing the country. After that, Zhuge Liang implemented a series of political and economic measures to make the territory of Shu Han prosperous. In order to achieve national unity, Zhuge Liang, after quelling the rebellion in the south of the State of Shu, decided to attack the State of Wei in the north in the fifth year of Jianxing (227 A.D.), intending to capture Chang An, the capital of the State of Wei. Before his setting off for the war, he wrote Liu Chan a letter, which is called *The First Memorial to the*

---

[1] 中文选自《古文观止鉴赏词典》，傅德岷 赖云琪主编，武汉：长江出版社，2011 年。
The First Memorial to the Throne Before Setting off for War，written by Zhuge Liang , selected from *A Selection of Classical Chinese Essays* from *Guwen Guanzhi*. Trans. by Luo Jingguo, Beijing; Foreign Language Teaching and Research Press, 2005.

King on his Expedition. This article, which is mainly expository, is blended with narrative and lyric, simple and concise language, sincere and loyal feelings. The whole text flows out of the author's innermost heart, which is thoroughly incisive in analysis, full of true feelings and deeply touching. And its emotional characteristics is intimately tied to his patriotism and loyalty to the throne, and its straightforward and plain language is inseparably connected with its content.

臣亮言：先帝创业未半，而中道崩殂[先帝：这里指刘备。崩殂(cú)：死。崩，古代称帝王、皇后之死。殂，死亡。]。今天下三分，益州疲弊，此诚危急存亡之秋也[益州疲弊：指蜀汉国力薄弱，处境艰难。益州，指蜀汉。疲弊，人力疲惫，民生凋敝。]。然侍卫之臣不懈于内；忠志之士忘身于外者，盖追先帝之殊遇，欲报之于陛下也。诚宜开张圣听，以光先帝遗德，恢弘志士之气；不宜妄自菲薄，引喻失义，以塞(sè)忠谏之路也[开张圣听：扩大圣明的听闻，意思是要后主广泛地听取别人的意见。遗德：遗留的美德。引喻失义：说话不恰当。引喻：引用、比喻。这里是说话的意思。]。

Your humble servant Liang begs to say:

Our late king passed away before the great undertaking founded by him was half accomplished. Now China is divided into three kingdoms. Yizhou(益州) is drained of its manpower and resources. This is a critical juncture of life or death for our country. Bearing the late king's special favor in hearts, the officials at court who guard Your Majesty dare not slacken in their vigilance and the devoted officers and soldiers at the front are fighting bravely disregarding their personal safety. They are now repaying to Your Majesty what they have received from the late king. It is advisable that Your Majesty should listen extensively to the counsels of officials in order to carry on the late king's lofty virtues, and heighten the morale of people with high aspiration. It is injudicious that Your Majesty should unduly humble yourself, and use metaphors with distorted meanings, lest you should block the way of sincere admonition.

宫中府中，俱为一体；陟罚臧否(zhì fá zāng pǐ)，不宜异同：若有作奸犯科及为忠善者，宜付有司论其刑赏，以昭陛下平明之治；不宜偏私，使内外异法也[陟(zhì)：提升，提拔。臧否：善恶，这里形容词用作动词。意思是"评论人物的好坏"。臧否：善恶。偏私：偏袒私情，不公正。]。侍中、侍郎郭攸(yōu)之、费祎(yī)、董允等，此皆良实，志虑忠纯，是以先帝简拔以遗(wèi)陛下[侍中、侍郎郭攸之、费祎、董允：郭攸之、费祎是侍中，董允是侍郎。侍中、侍郎，都是官名。此皆良实，志虑忠纯：这些都是善良、诚实的人，他们的志向和心思忠诚无二。简拔：选拔。简：挑选。拔：选拔。]。愚以为宫中之事，事无大小，悉以咨之，然后施行，必能裨(bì)补阙(quē)漏，有所广益。将军向宠，性行淑均，晓畅军事，试用于昔日，先帝称之曰"能"，是以众议举宠为督[必能裨补阙漏：一定能够弥补缺点和疏漏之处。裨(bì)：弥补，补救。阙，通"缺"，缺点。]。愚以为营中之事，事无大小，悉以咨之，必能使行(háng)阵和睦，优劣得所也。亲贤臣，远小人，此先汉所以兴隆也；亲小人，远贤臣，此后汉所以倾颓也。先帝在时，每与臣论此事，未尝不叹息痛恨于桓、灵也[桓、灵：东汉末年的桓帝和灵帝。他们都因信任宦官，加深了政治的腐败。]！侍中、尚书、长史、参军，此悉贞亮死节之臣，愿陛下亲之信之，则汉室之隆，可计日而待也。

The imperial court(“宫中”) and the Prime Minister’s Office(“府中”) are an integral whole. There should be impartiality in meting out rewards and punishments to officials from either administration(“陟罚臧否，不宜异同”). For both those who are treacherous and violate the law and those who are loyal and do some good deed, the same legally appointed officials should pass decision on how to punish or reward. This will make plain the equality and sagaciousness of Your Majesty’s rule. There should be neither prejudice nor partiality in Your Majesty’s attitude towards the officials inside and outside the court for fear that different laws be put into practice. Shizhong Guo Youzhi and Fei Yi as well as Shilang Dong Yun (侍中、侍郎郭攸之、费祎、董允) are kind and honest men with a strong sense of loyalty. The late king appointed them for your sake, and I respectfully opine that all political affairs at court, regardless of magnitude, be first subjected to their inquiry before actions are taken. Only in this way can errors be amended, negligence avoided, and greater results attained. General Xiang Chong(向宠) is well versed in military affairs and is kind and just by nature. After evaluating his performance of a trial basis, the late king praised his talent ability. That is why officials have elected him to be commander-in-chief. I humbly suggest that military concerns, regardless of weight, be first met with his consideration. Only in this way will there be harmony among the troops, and men both capable and incapable will each find his proper place in the camp. To be close to the virtuous and able officials and keep away from the vile and mean persons. That was the reason that the Western Han Dynasty(西汉/先汉) was prosperous. To be close to the vile and mean persons and keep away from the virtuous and able officials. That was the reason that the Eastern Han Dynasty(东汉/后汉) was collapsed. When the late king was alive and talked with me about these historical lessons, he used to heave a sigh in detestation for Emperor Huan(桓帝) and Emperor Ling(灵帝). Shizhong(侍中), Shangshu(尚书), Zhangshi(长史) and Canjun (参军) are faithful, upright, and ready to lay down their lives for honor and fidelity. As your humble servant, I hope that Your Majesty will retain close ties to them and trust them. Then the prosperity of the Han Dynasty(汉室) can be soon realized.

臣本布衣，躬耕于南阳，苟全性命于乱世，不求闻达于诸侯[躬耕：亲自耕种，实指隐居农村。南阳：东汉郡名。即今河南省南阳市。闻达：闻名显达。卑鄙：身份低微，见识短浅。卑，身份低下。鄙，见识短浅。与今义不同。]。先帝不以臣卑鄙，猥自枉屈，三顾臣于草庐之中，谘臣以当世之事，由是感激，遂许先帝以驱驰[猥(wěi)：辱，这里有降低身份的意思。枉屈：委屈。由是：因此。驱驰：驱车追赶。这里是奔走效劳的意思。]。后值倾覆，受任于败军之际，奉命于危难之间，尔来二十有(yòu)一年矣[倾覆：指兵败。尔来：那时以来]。先帝知臣谨慎，故临崩寄臣以大事也。受命以来，夙(sù)夜忧叹，恐付托不效，以伤先帝之明[临崩寄臣以大事：刘备在临死的时候，把国家大事托付给诸葛亮，并且对刘禅说：“汝与丞相从事，事之如父。” 临：将要。夙夜忧叹：早晚/整天担忧叹息。夙，清晨。忧，忧愁焦虑。夙夜：早晚。]。故五月渡泸，深入不毛[泸：水名，即金沙江。]。今南方已定，甲兵已足，当奖帅三军，北定中原，庶竭驽(nú)钝，攘除奸凶，兴复汉室，还于旧都[攘(rǎng)除：排除，铲除。奸凶：奸邪凶恶之人，此指曹魏政权。]。此臣所以报先帝而忠陛下之职分也。至于斟酌损益，进尽忠言，则攸之、祎、允等之任也[斟酌损益：斟情酌理、有所兴办。

比喻做事要掌握分寸。(处理事务)斟酌情理，有所兴革。]。愿陛下托臣以讨贼兴复之效，不效，则治臣之罪，以告先帝之灵[托臣以讨贼兴复之效：把讨伐曹魏复兴汉室的任务交给我。不效则治臣之罪：没有成效就治我的罪。]；若无兴德之言，则责攸之、祎、允等之咎(jiù)，以彰其慢[兴德之言：发扬圣德的言论。慢：怠慢，疏忽，指不尽职。彰其咎：揭示他们的过失。]。陛下亦宜自谋，以咨诹善道，察纳雅言，深追先帝遗诏[咨诹(zōu)善道：询问(治国的)好道理。诹(zōu)，询问。]。臣不胜受恩感激！

I was originally a commoner who had to wear clothes made of hemp, and tilled land in Nanyang(南阳). I merely managed to survive in times of turbulence(“苟全性命于乱世”) and had no intention of seeking fame and position from princes(“诸侯”). With an utter disregard for my low social status and meager fund of knowledge, the late king condescended to visit me at my thatched cottage three times to consult me about the current events of the country. I felt so grateful that I promised to serve him. Soon afterwards since I received my assignment at the time of the setback and was dispatched as an envoy at the moment of crisis. The late king knew my prudence, and entrusted me on his death bed with the duty of assisting Your Majesty in governing the country. Since then I have been worrying and sighing night and day lest I should do harm to the late king's illustrious fame if I fail to be effective. I was thus impelled to lead an army across the Lu River (泸水)in May and went deep into the barren district(“深入不毛”). Now the whole south is under our rule and we have plenty of fighters and armaments. It is time to reward our army men and lead them northward to conquer the Central Plains(“北定中原”). Although I am inferior in ability like a worn-out horse or a blunt knife, I would do my utmost to root out treacherous evildoers, rejuvenate the Han Dynasty, and move the capital back to the old city. I owe this to the late king and wish to demonstrate my loyalty to Your Majesty. As for government affairs such as the augmentation or repeal of certain measures, or the broadening of the way to receive exhortations, they are the duties of Gou Youzhi, Fei Yi, and Dong Yun. I hope Your Majesty would delegate to me the task of punishing the traitors and rejuvenating the Han Dynasty, If I should fail to achieve this, please punish me as to console the soul of the departed king. If Youzhi, Yi, and Yun fail to gather exhortations for the fostering of virtues, they should be held responsible for their negligence. Your Majesty should also make the most of your resources to solicit opinions on governing a country, to judge judiciously and accept good advices, and always bear in mind the imperial edict issued by the late king prior to his death. If this can be achieved, you will have my extreme gratitude.

今当远离，临表涕泣，不知所云。

I will be journeying far, and my eyes are full of tears in writing this memorial upon my departure. I can hardly express what else I should say.

《后出师表》The Second Memorial to the Throne on His Expedition [1]

《后出师表》载于三国时期吴国张俨的《默记》，一般认为是诸葛亮的作品，《出师表》（《前出师表》）的姊妹篇。全文以议论见长，传达出一股忠贞壮烈之气。诸葛亮在《后出师表》立论于敌强我弱的严峻事实，向后主阐明北伐不仅是为实现先帝的遗愿，也是关系到蜀汉的生死存亡，不能因"议者"的不同看法而有所动摇。正因为此表涉及军事态势的分析，事关蜀汉的安危，其忠贞壮烈之气，似又超过《前出师表》。表中"鞠躬尽瘁，死而后已"之句，正是作者在当时形势下所表露的坚贞誓言，令人读来肃然起敬。

[Introduction] The *Second Memorial to the Throne on His Expedition,* which is generally believed to be Zhuge Liang work, is a companion piece of the *First Memorial to the Throne on His Expedition.* It was recorded in *the Meditation* edited by Zhang Yan，a scholar of the State of Wu during the Three Kingdoms period. The full text which is distinguished by its argumentation conveys a spirit of loyalty and a sublimity of heroism. Founded on the grim fact that the enemy is strong and we are weak, Zhuge Liang declared to the latter King that the Northern Expedition was not only imperative to realize the last wishes of the late Emperor, but also related to the survival of the State of Shu Han. He could not be shaken by the different opinions of the "proponents. " Because this article involves the analysis of the military situation at that time, which is related to the peace of Shu Han, the sense of loyalty and the spirit of heroism emerged from it seems to be more sincere and wholehearted than the previous one. The staunch and upright oath is constantly resounding in the ears of Chinese people that "be entirely worn out in performing one's duties and do one's best till his heart ceases to beat," which shows the author's faithful determination under the grim circumstances and arouses a profound admiration from later generations of Chinese people.

先帝深虑汉、贼不两立，王业不偏安，故托臣以讨贼也[汉：指蜀汉。贼：指曹魏。古时往往把敌方称为贼。偏安：指王朝局处一地，自以为安。]。以先帝之明，量臣之才，固知臣伐贼，才弱敌强也。然不伐贼，王业亦亡。惟坐而待亡，孰与伐之[惟：助词。孰与：何如，用于比较，表示抉择，倾向肯定后一种(偏指一方)。孰，哪一个。]？是故托臣而弗疑也。

Having considered the fact that the House of Han (汉室) could not allow the insurgents to live under the same heaven and that its imperial activity ought not to be contented with the enjoying of one-sided peace and tranquility, the late emperor instructed your servant to have the

---

[1] 中文选自《古文观止鉴赏词典》，傅德岷 赖云琪主编，武汉：长江出版社，2011年。

Second Memorial to the Throne on his Expedition, written by Zhuge Liang, selected from *The Story of the Three Kingdoms,* trans. by Z. Q. Parker，North-China Daily News and Herald Ltd, 1925.

insurgents suppressed. His Majesty, though fully aware of your servant's inability to carry out this instruction, trusted him without hesitation; for the trend of events is that, should the rebels not be quelled, the imperial destiny would be bound to go to rack, so it would seem far much better to fight against them than succumb to them without resistance.

臣受命之日，寝不安席，食不甘味。思惟北征。宜先入南。故五月渡泸，深入不毛，并日而食；臣非不自惜也，顾王业不可得偏安于蜀都，故冒危难，以奉先帝之遗意也，而议者谓为非计[顾：这里有“但”的意思。蜀都：此指蜀汉之境。议者：指对诸葛亮决意北伐发表不同意见的官吏。]。今贼适疲于西，又务于东[“今贼”两句：指建兴六年(228)诸葛亮初出祁山(在今甘肃省礼县东)时，曹魏西部的南安、天水、安定三郡叛变，牵动关中局势；在魏、吴边境附近的夹石(今安徽省桐城县北)，东吴大将陆逊击败魏大司马曹休两事。]，兵法乘劳，此进趋之时也[进趋：快速前进。]。谨陈其事如左：

Upon receiving His Majesty's order, your servant was quite lost in thinking, enjoying no sound sleep and having no good appetite. He was of the opinion that in order to be able to dispatch an expeditionary force to the north, it was essential that matters should first be settled in the south, and he therefore ventured to cross the Lu River(泸水) in the fifth moon, entering right into the barren region and setting a dietary limit to himself. It is not that he did not know how to care about himself, but that the imperial dignity should not tolerate the maintenance of one-sided peace in Szechuen(蜀都); this is where he has endeavored to act upon the late emperor's instructions, though at his own risk. Such a course of action there are, however, many who are now disposed to criticize or deprecate. Now the rebels are being engaged in the east and getting exhausted in the west; this is certainly a most propitious time to start a campaign, for taking advantage of the adversary's misfortunes is a good policy in military tactics. Your servant begs to submit his views as follows:

高帝明并日月[高帝：刘邦死后的谥号为“高皇帝”。并：平列。]，谋臣渊深，然涉险被创[被创：受创伤。这句说：刘邦在楚汉战争中，屡败于楚军，公元前203年，在广武(今河南省荥阳县)被项羽射伤胸部；在汉朝初建时，因镇压各地的叛乱而多次出征，公元前195年又曾被淮南王英布的士兵射中；公元前200年在白登山还遭到匈奴的围困。被，同“披”。]，危然后安。今陛下未及高帝，谋臣不如良、平[良：张良，汉高祖的著名谋士，与萧何、韩信被称为“汉初三杰”。平：陈平，汉高祖的著名谋士。后位至丞相。]，而欲以长策取胜，坐定天下，此臣之未解一也。

With the acumen of Kao Ti (高帝) — which can be likened to the brilliancy of the sun and moon — and with the counsels of his wise advisers, peace and order was not maintained until many difficulties had been surmounted and untold sufferings sustained. Seeing that Your majesty is not such as Kao Ti and Your Majesty's advisers are not such as Chang Liang(张良) and Chen Ping(陈平), how is it possible to expect to win, while sitting tight and making no attempt to move? This is the first point not understood by your servant.

刘繇(yóu)、王朗各据州郡，论安言计，动引圣人，群疑满腹，众难塞胸，今岁不战，明年不征，使孙策坐大，遂并江东，此臣之未解二也。

While holding their respective counties, Liu Yu(刘繇) and Wang Lang(王朗) always quoted from the sages in discussing the situation and in laying their plans, but they were so prone to suspicion and so easily overwhelmed with fear that they failed to make up their mind to fight year after year, until Sun Ts'e(孙策) began to rise and annex the entire territory of Kiangtung(江东). This is the second point not understood by your servant.

曹操智计，殊绝于人[殊绝：极度超出的意思。]，其用兵也，仿佛孙、吴[孙：指孙武。吴：指吴起。]，然困于南阳，险于乌巢，危于祁连，逼于黎阳，几败北山，殆死潼关[殆：几乎]，然后伪定一时耳[伪定：此言曹氏统一北中国，僭称国号。诸葛亮以蜀汉为正统，因斥曹魏为“伪”]。况臣才弱，而欲以不危而定之，此臣之未解三也。

Notwithstanding the fact that his resourcefulness was almost superhuman and his proficiency in strategies could favorably be compared with that of Sun Wu (孙武) and Wu Ch'i(吴起), Ts'ao Ts'ao(曹操) was once besieged at Nanyang(南阳), then escaped narrowly from Wuchao(乌巢), then suffered seriously at Ch'ilien(祁连), and was finally vehemently pursued at Liyang(黎阳). At Peishan(北山) he was nearly put to rout; at T'ungkwan(潼关) his escape from death was by a hair-breadth. After all this, he was only able to find himself settling down to enjoy temporary peace. Now in the case of one of much weaker caliber such as your servant, how could settlement be expected without having to go through dangers? This is the third point not understood by your servant.

曹操五攻昌霸不下，四越巢湖不成，任用李服而李服图之，委任夏侯而夏侯败亡，先帝每称操为能，犹有此失，况臣驽下，何能必胜？此臣之未解四也。

In his attacks on Ch'angpa(昌霸) on five different occasions Ts' ao Ts' ao was repulsed; in his attempt to cross Lake Ch'ao(巢湖) for four times he met with no success. He employed Li Fu (李服) and Li Fu betrayed him; he trusted Hsiahow(夏侯) and Hisahow was killed. He was admired by the late emperor for his ability, yet he could not avoid such failures. Then how could one of your servant's inability be sure of success? This is the fourth point not understood by your servant.

自臣到汉中，中间期年耳[期(jī)年：一周年。]，然丧赵云、阳群、马玉、阎芝、丁立、白寿、刘郃、邓铜等及曲长、屯将七十余人，突将、无前、賨叟(cóng sǒu)、青羌、散骑、武骑一千余人。此皆数十年之内所纠合四方之精锐，非一州之所有；若复数年，则损三分之二也，当何以图敌？此臣之未解五也。

It is only a year since your servant came to Hanchung(汉中). During this time, however, generals such as Chao Yün(赵云), Yang Chün(阳群), Ma Yü(马玉), Yen Chih(阎芝), T'ing Li(丁立), Pai Shou(白寿), Liu Ho(刘郃), Teng T'ung(邓铜), etc., and seventy odd majors(曲长) and garrison commanders(屯将) have been dead, together with over a thousand brave generals of foreign birth and well-disciplined cavaliers. They were among the best of the elements, not belonging to one district only, but gathered together from various sources in all directions during the last tens of years. If it happens that another few years are allowed to pass without any action being taken, the result will be that two thirds of these elements will have been lost. Then with what will the enemy be attacked? This is the fifth point not understood by your servant.

今民穷兵疲，而事不可息；事不可息，则住与行劳费正等。而不及今图之，欲以一州之地，与贼持久，此臣之未解六也。

The people are now impoverished and the military strength is on the wane, yet we cannot afford to rest satisfied with the present condition of affairs. Under the circumstance, it would seem to involve the same amount of energy whether we stand still in the rear or take the offensive at the front. It is, therefore, inexplicable that while few appear to be prepared to take time by the forelock, there are many who are content with the keeping of one district to stand face to face with the rebels. This is the sixth point not understood by your servant.

夫难平者[平：同“评”，评断。]，事也。昔先帝败军于楚，当此时，曹操拊手，谓天下以定[拊(fǔ)手：拍手。以定：已定，以，同“已”。]。然后先帝东连吴越，西取巴蜀，举兵北征，夏侯授首[授首：交出脑袋。]，此操之失计，而汉事将成也。然后吴更违盟，关羽毁败，秭归蹉跌[秭(zǐ)归蹉(cuō)跌(diē)：蹉跌，失坠，喻失败。指刘备因孙权背盟，袭取荆州，杀害关羽，就亲自领兵伐吴，在秭归(在今湖北省宜昌市北)被吴将陆逊所败。]，曹丕称帝。凡事如是，难可逆见[逆见：预见，预测。]。臣鞠躬尽瘁，死而后已。至于成败利钝，非臣之明所能逆睹也[利钝：喻顺利或困难。逆睹(dǔ)：亦即“逆见”，预料。]。

It may be stated that it is exceedingly difficult to bring the current of events to a standstill. At the time when the late emperor was signally defeated in Ch’u(湖北/楚), Ts’ao Ts’ao chuckled with glee at the impression that the situation began to be settled in his favor. But later, when His Majesty threw in his lot with Wu and Yüeh(吴越) in the east acquired Szechuen (巴蜀) in the west, and launched a campaign in the north resulting in the killing of Hsia How, it appeared likely that Ts’ao Ts’ao’s plan was doomed to failure, while that of Han was going to be crowned with success. Shortly afterwards, however, Wu broke off its agreement; Kuan Yü(关羽) lost the day; the late emperor got the worst of it at Tzukuei(秭归) and Ts’ao P’i(曹丕) assumed the title of emperor. All this goes to show how this course of things is often too uncertain to admit of forecast(“难可逆见”). Your servant, therefore, desires to do all he can, even to the last drop of his blood(“臣鞠躬尽瘁，死而后已”), but without being able to foretell the consequences.

“约几个知心密友，到野外溪旁，或琴棋适性，或曲水流觞；或论些今古兴亡；看花枝堆锦绣，听鸟语弄笙簧。”

——沈复《浮生六记》

中国经典双语阅读

沈复《浮生六记》（选）

Unit 15

沈复《浮生六记》(选)

Selected from Shen Fu's Six Chapters of Floating Life[1]

《闲情记趣》Little Pleasures of Life

[思想指要]沈复(公元 *1763*—公元 *1825* 年)，字三白，号梅逸，清乾隆长洲(今江苏苏州)人。清代文学家，著有《浮生六记》。《浮生六记》描述了作者和妻子陈芸情投意合，想要过一种布衣蔬食而艺术化的生活，由于封建礼教的压迫与贫困生活的煎熬，终至理想破灭。《浮生六记》是一部水平极高影响颇大的自传体或忆语体随笔，在清代笔记体文学中占有相当重要的位置。该书特点在于真纯率真，独抒性灵，不拘格套，富有诗、思、情、意之创造性。所选《闲情记趣》是《浮生六记》中的第二卷。作者以朴实的文笔，记叙自己大半生的经历，欢愉与愁苦两相照应，真切动人。本节所选《浮生六记》中《闲情记趣》以《童趣》之名选入人教版的初中语文书中。

[Introduction] Shen Fu (1763 A.D.—1825 A.D.), born in Changzhou in Qianlong period of Qing Dynasty (now Suzhou, Jiangsu) , was a literator in the Qing Dynasty and the author of *Six Chapters of Floating Life*. In this book, the author describes the fondness of each other between him and his wife Chen Yun and their desire to live a life of coarse clothes and simple fare, and their readiness to find pleasure in the artistic engagement. However, their ideals were finally shattered because of the oppression of feudal ethics and the suffering of poverty. *Six Chapters of a Floating Life* is an autobiographical notebook with high artistic level and great influence, which occupies an important position in the notebook literature (*yiyuti, or Lament prose,* 忆语体) of the Qing Dynasty. The characteristics of the book is pure and sincere,

---

[1] [清]沈复著：《浮生六记·中英对照》，林语堂译，北京：外语教学与研究出版社，1999 年。

spiritually independent, informal and creative. The selected chapter is the second volume of *Six Chapters of a Floating Life*. With plain writing, the author narrates most of his life's experiences, joys and sorrows filling in the lines of writing and corresponding to each other, which is really touching. Furthermore, *the Little Pleasures of Life* has been selected into the Chinese textbook for the junior middle school students, in an excerpted form and in the title of *Fun For Children*, by People's Education Press.

余忆童稚时，能张目对日，明察秋毫，见藐小微物，必细察其纹理，故时有物外之趣。夏蚊成雷，私拟作群鹤舞空。心之所向，则或千或百，果然鹤也。昂周观之，项为之强。又留蚊于素帐中，徐喷以烟，使其冲烟飞鸣，作青云白鹤观，果如鹤立云端，怡然称快。于土墙凹凸(āo tū)处，花台小草丛杂处，常蹲其身，使与台齐；定神细视，以从草为林，以虫蚁为兽，以土砾凸者为丘，凹者为壑，神游其中，怡然自得。

I remember that when I was a child, I could stare at the sun with wide, open eyes. I could see the tiniest objects, and loved to observe the fine grains and patterns of small things, from which I derived a romantic, unworldly pleasure. When mosquitoes were humming round in summer, I transformed them in my imagination into a company of storks dancing in the air. And when I regarded them that way, they were real storks to me, flying by the hundreds and thousands, and I would look up at them until my neck was stiff. Again, I kept a few mosquitoes inside a white curtain and blew a puff of smoke round them, so that to me they became a company of white storks flying among the blue clouds, and their humming was to me the song of storks singing in high heaven, which delighted me intensely. Sometimes I would squat by a broken, earthen wall, or by a little bush on a raised flower-bed, with my eyes on the same level as the flower-bed itself, and there I would look and look, transforming in my mind the little plot of grass into a forest and the ants and insects into wild animals. The little elevations on the ground became my hills, and the depressed areas became my valleys, and my spirit wandered in that world at leisure.

一日，见二虫斗草间，观之正浓，忽有庞然大物拔山倒树而来，盖一癞虾蟆也，舌一吐而二虫尽为所吞。余年幼，方出神，不觉呀然惊恐。神定，捉虾蟆，鞭数十，驱之别院。年长思之，二虫之斗，盖图奸不从也。古语云“奸近杀”，虫亦然耶？贪此生涯，卵为蚯蚓所哈(俗呼阳曰卵)，肿不能便。捉鸭开口哈之，婢妪(bì yù)偶释手，鸭颠其颈作吞噬状，惊而大哭；传为话柄。此皆幼时闲情也。

One day, I saw two little insects fighting among the grass, and while I was all absorbed watching the fight, there suddenly appeared a big monster, overturning my hills and tearing up my forest — it was a little toad. With one lick of his tongue, he swallowed up the two little insects. I was so lost in my young imaginary world that I was taken unawares and quite frightened. When I had recovered myself, I caught the toad, struck it several dozen times and chased it out of the courtyard. Thinking of this incident afterwards when I was grown up, I understood that these two little insects were committing adultery by rape. "The wages of sin is death, " so says an ancient proverb, and I wondered whether it was true of the insects also—I was a naughty boy, and once my ball (for we call the genital organ a "ball" in Soochow) was bitten by an earthworm and became swollen. [Believing that the duck's saliva would act as an antidote for insect bites,] they held a duck over it, but the maid-servant, who was holding the duck, accidentally let her hand go, and the duck was going to swallow it. I got frightened and screamed. People used to tell this story to make fun of me. These were the little incidents of my childhood days.

及长，爱花成癖，喜剪盆树。识张兰坡，始精剪枝养节之法，继悟接花叠石之法。花以兰为最，取其幽香韵致也，而瓣品之稍堪入谱者不可多得。兰坡临终时，赠余荷瓣素心春兰一盆，皆肩平心阔，茎细瓣净，可以入谱者。余珍如拱璧。值余幕游于外，芸能亲为灌溉，花叶颇茂。不二年，一旦忽萎死。起根视之，皆白如玉，且兰芽勃然。初不可解，以为无福消受，浩叹而已。事后始悉有人欲分不允，故用滚汤灌杀也。从此誓不植兰。

When I was grown up, I loved flowers very much and was very fond of training pot flowers and pot plants. When I knew Chang Lanp'o(张兰坡), I learnt from him the secrets of trimming branches and protecting joints, and later the art of grafting trees and making rockeries. The orchid was prized most among all the flowers because of its subdued fragrance and graceful charm, but it was difficult to obtain really good classic varieties, At the end of his days, Lanp'o presented me with a pot of orchids, whose flowers had lotus-shaped petals; the centre of the flowers was broad and white, the petals were very neat and even at the "shoulders," and the stems were very slender. This type was classical, and I prized it like a piece of old jade. When I was working away from home, Yün(芸)used to take care of it personally and it grew beautifully. After two years, it died suddenly one day. I dug up its roots and found that they were white like marble, while nothing was wrong with the sprouts, either. At first, I could not understand this, but ascribed it with a sigh merely to my own bad luck, which might be unworthy to keep such flowers. Later on, I found out that someone who had asked for some off-shoots from the same pot, had been refused, and had therefore killed it by pouring boiling water over it. Thenceforth I swore I would never grow orchids again.

次取杜鹃，虽无香而色可久玩，且易剪裁。以芸惜枝怜叶，不忍畅剪，故难成树。其他盆玩皆然。

Next in preference came the azalea. Although it had no smell, its flowers lasted a longer time and were very beautiful to look at, in addition to its being easy to train up. Yün loved these flowers so much that she would not stand for too much cutting and trimming, and, consequently, it was difficult to make them grow in proper form. The same thing was true of the other flowers.

惟每年东篱菊绽，秋兴成癖。喜摘插瓶，不爱盆玩。非盆玩不足观，以家无园圃，不能自植，货于市者，俱丛杂无致，故不取耳。其插花朵，数宜单，不宜双。每瓶取一种，不取二色。瓶口取阔大，不取窄小，阔大者舒展。不拘自五七花至三四十花，必于瓶口中一丛怒起，以不散漫，不挤轧，不靠瓶口为妙；所谓“起把宜紧”也。或亭亭玉立，或飞舞横斜。花取参差，间以花蕊，以免飞钹耍盘之病。叶取不乱，梗取不强。用针宜藏，针长宁断之，毋令针针露梗。所谓“瓶口宜清”也。视桌之大小，一桌三瓶至七瓶而止，多则眉目不分，即同市井之菊屏矣。几之高低，自三四寸至二尺五六寸而止； 必须参差高下，互相照应，以气势联络为上。若中高两低，后高前低，成排对列，又犯俗所谓“锦灰堆”矣。或密或疏，或进或出，全在会心者得画意乃可。

The chrysanthemum, however, was my passion in the autumn of every year, I loved to arrange these flowers in vases instead of raising them in pots, not because I did not want to have them that way, but because I had no garden in my home and could not take care of them myself. What I bought at the market were not properly trained and not to my liking. When arranging chrysanthemum flowers in vases, one should take an odd, not an even, number and each vase should have flowers of only one colour. The mouth of the vase should be broad, so that the flowers could lie easily together. Whether there be half a dozen flowers or even thirty or forty of them in a vase, they should be so arranged as to come up together straight from the mouth of the vase, neither overcrowded, nor too much spread out, nor leaning against the mouth of the vase. This is called “keeping the handle firm.” Sometimes they can stand gracefully erect, and sometimes spread out in different directions. In order to avoid a bare monotonous effect, they should be mixed with some flower buds and arranged in a kind of studied disorderliness. The leaves should not be too thick and the stems should not be too stiff. In using pins to hold the stems up, one should break the long pins off, rather than expose them. This is called “keeping the mouth of the vase clear.” Place from three to seven vases on a table, depending on the size of the latter, for if there were too many of them, they would be overcrowded, looking like chrysanthemum screens at the market. The stands for the vases should be of different height, from three or four inches to two and a half feet, so that the different vases at different heights would balance one another and belong intimately to one another as in a picture with unity of composition. To put one vase high in the centre with two low at the sides, or to put a low one in front and a tall one behind, or to arrange them in symmetrical pairs, would be to create what is vulgarly called “a heap of gorgeous refuse. ” Proper spacing and arrangement must depend on the individual who has an understanding of pictorial composition.

若盆碗盘洗，用漂青、松香、榆皮、面和油，先熬以稻灰，收成胶。以铜片按钉向上，将膏火化，粘铜片于盘碗盆洗中。俟冷，将花用铁丝扎把，插于钉上，宜斜偏取势，不可居中，更宜枝疏叶清，不可拥挤；然后加水，用碗沙少许掩铜片，使观者疑丛花生于碗底方妙。

In the case of flower bowls or open dishes, the method of making a support for the flowers is to mix pitch and refined resin with elm bark, flour and oil, and heat up the mixture with hot hay ashes until it becomes a kind of glue, and with it glue some nails upside down on to a piece of copper. This copper plate can then be heated up and glued on to the bottom of the bowl or dish. When it is cold, tie the flowers in groups by means of wire and stick them on those nails. The flowers should be allowed to incline sideways and not shoot up from the centre; it is also important that the stems and leaves should not come too closely together. After this is done, put some water in the bowl and cover up the copper support with some clean sand, so that the flowers will seem to grow directly from the bottom of the bowl.

若以木本花果插瓶，剪裁之法(不能色色自觅，倩人攀折者每不合意)，必先执在手中，横斜以观其势，反侧以取其态。相定之后，剪去杂枝，以疏瘦古怪为佳。再思其梗如何入瓶，或折或曲，插入瓶口，方免背叶侧花之患。

When picking branches from flower-trees for decoration in vases, it is important to know how to trim them before putting them in the vase, for one cannot always go and pick them oneself, and those picked by others are often unsatisfactory. Hold the branch in your hand and turn it back and forth in different ways in order to see how it lies most expressively. After one has made up one's mind about it, lop off the superfluous branches, with the idea of making the twig look thin and sparse and quaintly beautiful. Next think how the stem is going to lie in the vase and with what kind of bend, so that when it is put there, the leaves and flowers can be shown to the best advantage.

若一枝到手，先拘定其梗之直者插瓶中，势必枝乱梗强，花侧叶背，既难取态，更无韵致矣。折梗打曲之法：锯其梗之半而嵌以砖石，则直者曲矣。如患梗倒，敲一二钉以管之。即枫叶竹枝，乱草荆棘，均堪入选。或绿竹一竿，配以枸杞数粒，几茎细草，伴以荆棘两枝，苟位置得宜，另有世外之趣。

If one just takes any old branch in hand, chooses a straight section and puts it in the vase, the consequence will be that the stem will be too stiff, the branches will be too close together and the flowers and leaves will be turned in the wrong direction, devoid of all charm and expression. To make a straight twig crooked, cut a mark half-way across the stem and insert a little piece of broken brick or stone at the joint; the straight branch will then become a bent one. In case the stem is too weak, put one or two pins to strengthen it. By means of this method, even maple leaves and bamboo twigs or even ordinary grass and thistles will look very well for decoration. Put a twig of green bamboo side by side with a few berries of Chinese matrimony vine or arrange some fine blades of grass together with some branches of thistle. They will look quite poetic, if the arrangement is correct.

若新栽花木，不妨歪斜取势，听其盆侧，一年后枝叶自能向上。如树树直栽，即难取势矣。

In planting new trees, it does not matter if the trunk comes up from the ground at an angle, for if let alone for a year, it will grow upwards by itself. On the other hand, if one lets the stem come up in a perpendicular line, it will be difficult later on for it to have a dynamic posture.

至剪裁盆树，先取根露鸡爪者，左右剪成三节，然后起枝。一枝一节，七枝到顶，或九枝到顶。枝忌对节如肩臂，节忌臃肿如鹤膝。须盘旋出枝，不可光留左右，以避赤胸露背之病。又不可前后直出。有名“双起”，“三起”者，一根而起两三树也。如根无爪形，便成插树，故不取。

As to the training of pot plants, one should choose those with claw-like roots coming above the surface of the ground. Lop off the first three branches from the ground before allowing the next one to grow up, making a bend at every point where a new branch starts off. There should be seven such bends, or perhaps nine, from the lower end of a tree to its top. It is against good taste to have swollen joints at these bends, or to have two branches growing directly opposite each other at the same point. These must branch off in all directions from different points, for if one only allows those on the right and left to grow up, the effect will be very bare, or “the chest and back will be exposed,” as we say. Nor, for instance, should they grow straight from the front or behind. There are “double-trunked” and “treble-trunked” trees which all spring from the same root above the ground. If the root were not claw-shaped, they would look like planted sticks and would on that account be disqualified.

然一树剪成，至少得三四十年。余生平仅见吾乡万翁名彩章者，一生剪成数树。又在扬州商家见有虞山游客携送黄杨翠柏各一盆，惜乎明珠暗投。余未见其可也。若留枝盘如宝塔，扎枝曲如蚯蚓者，便成匠气矣。

The proper training of a tree, however, takes at least thirty to forty years. In my whole life, I have seen only one person, old Wan Ts’aichang of my district(“吾乡万翁名彩章者”), who succeeded in training several trees in his life. Once I also saw at the home of a merchant at Yangchow(扬州) two pots, one of boxwood and one of cypress, presented to him by a friend from Yüshan(虞山), but this was like casting pearls before swine(“明珠暗投”). Outside these cases, I have not seen any really good ones. Trees whose branches are trained in different horizontal circles going up like a pagoda or whose branches turn round and round like earthworms are incurably vulgar.

点缀盆中花石，小景可以入画，大景可以入神。一瓯(ōu)清茗，神能趋入其中，方可供幽斋之玩。种水仙无灵璧石，余尝以炭之有石意者代之。黄芽菜心，其白如玉，取大小五七枝，用沙土植长方盆内，以炭代石，黑白分明，颇有意思。以此类推，幽趣无穷，难以枚举。如石菖蒲结子，用冷米汤同嚼喷炭上，置阴湿地，能长细菖蒲；随意移养盆碗中，茸茸(róng róng)可爱。以老莲子磨薄两头，入蛋壳使鸡翼之，俟雏成取出。用久年燕巢泥加天门冬十分之二，捣烂拌匀，植于小器中，灌以河水，晒以朝阳；花发大如酒杯，叶缩如碗口，亭亭可爱。

When arranging miniature sceneries with flowers and stones in a pot, design so that a small one could suggest a painting, and a big one the infinite. One should make it so that, with a pot of tea, one could lose oneself in a world of imagination; and only this kind should be kept in one's private studio for enjoyment. Once I planted some narcissus and could not find any pebbles from Lingpi for use in the pot, and I substituted them with pieces of coal that looked like rocks. One can also take five or seven pieces of yellow-brimmed white cabbage of different size, whose core is white like jade, and plant them in sand in an oblong earthen basin, decorated with charcoal instead of pebbles. The black of the charcoal will then contrast vividly with the white of the cabbage, quite interesting to look at. It is impossible to enumerate all the possible variations, but if one exercises one's ingenuity, it will be found to be an endless source of pleasure. For instance, one can take some calamus seeds in the mouth, chew them together with cold rice soup, and blow them on to pieces of charcoal. Keep them in a dark damp place and fine little calamus will grow from them. These pieces of charcoal can then be placed in any flower basin, looking like moss-covered rocks. Or one can take some old lotus seeds, grind off slightly both ends, and put them in an egg-shell, making a hen sit on it together with other eggs. When the little chickens are hatched, take the egg out also and plant the old lotus seeds in old clay from swallows' nests, prepared with twenty per cent of ground asparagus. Keep these then in a small vessel filled with river water, and expose them to the morning sun. When the flowers bloom, they will be only the size of a wine cup, while the leaves will be about the size of a bowl, very cute and beautiful to look at.

若夫园亭楼阁，套室回廊，叠石成山栽花取势，又在大中见小，小中见大，虚中有实，实中有虚，或藏或露，或浅或深，不仅在周回曲折四字，又不在地广石多，徒烦工费。或掘地堆土成山，间以块石，杂以花草，篱用梅编，墙以藤引，则无山而成山矣。大中见小者：散漫处植易长之竹，编易茂之梅以屏之。小中见大者：窄院之墙，宜凹凸其形，饰以绿色，引以藤蔓，嵌大石，凿字作碑记形。推窗如临石壁，便觉峻峭无穷。虚中有实者：或山穷水尽处，一折而豁然开朗；或轩阁设厨处，一开而可通别院。实中有虚者：开门于不通之院，映以竹石，如有实无也；设矮栏于墙头，如上有月台，而实虚也。

As to the planning of garden pavilions, towers, winding corridors and out-houses, the designing of rockery and the training of flower-trees, one should try to show the small in the big, and the big in the small, and provide for the real in the unreal and for the unreal in the real. One reveals and conceals alternately, making it sometimes apparent and sometimes hidden. This is not just rhythmic irregularity, nor does it depend on having a wide space and great expenditure of labour and material. Pile up a mound with earth dug from the ground and decorate it with rocks, mingled with flowers; use live plum-branches for your fence, and plant creepers over the walls. Thus one can create the effect of a hill out of a flat piece of ground. In the big, open spaces, plant bamboos that grow quickly and train plum-trees with thick branches to screen them off. This is to show the small in the big. When a courtyard is small, the wall should run in a series of convex and concave lines, decorated with green, covered with ivy and inlaid with big slabs of stone with inscriptions on them. Thus when you open your window, you seem to face a rocky hillside, alive with rugged beauty. This is to show the big in the small. Contrive so that an apparently blind alley leads suddenly into an open space and a closet-like door forms the entrance into an unexpected courtyard. This is to provide for the real in the unreal—Let a door lead into a blind courtyard and conceal the view by placing a few bamboo trees and a few rocks before it. Thus you suggest something which is not there. Place low balustrades along the top of a wall so as to suggest a roof garden. This is to provide for the unreal in the real.

贫士屋少人多，当仿吾乡太平船后梢之位置，再加转移其间。台级为床，前后借凑，可作三榻，间以板而裱以纸，则前后上下皆越绝。譬之如行长路，即不觉其窄矣。余夫妇乔寓扬州时，曾仿此法。屋仅两椽，上下卧房，厨灶，客座皆越绝，而绰然有余。芸曾笑曰：“位置虽精，终非富贵家气象也。”是诚然欤。

Poor scholars who live in crowded houses should follow the method of the boatmen in our native district who make clever arrangements with their limited space on the stems of their boats by devising certain modifications, such as making a series of successive elevations one after another, and using them as beds, of which there may be three in a little room, and separating them with papered wooden partitions. The effect will be compact and wonderful to look at, like surveying a long stretch of road, and one will not feel the cramping of space. When my wife and I were staying at Yangchow, we lived in a house of only two beams, but the two bedrooms, the kitchen and the parlour were all arranged in this method, with an exquisite effect and great saving of space. Yün once said to me laughingly, “The arrangements are exquisite enough, but after all, they lack the luxurious atmosphere of a rich man’s house.” It was so indeed.

余扫墓山中，捡有峦纹可观之石。归与芸商曰：“用油灰叠宣州石于白石盆，取色匀也。本山黄石虽古朴，亦用油灰，则黄白相间，凿痕毕露，将奈何？ ”芸曰：“择石之顽劣者，捣末于灰痕处，乘湿糁之，干或色同也。”

Once I visited my ancestral tombs on the hill and found some pebbles of great beauty, with faint tracings on them. On coming back, I talked it over with Yün, and said, “People mix putty with Hsüanchow stones in white stone basins, because the colours of the two elements blend. These yellow pebbles of this hill, however, are different, and although they are rugged and simple, they will not blend in colour with putty. What can we do?” “Take some of the worse quality,” she said, “pound them into small pieces and mix them in the putty before it is dry, and perhaps when it is dry, the colour will be uniform.”

乃如其言，用宜兴窑长方盆叠起一峰，偏于左而凸于右，背作横方纹，如云林石法；巉岩凹凸，若临江石矶状。虚一角，用河泥种千瓣白萍。石上植茑萝，俗呼云松。经营数日乃成。至深秋，茑萝蔓延满山，如藤萝之悬石壁。花开正红色。白萍亦透水大放。红白相间，神游其中，如登蓬鱼。置之檐下与芸品题：此处宜设水阁，此处宜立茅亭，此处宜凿六字曰“落花流水之间”，此可以居，此可以钓，此可以眺；胸中丘壑，若将移居者然。一夕，猫奴争食，自檐而堕，连盆与架，顷刻碎之。余叹曰：“即此小经营尚干造物忌耶！”两人不禁泪落。

So we did as she suggested, and took a rectangular Yi-hsing(宜兴) earthen basin, on which we piled up a mountain peak on the left coming down in undulations to the right. On its back, we made rugged square lines in the style of rock paintings of Ni Yünlin, so that the whole looked like a rocky precipice overhanging a river. At one corner we made a hollow place, which we filled with mud and planted with multi-leaf white duckweed, while the rocks were planted with dodder. This took us quite a few days to finish. In late autumn, the dodder grew all over the hill, like wistarias hanging down from a rock. The red dodder flowers made a striking contrast to the white duckweed, which had grown luxuriantly, too, from the pond underneath. Looking at it, one could imagine oneself transported to some fairy region. We put this under the eaves, and discussed between ourselves where we should build a covered terrace by the water, where we should put a garden arbour, and where we should put a stone inscription: “Where petals drop and waters flow.” And Yün further discussed with me where we could build our home, where we could fish, and where we could go up for a better view of the distance, all so absorbed in it as if we were moving to live in that little imaginary universe. One night, two cats were fighting for food and fell down over the eaves and accidentally broke the whole thing into pieces, basin and all. I sighed and said, “The gods seem to be jealous of even such a little effort of ours.” And we both shed tears.

静室焚香，闲中雅趣。芸尝以沉速等香，于饭镬[镬(huò)，是古代煮牲肉的烹饪铜器之一]蒸透，在炉上设一铜丝架，离火半寸许，徐徐烘之；其香幽韵而无烟。佛手忌醉鼻嗅，嗅则易烂。木瓜忌出汗，汗出，用水洗之。惟香橼(yuán)无忌。佛手木瓜亦有供法，不能笔宣。每有人将供妥者随手取嗅，随手置之，即不知供法者也。

To burn incense in a quiet room is one of the cultivated pleasures of a leisurely life. Yün used to burn aloes-wood and *shuhsiang* (a kind of fragrant wood from Cambodia). She used to steam the wood first in a cauldron thoroughly, and then place it on a copper wire net over a stove, about half an inch from the fire. Under the action of the slow fire, the wood would give out a kind of subtle fragrance without any visible smoke. Another thing, the “buddha’s fingers” (a variety of citron) should not be smelt by a drunken man, or it would easily rot. It is also bad for the quince to perspire (as under atmospheric changes), and when it does so, one should wash it with water. The citron alone is easy to take care of, because it is not afraid of handling. There are different ways of taking care of the “buddha’s fingers” and the quince which cannot be expressed in so many words. I have seen people who take one of these things, which have been properly kept, and handle or smell it in any old way and put it down again roughly, which shows that they do not know the art of preserving these things.

余闲居，案头瓶花不绝。芸曰："子之插花，能备风晴雨露，可谓精妙入神；而画中有草虫一法，盍仿而效之？"余曰："虫踯躅不受制，焉能仿效？"芸曰："有一法，恐作俑罪过耳。"余曰："试言之。"羞曰："虫死色不变。觅螳螂蝉蝶之属，以针刺死，用细丝扣虫 项系花草间，整其足，或抱梗，或踏叶，宛然如生。不亦善乎？"余喜，如其法行之，见者无不称绝。求之闺中，今恐未必有此会心者矣。

In my home I always had a vase of flowers on my desk. "You know very well about arranging flowers in vases for all kinds of weather, " said Yun to me one day. "I think you have really understood the art, but there is a type of painting commonly called 4 insects on grass blades, which you haven't applied yet. Why don't you try?" "I'm afraid, " I replied, "that I cannot hold the insect's legs still. What can I do?" "I know a way, except that I am afraid it would be too cruel, said Yün. "Tell me about it, "1 asked. "You know that an insect does not change its colour after death. You can find a mantis or cicada or a butterfly; kill it with a pin and use a fine wire to tie its neck to the flowers, arranging its legs so that they either hold on to the stem or rest on the leaves. It would then look like a live one. Don't you think it is very good?" I was quite delighted and did as she suggested, and many of our friends thought it very wonderful. I am afraid it is difficult to find ladies nowadays who show such an understanding of things.

余与芸寄居锡山华氏，时华夫人以两女从芸识字。乡居院旷，夏日逼人。芸教其家作活花屏法，甚妙。每屏一扇，用木梢二枝，约长四五寸，作矮条凳式，虚其中，横四挡，宽一尺许，四角凿圆眼，插竹编方眼。屏约高六七尺，用砂盆种扁豆，置屏中，盘延屏上，两人可移动。

When I was staying with my friend Mr. Hua at Hsishan with Yün, Mrs. Hua used to ask Yün to teach her two daughters reading. In that country house, the yard was wide open and the glare of the summer sun was very oppressive. Yün taught them a method of making movable screens of growing flowers. Every screen consisted of a single piece. She took two little pieces of wood about four or five inches long, and laid them parallel like a low stool, with the hollow top filled by four horizontal bars over a foot long. At the four corners, she made little round holes on which she stuck a trellis-work made of bamboo. The trellis was six or seven feet high and on its bottom was placed a pot of peas which would then grow up and entwine round the bamboo trellis. This could be easily moved by two persons.

多编数屏，随意遮拦，恍如绿阴满窗，透风蔽日，迂回曲折，随时可更；故曰："活花屏"。有此一法，即一切藤本香草，随地可用。此真乡居之良法也。

One can make several of these things and place them wherever one pleases, before windows or doors, and they will look like living plants, casting their green shade into the house, warding off the sun and yet allowing the wind to come through. They can be placed in any irregular formation, adjustable according to time and circumstances, and are, therefore, called "movable flower screens." With this method, one can use any kind of fragrant weeds of the creeper family, instead of peas. It is an excellent arrangement for people staying in the country.

友人鲁半舫，名璋，字春山，善写松柏或梅菊，工隶书，兼工铁笔。余寄居其家之萧爽楼一年有半。楼共五椽，东向，余居其三。晦明风雨，可以远眺。庭中木樨一株，清香撩人。有廊有厢，地极幽静。移居时，有一仆一妪，并挈其小女来。仆能成衣，妪能纺绩；于是芸绣，妪绩，仆则成衣，以供薪水。

My friend Lu Panfang's name was Chang and his literary name Chünshan. He was very good at painting pine-trees and cypresses, plum blossoms and chrysanthemums, as well as writing the lishu style of calligraphy, besides specializing in carving seals. I stayed in his home called Hsiaoshuanglou for a year and a half. The house faced east and consisted of five beams, of which I occupied three. From it one could get a beautiful view of the distance in rain or shine. In the middle of the court, there was a tree, the osmanthus fragrans, which filled the air with a kind of delicate fragrance. There were corridors and living rooms, and the place was quite secluded. When I went there, I brought along a man-servant and an old woman, who also brought with them a young daughter. The man-servant could make dresses and the old woman could spin; therefore, Yün did embroidery, the old woman spun and the man-servant made dresses to provide for our daily expenses.

余素爱客，小酌必行令。芸善不费之烹庖，瓜蔬鱼虾，一经芸手，便有意外味。同人知余贫，每出杖头钱，作竟日叙。余又好洁，地无纤尘，且无拘束，不嫌放纵。

I was by nature very fond of guests and whenever we had a little drinking party, I insisted on having wine-games. Yün was very clever at preparing inexpensive dishes; ordinary foodstuffs like melon, vegetables, fish and shrimps had a special flavour when prepared by her. My friends knew that I was poor, and often helped pay the expenses in order that we might get together and talk for the whole day. I was very keen on keeping the place spotlessly clean, and was, besides, fond of free and easy ways with my friends.

时有杨补凡名昌绪，善人物写真；袁少迂名沛，工山水；王星澜名岩，工花卉翎毛；爱萧爽楼幽雅，皆携画具来，余则从之学画。写草篆，镌图章，加以润笔，交芸备茶酒供客。终日品诗论画而已。更有夏淡安，揖山两昆季，并缪山音，知白两昆季，及蒋韵香，陆橘香，周啸霞，郭小愚，华杏帆，张闲酣诸君子，如梁上之燕，自去自来。芸则拔钗沽酒，不动声色，良辰美景，不放轻过。今则天各一方，风流云散，兼之玉碎香埋，不堪回首矣！

At this time, there were a group of friends, like Yang Pufan, also called Changhsü, who specialized in portrait sketches; Yüan Shaoyü, also called Pai, who specialized in painting landscape; and Wang Hsing-lan, also called Yen, good at painting flowers and birds. They all liked the Hsiaoshuanglou because of its seclusion, so they would bring their painting utensils to the place and I learnt painting from them. They would then either write "grass-script" or "chü an-script" or carve seals, from which we made some money which we turned over to Yün to defray expenses for teas and dinners. The whole day long, we were occupied in discussing poetry or painting only. There were, moreover, friends like the brothers Hsia Tan-an and Hsia Yishan, the brothers Miao Shanyin and Miao Chihpo, Chi-ang Yünhsiang, Loh Chühsiang, Chou Hsiaohsia, Kuo Hsiaoyü, Hua Hsingfan, and Chang Hsienhan. These friends came and went as they pleased like the swallows by the eaves. Yün would take off her hairpin and sell it for wine without a second's thought, for she would not let a beautiful day pass without company. Today these friends are scattered to the four corners of the earth like clouds dispersed by a storm, and the woman I loved is dead, like broken jade and buried incense. How sad indeed to look back upon these things!

萧爽楼有四忌：谈官宦升迁，公廨时事，入股时文，看牌掷色；有犯必罚酒五斤。有四取：慷慨豪爽，风流蕴藉，落拓不羁，澄静缄默。长夏无事，考对为会。每会八人，每人各携青蚨二百。先拈阄，得第一者为主考，关防别座；第二者为誊录，亦就座；余作举子，各于誊录处取纸一条，盖用印章。主考出五七言各一句，刻香为限，行立构思，不准交头私语。对就后投入一匣，方许就座。各人交卷毕，誊录启匣，并录一册，转呈主考，以杜徇私。

Among the friends at Hsiao shuang lou, four things were tabooed: firstly, talking about people's official promotions; secondly, gossiping about law-suits and current affairs; thirdly, discussing the conventional eight-legged essays for the imperial examinations; and fourthly, playing cards and dice. Whoever broke any of these rules was penalized to provide five catties of wine. On the other hand, there were four things which we all approved: generosity, romantic charm, free and easy ways, and quietness. In the long summer days when we had nothing to do, we used to hold examinations among ourselves. At those parties, there would be eight persons, each bringing two hundred cash along. We began by drawing lots, and the one who got the first would be the official examiner, seated on top by himself, while the second one would be the official recorder, also seated in his place. The others would then be the candidates, each taking a slip of paper, properly stamped with a seal, from the official recorder. The examiner then gave out a line of seven words and one of five words, with which each of us was to make the best couplet. The time limit was the burning of a joss-stick and we were to tease our brains standing or walking about, but were not allowed to exchange words with each other. When a candidate had made the couplets, he placed them in a special box and then returned to his seat. After all the papers had been handed in, the official recorder then opened the box and copied them together in a book, which he submitted to the examiner, thus safeguarding against any partiality on the latter's part.

十六对中取七言三联，五言二联。六联中取第一者即为后任主考，第二者为誊录。每人有两联不取者罚钱二十文，取一联者免罚十文，过限者倍罚。一场，主考得香钱百文。一日可十场，积钱千文，酒资大畅矣。惟芸议为官卷，准坐而构思。

Of these couplets submitted, three of the seven-word lines and three of the five-word lines were to be chosen as the best. The one who turned in the best of these six chosen couplets would then be the official examiner for the next round, and the second best would be the official recorder. One who had two couplets failing to be chosen would be fined twenty cash, one failing in one couplet fined ten cash, and failures handed in beyond the time limit would be fined twice the amount. The official examiner would get one hundred cash "incense money." Thus we could have ten examinations in a day and provide a thousand cash with which to buy wine and have a grand drinking party. Yün's paper alone was considered special and exempt from fine, and she was allowed the privilege of thinking out her lines on her seat.

杨补凡为余夫妇写载花小影，神情确肖。是夜月色颇佳，兰影上粉墙，别有幽致。星澜醉后兴发曰："补凡能为君写真，我能为花图影。"余笑曰："花影能如人影否？"

One day Yang Pufan made a sketch of Yün and myself working at a garden with wonderful likeness. On that night, the moon was very bright and was casting a wonderfully picturesque shadow of an orchid flower on the white wall. Inspired by some hard drinking, Hsing-lan said to me, "Pufan can paint your portrait sketch, but I can paint the shadows of flowers." "Will the sketch of flowers be as good as that of a man?" I asked.

星澜取素纸铺于墙，即就兰影用墨浓淡图之。日间取视，虽不成画，而花叶萧疏，自有月下之趣。芸甚宝之。各有题咏。

Then Hsing-lan took a piece of paper and placed it against the wall, on which he traced the shadow of the orchid flower with dark and light inkings. When we looked at it in the daytime, there was a kind of haziness about the lines of leaves and flowers, suggestive of the moonlight, although it could not be called a real painting. Yün liked it very much and all my friends wrote their inscriptions on it.

苏城有南园北园二处，菜花黄时，苦无酒家小饮；携盒而往，对花冷饮，殊无意味。或议就近觅饮者，或议看花归饮者，终不如对花热饮为快。众议未定。芸笑曰："明日但各出杖头钱，我自担炉火来。"众笑曰："诺。"众去，余问曰："卿果自往乎？"芸曰非也。妾见市中卖馄饨者，其担锅灶无不备，盍雇之而往？妾先烹调端整，到彼处再一下锅，茶酒两便。"余曰："酒菜固便矣。茶乏烹具。"芸曰："携一砂罐去，以铁叉串罐柄，去其锅，悬于行灶中，加柴火煎茶，不亦便乎？"

There are two places in Soochow called the South Garden and the North Garden. We would go there when the rape flowers were in bloom, but there was no wine shop nearby where we could have a drink. If we brought eatables along in a basket, there was little fun drinking cold wine in the company of the flowers. Some proposed that we should look for some place to get a drink in the neighbourhood, and others suggested that we should look at the flowers first and then come back for a drink, but this was never quite the ideal thing, which should be to drink warm wine in the presence of flowers. While no one could make any satisfactory suggestion, Yün smiled and said, "Tomorrow you people provide the money and I'll carry a stove to the place myself." "Very well, " they all said. When my friends had left, I asked Yün how she was going to do it, "I am not going to carry it myself, " she said, "I have seen wonton sellers in the streets who carry along a stove and a pan and everything we need. We could just ask one of these fellows to go along with us. I'll prepare the dishes first, and when we arrive, all we need is just to heat them up, and we will have everything ready including tea and wine.' "Well, but what about the kettle for boiling tea?" "We could carry along an earthen pot, " she said, "remove the *wonton* seller's pan and suspend the pot over the fire by a spike. This will then serve us as a kettle for boiling tea, won't it?"

余鼓掌称善。街头有鲍姓者，卖馄饨为业，以百钱雇其担，约以明日午后。鲍欣然允议。明日看花者至，余告以故，众咸叹服。饭后同往，并带席垫，至座里，择柳阴下团坐。先烹茗，饮毕，然后暖酒烹肴。是时风和日丽，遍地黄金，青衫红袖越阡度陌，蝶蜂乱飞，令人不饮自醉。既而酒肴俱熟，坐地大嚼。担者颇不俗，拉与同饮。游人见之，莫不羡为奇想。杯盘狼藉，各已陶然，或坐或卧，或歌或啸。红日将颓，余思粥，担者即为买米煮之，果腹而归。芸问曰："今日之游乐乎？" 众曰："非夫人之力不及此。"大笑而散。

I clapped my hands with applause. There was a *wonton* seller by the name of Pao, whom we asked to go along with us the following afternoon, offering to pay him a hundred cash, to which Pao readily consented. The following day my friends, who were going to see the flowers, arrived, I told them about the arrangements, and they were all amazed at Yün's ingenious idea. We started off after lunch, bringing along with us some straw mats and cushions. When we had arrived at the South Garden, we chose a place under the shade of willow trees, and sat together in a circle on the ground. First we boiled some tea, and after drinking it, we warmed up the wine and heated up the dishes. The sun was beautiful and the breeze was gentle, while the yellow rape flowers in the field looked like a stretch of gold, with gaily dressed young men and women passing by the rice fields and bees and butterflies flitting to and fro —a sight which could make one drunk without any liquor. Very soon the wine and dishes were ready and we sat together on the ground drinking and eating. The *wonton* seller was quite a likeable person and we asked him to join us. People who saw us thus enjoying ourselves thought it quite a novel idea. Then the cups, bowls and dishes lay about in great disorder on the ground, while we were already slightly drunk, some sitting and some lying down, and some singing or yelling. When the sun was going down, I wanted to eat congee, and the *wonton* seller bought some rice and cooked it for us. We then came back with a full belly. "Did you enjoy it today?" asked Yün. "We would not have enjoyed it so much, had it not been for Madame!" all of us exclaimed. Then merrily we parted.

贫士起居服食，以及器皿房舍，宜省俭而雅洁。省俭之法，曰 "就事论事"。余爱小饮，不喜多菜。芸为置一梅花盒，用二寸白磁深碟六只，中置一只，外置五只，用灰漆就，其形如梅花。底盖均起凹楞，盖之上有柄如花蒂，置之案头，如一朵墨梅覆桌；启盖视之，如菜装于花瓣中。一盒六色，二三知己，可以随意取食。食完再添。另做矮边圆盘一只，以便放杯、箸、酒壶之类，随处可摆，移掇亦便。即食物省俭之一端也。

A poor scholar should try to be economical in the matter of food, clothing, house and furniture, but at the same time be clean and artistic. In order to be economical, one should "manage according to the needs of the occasion," as the saying goes. I was very fond of having nice little suppers with a little liquor, but did not care for many dishes, Yün used to make a tray with a plum-blossom design. It consisted of six deep dishes of white porcelain, two inches in diameter, one in the centre and the other five grouped round it, painted grey and looking like a plum flower. Both its bottom and its top were bevelled and there was a handle on the top resembling the stem of a plum flower, so that, when placed on the table, it looked like a regular plum blossom dropped on the table, and on opening, the different vegetables were found to be contained in the petals of the flower. A case like this with six different dishes would be quite enough to serve a dinner for two or three close friends. If second helping was needed, more could be added besides this, we made another round tray with a low border for holding chopsticks, cups and the wine pot. These were easily moved about and one could have the dinner served at any place one wished. This is an example of economy in the matter of food.

余之小帽领袜，皆芸自做。衣之破者移东补西，必整必洁；色取暗淡，以免垢迹，既可出客，又可家常。此又服饰省俭之一端也。初至萧爽楼中，嫌其暗，以白纸糊壁，遂亮。夏月楼下去窗，无栏干，觉空洞无遮拦。芸曰："有旧竹帘在，何不以帘代栏？"

Yün also made me my collars, socks and my little cap. When my clothes were torn, she would cut out one piece to mend another, making it always look very neat and tidy. I used to choose quiet colours for my clothes, for the reason that dirty spots would not show easily, and one could wear them both at home and abroad. This is an instance of economy in the matter of dress. When I first took up my residence at the Hsiaoshuanglou, I found the rooms too dark, but after papering the walls with white paper, they were quite bright again. During the summer months, the ground floor was quite open, because the windows had all been taken down, and we felt that the place lacked privacy. "There is an old bamboo screen, " suggested Yün, "why don't we use it and let it serve in place of a railing?"

余曰："如何？"

芸曰："用竹数根，黝黑色，一竖一横，留出走路。截半帘，搭在横竹上，垂至地，高与桌齐。中竖短竹四根，用麻线扎定，然后于横竹搭帘处，寻旧黑布条，连横竹里缝之。既可遮拦饰观，又不费钱。" 此就事论事之一法也。以此推之，古人所谓"竹头木屑皆有用"，良有以也。

"But how?" I asked.

"Take a few pieces of bamboo of black colour," she replied, "and make them into a square, leaving room for people to pass out and in. Cut off half of the bomboo screen and fasten it on the horizontal bamboo, about the height of a table, letting the screen come down to the ground. Then put four vertical pieces of short bamboo in the centre, fasten these in place by means of a string, and then find some old strips of black cloth and wrap them up together with the horizontal bar with needle and thread. It would give a little privacy and would look quite well, besides being inexpensive." This is an instance of "managing according to the needs of the occasion. " This goes to prove the truth of the ancient saying that "slips of bamboo and chips of wood all have their uses."

夏月荷花初开时，晚含而晓放。芸用小纱囊撮茶叶少许，置花心。明早取出，烹天泉水泡之，香韵尤绝。

When the lotus flowers bloom in summer, they close at night and open in the morning. Yün used to put some tea leaves in a little silk bag and place it in the centre of the flower at night. We would take it out the next morning, and make tea with spring water, which would then have a very delicate flavor.

部分中国经典英译补充阅读书目

Some Chinese Classics in English Translation are Added to the Reading List

1. 韩愈《原道》(选)

[1]石峻主编：《汉英对照中国哲学名著选读》，北京：中国人民大学出版社，1988。

2. 司马谈《论六家要旨》

[1]*Sima Tan: The Discussion of the Essentials of the Six Schools,* selected from *Si-ma Ch'ien: Grand Historican of China,* trans. by Burton Watson. New York and London: Columbia University Press, 1958.

3. 王充《论衡》(选)

[1]*Philosophical Essays Of WANG Ch'ung*, trans. by Alfred Forke,Paragon Book Gallery, New York, 1962. Book XVIII.

4. 王弼《老子指略》

[1]*Wang Bi: "The Structure of the Laozi's Pointers"* (*"Laozi weizhi lilüe"*) — *A Philological Study and Translation,* by Rudolf G.Wagner. from *Toung Pao*, Second Series, Vol. 72, Livr. 1/3 (1986), 72 (1): 92-129.

[2]Rudolf G.Wagner. *A Chinese Reading of Daodejing: Wang Bi's Commentary on the Laozi with Critical Text and Translation*, Albany: State University of New York Press, 2003.

5. 公孙龙子《白马论》(选)

[1]公孙龙：《公孙龙子英译本》，孙启勤译，杭州：浙江工商大学出版社，2014。

6. 朱熹(选)

[1]*A Source Book in Chinese Philosophy*, trans. and compiled by Wing-tsit Chan, Princeton: Princeton University Press, 1969.

7. 王阳明(选)

[1]*Instructions for Practical Living and Other Neo-Confucian Writings by Wang Yang-Ming,* trans., with Notes, by Wing-tsit Chan, New York and London: Columbia University Press, 1963.

[2]*The Philosophy of Wang Yang-ming,* trans. by Henke, Frederick Goodrich, London & Chicago: The Open Court Publishing Co., 1916.

8. 《黄帝内经》(选)

[1]*The Yellow Emperor's Classic of Medicine: A New Translation of the Neijing Suwen with Commentary*, trans. by Maoshing Ni, Ph.D., Boston and London: Shambhala Publications, Inc., 2011.

[2]*Introductory Study of Huang Di Nei Jing,* trans. by Luo Xiwen, Beijing: China Press of Traditional Chinese Medicine, 2009.

[3]*Huang Di Nei Jing Su Wen: An Annotated Translation of Huang Di's Inner Classic*——Basic Questions: 2 Volumes, trans. by Paul Ulrich Unschuld, California University press, 2011.

[4]*The Yellow Emperor's Classic of Internal Medicine,* trans. by Veith Ilza, Newed Berkeley, Los Angeles and London: University of California Press.2002.

[5]*Huang Di nei jing su wen*（*An Annotated Translation of Huang Di's Inner Classic-Basic Questions*, trans. by Unschuld Paul U & Hermann Tessenow & Zheng Jinsheng, Los Angeles: University of California Press, 2011。

[6]李照国译，*Yellow Emperor's Canon of Medicine-Plain Conversation*，西安：世界图书出版公司，2005。

[7]吴连胜，吴奇译，《黄帝内经：英汉对照》，北京：中国科学技术出版社，1997。

9. 《僧肇》(选)

[1]*Chao Lun*: *The Treatises of Seng-chao*, trans. by Walter Liebenthal, Hong Kong: Hong Kong University Press, 1968.

10. 慧能《坛经》(选)

[1]*The Sixth Patriarch's Dharma Jewel Platform Sutra With the Commentary of Tripitaka Master Hua*, edited by Martin Verhoeven, Ph.D, University of Wisconsin and trans. by Buddhist Text Translation Society, Burlingame, California, 2001.

[2]*The Platform Sutra of the Sixth Patriarch,* trans. by McRae, John R., Berkeley: Numata Center for Buddhist Translation and Research, 2000.

[3]*A Buddhist Bible,* trans. by Dwight Goddard, New York: Casimo Inc, 2007.

[4]黄茂林译，《坛经英译本》，上海：上海有正书局，1930。

[5]蒋坚松译，《坛经英译本》，长沙：湖南人民出版社，2008。

11. 屈原(选)

[1]*The Songs of the South and Anthology of Ancient Chinese Poems* by Qu Yuan and Other Poets, trans. by David Hawks, Penguin Classics, 1985.

[2]*The Columbia Book of Chinese Poetry: From the Early Times to the 13th Century*，trans. by Burton Watson, New York: Columbia University Press,1984.

[3]孙大雨译，《屈原诗选英译》，上海：上海外语教育出版社，2007。

[4]许渊冲译，《楚辞：汉英对照》，北京：中国对外翻译出版公司，2008。

[5]杨宪益、戴乃迭译，《楚辞选》，北京：外文出版社，2010。

[6]卓振英译，《楚辞》(汉英对照)，长沙：湖南人民出版社，2006。

12. 刘勰《文心雕龙》(选)

[1]*Readings in Chinese Literary Thoughts,* written and translated by Stephen Owen, Harvard University, Cambridge, Massachusetts, 1992.

[2]*The Literary Mind and the Carving of Dragons,* trans. by Shih,Vincent Yu-chung. New York: New York Columbia University Press, 1959.

[3]刘勰，《文心雕龙》，杨国斌译，见《大中华文库》(汉英对照)，北京：外语教学与研究出版社，2003。

13. 王羲之《兰亭集序》

[1]《古文观止精选(汉英对照)》，罗经国译，北京：外语教学与研究出版社，2005。

[2]《中国历代散文选(汉英对照)》，戴抗编选，谢百魁英译，北京：中国对外翻译出版公司, 2008.

[3]林语堂，《林语堂英译精品：扬州瘦马》(英汉对照)，合肥：安徽科学技术出版社, 2012。

14. 诸葛亮(选)

[1]*The First Memorial to the Throne Before Setting off for War,* written by Zhuge Liang , selected from *A Selection of Classic Chinese Essays from Guwenguanzhi*. Trans. by Luo Jingguo, Beijing: Foreign Language Teaching and Research Press, 2005.

[2]《中国历代散文选(汉英对照)》，戴抗编选，谢百魁英译，北京：中国对外翻译出版公司, 2008。

15. 沈复《浮生六记》(选)

[1][清]沈复著：《浮生六记·中英对照》，林语堂译，北京：外语教学与研究出版社，1999。

[2]*Chapters from a Floating Life,* trans. by Black Shirley M., Oxford：Oxford University Press, 1960.

[3]*Six Records of a Floating Life,* trans. by PRATT L, CHIANG S., New York：Penguin Publishing, 2004.

[4][清]沈复著：《浮生六记》，(美)白伦，江素惠，英译. 汪洋海，今译. 南京：译林出版社，2006。